Hindustani Sangeet and a Philosopher of Art

Music, Rhythm, and Kathak Dance *vis-à-vis* Aesthetics of Susanne K. Langer

By the same author

Studies in the Metaphysics of Bradley
George Allen & Unwin, London
and
Humanities Press, New York, 1967
(Muirhead Library)

The Winged Form: Aesthetical Essays on Hindustani Rhythm
Sangeet Natak Akademi, New Delhi, 1979

Aesthetical Essays
Chanakya Publications, Delhi, 1981

Ever Unto God: Essays on Gandhi and Religion
Indian Council of Philosophical Research, New Delhi, 1988

Swinging Syllables: Aesthetics of Kathak Dance
Sangeet Natak Akademi, 1991

Art and Philosophy: Seven Aestheticians
Indian Council of Philosophical Research, 1994

New Vistas in Indian Performing Arts, no. 2

Hindustani Sangeet and a Philosopher of Art

Music, Rhythm, and Kathak Dance *vis-à-vis* Aesthetics of Susanne K. Langer

by

Sushil Kumar Saxena

PRINTWORLD

Publishers of Indian Traditions

Cataloging in Publication Data — DK

[Courtesy: D.K. Agencies (P) Ltd. <docinfo@dkagencies.com>]

Saxena, Sushil Kumar, 1921 –

Hindustani sangeet and a philosopher of art.
(New vistas in Indian performing arts; no. 2).
Includes bibliographical references (p.).
Includes index.
ISBN 9788124601808

1. Langer, Susanne Katherina Knauth, 1895-1985 — Aesthetics. 2. Music, Hindustani — Philosophy and aesthetics. 3. Kathak (Dance) — India. 4. Aesthetics. 5. Rhythm. I. Title. II. Series: New vistas in Indian performing arts; no. 2.

ISBN 978-81-246-0180-8

First published in India in 2001
Second impression published in 2013

Printed and published by:
D.K. Printworld (P) Ltd.
Regd. office : *'Vedaśrī,'* F-395, Sudarshan Park
(Metro Station: Ramesh Nagar)
New Delhi - 110 015
Phones : (011) 2545 3975, 2546 6019; *Fax* : (011) 2546 5926
e-mail : indology@dkprintworld.com
Web : www.dkprintworld.com

To the Memory of
Susanne K. Langer
and
Rahimuddin Khan Dagar
to whom I owe,
respectively,
The dawn of my interest in Philosophical Aesthetics
and in
Ālāpa of the Dhruvapad idiom

Preface

INTERNATIONALISM in aesthetics is a growing demand of the day, and work in this direction has already begun paying dividends. I say so on the basis of my own experience. My studies in philosophical aesthetics began in 1964, when I was asked to start the teaching of this young and very promising discipline to postgraduate students of my university, that is, the University of Delhi. Ever since that year I have tried to make a close study of the basic writings of some of the greatest aestheticians of the West with a threefold purpose. First, I wanted to get familiar with their analytic ways of looking at problems relating to art, — ways which are necessary for authentic understanding, and so also for avoiding obfuscatory metaphysical jargon to which we in India have freely resorted in our traditional, scholarly concern with the arts, with not very happy results. Second, with the help of this supplement to my own habits of thinking, my aim has also been to gain a better understanding of Hindustani music, rhythm, and Kathak dance — three aspects of *Sangeet* with which I have been quite actively, and not merely theoretically concerned for long. Thirdly, I have been keen to determine how the leading Western theories of art relate to our own music and dance.

None of these aims has remained quite unattained by the work I have already published. My first step in this direction was my little book on rhythm, *The Winged Form: Aesthetical Essays on Hindustani Rhythm*, brought out by our central Sangeet Natak Akademi in 1979. It is admittedly a mere primer. But, as an *analytic* study of Hindustani rhythm taken generally, and not only of the idiom and repertoire of any particular *gharānā* (traditional family-school), it has neither any precedent, nor even a rough analogue so far. I think I can fairly say the same of my second attempt in the way of contemporary aesthetics, namely, *Swinging Syllables — Aesthetics of Kathak Dance* (Sangeet Natak Akademi, 1991). To the best of my knowledge, it is the first ever analytic study of an important classical dance of India; and it too is yet to stimulate similar work in respect of our other dance-forms, all alike beautiful and open to aesthetic analysis. A subsequent work, an essay in both understanding and evaluation, has also gratified me. *Art and Philosophy — Seven Aestheticians* (Indian Council of Philosophical Research, New Delhi, 1994) is, in fact, my first sustained attempt to look at some leading aestheticians of the West — from Benedetto Croce to L.A. Reid — not merely in the context of their original writings, but in relation to the three facets of *sangeet* I have distinguished, and have been keenly interested in for a number of years. Luckily, this recent book has been liked by some top aestheticians of the day. Jerome Stolnitz, sometime President of the American Society for Aesthetics, believes it is 'admirably comprehensive [and] uniformly thoughtful'; and adds that 'there is nothing in the current literature that does the same thing in the same way'. This has surely encouraged me to keep working on the lines I have chosen.

The present book, however, follows a path which is a little different, and is perhaps of direct value to us in India. It is a detailed attempt to interpret and examine a fair part of the aesthetics of Susanne K. Langer, an important 'systematic' aesthetician of recent times, in the light of the evidence of our Hindustani music, rhythm and Kathak dance. I indeed expect this book to enable us to adjudge her work a little more thoughtfully than we have done so far; and to improve our own understanding of the three allied arts I propose to focus on, namely, music, rhythm, and dance.

What lends aesthetic substance to this work is, in the main, my fellowship of fifty long years with Hindustani *sangeet* in a multiple capacity, that is, as a *rasika*, critic and as an aesthetician; and also as a composer of sorts. At quite a few places in this work, I have drawn upon my 'critical' write-ups contributed (since 1950) to the following: *The Hindustan Times, The Pioneer, Asian Age*, and *Śruti* (Madras) for which I still write as a contributing editor. I have also availed of some of my essays published (and debated) in leading Western journals; and, above all, in *Sangeet Natak*, official journal of our central Sangeet Natak Akademi which has all along been very helpful to me. Further, the recordings of some select musicians that I have done in the last few years on behalf of the Akademi and the Indira Gandhi National Centre for the Arts have also provided some good material for the present work.

But I see it clearly that the basic impulse to take to philosophical aesthetics as a lifelong commitment has come from my careful and repeated reading of the works of Susanne K. Langer; and that, if not quite openly, the fillip to go on has been provided, in a measure, by her following moving and reassuring words in a letter written to me more than eighteen years ago (30.4.1982):

> I am sorry there has been such a long delay in thanking you for sending me your book [*Aesthetical Essays*, 1981] *which I have read as far as my failing eyesight has allowed.* Among all the reactions to my own ideas which I received, yours has been one of the most gratifying. Unlike most of the others who have put their previous ideas into my words, I feel that you have understood what I have actually said. Perhaps your Indian background is more conducive to understanding than our Western habits of thought. I am sorry that we have never met each other.

Therefore, it is not without reason that I have dedicated this book to her memory. The sense that I am deeply indebted to her work is also the reason why my disagreement with her views, which recurs freely in this book, has in every case come about after very close attention to the text of her books; and perhaps never without a touch of regret.

To the other dedicatee, Ustad Rahimuddin Khan Dagar, I am just as indebted. He was a consummate *ālāpīyā*, and the first to open my eyes to the glories of the severely 'pure' in Indian vocal music, that is, of *ālāpa* which needs neither rhythm nor any words to spellbind the listener. In respect of *sheer fineness of musical utterance and impact*, I have not come across anything preferable to *ālāpa* of this maestro of the Dagar *gharānā*.

But as I say so, I cannot help recalling, very gratefully, how much I owe to the following artistes as well, for making me see some of the subtlest charms of the different aspects of our *sangeet*: Ustads Chand Khan, Hilal Ahmad, and Nasir Ahmad (*khyāl-gāyakī* of Delhi *gharānā*); my brother, Prof. Sudhir Kumar Saxena and Ustad Chhammā Khan (*tablā*-rhythm); and Nṛtyācārya Nārāyan Prasād and Akademi Award winner Rani Karnaa (Kathak Dance).

All this, however, could not see the light of day without the kindly co-operation of my publishers, D.K. Printworld (P) Ltd. They have taken pains to ensure correct printing and also to make the book look good. Further, to lessen the strain on my ageing eyes, in the first two proofs of the manuscript submitted to me, they used a bigger font than the one which appears in the book. This has touched me deeply.

Delhi
14.01.2001

S.K. Saxena

Acknowledgments

IN working at this book, help has been received from various sources; and I happily acknowledge that I am indebted to the following:

The Indian Council of Philosophical Research, New Delhi: for the monetary assistance of a three-year Senior Fellowship.

The Librarian, Connecticut College, New London, Connecticut: for providing clues to secure some essays published *by* Susanne K. Langer and some critical writing *on* her work.

Sangeet Natak Akademi, New Delhi: for letting me record the music of some maestros of Hindustani *Sangeet* for our National Archives, and so providing some first-hand material to illustrate a few points of aesthetic theory made in this work.

Editors of *Sangeet Natak,* official journal of Sangeet Natak Akademi (New Delhi) and *Śruti* (Madras): for permission to draw upon my essays and write-ups published in their periodic issues.

Indira Gandhi National Centre for the Arts, New Delhi: for giving me a chance to do some elaborate recording of the repertoire of Ustad R. Fahimuddin Dagar at the Central Production Centre of Delhi Doordarshan, thus enabling me to make my references to *ālāpa-dhruvapad* in this book more authentic than they would have been without this help;

Dr. (Mrs.) Ujwala Sharma and Dr. Mrs. Anjali Mittal: for notating my compositions discussed in the book;

Mrs. Smrti Srivastava for help in preparing the Index; and Dr. P. Kumar for designing the jacket.

Contents

1

Langer's Theory of Art
Some Essentials

PERHAPS more than the artists themselves, philosophers, 'consumers' and critics of art have often put forth divergent definitions of art. The view that art is a conscious and disciplined effort to create *beauty* has for long dominated traditional thinking in India. In the region of classical Indian music and dance it still holds sway, though admittedly along with the view that art is a kind of self-expression. A much greater variety of views is to be found in Western thought. Here, some have held that the essential function of art is to meet the canons of composition, such as unity in diversity, for the lack of which the Pyramids have been denied the status of architectural works by Herbert Read.[1] Others, like Dewey and Roger Fry, have taken pains to argue that art owes its unique significance to its ability to exalt and prolong our perceptual experience of things or of their form. Finally, there are those who profess the view that art is essentially a kind of expression of one's own immediate feelings or emotions.

Art as expression

It is specially to the last conception of art that Susanne Langer's theory of art is explicitly opposed. According to her, art is the 'expression of *conceived* feeling,[2] not of any feeling presently experienced. She refuses to regard artistic expression as a mere symptom of the artist's own immediate state of mind. Nor is

1. Langer, *Mind — An Essay on Human Feeling*, vol. I, p. 140.
2. *Ibid*.

she importantly concerned with the expression of the life of a particular society or age in works of art. The views she opposes or ignores may well be said to have used the word, *expression*, quite meaningfully; but none of these uses, Langer rightly says, is *uniquely* relevant to art.[3] We are generally right in reading the frown on a man's face as an expression of his anger; and a purely historical account may well succeed in giving utterance to the life and thought of a particular age; but in neither case is the expression regarded as a work of art. Yet, though she surely gives to *expression* a new and important meaning in the context of art, it is not the only concept of value in the rich fabric of her aesthetics. So, as I open this work by focusing on *expression* alone, I must argue a little for the choice.

Historically, the expression theory of art has been pre-eminent, and Susanne Langer is generally regarded as its most important recent advocate. Her work is distinctive too, in respect of the uniqueness and detail of the way she explains *what* art expresses (the life of feeling) and *how* it expresses (symbolically) what it does. This is not to suggest that nobody has anticipated any major emphasis of her theory of art. If only by way of indicating that she is not quite without support from respectable sources, Langer herself speaks of some authors from whom she has drawn

> some of . . . [her] own philosophical ideas . . . such as the concept of expressiveness . . . and the concept of 'semblance'.[4]

But, at the same time, her work may perhaps be said to be noteworthy because of its analytic rigour, adequacy of concern with a wide variety of art, and novelty and cohesion of its conceptual framework.

Further, though it is true that expression is not *the only* important aesthetic concept — and that, therefore, as upon Langer's own view, aesthetics cannot be defined as merely the science of expression,[5] it is just as unquestionable that it is a

3. Langer, *Feeling and Form*, p. 26.
4. Langer, *Philosophical Sketches*, p. xi.
5. Langer, *Feeling and Form*, p. 12.

key concept in her total view of art; for where she speaks of art as the symbolic expression of the forms of feeling, the forms in question are to be taken as what art *expresses*, and 'symbolic' as qualifying the way they may be said to be *expressed*. On the other hand, the claim of expression to centrality in aesthetics has been strongly challenged by quite a few aestheticians, including L.A. Reid who criticises Langer at length and with a fair show of reason. So the concept of expression in art demands critical reflection.

Such reflection, it is obvious, has to address three basic questions. What does expression mean? What is it that art may truly be said to express? And how exactly does expression become *artistic*? It is indeed around these three questions, in the main, that I propose to discuss Langer's views in the present chapter. Now, to begin with the first one, some commonly acknowledged meanings of 'express' are: *to press* or *force out*; to *emit*, to represent or reveal; to make known by some kind of likeness, in terms of words, signs, or symbols; and to put into words. Only the first three of these, we may note, suggest an ejection from within, and some looseness or separability of what is expressed from its original locus. On the other hand, when a face is said to be expressive, say, of joy, nobody commits the mistake of believing that the emotion in question is divided from the face.

But even this familiar and perfectly legitimate sense of expressiveness cannot be said to cover everything that is found to be expressive. As Otto Baensch rightly points out:

> We never think of regarding the landscape as a sentient being whose outward aspect 'expresses' the mood that it contains subjectively. [Further], the landscape does not express the mood [in the sense of ejecting the latter], but *has* it; the mood surrounds, fills, and *permeates* it, likes the light that illumines it. . . .[6]

On the other hand, meaning — as it is expressed by ordinary language — cannot be said to *inhere* in the words one uses;

6. Langer, *Feeling and Form*, p. 19; italics added.

they only *convey* or *indicate* what is meant; and the same meaning can be conveyed by a quite different, but synonymous set of words from another language. Nor does verbal expression *necessarily* invite notice to any *present* reality or reveal anything about the person who makes the utterance. A woebegone face may be truly said to reflect the unhappiness that besets one presently, but should he express himself verbally as follows, 'sorrow is as much an integral part of life as joy', he would neither reveal anything about his present state of being nor invite us to notice anything nearby. What language here does is only to present a definite thought to our understanding.

To conclude, it is quite possible to speak of *expression* sensibly without suggesting that what is expressed is a state of the self or an invitation to look at something present; and so far as *verbal* expression is concerned, what is always necessary (according to Langer) is only a projection of some ideas for our contemplation.

In the theory of art, however, *expression* has often been conceived quite differently not only by aestheticians, but by quite a few artistes of eminence. Specially in respect of music and dance, it has been freely held that the essence of these arts is direct (or 'sheer') *self-expression*. Langer's formulation of this view is clear, if not all along guarded; and her opposition to it, well grounded. All this, however, will be brought out later — I mean, in chapters which aim at a detailed discussion of Langer's aesthetics of music and dance; and here we may simply note that investing a musical passage with a tinge of grief — say, through a subtle regulation of aesthetic pace and vocal volume — is clearly not the same thing as the effortless act of crying out of grief. But if a little attention is enough to expose the falsity of the self-expression theory of art, why is it that people yet find it easier to accept this view than Langer's own thesis, to be discussed at length a little later, that what art expresses is not the artist's *present experience* of some feeling, but his *imagination* of some form of felt life? The explanation, as given by Langer herself, may be put thus:

Where what is presently imagined is a thing which has been previously *perceived*, the two experiences can be discriminated with ease; for whereas the imagining is, so to say, essentially an inner experience, the perception relates to what is clearly outside of us. On the other hand, the actual having of an emotion and the subsequent imagining of it are both 'inner' experiences, in the main; and, therefore, they cannot be easily distinguished. This is why the common man finds it difficult to see that what art expresses is the artist's *imagination or conception of a feeling, and not his own present experience of it*.[7] The difficulty is heightened by the fact that

> creative work [involving imagination] always produces an actual excitement, which is coloured by the [thought of the] feeling to be projected, and is sometimes more massive than the intended import.[8]

To illustrate, the involvement required, and the delight taken in being able, to invest the *gāndhār* of *rāga darbārī*[9] with a look of faded tint or tentativeness, together dominate more of consciousness than the actual 'look' itself; and so the feeling *creatively evoked and projected* is likely to be confused, because it is subduedly contiguous, with what is *actually felt*. Building upon Campbell Fisher's view that the intellectual excitement and feeling of heightened sensibility — accompanying 'acts of insight and intuitive judgement' — which the artist himself experiences during the act of creation are not the import of art, and that

> what the created form expresses is the nature of *feelings conceived, imaginatively realised*, and rendered by a labor of formulation and abstractive vision,[9a]

Langer adds that the

> envisagement [of feelings] may be spontaneous and easy or very arduous and slow; [and that] the result need not show

---

7. Langer, *Mind — An Essay on Human Feeling*, vol. I, p. 89.

8. *Ibid*.

9. A *rāga* may roughly be called a melody-type. For a fuller and better understanding of this concept, see Ch. II. *Darbārī* is one of our more serious *rāga*s and is, therefore, meant to be sung preferably at a reposeful pace.

9a. Langer, *Mind — An Essay on Human Feeling*, vol. I, p. 90.

the way it was achieved.[10]

Langer on expression: Some questions

The way is now paved to consider some such utterances of Langer as project the essentials of her own positive view of art unequivocally. The following may be picked, to begin with:

> (1) What art expresses is *not* actual feeling, but ideas of feeling; as language does not express actual things and events but ideas of them. (2) Art is expressive through and through — every line, every sound, every gesture; and therefore it is a hundred per cent symbolic. (3) It is not sensuously pleasing and *also* symbolic; the sensuous quality is in the service of its vital import. (4) A work of art is far more symbolic than a word which can be learned and even employed without any knowledge of its meaning; for a purely articulated symbol *presents* its import directly to any beholder who is sensitive at all to articulated forms in the given medium. (5) [Even] pure decorative design is a direct projection of vital feeling into visible shape and color. . . . [Quite unlike geometric forms such as a triangle, the design] always has . . . motion and rest, rhythmic unity, wholeness . . . it is 'living' form, though it need not represent anything living. . . . Decorative lines and areas express vitality in what they themselves seem to 'do' . . . the design itself expresses life. Lines that intersect in a central point 'emanate' from that center, although they never actually change their relation to it. Similar or congruent elements 'repeat' each other. Colors 'balance' each other, though they have no physical weight. (6) All these metaphorical terms denote relationships that belong to the virtual object, the created illusion.[11]

Let me now see if what Langer says in the above is all quite acceptable, or even intelligible.

A part of her basic view of art is quite clear. The essence of art, she insists, is *expression*. But *what* does it express? To this question, Langer gives the following different answers in the extract cited: 'ideas of feeling' (1), vital feeling, vitality (5). So

10. Langer, *Mind — An Essay on Human Feeling*, vol. I, p. 90.
11. Langer, *Feeling and Form*, pp. 59, 63. Bracketed numbers added.

according to her, the significance of art may be said to be '*vital* import' (3). By way of explaining how even a decorative design may be said to express 'life' or 'vitality', Langer says that the "decorative lines and [coloured] areas in such a design, do so [or express 'life'] by virtue of what they appear to *do*". Lines may seem to *emanate* from a common centre; and colours, to *balance* each other. Now, if we speak thus, as indeed we commonly do, our meaning would clearly be that these elements of a design express certain directions, movements or activities that we come across in daily life, such as arising from the same point, and balancing things or alternatives. But, then, how is this suggestion to be squared with Langer's explicit view that what art expresses is *ideas of feeling* (1)? Activity as such is surely not the same thing as an *idea* of feeling. An attempt may be made to meet the difficulty by saying, as Langer does elsewhere,[12] that by *feeling* we may mean not merely emotions, but 'everything that can be felt'; and that, therefore, a decorative design may be said to express ideas of activity *as felt*. But, though such a suggestion may well seem to lessen the distance (so to say) between 'activity' and 'feeling', it will not really serve the purpose. It will require us to say, I repeat, that by virtue of what its elements seem to 'do'— such as balancing or repeating each other — a decorative design expresses ideas of activity *as felt*. But, one may at once ask, how is 'activity as felt' to be understood? In the sense of activity as *directly experienced*, as opposed to activity that we merely *visualise or think of*? Probably yes; but the concept of 'activity as directly experienced' would itself call for some explanation. Is it to be taken in the sense of activity as experienced in the process of being personally undergone *or* as activity that we see in the outer world, quite close to us, may be, but not as a part of our inner life? In respect of the former kind of activity as experienced we use words like 'interesting', 'exciting', 'boring'; and for the latter kind, words like the ones that Langer herself has used in the context of the matter being discussed: (lines) *emanating* from a common centre, (congruent elements) *repeating* each other, (colours) *balancing* each other. But if, following Langer, we choose to use the second set

12. Langer, *Problems of Art*, p. 15.

of words, why should we not be content with speaking thus: 'In a good decorative design lines appear to emanate; congruent elements, to repeat each other; colours, to balance each other'? What is the need, and how would it be proper, to say that a design which is artistically good *expresses ideas* of activity? And why not choose to wind up the matter by putting it simply as follows: 'The elements and colours *appear* to be doing something, and the design, as a whole, therefore, *seems* to have a life of its own, quite unlike, say, tables and chairs'? Here, 'appear' and 'seems' will duly provide for the element of semblance on which Langer rightly insists; and, what is more, the perceptual character of the experience will be duly retained, because the words 'ideas of —' (feeling/activity) will be kept out.

Langer, however, would not agree to this exclusion. It is her considered view that artistic expression is symbolic; that a symbol is a vehicle *of ideas*; and that a work of art is 'far more symbolic than a word' (4). But the way she puts this emphasis (2, 3, 4) is not clear, much less acceptable. So, let me deal with it piecemeal:

Consider, first, the emphasis that 'art is expressive through and through — every line, every *sound*, every *gesture* . . .' (2). This remark is, in my view, too sweeping to be true. How can expressiveness be ascribed to the tonic with which a vocal recital may directly open? *What* does it express? In the case of Hindustani music, the note in question may well be able to *indicate* — I would not say, *express*, for *express* suggests as in-out relation, or some projection, which is not present in the case being considered — what *rāga* is going to be sung; but this indication too would be possible only if the *svara* (note) in question takes the help of some other notes, *which it does not always do*. Further, the practice of Hindustani music does not warrant the view that 'the sensuous quality [of a *svara*] is [always] in the service of its vital *import*'. It is, for instance, common knowledge that the singing of the upper tonic may well be admired as intensely tuneful without the slightest suggestion that it is expressing something.

And to turn to our classical dance for a while, nobody who

is really familiar with it would say that dancing is expressive 'through and through'. There is, generally, a whole distinct section of a classical dance recital which has nothing to do with expression. It is called *nṛtta*, and is only a skilful creation of ever more various rhythmic patterns within and across the chosen cycle. Nor can expressiveness be said to qualify every *gesture*. Where a Kathak dancer gently *nods* his head as a definite *footfall* marks the focal beat, the two gestures alike *indicate* or acknowledge attainment of the *sama*, but do not express anything.

Finally, it is difficult to accept Langer's way of opposing 'a work of art' to a word in respect of symbolic quality. First, it is hardly fair to pit a single word against a complete work of art; and should a meaningful *complex* of words be taken into account, it would not be possible to say that it is less meaninful than a simple work of art, necessarily and categorically. Secondly, it is not clear what Langer means by saying that a work of art is *far more symbolic* than a word. Her argument here is that whereas 'a purely and wholly articulated symbol' — that is (in her view) a work of art — '*presents* its import directly to any beholder' who knows how to react to works 'in the given medium', a word may well 'be learned and even employed without any knowledge of its meaning' (4). But, even if we accept it, such a way of arguing would only mean that a work of art reveals its meaning *more readily*, not that it has *more meaning*, than a word. Further, in the very next para (on p. 59 of *Feeling and Form*) Langer says that 'an articulate form must be understood before it can convey any import. . . .' But, then, if we are to level up the comparison, we should allow ourselves to speak similarly in respect of a verbal complex too, say, as follows: it reveals its meaning only to him who is conversant with the language to which it (the complex in question) belongs; and this revelation (of its full or deeper meaning) will be had only when its (obvious or literal) meaning has been understood. So, I conclude, by opposing *a whole work of art* to a word in the way she does it here, Langer is not really able to argue for the superiority of the former in respect of symbolic value.

Creation of art

The extract we have just discussed relates, in the main, to the expressiveness of a work of art. It does not throw any light on the *creation* of art. But there *are* quite a few passages in Langer's writing which project her views on the making of art quite clearly. See, for instance, the following:

> *a.* [In so far as seizing the import of a work of art consists in perceiving] the congruence of the symbolic form and the form of some vital experience . . . by the force of Gestalt alone . . . [*b.* the importance is paramount] of *abstracting the form* . . . and divesting it of all its usual meanings so it may be open to new ones. *c.* The first thing is to estrange it from actuality, to give it . . .' self-sufficiency' . . . by creating a realm of illusion in which it functions as *Schein*, mere semblance free from worldly offices.[13] *d.* The second thing is to make it plastic, so [that] it may be manipulated in the interests of expression . . . [again] by uncoupling it from practical life, abstracting it as a free conceptual figment. . . . *e.* And finally, it must become 'transparent' — which it does when insight into the reality to be expressed, the *Gestalt* of living experience, guides its author in creating it. Wherever craftsmanship is art, these principles — abstraction, plastic freedom, expressiveness — are wholly exemplified. . . .[14]

Here, it is obvious, Langer is talking mainly of the basic principles of artistic creation taken generally, that is, of *creation* in every medium, though where she speaks of the seizure of import (*a*) what she seems to have in mind is the *contemplation* of art. So let me see if what she says makes sense even in the context of Hindustani music:

Take the case of *ālāpa*[15] as it is done by a *dhruvapad*[16]-singer

13. Langer, *Feeling and Form*, p. 59.
14. *Feeling and Form*, pp. 59-60.
15. *Ālāpa* in Hindustani music is the speciality of a *dhruvapad* singer. It is singing without the help of both words and rhythm as drummed. Yet it can be very appealing and expressive.
16. *Dhruvapad* is the oldest existing form of Hindustani or north Indian vocal music. It is admirably suited to produce deeper effects.

(and contemplated by a *rasika*).[17] As the vocalist begins, he already has a form in mind which he is required to keep to, all along, — namely, the form of the *rāga* chosen for musical treatment. No 'form' *has to be* abstracted and *divested* 'of all its usual meanings'. The (*rāga*-) form, I repeat, is (so to say) given to the singer, readymade. And if we may at all talk of the *meaning* of a *rāga*-form, it could only be the emotion (or *rasa*) which it is (at least in some cases, and in principle) required to express, rather than to be *divested of*. (So *b*. is not relevant to the case being considered). But this is undeniable that the ongoing *ālāpa*, which is at once and necessarily an unfoldment of the *rāga*-form, is 'self-sufficient' and quite freed 'from worldly offices' (*c*.) in the sense that we attend to it and value it for its own sake, without at all thinking as to how it can be of use to us in life. It is also an illusion in a specific sense, illusion as '*Schein*' or *mere* appearance, not as the appearance *of a thing* as something else. (*d*.) Further, the *rāga*-form is, in actual singing, also made plastic in the sense that, instead of remaining confined to its written or notational form, it here admits of plenty of creative treatment — in respect of aesthetic pace, abidance at individual *svaras*, and ways of linking or traversing them — exactly as the implications of a big thought may be worked out freely without any pressure from outside. But, though a good *ālāpīyā* (or *ālāpa*-singer) may well be able to evoke an intense, soul-filling sonant atmosphere, identifiable as the realisation of the aesthetic potential of a particular *rāga*, and so transparent (*e*.), I am not sure if he can be said to be guided, in the course of creation, by any '*Gestalt of living experience*'. If he is supposed to be so guided, he must be also be credited with the ideal possession of *such* a *gestalt* from the very opening of song. But what he, in fact, has at the very outset is simply an ideal grasp of the form of the *rāga*, besides of course the accumulated fruits of training and a keen desire to do his best by way of translating the vision into overt singing. The praise that is generally showered on good *ālāpa* relates to its orderly progression, methodical build-up, sensitiveness and variety of musical treatment, and its eventual look of pervading every

---

17. A *rasika* is a qualified contemplator of the arts.

corner of the concert hall, but never to the *gestalt* of a living experience. A *gestalt* is a shape, an organised *whole* or unit. The crowning effect of top class *ālāpa* is, on the other hand, one of 'an intense diffusion, a serene omnipresence', to use Shelley's words; or one of a sweet, even elevating atmosphere, in our common musical parlance.

Our account of Langer's view of creation in art is, however, yet quite sketchy; and I think it necessary to make the following supplementary remarks — at places, with some comments of my own:

(a) It is only in the *creation of art*, not in the *making of things*, that the material used loses its original, independent character. This is why whereas it is common and proper to speak of a shoe as an article of leather, nobody ever refers to a painting as a colour-and-canvas structure, or of a dance as a collocation of bodily power, light, and gravity, though these are all alike necessary as its materials. The simple truth (according to Langer) is that in the creation of art the material is so swallowed up in the process that it does not remain a distinct object of attention.

Here, I have no qualms in accepting Langer's account of how we do *not* generally talk of a work of art; but I wonder if the way she speaks of the disappearance of the material's independent status in creation is true of every art. For instance, if a singer's voice is sweet, however captivating be the overall form of music and its magical or illusory features, does it not remain possible to occasionally point to the fact of its pervasive tonal sweetness?

(b) Further, quite unlike things *made* for daily use, all works of art are creations because (in Langer's view) they objectify some details of life as felt or directly experienced. Consider, for instance, the way a painting takes shape on the canvas. The moment the pigment used appears as a coloured line, it comes *to do* something, to divide space, and possibly even to *express* a little tension, nervousness or fineness and serenity. In other words, it loses its utter materialness and acquires a living character, some semblance of life. This is what the creative treatment of material really means. It is not that the artist has to try to put some 'feeling' into the work; rather the material itself, because of creative handling, comes to acquire a semblance of lived experience. No work of art, however indifferent it be, is a mere thing; and in the case of every work of art, material cannot but be creatively treated. So, *all* art is creation. 'Creation is not properly a value-concept'[18] and its relevance is by no means confined to *good* works of art.

Now, this is not a very common view of creation in art. But the way Langer projects the difference between everyday objects and works of art is even more striking, partly because she uses some quite new terms, such as 'illusion' and 'apparition' in respect of art. She argues that a work of art is an apparition, in the sense of being a *mere* appearance, not as an appearance *of* any hidden reality. True, it is (in her view) *expressive* of some meaning; but this meaning, she insists, is nothing behind or beyond — nor merely conjoined with — the work, but is perceived *in* it, as the work's own distinctive look, so to say. Mere appearance is, however, no monopoly of the region of art. In nature too we find objects which are 'merely apparent'.[19] Rainbows and mirages are good examples here. Yet, as apparitions, these are different from a work of art; for the latter is *created*. However, the work is a creation not merely because it is actively brought into being, but because it never existed before *and* is not an actual object. It is only because of this doubly negative character of both its parts and its total form — that is, its clear remoteness from the world of actuality — and *not because it deceives us in some way*, that a work of art may be said to be 'illusory'.[20] The organised space that we see in the picture is no real space. We cannot traverse it. Nor does it permit any echoing of sounds. And the 'things' that may be

18. Langer, *Problems of Art*, p. 28.

19. *Ibid.*, p. 29.

20. *Ibid.*, p. 30.

there in the picture — say, figures and fruits — do not relate to us in the same practical ways as people and objects in real life do. 'The whole picture is a *purely visual* space', 'nothing but a vision'. Such space and such 'things', which are objects of vision *alone,* are clearly no parts of the actual world. In this sense 'the picture . . . is an apparition . . . [a] spatial illusion'. It is surely not mere nothing; we really see it and register its expressiveness. But it is an abstraction. What is more, we know that it is only meant to be seen, and we accept it as such. The picture does not seek to make us believe, nor are we ever deceived into believing, that what it presents is merely some actual content bodily lifted from life. It abstracts and presents the merely visual, and we acquiesce in the visual abstraction. As a creative activity, art abstracts 'the elements of sensory appearance from the fabric of actual life and its complex interests' and projects 'a datum that is nothing but appearance'. We take delight in the play of such appearances; and, what is more, we come to learn something about felt life thereby. It is in this sense that 'illusion' may be regarded as a principle of *both* creation and contemplation of art. 'To create a sensory illusion' and to make us see 'abstractly' — this is the artist's normal function.[21]

But, as the very first step in creation, abstraction in art is not simply a matter of taking something out of, or abdicating given reality. A work of art does not come into being as a *mere* extraction from the world and its contents. What motivates the act of abstraction and makes it aesthetically significant is a positive, creative purpose. An artist focuses on how life feels, or how things and events appear, and projects this feeling or appearance through the form abstracted, producing *the expressive form that a work of art work essentially is* — a form which makes felt life more manifest and open to understanding. To call the 'art-image' illusory is not to make it inferior in value to actual objects; it is not merely to mean 'that it is not material' but also, and more importantly, that it is such an expressive form — that is, such a whole of 'dynamic relations'[22] — that it enables us *to comprehend what we only undergo and see but dimly*

21. Langer, *Problems of Art*, p. 32.

22. *Ibid.*, p. 34.

in real life. As Roger Fry pointed out, our practical needs are so imperative that, ordinarily, we see and hear only so much as is needful for our everyday purposes. The creation of *art liberates the 'living' or felt character of things from this yoke of necessity and projects it for our contemplation*. It does not merely project some feature of felt life, but does it in such a way that what is expressed becomes amenable to our understanding.

Some basic distinctions

A fuller understanding of Langer's own positive view of art, however, calls for detailed attention to some such distinctions drawn by her as are implicit in her negative emphases. She insists that art is not expressive in the sense of being *signific*. In other words, it does not point to a matter of fact — 'how someone felt, what he believed, when and where he lived. . . .'[23] Now, this is clearly true of (the bulk of) instrumental music which, because it does not use any language, is quite *non-representational*. Even where such music appears to be expressive of some feeling, we do not tend to believe that the feeling which the strings seem to breathe is a mere extension of what presently besets the heart of the instrumentalist himself. But, according to Langer, even a *representational* painting, if taken in its wholeness and as a work of art, is not essentially a pointer to any matter of fact. What is more, she would like us to believe that even an actor's projection of a particular emotion — say, fierce anger — through due bodily adaptation, is not a direct *symptom* of some fire actually raging within his heart, or a *signal* to us to be on our guard. The truth (for Langer) is that art is, in every case, a *symbolic* projection of some detail of life as felt. But then it should be made clear how she distinguishes sign, symptom, signal, and symbol from one another; and this is precisely what I now set out to do.

Langer prefers to use *sign* as a generic term to cover both 'signal' and 'symbol'.[24] Taken generally, the *signific* function may be explained as the indication of a fact by some *natural*

23. Langer, *Feeling and Form*, p. 26.

24. *Ibid.*, footnote.

symptom or *invented* signal. To illustrate, the shivering of a man in sickbed is often rightly taken as a natural symptom of malaria because it betokens the fact that he is *presently* in the grip of the fever; and even (invented) signals, such as the ones which regulate traffic, indicate what the *immediate* situation requires us to do, that is, to come to a halt or to proceed. No such relatedness to some present fact is meant by a symbol. A pair of scales is commonly taken to symbolise justice, but it does not make us look for any actual act of equitable distribution close by; we only take it to stand for the idea of justice. So Langer says:

> A *signal* is comprehended if it serves to make us *notice the object* or situation it bespeaks. A *symbol* is understood when we *conceive* the idea it presents.[25]

Take the case of language. It is a paradigmatic system of *symbols;* but this is so only because its paramount function is the formulation of *ideas* for presentation to our understanding. It is, of course, easily possible for a man to say something about himself in a way that may clearly relate the 'expression' to his own present state; but in everyday conversation our language is, by and large, meaningful only as an 'articulation and presentation of *concepts*'.[26] Even where a reference to what is not far-off is involved, as in the statement: "We need a hundred chairs for *this* evening's function" most of the words used — 'hundred', 'chairs', 'function' — are meaningful as concepts rather than as denoting any particular object. They are all symbols, that is, vehicles of meanings that are general. But, we may note, the meaning here is *separable* from the specific words used. The ones we have listed can all be replaced with synonyms from other languages, and without any detriment to meaning. But the same just cannot be said of a work of art. The overall significance of a poem is *in*separable from even the specific sounds of the words it builds upon. This, incidentally, is the main reason why Langer refuses to regard a work of art as symbolic *exactly* in the way of language.

25. *Feeling and Form*, p. 26.

26. *Ibid*.

But, one may wonder if she is quite right in the way she distinguishes signal, symptom, and symbol. The symptoms of a difficult disease may all be said to be 'natural' in so far as they are not 'invented' by us; but instead of directly suggesting the presence of a *specific* ailment, sometimes their very number may only leave a homeopath wondering as to what precise ailment they could all be said to point to jointly. And, to turn now to *signal*

> what shall we say of a boy scout's attempt, during training, to convey a message to his partner by *signalling* with flags? On the one hand, the use of flags (in varying positions) may have to be understood by conceiving the ideas they present, a requirement which Langer associates with attention to *symbols*; and, on the other hand, the communicative device, even when rightly decoded, may *not* require us to notice or perceive — as, according to Langer, a signal should — any present object or situation. The signalling has only to be understood like sentences in everyday conversation. Therefore, the signal-symbol distinction, as Langer draws it, is not beyond question.[27]

Further, it is not enough to say that a signal is a kind of sign. The two should also be distinguished, because they surely differ in one respect at least. As Ducasse rightly points out, a *signal* is a sign made with the intent to affect someone; 'it is in its very nature communicative' and has, in general, to be decoded.[28] A *sign* like

> smoke, on the other hand, is not *intended* by anyone to convey meaning. Nor is any decoding ordinarily involved in expecting the presence of fire at a place which emits smoke. If, however, it is predetermined for some men in arms that the moment they see the rise of a cover of smoke they have to set out to launch an attack on the enemy, the smoke becomes a *signal, because it is now the vehicle of an intent* and ceases to be a mere sign.[29]

But, in spite of such possible objections to what Langer has to

27. S.K. Saxena, *Art and Philosophy — Seven Aestheticians*, pp. 264-65.
28. C.J. Ducasse, The *Philosophy of Art*, pp. 31-2.
29. Saxena, *Art and Philosophy*, pp. 262-3.

say by way of distinguishing sign, symptom, and symbol, this is unquestionable that a work of art cannot be regarded as a direct sign or symptom, or as a mere spillover of some presently experienced emotion of the artist himself. Physiognomic (self-expression) of personal emotion is, of course, an everyday occurrence; and it can be easily genuine (or *sāttvika*) instead of being merely enacted. But the perception of 'intrinsic expressiveness' in a *sensory presentation*, be it a drooping flower or the painting of a serene Dutch interior, is something quite different:

> In the former, [that is, in physiognomic self-expression] feeling is always understood as actually felt by someone else, but in the latter it is experienced as 'impersonal', not actually besetting any one, not even oneself.[30]

Artistic expression as logical

What is, however, not so easy to understand is Langer's positive emphasis that artistic expression is *logical* rather than psychological, and that (yet) the import of art is presented 'homogeneously'[31] and not discursively. However, if due attention is paid to utterances of some artists that she cites in support of her view, the task becomes a little easier. But let me explain:

Artistic expression may be said to be logical in the sense of being *conceptual*. This, in turn, can be explained by saying that in creating a work of art an artist expresses not what or how he himself feels at the moment of creation, but how he *understands* or *conceives* some general features of the life of feeling. See, here, the following:

> Painters must paint for their own edification and pleasure, and what *they have to say, not what they are impelled to feel,* is what will interest those who are interested in them. The *thought* of the time is the emotion of the time.[32]

30. Langer, *Mind — An Essay on Human Feeling,* vol. I, p. 176.
31. *Ibid.*, p. 65.
32. Marsden Hartley's view cited by Langer in *Feeling and Form*, p. 82. Italics added.

Further, artistic expression is not psychological, but logical also because whereas *psychological* expression, as of genuine sadness in terms of tears, is automatic and not actively organised, *artistic* expression involves a careful integration of all that is there in a work. This is the truth which Matisse emphasises in speaking as follows:

> Expression, to my way of thinking, does not consist of the passion mirrored upon a human face or betrayed by a violent gesture. The whole arrangement of my picture is expressive. The place occupied by the figures or objects, the empty spaces around them, the proportions — everything plays a part.[33]

All this is very much in line with Langer's conception of art as expressive *form*, for what she means by this keyword is not mere shape, but the unique interrelatedness of all that is there in a work. But before we develop this emphasis of hers, it seems necessary to pay some attention to her view that artistic expression is *symbolic*, so as to provide the positive supplement to her negative thesis, which we have already discussed, that a work of art is neither a symptom nor a signal of some present fact.

Art as symbolic

How, if at all, is art *symbolic* in character? And what is a *symbol*? Now, a simple dictionary meaning of the word is: 'that which by custom or convention represents something else'. But, psychologically, a symbol may be taken to mean 'an object or act representing an unconscious or repressed conflict'. In this (second) sense, symbols are said to make for a kind of wish-fulfilment. They serve to give us some emotional relief, if only in a way which hardly ever makes for a better adaptation to the demands of waking life. Art too has sometimes been regarded as a way to provide such relief. The positivistic thinkers, in particular, generally look on all artistic expression

> as an exhibition of the artist's own emotions, either in lyrical signs and confessions, or by representation of things which evoke his emotive responses.[34]

33. Langer, *Feeling and Form*, p. 83.
34. Langer, *Mind — An Essay on Human Feeling*, vol. I, p. 80.

See, for instance, the following:

> The suppositious sentences of metaphysics, of the philosophy of *values*, of ethics are pseudo-sentences; they have no logical [meaning 'conceptual'] content, but are only expressions of feeling which in their turn stimulate feelings and volitional tendencies on the part of the hearer.[35]

To this view, however, Langer is stoutly opposed. She protests that philosophers of science and mathematics have been a bit too sweeping in lumping artistic expression with symbolization of wishes and fears in dream or fantasy.[36] But, then, how exactly is art symbolic *in her view*? In the way of language, or otherwise — or partly like language?

Now, Langer is very clearly aware of the difference between art and language; she, in fact, takes pains to heighten this difference. As used ordinarily, language becomes meaningful only as an *additive* whole of the individual *and more or less determinate* meanings of the words it builds upon. A work of art, on the other hand, is symbolic essentially as an *indivisible* whole. Langer argues for this point, in part, by proposing a distinction between *the art symbol* — that is, the complete work as itself the vehicle of some specific meaning — and *symbols in art*. This distinction, however, is by no means self-evident. So I have to bring it out, following Langer in the main.

The use of symbols *in* art is common knowledge. The halo of sacrosanct personages, for instance, symbolises holiness; and the rose and the lily, womanhood and chastity, respectively. Indian classical dances avail of whole systems of gesture-symbolism. What is more, here a symbol may connote more than one literal meaning. To illustrate, depending on how it is related to the total dance-fabric — and on how exactly the hands are positioned in making the gesture — the *patākā-mudrā* (or the 'flag' gesture-symbol) may signify the beginning of dance as an activity that is quite different from everyday business, or

35. Rudolf Carnap, *The Logical Syntax of Language*, (1937) p. 278; cited by Langer in *Mind — An Essay on Human Feeling*, vol. I, p. 80, f.n.

36. Langer, *Ibid.*, main text.

welcome, or the undulating waves. Such symbols, or units of more or less determinate meaning, do not merely occur in the dance, but actively help the creation and articulation — that is, the diversified oneness — of its organic form. This truth is specially manifest in those numbers of our classical dance which seek to tell a story or project an emotional situation, that is, in *nṛtya*. But the meaning of these (subsidiary) symbols is not as such a direct part of the dance-work's overall import. *Their* meaning is literal, matter-of-fact, not figurative. Very much like words, they refer to *facts* or state of affairs as such. On the other hand, what the Art Symbol formulates for contemplation is (according to Langer) only the *appearance* of feeling or subjective experience, not the fact of such experience. (Thus, though the traditional opening number of a Bharatanātyam recital, *alārippu*, opens with the *patākā-mudrā*, a gesture-symbol which literally means a flag, *as a part of the dance* it is apprehended as the fixation of a frame, so to say, whereby the subsequent figural dynamics appears to push and keep the daily world apart, and to create for the *rasika* a beautiful, autonomous apparition objectifying as Langer would say, the felt efflorescence of organic vitality.) Further, the Art Symbol, and the symbols it may build upon, are different not only in respect of *what* they mean, but also from the viewpoint of *how* they mean what they do. The symbols function in the way of words; 'what they mean is something beyond what they present in themselves'. The Art Symbol, on the other hand,

> does not stand for something else nor refer to anything that exists apart from it.[37]

> Its import is seen in it; not, like the meaning of a genuine symbol, by means of it but separable from the sign.[38]

At this point, however, reflection along the following lines may give rise to a question. A *genuine* symbol — that is, a symbol that is commonly accepted as such, say, a word — stands for, or refers to something 'that exists *apart* from it'. Indeed

---

37. Langer, *Problems of Art*, p. 132.
38. *Ibid.*, p. 139.

> the [meaning of a word] . . . lies elsewhere, and once we have grasped its connotation or identified something as its denotation, we do not need the word any more. But [as Langer herself takes pains to emphasize] a work of art does not point to a meaning beyond its own presence.[39]

But, if this is so, how can a work of art be said to be a symbol *in an acceptable sense*? Langer answers this question as follows:

The chief functions of language, as we use it ordinarily, are reference and communication. This has led semanticists to believe that symbols (or words) do nothing else, and that a symbol is essentially 'a sign which stands *for* something else and is used to represent that thing in discourse'. But 'to refer to things and communicate facts' is surely not the *only* function of language. Its 'second great office' . . . [is] 'the formulation of ideas, or conception itself . . . giving form and connection, clarity and proportion to our impressions, memories. . . .' It is indeed a primitive function of language '*to formulate experience* as something imaginable — to fix entities, and formulate facts. . . . This function is *articulation* . . . [Even a name which is an] arbitrarily assigned symbol] serves this purpose';[40] for in the very act of naming, say, an individual, do we not isolate and fix him for thought as a being with a distinct appearance or character? And in the act of imagining a pleasant experience of the past, or in *saying* (meaningfully) that this experience was pleasant, do we not at once mark off its bounds (so to say) and distinguish it from the general run of experience? To refer to *something*, or to communicate an *experience* (by means of language) is at once to put the thing in question in a meaningful relation and to give an intelligible form to the experience communicated. This is *formulation* in the sense of 'giving form to', and, of course, also as specifying or individualizing. It may also be said to be articulation regarded as a joining of distinct parts or details with an eye to clarity of understanding. The crux of the matter, here, is that *articulation* is necessarily presupposed in all reference and communication. And, what is more,

39. Langer, *Problems of Art*, pp. 133-4
40. *Ibid*., p. 132; italics added.

this function may outlast the other functions of language commonly recognised and emphasised by semanticists. The name of a man who died long may not longer be used to recall him or to *refer* to him; but, precisely because he has been named in the past, he still remains thinkable or *imaginable* as a distinct individual.

Now, this function of articulation or 'logical expression' is, according to Langer, necessarily performed by 'every good work of art'.

> It formulates the appearance of feeling, of subjective experience, the character of the so-called 'inner life', which discourse — [or] the normal use of words — is peculiarly unable to articulate, and which therefore we can only refer to in a general and quite superficial way.[41]

Artistic expression is *logical* in the sense that it presents 'objectively for contemplation . . . [and] understanding . . . the actual felt process of life'.[42] So, if not in its popular meaning, at least in its 'prime' [or necessary] sense of formulating experience for 'recognition and understanding', the word *symbol* may be used to characterise a work of art. But how exactly does art become symbolic *of human feeling*? Here, Langer lays down a basic requirement:

> Formal analogy, or congruence of logical structures, is the prime requisite between a symbol and whatever it is to mean. The symbol and the object symbolised must have some common logical form.[43]

Here, my immediate reaction is one of doubt. Where they signify an operation, and are not intergral to a number (as in — 5), the plus and minus signs that we use in mathematics may be said to be symbols upon Langer's own view, because they make us think of addition or positivity and subtraction or negativity, respectively. But where do we find *in these symbols* the 'logical structures' which could be said to have parallels in

41. Langer, *Problems of Art*, p. 133.

42. *Ibid*.

43 Langer, *Feeling and Form*, p. 27.

what they mean? But perhaps the sceptical question is unwarranted, because irrelevant to art. Mathematical symbols are 'arbitrarily posited';[44] in art, on the other hand,

> the symbolic function is not conventionally assigned . . . the presented form is significant simply by virtue of its articulate [or relational] character.[45]

So we may focus on *symbol* in relation to *art.*

Before, however, we turn to do this, let us see what the extract cited really means. The key is here provided by the way Langer interprets (logical) structure or form (ref. no. 43 on the previous page): that is, as an arrangement which heightens relations between qualities, and not as mere abstractable shape which may admit of description in geometrical terms. 'Congruence of logical structures' or 'common logical form' may, therefore, be taken to mean similarity or equivalence of arrangement, *not identity of content*. The 'feeling' that we may find in a work of art is clearly not the same as that which brings about a change in our blood pressure, or lends, say, a little warmth to our dealings with our fellow-beings.[46] The analogy of which Langer here speaks relates to something quite different. The *disposition or arrangement* which brings about the appearance of feeling in the (art) symbol has to be similar to what is symbolised, namely, to some form of feeling or some distinct way in which life as lived is really felt.

An example may be taken here. *A pair of scales* is commonly taken to symbolise *justice*. The two terms are obviously quite unlike each other. We cannot deal with the virtue of justice in the way we handle a balance; and, again, it is only in the latter that we find a beam which may seem titled to the eye. So if yet

44. Langer, *Problems of Art*, p. 132.

45. *Ibid*., p. 176.

46. See, here, the following: "A work of art . . . presents the semblance of feeling so directly to logical intuition that we seem to perceive feeling in the work; but of course the work does not contain feeling any more than a proposition about the mortality of Socrates contains a philosopher". Langer, *Mind — An Essay on Human Feeling*, vol. I, p. 67.

the symbolic relation holds, as it clearly does, it is only because of a relational sameness. To put it clearly, just as (in everyday use) the two halves of the beam are expected to remain on a level *with each other*, instead of inclining to any side, so justice demands (or means) that no bias be shown *in favour of, or against*, any of the individuals or parties that expect their claims to be properly weighed.

To turn to the specific congruence *we* are concerned with, that is, the one between artistic form and feeling, our doubts in respect of it may diminish if we realise (as Langer wants us to) that the life of feeling is not formless or chaotic.[47] Life is a natural process of . . . tensions [and resolutions], balance [and] rhythms.[48] This is manifest in such everyday states of experience as expectation and fulfilment, excitement sought as a recoil from depression, and the never-ending cycle of satisfaction and cravings anew.

On the other hand, a work of art too 'is a composition of tensions and resolutions, balance and unbalance, and rhythmic coherence'. This is manifest in quite a few works in the region of every art. A clear instance of balanced segments in patterns is provided, in the region of *khyāl*-singing, by what is called *sawāl jawāb kī tāna*; and unbalance may as properly be said to be there in a vocalist's over-indulgence in torrential *tāna*s — and neglect of *sthāyī* as a refrain and relief — as in a gourmet's enslavement to the palate. Nor is the coherence of a rhythmic flow confined to music. It may be equally present in a work of decorative art, in *alpanā*s on the floor or in arabesques of henna on the palm of a lady. But, as is common knowledge, balance may be freely found in poetry and drama as well; and a human life, too, may feel as one and inwardly balanced because of its proportionate emphasis on the various needs of life and personality. To conclude, the presence of formal congruence between (some or quite a few) works of art and subjective life is more or less obvious. But this is, of course, not to suggest that the presence in question is ubiquitous in the region of art.

47. Though the number of 'forms of subjectivity' or of 'the actual felt process of life' is myriad. Langer, *Problems of Art*, p. 133.

48. *Ibid.*, p. 8; bracketed words added.

What is much more acceptable is Langer's emphasis on the non-discursive character of a work of art.

Three important emphases of Langer's aesthetics of art have been discussed by now: first, that art is essentially a form of expression, but not in the way of a signal or symptom;. second, that it may be said to be symbolic in a primal, if not quite popular sense of the word *symbol* — a sense that is implicit in the use of language which is commonly regarded as a paradigmatic system of symbols; and, thirdly, that a complete work of art — as distinguished from the symbols it may build upon — is yet to be distinguished from language, because it is a presentational and not a discursive symbol.

Langer takes pains to distinguish the two kinds of symbols; and in so far as the distinction is of help in understanding her emphasis that a work of art — or, in her own words, the Art Symbol — is (in principle) indivisible, I think it necessary to outline how she projects the differences. This is required also by the fact that, on Langer's own view, the two kinds are not totally dissimilar either; for, as a symbol, art too serves to *articulate* or *objectify* experience, if not exactly in the way of language.[49]

(a) Discursive symbols are words, so necessary for everyday discourse. They make for determinateness and economy in thought. Words like 'triangle' and 'table' cover all individual figures or things which exemplify these concepts and have something specific in common. The *drawing* of a triangle, on the other hand, 'represents just one object — real or imaginary . . . [but necessarily] a unique object'.

> The definition of a triangle [or a triangle as understood] fits triangles *in general*, but a drawing always presents a triangle *of some specific kind and size.*[50]

The fact that we can define a *triangle* — say, as a figure bounded

49. From here on, the three points that I set out to make have all been developed essentially in the way I followed in my earlier work, *Art and Philosophy: Seven Aestheticians*, pp. 268-70.

50. Langer, *Philosophy in a New Key*, p. 96; italics added.

by three straight lines — means that this discursive symbol can be understood in terms of other words (*figure, straight, lines*) which are themselves symbols or general in meaning. But a presentational symbol — say, *an actual* work of art, as distinguished from the mere *concept* of art — cannot be defined in terms of other non-discursive symbols.[51] No two works of art are identical in significance. Repeated and discriminating reading of poetry, *generally*, may well enable us to look for the right excellences in *a* new poem; but what this particular poem has to say, or its own meaning as a work of art, can be realised only by comprehending how *it* organises in *its* own way the details *it* comprises.

(b) Further, the meaning of a *discursive* symbol, (or a word) is clearly not inseparable from its perceptual character, or its sound or look. In fact, the same meaning can with ease be conveyed by a synonym — say, from a different language; and so conjoined with a quite different appearance to the ear and the eye. But what a *presentational* symbol, or a work of art, means (or expresses) is *in*separable from all its perceptual details. It is indeed the solid evidence of listening to Hindustani music that the same composition presented by two singers strikes us differently simply because their *voices* differ in quality. This gives us a clue to distinguish works of art from holy Names which too can operate as presentational symbols. In the life of religion it is the settled quality of one's faith, and the intensity of devotion at the moment, which make the very utterance of His name feel like addressing God *Himself;* in art contemplation, on the other hand, it is the exercise of imaginative sympathy and percipience acquired over years that enables us to see the meaning embodied in the work. But, in either case, what is felt or realised as the deeper meaning of the experience is indivisible from, and so is taken to be intrinsic to, rather than merely indicated by the symbol. It should now be easy to follow Langer's emphases that a work of art is a presentational symbol, not a discursive one like language as ordinarily used; and that it is better to speak of it as an *expressive* rather than as a merely significant form:

51. Langer, *Philosophy in a New Key*, p. 95.

> [What is commonly regarded as] a genuine symbol, such as a word, is only a sign. . . The word is just an instrument. Its meaning lies elsewhere. . . . But a work of art does not point us to a meaning *beyond* [or as separable from] its own presence. [Here,] what is expressed cannot be grasped apart from the *sensuous* or poetic form that expresses it. In a work of art we have the direct presentation of a feeling, not a sign that points to it. That is why 'significant form' is a misleading . . . term. An Art Symbol does not signify, but only articulate[s] and present[s] its emotive content; hence the peculiar impression one always gets that feeling is *in* a beautiful and integral form. The work seems to be *imbued with* the emotion or mood or other vital experience that it expresses. That is why I call it an '*expressive* form' and call that which it formulates for us not its meaning, but its *import*.[52]

(c) What is more, whereas in getting at the meaning of a complex of discursive or verbal symbols (or words) we have to follow a definite before-after order, or to begin with words that open a sentence and then to turn to the ones that follow, no such binding is there in attending to presentational symbols (or works) in the region of visual arts like sculpture, painting, and architecture. And (I may add) where, as in the case of reading poetry or listening to music, one has to follow a definite order, it being obvious that one just cannot *begin* by attending to words or notes that come *at the end*, a kind of cyclic upgathering of the material which precedes the part presently attended to is more importantly required for the perception of the overall form — and is, in addition, much more conducive to the seeing of richer meaning — than in getting at the meaning of an everyday sentence, so that the sequential character of art contemplation is always vitally tempered with an interplay of elements, lending cohesion to our experience.[53]

(d) Finally, whereas the meaning of a complex of discursive symbols (or of a sentence) can be had by merely adding their

52. Langer, *Problems of Art*, pp. 133-4; only the last italics is original. Bracketed words too are mine.

53. This reflection concerning the intensification of our experience is mine, not Langer's. But I think it is warranted by her emphasis on the organic form of art. See her *Problems of Art*, p. 135.

determinate individual meanings, a presentational symbol—that is, according to Langer, a work of art — cannot be so understood. The elements of art have no fixed, exclusive meanings. They come to *acquire* meanings in the making of a work; and these meanings emerge from its unique organisation. Wavy lines may highlight the grace of flowing tresses in one picture, and merely an undulating surface in another. A whole work is indivisible in respect of its import; that is, it cannot be broken up into elements of set, independent meanings. Langer seeks to emphasise the essential singleness of a work of art, as also her view that art is expressive of 'the character of life', by using the concept of *living* or *organic* form.

'Livingness' and organic character of art

The concepts of living or organic form and expressive form are, in fact, closely related in her theory of art. I say so on the basis of quite a few explicit remarks of hers, such as the following one:

> [A poem is] not a report or comment, but a constructed form; if it is a good poetic work it is an *expressive form* in the same way that a work of plastic art is *expressive form* — by virtue of the tensions and resolutions, balances and asymmetries among its own elements, which beget the illusion of *organic nature* that artists call 'living form'.[54]

Here, at once, a question may be put. How is the relation of life *to form* necessary? Langer answers this question in the way of Aristotle:

> . . . Life, once put in motion, achieves certain forms inevitably, as long as it goes on at all: the acorn becomes an oak, . . . the sparrow's egg a sparrow. Other accretions of matter may *have* usual forms, but do not *strive* to achieve them, nor maintain themselves in them. . . . A creature broken in half either dies . . . or repairs one part, or both parts, to function again a whole.[55]

---

54. Langer, *Problems of Art.*, p. 148; italics added.
55. Langer, *Feeling and Form*, p. 89. Italics added.

So the relation of life to form may be said to be a literal fact. But in respect of art, on the other hand, the concept of 'living form' is but a metaphor. Here, again, Langer is explicit:

> Pictures do not really pulse and breathe[56]. . . . [But] if a picture is successful it [necessarily] presents us with something quite properly, even though *metaphorically called* 'living form'.[57]

But, if this is so, why can't we dispense with this metaphor straightaway? Why do we have to use it at all? Langer's answer is that "every artist finds 'life', 'vitality' or 'livingness' in a good work of art . . . ; [that] his first task is to 'animate' the canvas";[58] and that the whole literature of art uses the metaphor in question, and develops it at length.[59] *I* may at once add that this emphasis of Langer is strongly supported by the way we talk about our *Sangeet*.[60] To take a familiar instance, if a rhythmic pattern is played on the *tablā* or danced by a Kathak correctly in respect of its extent, *but without due accentuation of some syllables*, the presentation is likely to be called cold (ठंडा) or spiritless (बेजान) by a *rasika*, because a semblance of 'life' in rhythm is produced, in the main, by a blend of tension and release which, in turn, arises (in part) from a judicious accentuation of some select syllables and regulation of aesthetic pace.

Another metaphor of the studio, borrowed from the biological realm, is implicit in the view that every work of art must have the character of an organism, or that it must be internally unified. Good music is often acclaimed not only for its expressiveness, but for the fact that the *bandish* (composition) — or the *sthāyī-antarā* jointness — is tightly structured on the inside. At this point one may contend that whereas the concept of *organic unity* is widely acceptable to theorists of art, the concepts of *living and expressive form*, as applied to art *taken generally*, seem suspect to many; and that, therefore, it may be

56. Langer, *Problems of Art*, p. 45.
57. *Ibid.*, p. 128; italics added. Also see Langer's *Mind — An Essay on Human Feeling*, vol. I, p. 199.
58. Langer, *Problems of Art*, p. 44.
59. Langer, *Mind — An Essay on Human Feeling*, vol. I, p. 149.
60. A popular Indian word for music (both vocal and instrumental) *and* dance.

better to eschew these two concepts altogether. But at least in respect of 'living form', the suggestion, I believe, would be unacceptable to *rasikas*, that is, to those who have actual and substantial experience of contemplating art knowledgeably. Langer refers to *but one*

> serious reflective artist . . . [probably a painter, known to her, who was] actually shocked at such philistine statements as . . . calling these terms [mere] metaphors.[61]

But I have seen such metaphors used freely by quite a few of our eminent artists in respect of every form of *sangeet*. And the warrant for this usage will become clear as we turn to consider, with Langer, how exactly a work comes to appear 'alive' (and expressive) by creating the semblance of an *organic* form or unity. But, first, we must bring out the character of this form (or unity) itself. Langer's account of the matter may be summarized thus.

Organic form is *dynamic* and integrated, beside being sentient. It is dynamic because the unity, here, is the functional accord of a *process*,

> the organic process — [that is,] the constant burning up and equally constant renewal of . . . substance. Every cell, and indeed every part of every cell . . . is perpetually breaking down, and perpectually being replaced. . . . An organism . . . is really not a [stable] thing at all. Its individual, separate thing-like existence is [but] a pattern of changes; . . . . [62]

Organic form and rhythms: Primary, secondary

Further, organic form is richer, because more visibly integrated than the dynamic forms that we find in nature. It is true that a waterfall is a dynamic form. It is a 'moving somewhat, its long streamers seeming to shift like ribbons in a wind'; and so it may be said to be 'a mobile shape . . . a permanent datum in the landscape, among rocks and trees'.[63] Lines too can appear to

61. Langer, *Problems of Art*, p. 45.
62. *Ibid.*, p. 47.
63. *Ibid.*, p. 48.

have a dynamic form.[64] But *organic* form is dynamic in a special sense; it comprises changes in such a way that the very disappearance of one state makes for the emergence of the next. Therefore, such form may be said to be not only dynamic but *rhythmic*, rhythm (according to Langer) being *essentially* a matter of complementation or mutual conditioning of passing-out-of and coming-into being, and not of merely a regular and periodic succession.[65] Yet the fundamental or primary rhythm of organic (or living) form is (again, in Langer's view), the complementary alternation of growth and decay.

> [Even the] basic forms [of our feelings, emotion and desire] are vital forms . . . [;] their coming and going is in the pattern of growth and decline, not of mechanical occurrences [such as the failure of a vehicle to start, we may say, because of some mechanical defect].[66]

Secondary rhythms develop as 'specialised responses to the surrounding world'. Some of the commoner ones of these are: concentration and relaxation of attention, the former calling for the latter, and the latter releasing energy for focusing of attention anew; the build-up and release of the tension of desires, so that every such exercise is at once a quiet preparation for the emergence of new desires; and the rhythm of moments of renewed endeavour and piecemeal attainment and repose. However, all such rhythms can remain in periodic abeyance *without* damaging life. On the other hand, the rhythm of the 'breaking up and reconstitution of every living part' is such that if it is 'greatly disturbed, or suspended for more than a few moments, the organism collapses, life stops'.[67] This is, therefore, the primary rhythm; it is inviolable not in the sense that it *cannot* be disrupted, but in the sense that it *should* not be grievously affected if life is to continue. 'Its fundamental traits [are] . . .' dynamism, inviolable unity, organization, rhythmic

64. Langer, *Problems of Art*, p. 54.
65. For a detailed discussion of this point see chapter III on Rhythm.
66. Langer, *Problems of Art*, p. 46. Bracketed words and marks are all my addition.
67. *Ibid.*, pp. 52-3.

continuity . . . growth [and decline].' These are, in Langer's view, 'the [basic] principles of living form'.[68]

An important distinction

Our main task, now, is to see how these primary and secondary rhythms of life are projected in art. But as we set out to do so, Langer would like us to mark and remember an important distinction. All the principles of living form we have just listed

> have their analogues in those of artistic creation . . . (1) But . . . *analogous principles are not identical.* (2) The semblance of life need not be constructed on the same plan as life itself; (3) a device that serves to create a sense of change need not involve any actual change, (4) nor the most forcible presentation of growth any actual accumulation. (5) Artistic form is a *projection, not a copy* . . . (6) There is no direct correlation between the constituents of an organism and the elements in a work of art. Art has its own laws, . . . of expressiveness. [Further,] its . . . elements are all created forms, not material ingredients; such elements cannot be compared to physical factors, nor their functions to physical functions. (7) Only their product — the expressive form, the work of art — has characteristics symbolically related to those of life itself.[69]

This passage is too close a catalogue of some major views of Langer to be readily intelligible. It is, therefore, necessary to bring out its meaning at some length. I may do it thus, mostly in accordance with the order in which the individual points have been numbered (by me) in the passage.

To begin with, an analogy (we may note) is an agreement or correspondence in certain respects between things *that are otherwise different.* It is a parallelism, a resemblance of relations. Resemblance is likeness, not identity or sameness. Now, to turn to the basic distinction made in the passage cited, it is easy to see that the principles which make for the preservation or conduct of life are only similar to, but surely not the same as

---

68. Langer, *Problems of Art,* p. 53.

69. *Ibid.*, pp. 53-4. Italics and breaking-up of the passage into numbered portions are both my work.

those which underlie the creation of art. Some simple illustrations should bear out the point. Accentuation is a principle (or device) of both everyday talk *and* rhythm in the region of *sangeet;* and in either case it makes for clarity of utterance. But the material it works upon is language in one case, and beats and *bols* or mnemonic syllables in the other. Nor is the net purpose served *exactly* the same in the two cases, though it may *quite generally* be said to be improved following; for whereas the precise end achieved in speech is greater manifestness of verbal meaning, in rhythm the device of accentuation makes for an utterly non-semantic pattern of winsome articulateness. So the principle of accentuation as it works in everyday speech can only be said to be *analogous* to the way it operates in rhythm (point 1 on p. 33).

Take, next, the principle of balance as it works in a living organism — say, the human body — and in rhythm. In either case the principle makes for complementariness of acts, processes or segments. But the way it works and the precise ends achieved are again clearly dissimilar in the two cases. The heart balances itself through rhythmic *and physiological* alternation of systole and diastole. But a rhythmic phrase may do the same through an artistic juxtaposition of tufts of *bols* which take an equal number of beats; and which, it is obvious, do not involve contraction or dilatation of any bodily organ. Yet, I hasten to add, if the *bols* are also neatly cut, because of the very balance of compression (or quickening) and deceleration (or relaxation) of its constituent syllables, the whole phrase or pattern may well seem to be alive. So the principles on which real life depends and those which make for the semblance of life in art are only analogous, not identical. No literal 'livingness' is there where a rhythmic pattern appears to be *toying with the basic laya mischievously* or where a female figure in marble bewitches us with its look of 'living' flesh. Yet the semblance of life may be clear and irresistible in either case. It is produced here, respectively, by deviating from the basic rhythm for a moment *and designedly,* that is, expressly and according to a plan; and by polishing the material substance to the requisite degree of fineness.

Art-reality difference (contd.)

The difference between what we find in reality *and* as mere semblance or appearance in art is indeed undeniable. To illustrate, it is common knowledge for those who are conversant with the subtleties of our art of rhythm that where the drummer returns to the basic *laya* immediately after executing a very fluent pattern, the *ṭhekā* appears to have *grown a little steadier*, though the pace has not undergone any *actual* change. So, it seems proper to say that a device which serves to create a sense of change need not involve any actual alteration (point 3 in the extract being discussed p. 33). Even in the region of nature, a suggestion of flow and change can be easily provided by what is, in fact, presently inert. Thus, lines in the bed of a river which has deflected or dried up are quite static; yet they may clearly express 'the dynamic form of the river'.[70]

Luckily, the practice of Hindustani rhythm also provides some clear illustrations of how, in the region of art, the most forcible presentation of growth . . . [may not] 'involve any actual accumulation' (point 4). Thus, when a *chakradār paran* (an elaborate rhythmic pattern) is played on the *pakhāwaj* (a big drum) in the duly robust and accentuated, yet billowy manner, the pattern appears *to gather and elongate itself* as it moves from one segment to the next. But nothing here stays to be amplified; there is no growth or accumulation in actuality; that is, no accretion to the prefixed form of the *paran*. In other words, the form of the pattern as played projects or expresses a mere semblance of growth. Artistic form is surely a projection, that is, a disciplined expression of artistic intuition; but neither in the details of its making, nor in respect of its ultimate purpose, can it be said to be a mere imitation of given reality (point 5). It *is* organic in character in the sense of being an indivisible unity of whatever it contains. Yet it is not the same thing as an organism. The constituents of an organism are all 'material', tangible; the elements of a work of art, on the other hand, are all *created forms* that are meant to be contemplated and understood, and not for handling. Further, the two kinds of

---

70. Langer, *Problems of Art*, p. 19.

constituents do not serve identical ends. Our bodily organs and processes *keep us alive*, and fit in body and mind. Art elements, on the other hand, conjoin to *make a work expressive* (point 6; again, p. 33). Yet though 'there is no direct correlation between the constituents of an organism and the elements in a work of art . . . the expressive form . . . [or the work itself] has characteristics symbolically related [that is, not literally, but as semblance] to those of life itself' (point 7).

How art can (yet) symbolize life

Is this positive view (point 7) artificial? Not really; for it is easy to think of supportive instances. There is no living flesh in the material of a plant. Nor does the human body grow in the way of a plant, say, by drawing nourishment directly from the soil. Yet the faded tint of a fallen leaf may be easily taken as a symbol of the transience of the bloom of youth. But if the semblance of a form of (a phase of) life can thus arise from a commonplace working of imagination, why should it be difficult to envisage the same possibility in the region of art where imagination operates *along with manipulative power*, and is given some external material to work upon and to serve as the plastic substrate of creative embodiment? However, such a rhetorical question is hardly enough for our purpose. We have to show positively and at some length how a work of art can appear 'living' or project 'characteristics of life itself'.

Langer cites, with obvious approval, the following words of Edward Wardsworth:

> A picture is primarily the animation of an inert plane surface by a spatial rhythm of forms and colours.[71]

But, by way of clarifying what this 'animation' really is, I think it necessary to put together some of Langer's own remarks:

Take, first, the case of a picture. Here, some 'actual spatial datum, the canvas or paper surface' is surely used. But it is not allowed to remain what it is in its original character. By means of 'lines or volumes, or intersecting planes, or shadows and

71. Langer, *Feeling and Form*, p. 80.

lights', it is transformed into 'virtual space', that is, space which, though it appears to be spread out on the canvas, is quite different from the space of everyday life. Nobody thinks of putting things in this *created space*; nor does it let a sound carry in the way of actual space. What is more, the moment this virtual space, which is meant only for the eye and not for exploration by bodily movement, makes its appearance, it also 'dissociates itself from the actual space in which the canvas or other physical bearer of it exists'.[72] It is surely not taken into account while measuring the floor area of the gallery where it is put. However, the fact of this space's being different from, and discontinuous with actual space is not the same thing as the work's having a 'life' of its own. Yet the two appearances *are* closely related. This is so because virtual space arises from the creative ordering of, say, lines, colours, and volumes; and the skilful integration not only makes the work appear quite different from things of daily use, but significant in itself and, in a way, 'alive' to contemplation, may be because of suggestions of movement, thinning out or recession. In daily life the rim of a rectangular table is rarely, if ever, made an object of explicit attention; we just use the whole table as and when the need arises. But where what we contemplate is, say, a *painted* table or landscape which (we know) is not an existent, the formal elements are noticed for their own sake; and what they *appear to do* can easily draw and hold attention. Thus, in 'a purely decorative design, a wavy line adorning the rim of a pot' may look like *running* 'around the rim'; and in a picture a colour may not only seem to be a seamless expanse as compared to a tiny figure in the foreground, but also *to recede* into an infinite background.

Sources of 'livingness' in art

But perhaps the clearest suggestion of (what Langer calls) 'livingness' in a work of art arises from the creative use of tension *and* such an arrangement of details that they appear to be internally related and interactive. Langer puts emphasis on both these features, though not always at the same time. In *Feeling and Form* we are told that (visual) art is admirably suited

---

72. Langer, *Feeling and Form*, p. 83.

to 'exhibit tension and resolution simultaneously through the illusion of space-tensions and space-resolutions' because it 'creates its elements instead of taking them from the world';[73] and that the symbolic power of music — that is, its ability to project the character of life — lies in the fact that it creates a pattern of tensions and resolutions.[74] And, again in the same work, Langer explains that 'the oft-remarked quality of "livingness" *in all successful works*'[75] arises from the integral relationship of elements, that is, from the fact that 'every element . . . [seems] at once distinct, i.e., itself, and also continuous with a greater, self-sustained form'.[76]

Now, as I seek to understand these two emphases essentially in the light of Hindustani *sangeet*, I find it necessary to make the following remarks:

(a) In the case of art, it is obvious, tension is not a feature of interpersonal relations. Yet a look at what it is in actual life is surely of some help in understanding how it appears in our *sangeet*. Often we become tense after a long *waiting for* something to happen or for someone to arrive; and, what is more, in every case we keenly wish for a release from the keyed mental state. Together, the two attitudes make the experience feel oriented *and* a little compulsive. Now, if only as semblances, both these features occur freely in our music and rhythm, particularly in the way of gaining access to the *sama* designedly. This too is borne out by actual experience of listening to Hindustani music, and of watching Kathak dance, that (as Toch points out) the tension segment is generally longer than the relaxation segment.[77] We may further agree that form (in music) appears as 'polarity, as lines of force, as tensions perhaps

73. Langer, *Feeling and Form*, p. 373.
74. *Ibid*., p. 372.
75. *Ibid*., p. 373.
76. *Ibid*.
77. Langer, *Mind — An Essay on Human Feeling*, vol. I, p. 163.

as *longing'*.[78] Every good *bandish* (or composition) builds upon *āroha* and *avaroha* (polarity of ascent and descent) visibly; and so do the more appealing *tāna*s (or patterns) of the *khyāl*-singer. Lines of force and the appearance of tension strike the listener, I repeat, mostly in approaches to the *sama*; and 'longing', just mentioned along with other determinants of musical form, is to be taken, I suggest, not in the familiar conative-affective sense of human psychology, but as the aesthetic demand of a note or phrase for a specific supplement, may be for bringing out the distinctive nature of the *rāga* being presented, as when the course of singing appears to press for due projection of *pa-ga* or *dha-re* linkages in *rāga*s *bhūpāli* and *śrī*, respectively. And in so far as these are all ways in which our music is in fact organised, they may well be said to be indices of musical form.

(b) Tension, however, is only one of these ways; and so Langer would not like us to regard it as the sole essential of music. Indeed, there is a good deal in *our* music which is quite without a semblance of tension. In its initial stages, *ālāpa* of the *dhruvapad* manner is distinguished by the charm of tranquil passages;[79] and if our *ārādhanātmaka dhruvapads*[80] seem to be imbued with a spiritual quality, as they surely do, it is importantly because of their evenness, poise, and structural lucidity, as distinguished from compositions which excite and please us by working up a semblance of the tension of opposing pulls.

(c) It is, therefore, only proper that Langer regards 'the integral relationship' of elements within and with the

78. W. Harburger's words cited by Langer, in *Mind — An Essay on Human Feeling*, vol. I, p. 163; italics added.

79. See, here, my essay, 'Master of Tranquil Musical Passages' on Ustad N. Zahiruddin Dagar in *The Pioneer* of 11.10.'1995.

80. Such *dhruvapad*s are meant more for personal devotion than for presentation on the stage.

whole work as the *basic* source of the appearance of 'livingness in all successful works'. At the same time, she insists that every element retains a measure of self-existence in the whole form of the work. It may be noted that the two aspects of an element we have just distinguished — that is, its self-existence and self-transcendence — may well operate together without the slightest hint of collision or tension. Being onself is surely not the same thing as *asserting oneself against* the other; and being helpful to the other is not necessarily the upleasant state of *being forced to help* against one's will. All the members of a close-knit family may, in general, be willingly helpful to one another in their own individual ways, so that there is neither any loss of self-existence nor any sense of constraint. Even in such a family, of course, tensions may arise at times and be resolved; but simply on the basis of this occasional happening, tensions and their resolutions cannot be said to be the pervasive feature of the family in question.

Langer is indeed emphatic on the point that what gives a work the 'semblance of organic structure' is the 'many-sided involvement of every element with the total fabric . . . [of the work]'; and that though it

> does not really have organs and vital functions . . . like living substance, a work of art is inviolable; break its elements apart, and they no longer are what they were — the whole image is gone.[81]

This emphasis on the deep, inner unity of a work of art will be acceptable to many. But this is not the only major emphasis in Langer's view. She insists that art is a symbolic projection not only of the rhythm of *organic structure* but of that of *subjective life*. So it seems demanded that we bring out how life as lived and felt is also a dynamic unity of details that interplay and modify each other.

---

81. Langer, *Problems of Art*, pp. 55-7.

Felt life and art: A parallel

This is, in fact, fairly easy to see. No part of life as experienced retains (or can retain) its distinct character quite independently of its other parts or contents. To illustrate, one's being hopeful and keen in the present may, in fact, be related to one's feeling fit at the moment and also to the sense of what one has so far been able to achieve in the direction which promises further progress. But the attitude in question may lose its colour the moment one is told that what he hopes to achieve by further work has already been attained by another researcher. This change in attitude — say, as a passing subsidence of an excited looking forward-to — would itself owe its precise character to the quality of one's habitual attitudes, say, the meekness of a man who has been easily cowed down in the past by setbacks *or* the resilience of one who has responded to them spiritedly, as to a challenge. Nor is it immune to further influences from the outside. For instance, if the 'other' researcher approaches the individual in question with a proposal for co-operation in further work in the direction they have been pursuing independently, the chastened mood of the man approached may well regain its colour of cheer and hope.

In the same way, every 'part' — or rather virtual constituent — of a work of art is inseparable from the whole, as also from the other parts; and, what is more, it is for ever open to assimilation in, and transformation (not extinction) by other elements. But all this calls for some detailed explanatory comments, with the help of some illustrations from the region of art.

Let us begin by considering a detail of our rhythm, namely, the *sama* of the *tritāla* cycle-say, as providing 'accompaniment' to a Kathak dance recital. As only one of the 16 beats, it is simply a constituent. But as it is made to appear in the course of playing, recitation or replication of the cycle by the dancer, it is a virtual (or created) element; for now it appears not only as the beginning, but also as the *focal* beat of the cycle. But these two are not its only possible appearances. Where the cycle serves as the background or matrix of rhythmic patterns, the *sama* can assume quite a few other 'looks'.Thus, if it comes as the terminal beat of a pattern played, recited or danced at an *even* pace, it appears as merely the accent of due completion. But if it caps a shapely segment of approach it might appear as the *destiny* of the rhythmic passage. If the approach in question comprises footfalls (or musical passages) of gradually growing intensity, or segments of rising pace, the *sama* will probably appear as not only the terminus or destiny, but also as the *climax* of the pattern. If, on the other hand, its playing is purposely avoided — not inadvertently missed — the *sama* will appear as an accent which is merely apprehended in idea, instead of striking us as a sound, and will further ideal attunement with the basic *laya*. Further, if, as in the case of an *anāgat* pattern, the *sama* (as normally located) comes a little after the end of the pattern as played, it will appear as something that, so to say, eludes the grasp of playing or dancing; and if a (played) pattern — of the *atīta* kind — ends a little after the *sama* (of the cycle) the *sama*-beat will seem to be something which has been quietly overrun, without being effaced; for it continues to be apprehended in idea. Finally, if it comes immaculately at the end of a *chakradār paran*, it is likely to appear as *the coming-to-rest of an orderly ebullience*. To conclude, there is (in principle) no end to the variety of ways in which *sama*, with variations in its context, can appear to contemplation.

Further, though it is admittedly the focal beat of the whole cycle, the *sama* is not *directly* related to the whole *tritāla-ṭhekā*, for its centrality clearly arises from its occurring *in the context of 15 other beats*, thus lending point to Langer's explicit remark that 'no analysis can uncover a simple direct relation of an element to the work as a whole'.[82] Yet the *sama*'s character is not only determined by, but also determines, the function of the other beats. They will surely not appear to make a *cycle* without the *sama*. What is more, the very pace at which all the subsequent beats are to be played is determined by the *sama*'s own temporal extent as it appears in recitation or singing.

The net truth that emerges from the foregoing considerations is that, as in felt life, so in art, every detail is not

82. Langer, *Mind — An Essay on Human Feeling*, vol. I, p. 200.

only inseparable from, but owes and contributes character to others; and is, what is more, quite open to *changes* in its own character and conduciveness under the stress of its context. In other words, the unity of a work is not merely the togetherness of static parts, but a living or dynamic whole, so to say, of elements that interplay and are inseparable.

Organic unity and a poem

Langer seeks to illustrate the multiple relatedness of elements by analysing William Blake's poem, "Love's Secret".[83] But this analysis is not explicitly related to the points *I* have just made regarding the meaning of 'living form' in art. So I may do the needful by reflecting on another poem, say, Wordsworth's poem on daffodils, *I Wandered Lonely as a Cloud*, which has been acclaimed as

> Wordsworth pure and prime . . . [a poem which combines all the] obvious Wordsworthian characteristics . . . [and is] . . . strongly original.[84]

But before we turn to the poem I have picked, I think it necessary to put anew, but quite briefly and simply, what *organic unity* means. Be it a living animal or plant, an *organism* is a unified whole. But two distinct ideas are implicit in this concept: unity on the inside and manifest wholeness to outer view. As we have seen, the inner unity of an organism rests on what may be called the 'mutual conditioning' of processes that keep it alive. This conditioning is a blend of supplementation and contrast. Take the case of breathing, for instance. Exhalation is not only opposed to, but demands and paves the way to inhalation.

> As the oxygen of a breath is used up, it builds up the imperative need of oxygen that is really the beginning of the new breath.[85]

Outer wholeness, on the other hand, is indicated by a look of

83. Langer, *Problems of Art*, pp. 56-7.

84. Louis Coxe's essay on '*I Wandered Lonely as a Cloud*' in *Master Poems of the English Language*, pp. 416-18.

85. Langer, *Problems of Art*, p. 52.

self-completeness arising from the presence of clear termini. Now, all this is easily traceable in the poem I propose to analyse; but first let me put it as it is:

I WANDERED LONELY AS A CLOUD

I wandered lonely as a cloud
That floats on high o'er vales and hills,
When all at once I saw a crowd,
A host, of golden daffodils;
Beside the lake, beneath the trees.
Fluttering and dancing in the breeze.
Continuous as the stars that shine
And twinkle on the milky way
They stretched in never-ending line
Along the margin of a bay;
Ten thousand saw I at a glance,
Tossing their heads in sprightly dance.

The waves beside them danced, but they
Out-did the sparkling waves in glee;
A poet could not but be gay,
In such a jocund company;
I gazed — and gazed — but little thought
What wealth the show to me had brought:

For oft, when on my couch I lie
In vacant or in pensive mood,
They flash upon that inward eye
Which is the bliss of solitude;
And then my heart with pleasure fills,
And dances with the daffodils.

Now, even a casual look at the opening and closing pairs of lines in the above poem should make it clear that they provide a definite beginning and just as clear an end to the whole form, and that the definiteness arises from the mutual opposition of what the pairs in question say. Thus, whereas in the beginning the poet (as the bearer of the experience which the poem projects) appears to be wholly indifferent to the most pronounced *differences* in outer nature (see 'hills and valleys'), the lines which wind up the poem project him as lit up with a sudden recall, and as sucking the bliss of a rapt communion with the beauty of flowers *of but one kind* so deeply that the initial abstraction is utterly set off by the plenitude of an intense and highly satisfying personal experience. Merely to 'float on high' is one thing; 'dancing with' quite another. Even between its *two* termini the poem builds upon the principle of contrast quite freely, if a little less openly. One way in which the principle is seen to operate is as covert (implied) opposition of the momentary or immediate to the ongoing or laid out. The *suddenness* (*of a momentary* impact) with which the beauteous 'show' is revealed to the poet ('all at once') contrasts finely with the *stretch and continuity* of the carpet of daffodils and of 'the margin of a bay'; and also, if a little later, with the *unblinking steadfastness* of simply gazing at the flowers. Further, though the experience is *one*, it flashes upon the poet's 'inward eye' *often* times ('oft, when on my couch. . . .') But a subtler use of the principle in question is provided by one express constriction of the movement of lines (as read) which at once heightens, by contrast, the ease with which the subsequent words extend themselves. The reference here is to the way the third line ends and the fourth one opens: 'a crowd, a host'. This little artifice, of such a quick segmentation of words, does not occur anywhere else in the poem; and it serves two clear ends. First, it invites us to leave out, from the meaning of 'crowd', the thought of *disorderliness* — which does not go well with that of *beautiful* flowers — and to hold on to numerousness alone (this being the primary meaning of 'host'); and, second, it throws into bolder relief the easy, flowing passage of the lines that follow, beginning with 'Beside the lake. . . .'

This facility of movement is kept up by all that appears later in the poem, except at the moment where the two dashes on either side of 'and gazed' obstruct the movement but minimally, and go rather *to add to* the thought of fixity implicit in the word *gazed*. Such supplementation is visible in the poem in at least in one other way. Words that express pleasure and degrees of pleasure — say, *sprightly, gay, glee, jocund* — are, of course, the key to the dominant feeling of the poem, which is joy or delight. But they would not be able to evoke the cheery atmosphere they presently do were they denied the assistance of such supportive images from the regions of colour, light, and movement as: *golden, fluttering, dancing, shine, twinkle, sparkling* and *flash*.

In sum, the poem is organic in character, or an analogue (not an imitation) of a living creature, first, because it appears to be self-complete; and, second, because it is tightly structured on the inside. Not only this poem but every work of art is 'like actual life . . . an indivisible phenomenon'.[86] This is why

> every artist finds 'life', 'vitality' or 'livingness' in a good work of art. He [likes to refer] to the 'spirit' of a picture, not meaning the spirit in which it was painted, but its own quality; and his first task is to 'animate' [or to put 'life' into] his canvas.[87]

Our task, however, is not yet complete. For a clearer understanding of Langer's emphasis on the 'livingness' of a good work of art, we have still to bring out how the poem we have just analysed may be said to reveal the following features which she regards as the distinguishing marks of living form.[88] Or, to put it simply, I must explain

(a) how the poem in question may be said to be a dynamic form, that is, a form whose permanence is really a pattern of changes;

(b) how it is organically constructed;

(c) how it is held together by rhythmic processes;

(d) how it could be said to reveal the dialectic of growth and decay which is the basic rhythm of living form, and, finally;

(e) how it may be shown as projecting a portion of felt life in such a way that this 'life', to which ordinary language

86. Langer, *Problems of Art*, p. 135.

87. *Ibid.*, p. 44.

88. *Ibid.*, pp. 52-3.

can refer but generally and superficially, becomes amenable to our understanding or clear, objective grasp.

The last point (e), which I propose to clarify a little later, deserves our special attention; for Langer does not touch it in her analysis of Blake's poem. She just concludes with the following remark:

> This many-sided involvement of every element with the total fabric of the poem is what gives it a semblance of organic structure. . . .[89]

Before, however, I set out to answer the five questions I have posed it is necessary to recall Langer's cautionary emphasis, already brought out, that *analogous* principles are not *identical,* and that when a work of art is regarded as organic and as somehow imbued with feeling, however irresistible be its look of 'livingness', it is surely not supposed to live and behave exactly as living creatures do.[90]

'Transformation' of life in art

Langer is indeed not unmindful of the *difference* between art and real life. Yet she is emphatic in her view that the essence of art is to express felt life. She reconciles the two sides of the matter by suggesting that the expression of life in art is not literal, but indirect and analogous; and she argues for the point by introducing an important aesthetic concept, *transformation,* regarded not as I have taken it earlier — that is, as the susceptibility of elements to change under the stress of their context — but as:

> . . . the rendering of a desired appearance without any actual representation of it, by the production of an *equivalent* sense-impression rather than a literally similar one, in terms of the limited, legitimate material which cannot naively copy the desired property of the model.[91]

---

89. Langer, *Problems of Art,* p. 57.

90. *Ibid.,* pp. 44-5.

91. *Ibid.,* p. 98.

Langer makes her meaning quite clear and acceptable by citing some familiar examples:

> To convey a sense of motion by dynamic lines, without picturing attitudes or events that connote it; to convey a dramatic situation by well-timed silences instead of exciting statements; . . . [or] to get a spatial effect through a medium of sound . . . — that is what I mean by *transforming* the appearance of the model into sensory structures of another sort.[92]

I may illustrate the last of the three ways of artistic transformation just cited by referring to a beautiful creative possibility in the region of Hindustani music. If in an exposition of *rāga sohnī* the *tāra ṛṣabha* is projected finely and sweetly, and is held on to for a while as a beam of light; and if, what is more, the immediately preceding *sa* is sung as a mere instant of sweetness, the overall effect will be one of a far-away look, suggesting distance unmistakably, though the two notes in question are in fact quite close to each other.

Yet another instance of 'transformation' in the region of Hindustani music is provided by the following extract from a music critic's essay on our classical music:

> I have seen Ustad Rahimuddin Khan Dagar delighting an audience of university teachers with a projection, through *ālāpa*, of the image of a flower opening up gently to the rays of the sun [, by just relieving a sweetly sustained *svara* with a momentary, yet noticeable accent]. In such cases the audience has, of course, to be notified in advance. But the interruption . . . is more than set off by the completeness of delight which follows.[93]

Of course, there are many other ways in which the principle of transformation may be seen to function in *ālāpa*. Here,

> depth may be manifest in the manner of a sigh, as a reflex of inwardness, not of physical bulk; and . . . [an] overall purity

92. Langer, *Problems of Art*, pp. 98-9.

93. Cited from my essay, 'Our Classical Music' published in the Independence Day Supplement of *The Hindustan Times*, New Delhi, on 15.8.1955.

> of effect, in the absence of [ethico-religious] words, . . . as a pervasive daintiness of manner that . . . [speaks] to the spirit, instead of titillating sense or amorous fancy.[94]

Reflections such as these make it clear that creative effects in the region of art are but appearance, and that it is vain to expect in a work that fundamental rhythm of a living organism which consists in the break-up and emergence of cells and because of which an organism has to be regarded as a permanence of *literal* changes or as a being which *actually* grows and decays in time.

The poem-again

The moment we realise this it becomes easy to answer the five questions [(a)-(e)] I have posed (on p. 46). Thus, (a) the form of the poem we have analysed is dynamic not because its words exchange places or get replaced by other words — neither of which can be an actual happening here; but because, as we have seen, besides contributing to the import of the total poem, the words and phrases interact and themselves suffer changes of meaning or emphasis through both supplementation and contrast, so that what seems to be a single, changeless poem to a superficial look comes to be apprehended, on a little close analysis, as a dynamic whole which, so to say, attains to rest because of an equilibrium of the diverse forces that go to make it. (b) has been already brought out by our analysis of the poem (on daffodils). Nor is it difficult, in this context, to argue for (c) As I have already hinted, the essence of rhythm, according to Langer, is not regularity of recurrence but such a mutual conditioning of elements or processes that the disappearance of one naturally paves the way to the next one's appearance. To illustrate, as we run through the full twenty-four lines of the poem discussed we nowhere feel that the transition is abrupt. Even in the last six lines, where the poet's attention turns from the outer to the inner, the shift is nowhere a leap.

94. My essay, 'Ustad A. Rahimuddin Khan Dagar' in *Sangeet Natak*, official journal of Sangeet Natak Akademi (new Delhi), No. 39, Jan-March, 1976, pp. 5, 22. I may add that 'A' here stand for 'Allābande', the first name of Rahimuddin Khan's father; and that Rahimuddin Khan would insist on opening the writing of his own name with A.

The mention of a 'pensive mood' suggests a little introversion; and, therefore, when the following lines speak of (1) the bliss of falling back upon the subjective resource of happy memories —brought about, as a kind of reflex, by isolation on the outside, and also (2) of the 'inward eye' and an ecstatic heart, we do not feel we are being wrenched away from outer nature. As for (d), in so far as a poem is obviously not a living creature, the concepts of growth and decay can only be taken to mean the origin, efflorescence, and fulfilment of an experience; and these three stages are clearly there in the poem we have analysed.

But (e) does not appear to be so easy to deal with, partly because the projection of felt life is likely to be equated with expression of *emotions*. However, the equation is by no means necessary or unavoidable; for life as felt may be quite properly taken as the feel of *naïve* experience, that is, of experience which is not yet sundered into perception and affective responses, or into opposition of moods of vacuity or indifference and involvement and communion. And in *this* basic sense, felt life may well be said to have been projected admirably by the poem we have reflected on; for, by means of the very rhythmic movement of the lines and other devices we have distinguished, the poem surely presents to contemplation a *seamless* fabric of diverse moods, of seeing and sensitiveness, and of a happy *recall* as suffusing the *present* with delight. To conclude, the very organic structure of the poem may be said *to project the immediate feel of life*.

Why *such* projection is beyond the power of language as ordinarily used is easy to show. I may here cite the following argument from one of my earlier works:[95]

The subject-predicate form of language distinguishes and relates. Words here occur as a succession, or before or after one another; and most of them have a fairly determinate, isolable meaning. How, then, can they present (in this everyday, inartistic manner) the felt quality of such experiences as, say, the self-division of being *at once* between two opposing temptations or the *instant* radiation of being with relief on

95. Saxena, *Art and Philosophy: Seven Aestheticians*, p. 298.

accomplishing a task long overdue? If we *speak* of self-division we miss the tempting quality of the opposites faced; and if we take care to mention the quality in question too, we do so only as a supplement, and (so to say) loosen what is, in fact, intense and unified. Our everyday speech indeed cannot make us *see* the tension of a waiting or the happy suffusion of being that is one with, *and does not only follow,* the ending of a tension. The 'inward life of human beings'[96] is too intricate, nimble and conjoint to brook presentation in the usual spread-out arrangement of words with often quite exclusive meanings.

But, one may ask, if that is so, how can poetry which must work *through language* re-create, say, the seamlessness of naïve experience? Langer's answer is: through that cohesive inner organisation of details which is the essence of artistic form, scrupulous omission of irrelevant details, and such a deft choice and knitting of words and other materials — say, 'metrical stresses, vowel values, rhymes, alliteration'[97] — that the 'look' of whatever content is picked for artistic treatment is at once vivified. *I* may add that the cohesiveness of felt life is perhaps projected more clearly by rhythm in music than by poetry. Thus, during the course of the actual playing of a *ṭhekā* the beat which marks the end of a rhythmic round is *at once* the beginning of the next round; and, where it is sweetly sung, the upper tonic which caps the *puriyā* phrase, *ni re ni ni re* (*sa*) does not only complete the passage, but makes it appear to bloom — instantaneously.

'Life' or import of a work of art

For Langer, indeed, the basic sense in which a work of art may be said to be 'alive' — and its form, 'living' — is not that it is a truthful representation of something in real life, but that its own structure is as deep or cohesive a unity of details or dynamic relations (or processes) as the life of an organism. And when we speak of a work's own 'life' we should only mean the work's own unique import or expressiveness arising, in the

96. Langer, *Problems of Art*, p. 22.

97. Langer, *Feeling and Form*, p. 213.

main, from its form or integrated structure. Langer puts the point graphically:

> The import of a work of art is its 'life', which, like actual life, is an indivisible phenomenon. Who could say how much of an organism's life is in the lungs, how much in the legs . . . ? The Art symbol is a single symbol, and its import is not compounded of partial symbolic values.[98]

The meaning, here, is clear. Just as one cannot indicate exactly how much life is contributed by a particular bodily organ to the life of the total organism, so it is impossible to fix the precise amount of meaning that the individual elements may be said to provide to a work's overall import. The truth is that a work of art's net import cannot be regarded as a mere aggregate of the meanings of its elements. These meanings are not a *direct* part of the work's own significance. They, of course, go to make the total form of the work; but in the process — that is, as built upon in the organisation of the work's details — their own individual significance changes through sheer interplay; and when the work's final form appears, *its* meaning or expressiveness cannot be said to issue directly from the individual character or meaning of the elements. When their own meaning changes during the making of the form, how can the import or expressiveness of the form, as it finally emerges, be regarded as the mere totality of what the elements signify in themselves or originally?

The 'expressed' in art: Interpreting Langer's view

But *what* exactly does a work express or formulate objectively for our contemplation? Here, Langer gives so many and so various answers that it needs quite an effort to integrate them. But let me first cull them from some of her works:

I. PROBLEMS OF ART

> 'human feeling';[99] 'inward life'; the *subjective aspect* of experience, the direct feeling of it — what it is like to be

98. Langer, *Problems of Art*, p. 135.

99. *Ibid.*, p. 15

working and moving, to be drowsy, slowing down or to be sociable, or feel self-sufficient but alone';[100] what it feels like to pursue an elusive thought or to have a big idea;[101] 'felt life';[102] the steady feeling-tones of a conscious human life; the actual felt process of life; the tensions interwoven and shifting from moment to moment; the flowing and stowing; 'the drive and directedness of desires, . . . the rhythmic continuity of our selfhood . . . the myriad forms of subjectivity; the infinitely complex sense of life . . . vitality, in all its manifestations from sheer sensibility to the most elaborate phases of awareness and emotion. . . .'[103]

II. MIND: AN ESSAY ON HUMAN FEELING, VOL. I

'how vital and emotional and intellectual tensions appear, i.e., how they feel';[104] 'the mere feeling of vitality, energy or somnolence; or the sense of quietness, or of concentration; or any of the countless inward actions and conditions which are felt in the living fabric of mental life';[105] 'the *feeling* of rational thought, which the discursive record of rational order has to omit'.[106]

III. FEELING AND FORM

Forms of human feeling — forms of growth and attenuation, flowing and stowing, conflict and resolution, speed, arrest, terrific excitement, calm, or subtle activation and dreamy lapses — not joy and sorrow perhaps, but the poignancy of either and both — the greatness and brevity and eternal passing of everything vitally felt . . . the logical form of sentience . . .[107]; 'the great vital rhythms and their emotional overtones and undertones.[108]

---

100. *Problems of Art*; p. 22.
101. *Ibid.*
102. *Ibid.*, p. 25.
103. *Ibid.*, p. 133.
104. Langer, *Mind — An Essay on Human Feeling*, vol. I, p. xix.
105. *Ibid.*, p. 84.
106 *Ibid.*, p. 104.
107. Langer, *Feeling and Form*, p. 27.
108. *Ibid.* , p. 227.

Now, by way of clarifying the point at issue, I may comment on the above extracts as follows:

(a) To begin with I., (p. 52) we have to mark that by *feeling* Langer means not only the distinctive *idiom*, but *the whole fact* of feeling. As distinguished from the discursive manner of logical thinking, feeling is experience as immediate. The details or steps of an act of thinking are more or less held apart by relations; the content of feeling, on the other hand, is sensed as a fusion, and as closer to the self than the objects of thought, which is why the actuality of what is felt is never questioned by the person who feels. If in part implicitly, what I have just said is borne out by the following words of Langer herself:

> The word 'feeling' must be taken here in its broadest sense, meaning *everything that can be felt*, from physical sensation, pain and comfort, excitement and repose, to the most complex emotions, intellectual tensions, or the steady tones of a conscious human life.[109]

Here the italicized words make it clear that, as Langer uses the word, *feeling* includes *what is* felt or the content of feeling; and that, therefore, what is meant is feeling in its entirety. At the same time, we may note, she wishes to *emphasize* the subjective aspect of feeling, or its immediacy; I say so because she equates feeling with 'inward life', 'the subjective aspect of experience, the direct feeling of it', or 'felt life'.[110] Further, in so far as every content or detail of experience is also felt because its bearer is a sentient individual, *feeling* (as we have just interpreted it above) may be taken to cover both 'sheer sensibility' — say, as the mere feel of the weather — and 'the most elaborate phases of awareness and emotion', the pursuit of 'an elusive thought', or the dawn of 'a big idea'. All these, along with whatever else we have listed in I., II. and III., (on pp. 52, 53) are covered by the words, 'myriad forms of subjectivity' and 'the infinitely complex sense of life' provided *life* is taken not to signify the circumstances a man finds himself in — as in the question, 'How

109. Langer, *Problems of Art*, p. 15.

110. The last of these, felt life, may be put thus in simple Hindustani: 'ज़िन्दगी लगती कैसी है' or 'ज़िन्दगी का अहसास'.

is life with you?' — but as meaning the essentially personal impact of experience and circumstance.

(b) Similarly, none of the extracts which make group II. (on p. 53) is left uncomprehended by 'myriad forms of subjectivity'.

(c) But, we may note, III. brings in a quite new concept: '*forms* of human feeling'. A look at the context of these words[111] makes it clear that, here, Langer is not thinking of form in the 'most abstract sense' of the word which, she believes, 'is involved in the notion of expression'[112] and which regards *form* as the inner structure . . . [or] *articulation* of a whole, but as pattern. I think it necessary to make this distinction. But let me explain:

Articulation means jointing of distinct details. As such, it cannot be said to characterise the following which Langer includes in her list of forms of feeling: arrest, terrific excitement, calm, and subtle activation. Intensive psychological or phenomenological analysis may well reveal some orderly disposition of distinct feelings or impulses in each one of these states (and courses) of experience; but though they may all be *complex and orderly in themselves*, they are *not felt as such*, and so cannot be said to be forms of human feeling or of *felt* life. Shall we then call them patterns (or logical form) of sentience, as Langer herself does in *Feeling and Form*'?[113] In *Philosophical Sketches*, we may note, Langer speaks of the whole of human feeling as a fabric or 'dynamic pattern . . . of organically interdependent and interdetermined tensions and resolutions, a pattern of almost infinitely complex activation and cadence'.[114] Now, is there any difference between the two ways of speaking about 'feeling', that is, as signifying forms in the sense of articulated wholes *or* as patterns? Perhaps there is. The former way of speaking directly conveys a suggestion of inclusiveness which the word *pattern* does not. But the verbal shift will hardly be of help. For a pattern is simply an arrangement, design, or

111. Langer, *Feeling and Form*, p. 27.

112. Langer, *Problems of Art*, p. 16.

113. Langer, *Feeling and Form*, p. 27.

114. Langer, *Philosophical Sketches*, p. 90.

sequence; and a state of 'terrific excitement', which Langer includes in her list of *forms* of feeling, is never *felt* as a pattern or design. On the other hand, do we not commonly and fairly speak of *growing wild* with excitement?

I admit there is nothing mythical about the 'forms of subjectivity' which Langer picks for mention. They are all, in fact, possible states of actual experience; and, what is more, our music freely provides 'analogues' of quite a few of them. Thus,

> [the] *tablā*-player's moment of intentional deviation — during the playing of a *quāyedā* — from the set pace of the cyclic flow (or *ṭhekā*) chosen, may make us 'see' how a 'dreamy lapse' feels or looks; and the *ālāpiya*'s intensely tuneful but momentary pecking of the *tāra shadja* in the *dyut* manner, so that the *svara* appears to twinkle like a star, may seem to be imbued with 'the greatness and brevity of everything *vitally* felt'. Again, the first few passages of *ālāpa* on the *veenā* (I have in mind *Vichitra veenā* in particular) often appear as the alternating surge and recession (or, in Langer's words, 'growth and . . . attenuation') of powerful feeling in sonorous majesty, just as in the hands of a *sitar* maestro the sudden execution of a little [creative] turn at a point where one does not commonly expect it (called जगह निकलना or जगह दिखाना in our musical parlance) may *either* 'show' us how the 'subtle activation', say, of a sudden but suggestive thought feels or looks; *or* appear to tickle us in the way of a twinkle of mischief in the eyes of a child.[115]

Yet, I cannot agree with Langer's sweeping remark that 'music is [essentially] a tonal analogue of emotive life'.[116] I shall argue for this disagreement in the next chapter; and here I may only reiterate that quite a few of Langer's 'forms of subjectivity' *are not felt* as forms or patterns at all. But to see the point of my protest it is, of course, necessary to remember that, according to her view, art only projects — but does not create — the forms of *felt* life; which means that these forms are already present in everyday experience in their full dual character, that is, as both

115. Saxena, *Art and Philosophy: Seven Aestheticians*, p. 278.

116. Langer, *Feeling and Form*, p. 27.

forms *and felt as such* — before art articulates them.

I may also add, if in passing, that the 'forms' distinguished by Langer perhaps cannot find a locus *in every art with equal ease*. One may admit the presence of some semblances of poignancy of feeling — of penance and martyrdom — in works like *St. Peter Weeping* and *Crucifix* by EL Greco; but I can only wonder how an appearance of *subtle activation* can be created in the plastic arts.

Form in art

Subjective life, however, is not the only context in which Langer uses the word *form*; quite as purposefully she also discusses the concept in relation to works of art. And the concept is integral to her overall view of art. If a work of art is expressive of felt life, as it surely is in her view, it is so (she insists) primarily because of its overall form. (See, here, Langer's explicit remark that a poem expresses 'feeling' essentially by 'weaving a pattern of words', and 'not by recalling objects which would elicit the feeling itself'.)[117]

But how are we to take *form* in the artistic sense? Langer's answer, here, is both detailed and fair; and I think it necessary to outline it clearly:

(a) To begin with, a work's *form* is not a mere constituent of it, but its very constitution or relational structure.[118] The word is surely used in quite a few other senses, say, as meaning shape, appearance, or mould; but the abstract sense that is 'involved in the notion of *expression*'[119] — which (we have seen) is a key concept of Langer's aesthetics — is, in her own words, the following:

> structure, articulation, a whole resulting from the relation of mutually dependent factors, *or more precisely*, the way that whole is put together.[120]

---

117. Langer, *Feeling and Form*, p. 230.
118. Langer, *The Practice of Philosophy*, p. 92.
119. Langer, *Problems of Art*, p. 16.
120. *Ibid*.

A little close attention to this extract reveals that, of the two possible aesthetic senses of *form* — *a whole* that results from the integration of some factors or the *integration* itself — Langer *prefers* the latter. She admits that the former is a legitimate meaning of the word, and that when aestheticians like Bell and Fry speak of significant *form* what is meant is

> a visible individual form produced by the interaction of colours, lines . . . or whatever entered into a specific work . . . [that is,] *something formed* . . . as a pot is formed out of clay.[121]

But, then, why does she *prefer* to take 'form' in the sense of relational *structure*? The reason perhaps is that if we speak of a work of art as some*thing* formed, we may be easily tempted to take *form* in the sense of mere (outer) shape — in which sense the word in question would be inapplicable to numerous works of art, most obviously to literary works. Further, if we look at a work of art simply as an agreeable *shape* we are likely to give no thought at all to the quality of its being deeply and creatively organised on the inside which alone is common to all successful works of art. Langer, therefore, finds it necessary to say that the 'strict' (or theoretically proper) way to take 'form' in the context of art is as relational structure. But, on the other hand, if our thinking is to be true to the evidence of actual art-making, we have to remember that *the structure* in question is not a pre-fixed — and so abstractable — mould into which the materials of art have only to be put to produce a work, but itself arises out of them as the artist goes on realising their aesthetic potential by creatively handling and interrelating them. So Langer insists:

> Artistic forms are . . . not abstractable from the works that exhibit them. We may abstract a shape from an object that has this shape, by disregarding color, weight . . . [or] even size; but to the total effect that is an *artistic* form, the color matters, the thickness of lines matters, and the appearance of texture and weight.[122]

---

121. Langer, *Problems of Art*, p. 128. In the original, I may add, only the word, *formed*, is italicised.

122. *Ibid.*, pp. 25-6; italics added.

The meaning, here, is clear. The shape of everyday objects is abstractable; that is, it can be spoken or thought of, quite fairly, without at all referring to their material, colour, or weight. Thus, it would make perfect sense if one only said that the table in the room is oval in shape, that is, without making any mention of its other features or qualities. But, it is obvious, no one can speak of the form of a work of art — say, a poem — without meaning, if not openly affirming, that the factors or elements that go to make it are all interconnected. In other words, the form of a poem cannot be abstracted (even in thought) from what the poem is as a whole. But, of course, the two *can* be distinguished. This is indeed done, if implicitly, when artists speak of 'achieving form' in the work regarded as 'a visible and tangible . . . object'.[123]

(b) Langer would like to add that, though it *is* a kind of togetherness, the relational structure (*or* form) of a work of art is no mere *additive* unity. It is rather a fabric of 'mutually dependent factors', 'produced [in the case of painting] by the interaction of colours, lines . . . or whatever entered into . . . [the] work;[124] and the interplay is special, because productive. It is quite unlike the random jostling of pebbles in a bag or the unconstrained mixing of paints simply for the sake of making a new colour. The pebbles do nothing to determine or modify each other, and the emergent colour may not at all reveal the diverse paints that have gone into its making. In a work of art, on the other hand, the interaction of its *elements* is dynamic and creative; and it makes for articulateness of artistic form.

But what all this means, and how exactly it happens, has to be brought out at some length, partly by reflecting on the distinction that Langer draws between the elements and materials of art, but all along in the light of her own relevant remarks, such as the following:

> Pigments, clay . . . the vocabularies of language . . . are materials of art; colours, volumes, accents, word uses . . . are

123. Langer, *Problems of Art*, p. 16.

124. *Ibid.*, p. 128.

> elements.[125] Materials are actual, but elements are always virtual; and it is elements that an artist composes into an apparition, an expressive form. . . .[126] [The form of a work] involves *all* the relationships of its elements to one another, all similarities and differences of quality, not only geometric . . . relations. That is why qualities enter directly into the form itself, not as its contents, but as constitutive elements in it. . . . A work of art is a structure whose interrelated elements are often qualities, or properties of qualities such as their degrees of intensity; . . . qualities enter into the form and . . . are as much one with it as the relations which they . . . have. [So], to speak of them as 'content', from which the form could be abstracted logically, is nonsense. The form is built up out of relations peculiar to them; they are formal elements in the structure, not contents.[127]

Quite a few points are made in the extracts just cited, and I think it necessary to explain them as follows:

Take, first, the material-element distinction. Materials are available or given to the artist right as he sets out to make the work; but elements are created by him. Consider, for instance, the very opening of a *khyāl* recital. The vocalist is, of course, aware of the *svara*s that make the *rāga* he is going to sing; they are clearly the given material of the music. But the *way* he begins, that is, the precise manner in which he applies his voice onto the first one or two notes (called *sur kā lagāo*, in our musical parlance) is *his* work. And this detail of manner invests the notes in question, may be, with a look of (the vocalist's) self-attunement with the act of singing, or (at least) makes them appear sweet-*sounding* to the ear, which quality certainly does not belong to them in the notational scheme or as merely contemplated. The same may be said of the *sthāyī-antarā* pair, and of all the *tāna*s as actually sung, as against being merely contemplated. The polarity of ascent and descent (*āroha-avaroha*), which is perhaps the most important source of form

125. Langer, *Mind — An Essay on Human Feeling*, vol. I, p. 66. The way the extract is cited here differs from the order of its words in the book referred to.

126. Langer, *Problems of Art*, p. 42.

127. Langer, *Feeling and Form*, pp. 51-2.

in music; some passages of subtly regulated volume that look like the surge and subsidence of feeling; quite a few others that terminate at the *sama* and evoke the suggestion of orientation and attainment, — these elements of music are all virtual in so far as they are created by the singer at work, and are surely not identical with the up-and-down movement, rise and abatement of emotion, and the getting of targeted goals that we see in daily life.

(c) Yet, important though they all are as marks of creativity, elements as such are not the form of art. Form arises from all the mutual relationships of the work's elements. These relations may be geometric, such as those arrangements of lines, colours, volumes, and figures which produce a centripetal or centrifugal look, or symmetrical and asymmetrical balance; or 'similarities and differences of quality'. But whatever be its precise nature, a relation cannot be separated from what it relates, neither in thought nor in fact. Differences in music are necessarily difference *of* pitch, pace, or volume; and similarities, equivalences of the number of *svara*s or *mātrā*s, respectively, in musical phrases or in segments of the rhythm-cycle.

(d) But if form is necessarily a matter of the ways in which a work's elements are related, and if — as is unavoidable — the relations here obtain between terms, may be shapes, or (in the case of literary work)' degrees of importance in events', or different speeds[128] in musical passages which are all distinct or distinguishable, form in art must be said to be articulate in the sense of a *joining* of *distinct* parts. In Langer's view, the linkages and the individuality of elements integrated are both of vital importance for form in art. On the one hand, the

> parts [of a work of art regarded as a form] . . . fuse together to yield a greater unity . . . [and on the other hand] in doing so they maintain *some* degree of separate existence . . . [though] the sensuous character of each element is affected by its function in the complex whole. This means that the greater entity we call a composition is not merely produced by mixture, like a new color made by mixing paints, but is

128. Langer, *Feeling and Form*, p. 51.

> *articulated*, i.e., its internal structure is given to our perception . . . [As a complex symbol, music is] an *articulate form*. Its characteristic symbolic function is . . . *logical expression*. It expresses relations. . . .[129]

The thrust of this extract is clear. Langer here affirms that form in art may be said to be both articulate and logical. One may here protest against the addition of 'and logical' to 'articulate', because logic is commonly regarded as being quite dissimilar to art. But Langer could here rejoin that by calling the form of art *logical* she only means that such form expresses relations; and that, in so far as articulateness also means relatedness of distinct details or elements, the protest may be ignored.

Yet I doubt if all that she says (in the extract cited above) by way of vindicating the emphasis is quite intelligible. Consider, to begin with, the very opening word, *parts*. How exactly is it to be taken? 'Part' as a particle, or fragment, or as a segment; or, quite generally, as a component or element? It is usual to think of a segment as having a measure of self-completeness which is generally denied to a mere fragment; and a particle too is neither a portion nor a segment. Understood as 'component' or 'element', the word (*part*) may be taken to cover all its other senses we have distinguished. But, to turn now to the art of music, what shall we say of a single note? A component it assuredly is — of the total music. But would it be proper to call it, quite generally, a part of the melodic whole? Or, do we have to go back again to the word *element* regarded as an *essential* part or unit? But, quite apart from this verbal quandary, how exactly a *svara* (as a part, in the sense of *element*) may be said to 'maintain *some* degree of separate existence' throughout the course of a music recital?

Where the singer avails of a *mīṇḍ* (glide) traversing three or four notes, none of them is projected as being self-existent, though all of them are registered in idea, and *can be* named by a discriminating listener, by way of *sargam* (or recitation of note-

---

129. Langer, *Feeling and Form*, pp. 30-1. Except the first, all emphases occur in the original too. However, in the extract as here cited, its words as they occur in the book referred to have been slightly re-arranged.

names). The noteworthy point, I may add, is that here the 'internal structure [of an element or of the whole] composition is given to our perception[130] *only in principle*, because it can be apprehended only by a trained listener. And where he executes a fluent *āroha-avaroha* (ascent-descent) *tāna*, though (a part of) the norm here certainly is that the *dānā* or individuality of the constituent *svaras* should not be bedimmed, no one of them can be said to have any 'degree of *separate* (as against *distinguishable*) existence' because the pattern, we have posited, is a fast one, and is, therefore, required to appear as a seamless string of beady accents, the *complete* ideal here being that in the singing of a *drut tāna* (or quick pattern) the individuality of notes should neither be subdued nor so projected that the run of the *tāna* may suffer the slightest arrest.[131] And if, as Langer herself admits, 'the sensuous character of each element is affected by its function in the complex whole', how can any element be said to maintain a degree of *separate* existence? A possible rejoinder here is that its sensuous character — or how it appears to the ear, tender or firm, as against the adjacent elements — is not everything about an element, and that at least in respect of its *existence* it may be said to be separate or independent. But this, again, would not be defensible, for the right location of any *svara* in the scale depends upon the propriety of the intervals that *relate* it to its neighbours.

(e) Its articulateness, however, is not the only feature of form in art that Langer emphasizes; she takes pains to highlight its expressiveness too and even proffers the view that the problem of expressive form is pivotal to aesthetics.[132] What exactly she means by expressive form may be put in her own words:

> An expressive form is any perceptible *or* imaginable whole that exhibits relationships of parts, or points, or even qualities

---

130. Langer, *Feeling and Form*, p. 31.

131. Put in *our* musical parlance, the total requirement runs thus 'दाना दबे नहीं, और तान फंसे नहीं'. I made this point during the course of my talk: 'The Essence of Bade Ghulam Ali Khan's *gāyakī* at India International Centre, New Delhi, on 15.9. 1996.

132. Langer, *Problems of Art*, p. 149.

> or aspects within the whole, so that it may be taken to represent some other whole whose elements have analogous relations. The reason for using such a form *as a symbol* is usually that the thing it represents is not perceivable or readily imaginable. We cannot see the earth as an object. We let a map or a little globe express the relationships of places on the earth, and think about the earth by means of it.[133]

The passage is significant and calls for the following comments:

First, an expressive form may be an essentially perceptible whole, as in the case of the visual arts, or an imaginable one, as in the case of literary works. From this is follows that the form of a work of art can be grasped only by means of percipience or (/and) imaginative sympathy.

Second, form which is expressive is so not by virtue of giving a direct vent to some particular feeling, but by being similar to the general feature of feeling which it is meant to 'express' or symbolize. This similarity, however, is not the similitude of a photocopy, but only one of analogous *relations*. What these relations relate may be parts or aspects, or specific points or qualities, within the whole. But what is of *crucial* value for a form's expressiveness is not *what* the relata in their individual character are, but *how* they are put together. It is form or organisation which is really vital here.

Thirdly, though elsewhere Langer speaks freely of the 'function [which] every good work of art does *perform*' — that is, articulation or logical expression[134] — in the passage being discussed she speaks of art as an *expressive* form. Now, this verb-adjective (*perform-expressive*) distinction is significant. When we think of art as a distinct kind of *activity* it may well be said to seek to *express* what it does in a particular way; but to direct contemplation a completed work of art is only an *expressive* something. And in so far as a work's true significance is revealed when we contemplate it as art, the adjective *expressive* — as against verbs like *express, formulate,* and *articulate* — may be

133. *Problems of Art*, p. 20.

134. *Ibid.*, p. 133.

taken to underline the truth that, as directly realised, the expressiveness of a work of art involves no loosening of what is expressed from its material or verbal base. This emphasis on the fusion of material and meaning in art is unchallengeable, though it yet remains open to question if *all* art is expressive, and expressive *of feeling*.

Form, artistic import, and logical intuition

In the context of other details of her aesthetics, indeed, Langer's view of form raises quite a few problems. Take it, for instance, along with what she has to say on artistic import and logical intuition. The total linkage may be put thus, as a possible definition of art developed in her works:

> A work of art is an *expressive form*, and its *import* — that is, what it objectively projects of felt life — is seized by an act of *logical intuition*.

Let me now see if such a conception of art can be said to be true to the practice and contemplation of Hindustani music.

(a) Take, first, the concept of logical intuition, Langer contends that "intuition is not a 'method' at all, but an event".[135] Now, as an occurrence, an event may be instantaneous like a sudden death — a tragic event; or it may spread over a period of time like a week-long, international seminar on aesthetics which may be later remembered as quite an event. Langer seems to opt for the first meaning, for she speaks of (logical) intuition as insight, and of insight as a *sudden* emergence of meaning.[136] I say so also because, as in the following extract, she heightens the *instantaneousness* of (logical) intuition — as it seizes the import of a work of art — by opposing it to the *gradual* way in which contemplation later draws attention to the work's details:

> I. The import of an art symbol cannot be built up like the meaning of a discourse, but must be seen *in toto* first; that is, *the 'understanding' of a work of art begins with an intuition of the whole presented feeling*. Contemplation *then gradually* reveals

135. Langer, *Feeling and Form*, p. 378.

136. *Ibid.*, p. 379.

> the complexities of the piece, and of its import. In discourse, meaning is synthetically construed by a succession of intuitions; but in art the complex whole is seen or anticipated first.[137]

But what is *logical intuition*? Langer's answer, here, is clear. Logical intuition, she believes, is the (immediate) recognition of certain 'relational factors in experience' which are either sensed at once or not al all. Some of these factors are

> distinctness, similarity, congruence, relevance. These are all formal characteristics which are protological in that they 'must be seen to be appreciated.' One cannot take them on faith.[138]

Langer adds that the synthesis of details 'in a total Gestalt' is also registered by logical intuition. To take an instance, understanding the meaning of the relational complex, ' Socrates is a man', by welding the sense of its individual words 'into a single concept', is an act of *logical* intuition, as distinguished from the *simple* intuitions of Croce such as '*this* thing', '*this* event'.[139] What is more, not only form but *formal significance,* or import, is (according to Langer) seen intuitively.

(b) But she would like us to mark that though the intuitive seizure itself of a work's import is instantaneously accomplished, what the work may thereupon be said to 'do . . . to us'[140] is a vital quickening of being which is by no means momentary, even as the sudden dropping of a pebble into a placid pool may generate ripples that go on widening for a while. Langer elaborates the point as follows:

> II. What it [the work] does to us . . . [is not evoking 'emotions and moods'; it is rather] to formulate our conceptions of feeling and our conceptions of visual, tactual, and audible reality together. It gives us *forms of imagination* and *forms of feeling,* inseparably; that is to say, it clarifies and organises intuition itself. That is why it has the force of a revelation, and *inspires*

---

137. Langer, *Feeling and Form,* p. 379; 2nd and 3rd italics added.
138. Langer, *Problems of Art,* p. 166.
139. Langer, *Feeling and Form,* p. 378.
140. *Ibid.,* p. 397.

> *a feeling of deep intellectual satisfaction*, though it elicits no . . . reasoning. *Aesthetic intuition seizes the greatest form*, and therefore the main import, at once; there is no need of working through lesser ideas and serried implications first without a vision of the whole, as in discursive reasoning where the total intuition of relatedness comes as the conclusion. . . . In art, it is the impact of the whole, the immediate revelation of vital import, that acts as the psychological lure to long contemplation.[141]

The third italics in the above may be marked at once, because the words it covers do not say exactly the same thing as the following utterance of Langer:

> 'The aesthetic emotion' is really a pervasive feeling of *exhilaration*, directly inspired by the perception of good art.[142]

As for the other points made in the extracts cited, I think it necessary to comment on them at some length, but all along with reference to *ālāpa* of the *dhruvapad*-singer which provides the best instance of how the appeal of even *vocal* music can be quite independent of its usual linguistic content.

Now, philosophers may not all agree that 'intuition is not a method at all'; but in the light of the simple fact that we speak of a truth's being intuited only when we come to see it (seemingly) quite suddenly, it seems fair to suggest that (the working of) intuition is an *event*. Nor does it seem odd to speak of the intuitive apprehension of a *relational* complex. That which involves, and becomes possible through a relation may yet be experienced intuitively, that is, forthwith; and not as relational or operating visibly through a discursive movement of thought. Recognition, for instance, can be quite instantaneous, though it must ever involve a relating of the present experience to some past meeting with the person recognised. To take an instance from the practice of our music, after listerning to the first two or three rounds of a *tritāla ṭhekā* as played by the drummer, the vocalist goes on essentially by the visualised form of the

141. Langer, *Feeling and Form*, p. 397; all italics added, except the first two.

142. *Ibid.*, p. 395.

rhythmic round (called *chukkar*, in our musical parlance) without actively marking, though he sure does not forget, the beats and the segments (*vibhāgs*) that make the cycle. One may also accept Langer's insistence that, as a gathering of the meaning of words of a proposition 'into a single concept, . . . normal intuition' is involved at every step of discursive reasoning.

Some critical remarks

But when we turn to consider Langer's emphasis (in both I and II) that the 'understanding' of a work of art *begins* with an intuition of the whole presented feeling (see I on p. 65) or that 'aesthetic intuition seizes the greatest form, and, therefore, the main import, *at once*' (II p. 67); and that 'it is . . . the immediate revelation of vital import . . . that acts as the psychological lure to long contemplation' (II, *ibid.*), it does not require any great effort to see that nothing that is meant by the words cited is warranted by the practice and contemplation of what is called *ālāpa* in Hindustani music. But I must explain why I so.

Ālāpa, as a traditional *dhruvapad* singer does it, begins at a leisurely pace and proceeds, so to say, stepwise. Every individual *svara* and passage has to be carefully attended to; and at the early stages of *ālāpa* it would make no sense at all to say that we 'begin with an intuition of the *whole* presented feeling' or 'seize the greatest form . . . [and so also] the main import [of the music] at once'. The 'whole presented feeling' — if one can at all speak of such a feeling, as distinguished from the overall impact of music — comes towards the end of the recital. Nor can we say that we seize *the greatest form* 'at once', that is, as soon as the *ālāpa* in question begins. It is, of course, possible that a few deft phrases at the very commencement of singing may make the *rāga*-form quite clear to the discriminating listener. But this form, we may note, is merely the melodic matrix within and out of which the music develops; it is not the import or significance of the total recital which is to emerge much later. What is more, this eventual import cannot become manifest to those who do not or cannot focus on every detail of the ongoing course of music. This clear evidence of fact nullifies Langer's categorical view that 'in art the complex whole is seen or anticipated first'; and that it is the immediate revelation of vital import that acts as 'the psychological lure to long contemplation'.[143]

I must speak a little more fully of *ālāpa* as completed; for attention to this detail reveals other chinks in Langer's view. True, the net impact of a good exposition of *ālāpa* on a *rasika* is one of exhilaration; but, as I have said earlier, at this consummatory stage the music appears to be simply a melodic atmosphere, and not a *form* at all, in case we accept the Kantian emphasis that whatever is or has a form cannot but be limited.[144] Langer characterizes the crowning impact of a work of art in two, not quite identical ways: 'a feeling of deep intellectual satisfaction'[145] and 'a pervasive feeling of *exhilaration*.[146] Exhilaration is enlivenment, a quickening of being; and for the net impact of good *ālāpa* I prefer this word to 'deep intellectual satisfaction'. And I can justify my preference by availing of Langer's own view that sensible qualities are as important for the form of a work of art as the relations between them. A *svara* is, by definition, a sweet sound; and in so far as *svara*s are the basic bulding material of music, the final impact of good music, however adroit be its inner structure, cannot be predominantly intellectual, except in the case of a musicologist who cares only for the grammatical accuracy of *rāga*-rendering, and may therefore choose to admire the recital merely for the technical correctness with which the *rāga*, may be an *aprachalita* (or uncommon) one, has been handled. Indeed, after listerning to a consummate exposition of *ālāpa* no *rasika* says he has had a very satisfying *intellectual* experience. The words commonly used by *rasika*s, or by competent critics who are *rasika*s as well, are quite different. But before I cite some of these words I must make some distinctions.

---

143. Langer, *Feeling and Form*, p. 397.

144. How full-blown *ālāpa* may well be said to have a *form* in a different sense of the word, has been brought out in the next chapter.

145. Langer, *Feeling and Form*, p. 397.

146. *Ibid*., p. 395.

The relation of music to the listener or to the singer himself does not remain unchanging throughout. Take, first, the singer himself. His first few moments, as he sings, are of intense and wilful concentration, even visibly. As the *rāga* (melody) develops and begins to reveal its awesome, yet alluring potential for allowing *and inviting* tonal sustainment and passages of varying hue, the initial attitude of wilful attention changes into one of sweet absorption, and the *rāga* itself appears to take over the act of creation, with the result that when the singing eventually ends, the singer's feeling is one of being overwhelmed by what has come to overspread itself as a melodic ambience; and if, at this moment of consummation, the singer be complimented with the question, 'how could you sing so well'?, his answer would simply be, 'it just came off' (बस हो गया). And should a *rasika* be asked, without giving him time for critical reflection, as to how *he* is feeling, his answer would probably take one of the following forms: क्या कहने! (Good indescribably !); राग छा गया है (the *rāga* is all over; holds us spellbound). In neither case will the answer run as follows: "I am deeply satisfied at having been able to seize 'the greatest form' intuitively". Whatever be the way of our looking at intuition, Croce's or that of Langer, intuition is a cognitive experience, closer to perception than to that inner suffusion with delight touched with a little wonder, — or exhilaration (as Langer puts it), — which distinguishes the immediate aftermath of having listened to good *ālāpa*. It is Langer's penchant for words like *form*, *import*, and *intuition* that prevents her from seeing that the experience of listerning to good music may well be one of just opening up to, or being suffused with melodic charm, and not of having a meaningful intuition. The critic too, I may add, if he keeps close to how he actually felt after the experience, will not use the kind of language that Langer would like him to. He would rather speak probably as follows, as (I recall) two acknowledged music critics did by way of commenting on a glorious presentation of *ālāpa*:

> I. The finest recital of the day came from Rahimuddin Khan Dagar whose treatment of 'todi' [as *ālāpa*] was an embodiment

of spiritual repose and tranquillity.[147]

> II. The opening brought out the very basic pupose of *ālāpa*, and also how music [of this kind] is a formal art. *Ālāpa*, that is, rendition of a *rāga* independently of words, is required because . . . [to use some of the maestro's own favourite words] the quintessential finenesses of music cannot bear the blight of words. In music, as perhaps nowhere else, the linguistic minimum is the aesthetical absolute. . . . There are, of course, *no* words *in ālāpa*. But Rahimuddin Khan's very manner . . . was soft as dew . . . did it ever blight the *svara*?[148]

In I., I admit, there is a clear reference to the feeling projected in the music; and perhaps II. too may be said to indicate how softness and fineness feel — in music. But in neither case there is any hint of what Langer has spoken of as 'the greatest form'. Even during the ongoing course of *ālāpa* — that is, when it has not yet completed itself — the approbatory remarks of *rasika*s do not make any mention of what Langer calls 'the complex whole', but are likely to run generally as follows: "Wonderful! how skilfully is he doing *ālāpa* in such a narrow *rāga*";[149] 'What a charming use of *madhyama*s of *rāga Kedar*";[150] "How sweet and serene is his *ālāpa*".[151]

Yet, to keep balance, we have also to check what is of value in Langer's overall view of form in art and what needs some careful interpreting before we disagree with it finally, in case we have to. Now, I think she is justified in opposing the

147. Prakash Wadhera, today the leading critic of Hindustani music — whose column now appears in *The Hindu*, every Friday — writing on the maestro's recital in the Sunday morning session of Radio Sangeet Sammelan of 1956, in *The Times of India*, a leading daily of India.

148. S.K. Saxena's 'critical' reaction to the same recital appearing in *The Hindustan Times* of New Delhi, another important national daily of India.

149. The reference, in the case I have in mind, is to *rāga hindol* as it is sung quite without *niṣad*. In Hindustani, the comment may be put thus: "क्या कहने! कितने संकड़े राग में कैसा अलाप कर रहे हैं"!

150. क्या मध्यमें करती हैं केदार की।

151. कितनी मिठास और कितना चैन है इनके गाने में।

exaggerated polarities of 'expression and impression, *form and feeling*, and significance and sensation'.[152] Out of these three oppositions, the second one has often been accepted a bit too glibly. It has indeed been freely maintained that whereas 'form connotes formality . . . regulation . . . repression, and . . . [even] absence of feeling. . . . Feeling . . . [needs or is characterised by] . . . spontaneity . . . informality or indifference to form'.[153] This opposition is specially unacceptable to Langer. But she has her reasons to question the other polarities too. Take, to begin with, the first and the third ones. Langer puts the first opposition thus. Shall we judge a work of art as an utterance giving vent to its author's [own] feelings, *or* as a stimulus, producing sentiments in the spectator [or listener]?[154] Now, as she rightly comments, no critic at work goes by these alternatives. The evidence of *criticism* — as distinguished from that of the way *musicians* themselves may casually talk about their art — clearly is that whenever they speak of *feeling* in relation to a music recital they see it *in*, and as *of* the music itself. For when they set out to account for this appearance, they tend to focus on the following factors, all of which are the material and elements of *music* and not parts of the musician's own subjective life: intrinsic mellowness of the singer's voice, and the adroit way in which he regulates not only the duration of abidance at individual notes — and the pace and manner of passage across adjacent *svaras* — but the vocal volume too, so that a semblance of the rise and fall of (a tender) feeling may be created. And, of course, no critic would venture to suggest that the vocalist must have been pretty grieved himself when he made his music look so visibly sad. As for the *rasika* (the trained listener), he may well be moved as he registers the semblance in question. Yet *the overall feel of his experience* at the moment will not be one of sadness, but that of being moved into a state of *happy* approval, though it will surely include a clear notice of the (sad) character of the feeling. How, otherwise, could he give vent to his usual acclamation at such moments, *Wah, Wah*? *His* present feeling is

152. Langer, *Feeling and Form*, p. 22; italics added.

153. *Ibid.*, p. 17.

154. *Ibid.*, p. 18.

indeed not the same as the one he sees *in the music.* We may, therefore, conclude that, in cases like the one I have discussed, the aesthetic feeling or the affective look of the music is no direct pointer to how the musician and the *rasika* feel when the semblance is created and duly noticed.

But, be it noted, registering *a feeling* that music may project is not the same thing as being *generally impressed*. This is a distinction which the extracts I have cited appear to ignore. Langer seems to identify impression with 'producing sentiments in the spectator [or listener]'. I say so because it is soon after distinguishing the two alternative views of art, namely, as artist's expression of his own *feelings* or as a stimulus to produce *sentiments* in the contemplator,[155] that she lists the polarities of expression and impression.[156] But if *sentiment* be taken as feeling, as Langer here seems to do, evocation of feeling (as emotion) cannot be said to be the only way in which a work of art can *impress* us. In the region of Hindustani music, a *rasika* is often impressed by the sheer structural symmetry of a *bandish*, and may not see any feeling in the music nor experience any feeling himself — apart, of course, from the state of being gently pleased. This, indeed, is a basic point in my disagreement with Langer's view of art; and I may have to dwell upon it more than once when I turn to discuss her aesthetics of music and rhythm.

But as for her protest against the polarities of sensation and significance, and of form and feeling — which are often overdone — I think it can be shown to be justified by making some simple references to (Hindustani) music. The *significance* of a properly sung *svara* is precisely its *sweetness to the ear*. Here, the *auditory character* is indeed a criterion by which we judge the *value* of the note; and in musical listening, far from appearing opposed to each other, the two are inseparable. Similarly, in a picture, where a colour seems to be cool and recessive, how can one separate the colour as merely identified — say, as light blue — from the appearance it wears as an element of the work

155. Langer, *Feeling and Form*, p. 18.

156. *Ibid.*, p. 22.

and as suggesting, say, distance?

Nor is form necessarily opposed to feeling. If a *vilambit sthāyī* (the opening line of the song) seems a picture of serenity, it is generally because it runs at a leisurely pace and is held as one by unhurried *mīṇḍs* (glides), or is at least free from flirtatious embellishments. But to speak thus is clearly to explain the affective look of the line in terms of the elements of its form.

Further, it also makes sense to say, as Langer does, that form is quite important even in the case of representational art. As she points out, this is borne out by the very place which representation occupies in the evolution of visual art:

> A comparative study of decorative art and primitive representational art suggests forcibly that *form is first*, and the representational function accrues to it. Gradually the decorative forms are modified more and more to picture all sorts of objects — leaves, vines . . . flight of birds, people . . . rings become eye . . . triangles become bears, and spirals curls, . . . branches, breaking waves. . . . Decoration . . . [—] based on quasi-geometrical shapes that are 'congenial' to our spatial intuition, and guided by interest in felt continuities, rhythms and emotional dynamics . . . [—] is a simple but pure and abstract order of expressive form.[157]

Nor can we blink Langer's contention that 'fine representational art has always been formal too . . . [and that] Giotto's, Rembrandt's [and] El Greco's formal organizations are as great as those of Braque, Kandinsky or Picasso.[158]

I may add that the point here made is also true of Hindustani music, if not invariably. The singing of the late Ustad Bade Ghulam Ali Khan, rated by many as the best classical vocalist of independent India, was remarkable not only for its euphoniousness but for its articulate *form*, largely because of his fluent *tāna*s of bead-like shapeliness. Yet, and here I turn to disagree with Langer, with all their brilliance and charm, the meteoric patterns of the maestro could not be said to project

157. Langer, *Feeling and Form*, p. 70.

158. Langer, *Mind — An Essay on Human Feeling*, vol. I, p. 86.

any feeling; and, to lend further point to my protest, from the fact that fine *representational* art has been good in respect of formal organisation too, how does it follow that all art is 'the creation of forms symbolic of *human feeling*?'[159] The difficulty is surely not removed by Langer's ambivalent thesis that though in respect of its significance art is necessarily a projection of felt life, in the way of its making it is necessarily an *abstraction*. But let us first see, at some length, how she argues for the two sides of her view.

This is how she emphasizes the *second* aspect of the matter:

> All art is abstract. Its very substance, quality without practical significance, is an abstraction from material existence. . . . [The pictorial artist abstracts] the element of sensory appearance [that is, qualities, relations, volumes, shapes] from the fabric of actual life, and its complex interests . . . to create a sheer vision . . . an object meant only for sight. . . . [Even sculptures and buildings, though they do not] *so obviously* create an illusion as pictures do . . . exist [only] for vision in their own space unrelated to the space of science or practicality; and without representing anything, they *present themselves* so forcibly to vision that they seem to exist for vision alone. This fundamental abstractness belongs just as forcibly to the most illustrative murals and most realistic plays, provided they are good after their kind, as to the deliberate abstractions that are . . . entirely non-representative designs.[160]

Now, we may readily admit, the above emphasis is true to the *making* of art. It is obvious that art is no mere transference of the content of life in its fullness to the region of aesthetic treatment. Such a shift is, in fact, impossible; and some abstraction is unavoidable for art. But one cannot help tending to protest when, in respect of its positive and essential significance, Langer (yet) relates art to life as follows:

> Abstract form as such is not an artistic ideal. To carry abstraction as far as possible, and achieve pure form in only the barest conceptual medium, is a logician's business, not a

159. Langer, *Feeling and Form*, p. 40. Italics added.

160. *Ibid*., pp. 50-1.

> painter's or poet's. In art forms are abstracted only to be made clearly apparent, and are freed from their common uses only to be put to new uses: *to act as symbols, to become expressive of human feeling*.[161]

To this I have the following simple objection to make:

True, when the artist has freed a form from its context in real life he has to put it to some new use; but this 'new use' could simply be the projection of the form in question as a sensory appearance that invites and holds attention by virtue of being a close and singular wholeness. How is it fair and necessary to insist that this new use should *also* cover the expression of human feeling? Some of Langer's own utterances appear to concede the point of my protest; see, for instance, the following:

> The forms achieved by prose fiction are neither shapes nor logical system. . . . The artistic form is a *perceptual* unity of something seen, heard, or imagined — that is, the configuration, or *Gestalt*, of an experience.[162]

> The work has to be uncoupled from all realistic connections and its appearance made self-sufficient in such a way that one's interest does not go beyond it. At the same time, this purely apparent entity is *simplified* so that the ear, eye, or (in the case of literary art) the constructive imagination can take in the whole pattern all the time, and every detail be seen in a fundamental unfailing context — *seen related*, not seen and then rationally related.[163]

I may now scrutinize the extracts just cited. The first one is clearly right in its negative emphasis. It is obvious that the form of a novel or a short story — or of any work of art — is quite different from the shape of an everyday object. Nor is the form of a literary work a logical system, for such a system does not integrate happenings, feelings, character, and dialogues that form the content of a story or novel.

---

161. Langer, *Feeling and Form*, p. 51; italics added.
162. Langer, *Problems of Art*, p. 165; first italics added.
163. *Ibid.*, p. 178.

Positively, it is just as clear that a work of art presents some perceived or imgined content in a unified manner. It is also beyond question that a work of art has its own independent pull, and that we do not expect it to serve any purpose as things in daily life do. Yet the view that a work of art is cut off from *all* realistic connections cannot be taken categorically. Where a *dramatic character* appears convincing because of the consistency with which it has been portrayed, our approval of it may well be grounded in the sense that is appears lifelike. Yet, and this is what Langer would like to emphasize here, the play as a whole does not represent, much less duplicate, any part of given reality. But, to turn to her basic emphasis, how can a work be yet said to project some form of feeling? Maybe some answer can be had from the following words of Langer which seek to tell us how exactly the 'perception' of a work as 'significant of the nature of human feeling' *and* as a seemingly 'organic structure' proceeds:

> (a) Whether there is much detail or little [in a work of art], what there is must seem an articulation of the total semblance. (b) In the case of a piece that is not physically perceivable at one time, as for instance . . . a long drama . . . the proportion of the whole has to be established at all times by implication, which is a special and technical problem. (c) In any event, the perception of a work of art as 'significant form' — significant of the nature of human feeling — always proceeds from the total form to its sub-ordinate features. (d) This manner of perception, which the work is designed to elicit, causes it to appear organic; for the evolution of detail out of an indivisible, *self-sufficient* whole is characteristic of organisms and is the material counterpart of their function, life. And so the work of art seems to have organic structure and rhythms of life, though it is patently not a real organism but a lifeless object. . . . (e) When its proper material status is cancelled by the illusion of organic structure, its phenomenal character becomes paramount; the specific object is made to reveal its logical form.[164]

Now, there is a good deal in the above extract that seems

164. Langer, *Problems of Art*, pp. 178-9.

questionable to me; and I may argue for my dissent as follows, by reflecting on the points I have distinguished [as (a) (b) (c) on the previous page]:

Beginning with (a) and (c), I see that they share an emphasis, namely, the view that in perceiving the significance of a work we always proceed 'from the total work to its subordinate features'. But I fail to see how this can be true of a work of occurrent art. Where the object of contemplation is, let us say, a music recital, *awareness of the total work* comes only when the music ends. And the way we attain to it is by following the course of music and marking all its tones and tonal passages attentively, so that the perception of subordinate details must be said to come *before* we register the form of the total work and not vice versa. Point (c), however, also says that a work of art is 'significant' basically in the sense that it expresses 'the nature of human feeling'. But this, again, is questionable; and I may here cite two cases to prove my point. First, nobody ever uses the word *feeling* in relation to a *tarānā* which may use only mnemonic syllables and no language at all, though it surely represents an acknowledged genre of Hindustani classical vocal music, *and* squares all along with Langer's view of articulate form. Second, quite a few works of abstract art fall quite beyond Langer's view of art as expression of (forms of) feeling. Hospers rightly contends:

> Some works of art hardly touch 'the life of feeling' at all, but simply tease the eye or the ear: their impact is perceptual rather than emotional; consider some of Ganguin's and Matisse's color-harmonies or Mondrian's arrangements of straight lines intersecting at right angles. On the other hand, there are many works of art, especially literature, that appeal to the intellect and not to the senses, such as the long stretches of informational material in Tolstoy's War and Peace.[165]

Consider another well-known work: Mondrian's *Composition with Blue and White* (1935). It may well make sense to say of it that it looks clear, firm, and taut or tightly drawn; but it would surely look odd to speak of it as expressing the form of tightness as felt.

165. John Hospers: "Hartshorne's Aesthetics", in *The Philosophy of Charles Hartshorne*, p. 128.

What Langer says about a 'long' work of art is even more perplexing; and in respect of her belief that in the case of such works of art 'the proportion (or magnitude, relative measure) of the whole has to be established at all times by implication', I may at once make two critical remarks. First, if 'the proportion of the whole' is here 'established by implication *at all times*' (or all along), the determination in question may be said to begin from the earliest stages of the making of the work. But if we speak thus, we would be suggesting that the character of *the parts determines* the proportion of the whole, not (as Langer would like us to say) that *the parts* or details *seem* [not independent, but] an articulation of [and so *determined by*] the total semblance.

Second, even in respect of determination of the whole by the parts, we cannot speak unconditionally. In the case of a good dramatic play, the very opening scene may well appear to give us a feel of a pervasive feature of the whole; but the playwright alone, and no external observer can say if the *magnitude* of the entire work is established by its very beginning. It is true that the very opening scenes of Shakespeare's Twelfth Night and Macbeth give us an inkling of what they are going to project, that is, (respectively) the tendency to make a luxury of one's grief or loss of love *and* weirdness of ghoulish happenings, but such prefeeling of a feature of the play is clearly not the same thing as determination of the *proportion* of a whole by its constituents. What is more, the suggestion that the whole extent of a long work is determined at the very outset is not supported by the evidence of art-making taken generally. Thus, in the case of an exposition of Indian classical music, though the singer may well begin sedately and feel set to sing for about two hours, the notice of inappreciative audience-response to *vilambit* or slow singing may compel him to switch over to *drut* singing earlier than as preplanned, and so bring about a reduction of the originally intended length of the whole recital. And, again from the viewpoint of Hindustani music, one may find it difficult to accept, without questioning, Langer's *total* remark on the work's revelation of its 'logical form'(e). When a properly integrated *sthāyī* (first line of the composition) appears properly established after the first few rounds, it may well come to seem an *organic* structure, or reveal, as Langer would say, its 'logical form' as a compact whole of internally related details; but how can the 'proper material status' of the composition — which may be taken to mean the right location of the constituent notes in the scale, if not their experienced sweetness — be said to be '*cancelled* by the illusion of organic structure'?[166] And should it come to happen, will not such a cancellation at once turn the music into a mere jumble of undifferentiated sounds?

I, however, feel that the question may be answered, and our doubts dispelled, by considering the context of Langer's words which are troubling us. See. for instance, the following extract that precedes them:

> If the semblance [of organic structure] is forcible enough — that is, if the artist is successful — the impression of living form becomes commanding and the physical status of the piece insignificant.[167]

In the light of this extract one could say that where Langer speaks of the *cancellation* of the proper material status of the work by the illusion (or semblance) of organic structure, her meaning only is when the contemplator experiences the illusion in question — or seizes what Langer would call the artistic import of the work — he does not think of colours or tones as they are in their original individual character. Thus, if the source of the 'illusion of organic structure' is a musical work, the proper location of the notes in the scale, though it will surely not be unsettled in any way, may yet cease to be an object of the *rasika*'s explicit attention which will be held only by what the music appears to be, that is, an organic wholeness. He will, of course, duly register the rightness of the notes as sung (or played), but to him they will all alike appear as accents in, and as contributing to a flow, and not as detached existences in a mere series.

166. Langer, *Problems of Art*, p. 179; italics added.

167. *Ibid.*, pp. 178-9.

Art and the 'forms' of feeling

However, objections like the one I have just tried to meet are but little irritants and may well be ignored. But what cannot be passed over is the singularity of Langer's basic thesis that it is the essence of art to project forms of feeling or subjective life. But maybe the following extracts from her works can help us in seeing the truth of her view:

> *a.* [The] image of feeling . . . the 'life' of lines and colours themselves . . . is *the deepest principle* the arts have in common; the forward movement in drama, not the particular thing done; the articulate transience of music that makes us call fragments of music 'passages'; the self-defining masses of good architecture which possess life even if they happen to house nothing but lifeless things, or even death itself in a funerary shrine.[168]

> *b.* Our sense of change in permanence, the balance of becoming and passing is one of the profoundest aspects of human consciousness. [And yet this is precisely what] even the most elementary forms of visual art — say, a purely decorative design, a wavy line adorning the rim of a pot . . . [are able to project]. For instance, . . . the line, which is stationary, is said to 'run' around the rim [because it appears to do so].[169]

Langer here speaks of 'the deepest principle' which makes every art significant; so the extracts cited deserve close attention.

Now, what exactly is the *deepest principle* which the first extract emphasizes? It is (what is, for Langer) the truth that every art is an *image* of feeling:

> Every work of art is . . . an image [of subjective events], whether it be a dance, a statute, a picture, a piece of music, or a work of poetry.[170]

Here, it is obvious, the word *image*, is very likely to disturb us. How can *every* work of art be regarded as an image? As a

---

168. Langer, *Mind — An Essay on Human Feeling*, vol. I, p. 67; italics added.

169. Langer, *Problems of Art*, p. 54.

170. *Ibid.*, p. 9.

specimen of the art of architecture, and not as a mere memorial, a beautiful building does not represent anything. Nor is a 'patterned textile'[171] ordinarily a faithful imitation of any actual object in its wholeness. How, then, can the two be said to be *images*? Langer here offers two clear answers which are both alike ingenious, if not quite convincing or compatible with each other. I may put them as follows along with my comments on each one of them:

If an object, be it a building or a pot, 'presents itself purely to our vision, i.e., as a sheer visual form instead of a locally and practically related object . . . it *becomes* an image'.[172] Therefore, even a work of architecture may be regarded as an image, if we care only for its look, and quite without any thought to its 'physical and causal' context.[173]

Now, there is no doubt that, maybe because of intense focusing of attention on its distinctive configuration, any object can become 'a sheer visual form'. To illustrate, when a 'she' appears as 'a phantom of delight' to the poet's ravished eye, what happens is no literal

> vaporization of the figure, but just an utter engrossment of attention in the figure's appearance, as contemplated for a while in utter separateness from its variform relatedness to real life. . . . Even a massive structure of solid stone like the Taj Mahal may be registered for a few moments as just an eye-filling vision of beauty and may so become an image (in Langer's sense) to contemplation.[174]

But she may here protest that *so long as* we look at a building as sheer architecture, it *continues to appear* as an image, because we attend to it alone, *without any thought of its context in actual life*. Now, the emphasis Langer here puts on abstraction may be conceded; but a question would still remain open. Is it proper to *speak of* a building, thus contemplated as an *image*? Do not

171. Langer, *Feeling and Form*, p. 47.

172. *Ibid.*; italics added. This extract is slightly different in its order of words from the way they occur in the source.

173. *Ibid.*

174. Saxena, *Art and Philosophy: Seven Aestheticians*, p. 268.

the exigencies of common linguistic usage compel us to ask: image of what? And would it not be less questionable to say, as Langer herself freely does, that (as it appears to contemplation) a work of art is an apparition or pure appearance or 'a purely "virtual" object'?[175] One cannot help suspecting that it is only because she does not find the word, *image,* quite satisfactory (in the context of art) that she is compelled to use 'virtual entity', 'virtual object', 'appearance', 'apparition', and 'image' interchangeably.[176]

Langer, however, is able to offer another quite different argument in support of her view that a work of art is an image. I may put it thus. The notion that an image is 'a replica of sense-impression' is indeed quite popular. But it misses the most important character of images, which is that they are symbolic [and not merely imitative].[177] That is why, 'in point of sensuous character, they may be . . . indescribably vague . . . [and] quite unlike what they represent'.[178]

I see, in these words of Langer, a clear measure of truth. Where a poet speaks thus:

> *A little noiseless noise among the leaves,*
> *Born of the very sigh that silence heaves,*

his net purpose is to make us visualise a rustling of leaves so faint as to be hardly audible. But there is nothing like a *noiseless noise* in actuality; nor does it convey any determinate meaning to speak of *the sigh that silence heaves.* Yet the images enable us *to think of* a noise that is infinitely feeble. Even where they are not elaborate they can help visualisation of some details of felt life. In the opening scene of Hamlet, for instance, Shakespeare is able to project an eerie feel of absolute silence by availing of a minuscule image of movement:

> *Bernardo: Have you had quiet guard?*
> *Francisco: Not a mouse stirring.*

---

175. Langer, *Feeling and Form,* p. 48.
176. Langer, *Problems of Art,* p. 5.
177. Langer, *Feeling and Form,* p. 47.
178. Langer, *Problems of Art,* pp. 131-2.

Indeed, be they complex or brief, images articulate, and enable us to comprehend relations between details of lived experience. An Art Symbol functions likewise. A whole work of art may be said to be an *image* in the sense that it 'formulates experience, and expresses for our objective contemplation the actual felt process of life'.

This takes us to the key emphasis in the extracts being discussed, that is, the relation of art to feeling. Let us focus, first, on *feeling*. As we have seen, Langer requires us to take the word as signifying *felt life*; and 'felt life' as covering the content of both our outer world and inner subjective life, all *as directly felt*, instead of being merely visualised. Now, (as the extract b., on p. 81, says) it is indeed our common experience that, as it goes on, life is characterized by the felt recession of some events into the past and the occurrence or imminence of new ones. This *liquid* collocation of what is, has been, and is yet to come about, is indeed a basic and *permanent* datum of our consciousness. It is also 'profound' in the sense of being so deeply fused with our existence as sentient beings that we just cannot imagine ourselves being without it. And to turn now to art, we sure see something similar in the undulating wavy line that Langer speaks of; it does appear to 'run' around the border, though it does not really move. Similarly, 'the forward movement in drama', often sensed by us as the feeling that things are coming to a head, or as wonder in respect of what is going to happen next, may be likened to our feeling expectant in real life about the likely outcome of a long and directed endeavour. One may also acknowledge the similitude between the *articulate*, but '*transient* passages' of music and what Langer speaks of as a distinct form of human feeling, namely 'the greatness and *brevity* and eternal *passing* of everything *vitally* felt.[179] Further, by a simple exercise of imagination, '*the self-defining* masses of good architecture' may also be seen to be somewhat similar to another form of feeling distinguished by Langer, say, 'what it is like to . . . feel *self-sufficient* but alone'.[180] What is more, even a 'funerary shrine' may be taken to suggest

179. Langer, *Feeling and Form*, p. 27; italics added.

180. Langer, *Problems of Art*, p. 22. Italics added.

the finality of death which we experience in life as the poignant feeling that the one who has passed away has utterly ceased to be, 'leaving not a rack behind', so to say.

This focusing on likeness, I may add, is no fabrication; Langer herself resorts to it pretty often. Thus, see the following:

> 'Music sounds as feelings feel'. And likewise, in good painting, sculpture, or building, balanced shapes and colors, lines and masses look as emotions, vital tensions and their resolutions feel.[181]

Now, I am not sure if the arts of music and architecture provide any parallel to feelings of embarrassment and suspicion; but I will not press the point because it may well be that many other feelings have their equivalences in art. My protest is different; and I may put it straight. From the fact that there is a measure of clear sameness between what Langer calls the forms of feeling and some features that distinguish the various arts, how does it follow that imagined feelings and artistic treatment interfuse, and not merely correspond, to produce aesthetic semblances; and that the *supreme* function of art is to express the so-called forms?

Langer on poetry: A criticism

Langer would here point to the actual evidence of art; this is indeed her wont throughout her works. Of the many contexts in which she does this freely, I may choose her theory of poetry, for only a work of poetic art can be presented here — to serve as a check for her view. I do so also because the way she develops the theory in question projects some such concepts of her aesthetics of art as I have not discussed so far, such as those of vital rhythms, virtual life, and pure appearance. Moreover, it is here that she argues with fair reason how art alone can objectify for understanding the intricate fabric of our subjective life.

Now, the following may be taken to epitomise Langer's theory of poetry:

---

181. Langer, *Problems of Art*, p. 26.

> The poet uses *discourse* to *create* [and project] an *illusion* [or a sheer image or semblance of virtual life, 'life' as covering not merely immediate personal experience and forms of feeling, but 'the great vital rhythms' — all cast in the imaginative mode — that is, 'the mode of naive experience, in which action and feeling, sensory value and moral value, causal connection and symbolic connection, are still undivorced'] *a pure appearance*, which is a *non-discursive symbolic form* . . . [in which mere statements are used up, and transformed from vehicles of 'conversational interest' to those of literary interest, i.e., from actuality to fiction]. The *feeling expressed by this form* is neither his, nor his hero's, nor ours. It is the meaning [or import] of the symbol. . . . The appearances of events in our actual lives are fragmentary, transitory. The poet's business is to . . . organise them so they constitute a purely and completely experienced reality, a piece of *virtual life* [life, essentially in the social sense] . . . [and so] to create the appearance of 'experiences', the *semblance* of events lived and felt. . . . [The] illusion of life is the primary *illusion* of all poetic art.[182]

Let me now explain the concepts implicit in the words in italics.

(a) The poet surely uses discourse, or language generally, as the basic material of his art; but he does this not for narrating actual happenings, propounding theses, or evoking emotional reactions in the reader, but simply for the sake of creating an 'illusion' of virtual life comprising scenes, situations, recollections and events — all these in the imaginal mode.

(b) *Creation* of art, as distinuished from the *making* of things, is indeed to be taken as the evocation of a mere semblance or pure appearance, that is, something which is only meant to be contemplated, not to be used; and which, as appearance, is *pure* because it is not the appearance of any underlying substrate, but is just itself, a mere semblance, like the rainbow. Poetry creates 'a world of its own'. 'A world [that is] created as an

---

182. Langer, *Feeling and Form*, pp. 211-13. The way the extract is here put differs from its order of words in the parent work. But they are all Langer's words used at different places in Ch. 13 of *Feeling and Form*. Words within brackets have been interpolated to make for fulness of meaning.

artistic image is given us to look at, not to live in . . . [and] in this respect it is radically unlike the neurotic's private world'.[183]

(c) What exactly is meant by saying that the poet creates an *illusion* should now be easy to see. Here the word does not mean the misrepresentation of something actual; but only the projection of something which is not at all a part of given reality, though it is doubtless possessed of intrinsic charm *and significance.*

(d) But, though it is meaningful (or symbolic), what is created by the poet is a *non-discursive* form. It is (we have seen) 'a single symbol', a whole in respect of the 'life' (or meaning) of which we cannot decide as to how much is exactly contributed by the various elements (or limbs).[184]

(e) Above all,

> a poem always creates the symbol of a feeling, not by recalling objects which would elicit the feeling itself, but by weaving a pattern of words — words charged with meaning, and coloured by literary associations akin to the dynamic pattern of the feeling . . . the word 'feeling' here . . . [covering] more than a 'state'; for feeling is a process, and may have not only successive phases, but several simultaneous developments; it is complex and its articulations are elusive.[185]

The locus of the feeling is, therefore, the poem's whole form. The total piece looks as a vital experience may feel.

But is this true of poems generally? I find it difficult to say *yes* to the question. One may agree, by and large, with Langer's following comment on Wordsworth's "Ode: Intimations of Immortality":

> . . . There are [in this poem] no statements pro and con, no doubts and proofs but essentially the *experience* of having so great an idea — the *excitement* of it, the awe, *the image of holiness* it bestows on childhood, the explanation of the growing

183. Langer, *Feeling and Form*, p. 228.

184. Langer, *Problems of Art*, p. 135.

185. Langer, *Feeling and Form*, p. 230.

commonplaceness of later life, the resigned acceptance of an insight.[186]

But the way Langer relates (a particular) *feeling* to Blakes's 'The Echoing Green' is, in my view, clearly suspect even if it be kept in mind that the word 'covers more than a "state" ', and that 'feeling is a process and may have not only successive phases, but several simultaneous developments. . . .'[187] The art-feeling linkage is a key point in Langer's entire aesthetics; and so, at this juncture, I permit myself to repeat with some changes the protest I have already made in my earlier book, *Art and Philosophy: Seven Aestheticians*.[188] The poem in question is not a long one, and so I may cite it in full:

The sun does arise
And make happy the skies;
The merry bells ring
To welcome the Spring;
The skylark and thrush,
The birds of the bush,
Sing louder around
To the bells' cheerful sound.
While our sports shall be seen
On the Echoing Green.

Old John, with white hair,
Does laugh away care,
Sitting under the oak,
Among the old folk.
They laugh at our play,
And soon they all say:
"Such, such were the joys
When we all, girls and boys
In our youth time were seen
On the Echoing Green".

---

186. Langer, *Feeling and Form*, p. 219; italics added.

187. *Ibid.*, p. 230.

188. Pp. 303-310.

Till the little ones, weary,
No more can be merry;
The sun does descend,
And our sports have an end.
Round the laps of their mothers
Many sisters and brothers,
Like birds in their nest,
Are ready for rest,
And sport no more seen
On the darkening Green.

Now, what does this poem really mean? What is its *literary import*, as against its literal meaning? According to Langer, it is *'the feeling* [of fruition] *developed and revealed in' the poem;*[189] and, she adds, the fruition in question is

> the life process itself, and the direct experience of it is the profoundest harmony we can feel. This experience is what the poem creates in three short stanzas. Gratified desire is only the . . . end of this experience; the desire itself, the whole joy of beginning, freedom, strength, and then mere endurance, and finally weariness and the dark, held in one intensive view of humanity at play, are all equally important in creating the symbol of *life completely lived*. The completeness is felt; and the peculiar *elan* and progress of this feeling is the abstraction that the poetic form makes.[190]

Referring to the title of the poem, Langer says:

> The 'echo' is really that of the repeating life-story — the old laughing at the young and recalling their own youth, the young returning to a previous generation — 'Round the laps of their mothers, many sisters and brothers'; and there is another level of 'echoing' life — one form of life being typified in another; the children 'like birds in their nest', and the *aged* people gathered under the *oak*. . . . Even the line 'Old John with white hair' achieves the interweaving of age and youth, for 'John' means 'The Young'. . . . One can go on almost from word to word in this poem . . . that is completely organic, and

189. Langer, *Feeling and Form*, p. 226.

190. *Ibid*.

> therefore able to articulate *the great vital rhythms* and their emotional overtones and undertones. What such a symbolic form presents cannot be expressed in literal terms, because the logic of language forbids us to conceive the *pervasive ambivalence* which is characteristic of human feeling.[191]

Langer looks on the poem as a projection not of the mere *fulfilment* of desire to live a full life, but of '*the desire itself*, with some key features of its career in life'. But, I protest, no such reading is warranted by what one finds *in* the poem itself. Where *in the poem* do we find any hint of desire? The having of a desire is at once to look for something, and so it is always felt as a kind of tension, however slight it be. In the poem, on the other hand, even where it speaks of sport, there is not the slightest suggestion of aiming at any target. The relation or adaptation here found appears as a working for the sake of, a going well along with, or a willingness to receive something else (see: 'bells ring to welcome the spring'; 'sing louder to the bells' cheerful sound' 'and are ready for rest'), *but never as a pressing for or towards a goal*. So, a reader who prefers to go strictly by what is really there is the poem would find it impossible to agree that the poem projects the feeling *of desire* which is (in the end) gratified. But, one could rejoin (on Langer's behalf), may not desire be here taken as the very love of life that makes us quietly *look for* the next moment instead of trying to achieve some specific end? Perhaps yes; but if we choose to regard the fruition of desire *so taken* as the poem's keynote, almost the whole first stanza would be left quite unconsidered. For here, in the first eight lines, the poet speaks only of birds, bells and skies.

And yet it is these opening lines that give us a clear clue to what one may rightly regard as *the focus of the whole poem*, that is, *the idea of mutual accord and self-giving*. The daybreak gladdens the blue — with colour and light.[192] Nor do the bells ring only for themselves. They *welcome* vernal charm; and, what is more, themselves find an echo in the bird's louder singing.

---

191. Langer, *Feeling and Form*, pp. 226-7; italics added.

192 I am here reminded of Blake's colour print worked up with brush, *Glad Day*, 1794. See Kathleen Raina's *William Blake*, facing, p. 92.

One may also feel impelled, at this point, to make some comments on the title, and on the word 'echoing' in particular. Langer takes it to be integral to the poem. But it cannot be so if we take 'echo' as she wants us to: 'the repeating life-story — the old laughing at the young and recalling their own youth, the young returning to a previous generation'. For upon this interpretation the content of the first eight lines would again be merely ignored. On the other hand, the concept I have put up as the focal one may be said to cover both human and natural referents of the poem.

Nor is it fairly possible to accept the insistence that the word 'echoing', here, is not at all descriptive. The village green may well be flat in fact, and so many not be said to echo a sound literally. But in respect of a field which is enlivened with rustic sport, and where the players are all young girls and boys, would it appear quite improper to say that it *resounds* with their merriment?[193] Further, an echo, we may note, is a sound which is not only quite whole as it recoils, but a little more powerful in impact than at the moment of its origin. This is indeed an obvious hint in the poem's very opening:

> *The birds of the bush*
> *Sing* louder *around*
> *To the bells' cheerful sound.*

Many other details of the poem's inner weave also seem to be noteworthy. As here visualized, the beginning and the end of sport are no mere fringes. They strike the reader as clear termini, in part because they are made to go with the rise and descent of the sun, which are both *emphasized*. If there is nothing indefinite about the poem, it is partly because its details are in general so enframed. But what may here be said to be admirable, because of its subtlety, is the singular use of a device to vivify some features of 'our sports' obliquely. There is no direct mention of their kind or particulars. But the way Blake projects what sets the stage for sports, so to say — and also what comes

193. I may here point out that, according to Blake, delight is the essence of life, *William Blake*, p. 50.

in their wake — is so clear that the reader is directly enabled to visualize what intervenes, that is, the cheer and ebullience of the play itself, if not its details.

Langer, it appears, is a bit too impatient to look for deeper meanings. By way of arguing for my protest, I have already shown how no hint of desire may be said to be there in the poem; and, as a supplement, only the following from Langer may now be considered:

> . . . What the poem creates . . . is the direct experience of . . . the life process itself (which is) . . . the profoundest harmony we can feel . . . [The poem is a] symbol of *life completely lived.* The completeness is felt; and the peculiar elan and progress of this feeling is the abstraction that the poetic form makes. . . . What [this poem as] a symbolic form presents cannot be expressed in literal terms, because the logic of language forbids us to conceive the *pervasive ambivalence which is characteristic of human feeling*. Professor Tillyard speaks of 'the primal Joy-Melancholy'; and to indicate such feeling by a paradoxical name is about as much philosophy can do with it. [On the other hand, Blake's poem, because it is] completely organic, . . . [is] . . . able to articulate the great vital rhythms. . . .[194]

Now, it is not easy to see what Langer could here mean by a 'life *completely* lived'. At no point does the poem look crowded with (virtual) events. Nor does it anywhere project any wrestling with problems. So the completeness spoken of can only be taken lengthwise, or as a sign of the unobstructed attainment of a ripe old age. (Here the reference is to: 'Old John with white hair'.) But *such* an uneventful life can hardly be felt as an experience of 'profound' harmony. The poem, it is true, looks complete in itself. Nor can a careful reader here fail to register the hint of ambivalent feeling. It is surely easy to imagine that as they recall their own youthful joys 'the old folk' experience 'the primal joy-Melancholy'.[195] But one sees no *intenseness* about this recollection of the past, no sting or

194. Langer, *Feeling and Form*, pp. 226-7. I here diverge from the order of the original, but no violence is done to Langer's meaning. Second and third italics added.

195. *Ibid.*, p. 227.

poignancy. It rather opens leisurely:

> *Such, such were the joys,*
> *When we all, girls and boys,*
> *In our youth time were seen*
> *On the Echoing Green.*

Here, as indeed throughout the poem, the marks of punctuation are so used that they make for clear segments. *There is no interfusion of details,* and one is at a loss to see how, as Langer suggests, everything here could be said to be 'held in one *intensive* view of humanity at play'.[196] To an unbiased eye the poem is just a true projection of the 'look' (or feel) of a single typical day enlivened with the young at play, with very liberal, if unaddressed, support (so to say) from both village elders and nature.

But, though Langer's overall reading of this *particular* poem may thus seem suspect, it is yet possible to agree with her theory of poetry *in general.* Some of its emphases in fact appear borne out by the poem under review. The statements it includes do not merely inform: they all alike make for a single vision and evoke a pervasive feeling. The line: 'The sun does arise' betokens a general quickening of atmosphere; and the third line of the closing stanza, 'The sun does descend' not merely announces the end of the day and of sport, but is at once a call to return to the haven of maternal care. The poem's form, we may add, is also expressive in the sense that its very 'look' projects the self-completeness of a typical day. Again, the 'events' are all 'virtual' or cast in the imaginative mode. It is indeed easy to see how the very opening words of the poem 'effect the break with the reader's actual environment'.[197]

> *The sun does arise*
> *And make happy the skies.*

In everyday life we may well be struck by what goes along with a clear sunrise, that is, the upsurge of colour and light in

---

196. Langer, *Feeling and Form*, p. 226.

197. *Ibid.*, p. 214.

the heavens. But we do not really believe that the heavens rejoice at the dawn, or that the sun rises *with a view* to making 'happy the skies'. And in case we seek for literal truth it would be a further strain on our credence if we were told that the bells and the birds keep up their merry music '*while* (or as long as) . . . sports shall be seen'. The fact, however, is that the injection of a little feeling and purpose into nature is done so directly and so kept up throughout the first stanza that the reader's passage from the actual to the poem's virtual world is quick and secure. It is true that an *individual*, 'Old John', is named, and his 'white hair' *distinguished*. But the singleness is set off at once, for John is shown as sitting 'among the old folk' who laugh (as one) 'at our play'. A careful reader of this poem is bound to be struck by the liberal use of such words as suggest togetherness and collectivity. Thus see: '*our* sports shall be seen'; 'and soon they *all* say'; 'when we *all* girls and boys'; '*our* sports have an end', and '*many* brothers and sisters'.

Indeed, the entire poem is an *apparition*, that is, an *image* for contemplation alone, — an image (or apparition) in the way of a rainbow, not as an image (or imitation) of something in actual reality. There is nothing in it to impel us to check the veracity of its details with any outer fact. But though the poem may well be regarded as a powerful projection of the felt gathering of Nature and Man, so to say, around the village youth at play, one does not here see the *dominance* of any 'vital rhythm' or '*form*' of feeling.

Be it noted that what I deny only is that the poem as a whole is *dominated* by the projection of a vital rhythm, not that such that a rhythm does find *some* utterance here. Building upon some of Langer's own words,[198] we may say that the vital rhythm in the present context is the ambivalent one of 'the primal Joy-Melancholy', that is, the mixed feeling of joy and sorrow. A measure of such ambivalence may even be said to be 'characteristic of human feeling' for it is also seen to distinguish our experience in the form of love-hate relationship.[199] But what I wish to point out here is that the ambivalence

198. Langer, *Feeling and Form*, p. 227.

199. *Ibid*.

in question is effectively projected by the very first of the four lines that occur within double inverted commas in the poem: 'Such such were the joys'. Even an imagined utterance of such words is in fact an experience of both happiness, because what is recalled is 'joys' — and sorrow because they, 'the joys', are now a thing of the past (mark here the word, '*were*'). If the line is replaced with the everyday (discursive) statement: 'We feel both happy and sad', we would be incurring a double loss. The imaginative mode will get replaced with the literal one; and the *fusion* of feeling — of joy and sorrow — provided by the thought of 'joys that were' would disapper.

But turning to the way *I* have interpreted the poem, if it 'says' only what I have suggested it does, how is it significant? There is no great value in the thought that the young are playing merrily and that nature and the village elders are at one with them. Here, following Langer, our answer could be that the value of the poem lies not in any message that may be extracted from it, but in what it is able to create, that is, the image of a cheery day of village sport, of how it begins, attains to its zenith, and finally ends, quite as agreeably as it opened. The reader is enabled to *dwell on the cheer and the pervasive harmony*; he does not only read about them. But such a contemplative access to what is felt is granted only to those who are able to get at the poem's total form; only then does *it* appear to project the 'feelings' we speak of.

And as we seek to unravel the poem's form, its organic character becomes quickly manifest. We have already seen how some of its elements conduce to its overall import. But we must add that this build-up of significance is no mere accretion of pre-fixed, independent meanings. The elements contribute what they *come to* acquire in the knitwork, so that the overall form must be said to be non-discursive. Langer suggests that "the line 'Old John with white hair' achieves the interweaving of youth and age, for 'John' means 'The Young' ";[200] but one may wonder if the linkage in question would be so fully 'achieved' or manifest as it is without the help of the words that follow

200. Langer, *Feeling and Form*, p. 227.

immediately; 'Does laugh away care', and the prompt reiterative touch:

> *Among the old folk,*
> *They laugh at our play*

And we may be sure that the last line of the opening stanza:

> *On the* Echoing *Green*

would not make much sense unless we bear in mind the joyful; aspect of nature — *and its little 'virtual' acts of self-giving* — projected by the poem's very opening. But it is where the poem ends that the note of self-giving and accord rings audibly and clear:

> *Round the laps of their mothers,*
> *Many sisters and brothers,*
> *Like birds in their nest,*
> *Are ready for rest.*

It is the gathering of a need around its true source of succour. The weary ones look for rest; and their human nest, the mother's lap, is a ready refuge. It is easy for the reader to fill in this picture of a loving trust *returned*. What may be *emphasized* here, however, is not merely the echoing of a basic human feeling, but the subtle way in which these lines bring the poem to a close by providing a foil to the opening ones. Birds singing 'around' (to the bells' cheerful sound) and the sunrise that enlivens the blue, evoke images of *suffusion and free happy flight*. All this is reversed when we come to the following:

> *Round the laps of their mothers . . .*
> *Like birds in their nest.*

The poem does not merely end, but *gathers itself into a point of repose*.

Residual disagreements

It should be obvious that in interpreting the poem I have tried all along to go by 'the pattern of words' which are actually there in it; and *they* do not warrant, I repeat, Langer's conclusion that the poem is a symbolic *expression* of the ('profoundest') *felt* harmony of *life completely lived.*[201] What is more, quite generally too I have reason to question the way she relates art to expression of feeling; and, by way of closing this chapter, I think it necessary to put the residual points of my disagreement with her basic views as follows:

I. Take, first, her emphasis on *expression*. She regards it as the essence of art. But if this is really so, there must be a necessary relation between expression and whatever precedes and facilitates it, or provides a ground, source or impulse to it. According to Croce, this preceding something is intuition which, he insists, is inseparable from expression. In his view, however, expression (in the true sense) is not an overt, but an inner happening. This view, it is obvious, is difficult to square with the evidence of actual art-making. But Croce's basic thesis that art is intuition-expression as one, and not a mere sequential conjunction of the two, may be taken to point to the possibility that, if only in moments of consummate creativity, the very envisagement of what Langer calls 'the commanding form', or (to put it quite generally) the stirrings of the creative impulse, may themselves press for immediate, overt expression. This may not be said to be necessarily true, I repeat, of creation in the region of art, because here a watchful, intervening effort of the will is often found necessary; but in so far as it does hold with respect to cases where the making in question appears spontaneous and also effortlessly expressive to those who are conversant with the specific techniques it employs, I think it necessary to cite and explain some supportive evidence from the actual practice of art.

Consider, for instance, the case of a dancer (and singer) like Birju Maharaj, the Kathak maestro.[202] Whatever he does as a performing artist is done with intense focusing of all his creative

---

201. Langer, *Feeling and Form*, p. 226.

202. I here build upon my experience of recording Birju Maharaj's singing and drumming — on behalf of Sangeet Natak Akademi, and for our national archives — on August 19, and 21, 1996; and of watching him dance many a time.

powers; he puts himself into the act, so to say. Now, as in all other fields, so here too, the intensity of perfect absorption in the act generates *rasa* as the relish of *tasting* or of direct, personal experience. Relish is zestful enjoyment. Absorption in what one does is always an agreeable feeling, though it may not be zestful too. The nine *rasa*s distinguished by traditional aesthetical thinking in India are all cases of zestful enjoyment; but they are also all underrun by *rasa* in this basic, unitary sense because they emerge only as a sequel to — and flourish on the basis of — *tādātmya* or the *rasika*'s imaginative self-identification with the aesthetic object. In the case being considered, what is being done — namely, the dancing (or the singing) — is something that the individual in question is fond of, and has been doing for years. Further, he finds that he *is* able to do what he is trying to. This quiet sense of agency and concurrent achievement adds to the overall delight of his doing. Above all, the continual if implicit awareness that one is dancing (or singing) for *rasika*s, from whom a nod of approval is devoutly wished for, lends a gently projective tilt to the total experience, turning the basic absorption into rapture (or उल्लास). As agreeable feeling, rapture is not self-enclosed; it is ebullient and presses for release. This buoyancy of delight in creation enlivens the dancing of Birju Maharaj in (at least) two ways. *First*, it lubricates, so to say, the working of technical devices, making his dancing look delightfully effortless (or सहज), exactly as the natural buoyancy of water may make a trained man's swimming look like floating; and, second, it suffuses his visage with a gentle glow that captivates the (first few rows of) onlookers, accounting (in part) for the spellbinding quality of his dance. I venture to suggest that what is called *mukh-vilās* in Kathak jargon is, at its best, a direct bodily expression of the dancer's present feeling of delight in the course of dance. But because it is routed through the dancer's competent, and so self-satisfying handling of the technique of dance, the facial expression here matches the quality of dance, and is no mere appearance put on to cover some weakness. So it adds to the dance's own integrated look arising from internal design. I therefore disagree with Langer's *categorical* view that because, as *artistic* expression, it is actively organised, dance cannot be regarded as a direct projection of the dancer's own present feeling. Her reference to a detail of Pavlova's *The Dying Swan*[203] is not enough to support her sweeping view. Actual experience of *grief* while dancing a sad number will, of course, hinder disciplined movement which calls for a measure of composure. But the *joy* or rapture I have spoken of may only lift the quality of the total dance in the way I have indicated.

II. Consider, next, Langer's view of the relation of feeling to art. Two key utterances of hers in this context are as follows:

> (a) Art is the articulation, not the stimulation or catharsis, of feeling. . . . Abstract art seeks to convey . . . the morphology of vital and emotive experience.[204]
>
> (b) The function of art, like that of science, is to acquaint the beholder with something he *has not known before* . . . [;] the artistic symbol, *qua* artistic, negotiates insight, not reference. . . .[205]

Putting the two together we may say that, according to Langer, the essential function of art is not to evoke any feeling, but to give us some insight into, or to add to our knowledge of felt life, or of 'vital and emotive experience'.

From the viewpoint of this (positive) emphasis, the second extract may be said to be more striking, for it seeks to narrow the gap between art and science. So we may ponder over it. First, as is widely admitted, even the perceptual character of everyday objects — or of objects as they are directly 'felt' — can be made known to us much better by works of art than it is in humdrum experience. Second, art may be said to 'negotiate *insight*' in the sense of providing a direct awareness of the object's own quality, as distinguished from its functions and relations to other things in daily life. A simple illustration should make the point clear. When we say, the weather is *chilly*, some knowledge is surely conveyed. But the adjective only connotes a quality; and we apprehend the meaning with a

203. Langer, *Feeling and Form*, p. 177.

204. Langer, *Problems of Art*, p. 107.

205. Langer, *Feeling and Form*, p. 22. Here, only the second italics belongs to the original.

casual nod, and let it pass. It does not ordinarily invite us to dwell on the quality referred to. On the other hand, the opening lines of 'The Eve of St. Agnes' make us visualize very clearly how 'bitter chill' *feels*:

> *St. Agnes' eve, Ah, bitter chill it was!*
> *The owl, for all its feathers, was a-cold;*
> *The hare limped trembling through the frozen grass,*
> *And silent was the flock in woolly fold*
> *Numb were the Beadsman's fingers, while he told*
> *His rosary, and while his frosted breath . . .*

But, and now I take a critical turn, what are we make of the following:

> A wholly non-representational design, a happily proportioned building, a beautiful pot may, artistically speaking, be *just as expressive* as a love-sonnet. It has an import . . . a wordlessly presented conception of *what life feels like.*[206]

Langer is here explaining how 'every successful work' of art may be said to be expressive. It is, in her view, expressive in virtue of having some *vital import*; and this may be taken to mean that the work conveys 'some *mode* of feeling, sense, emotion, consciousness'.[207] But what could this *mode* be? The extract cited speaks of a '*happily proportioned* building' and 'a *beautiful* pot'. So, in all probability, by the (sentient) mode in question Langer simply means agreeableness to the eye. By so interpreting her view we cover almost every word — from *feeling* to *consciousness* — to which the word 'mode' is related by her. But if her meaning only is that a successful work of (visual) art is expressive in the sense that it *fascinates the eye*, what is the need, and how is it fair, to mystify the matter by saying that a work is expressive because it projects or expresses *what life feels like*, it being obvious that the word *life* is by no means unambiguous in meaning? And why complicate matters even more by propounding the rather grandiose thesis that art

---

206. Langer, *Problems of Art*, p. 59; first italics added.

207. *Ibid.*, p. 60; italics added.

is a *symbolic* projection of the *forms of feeling*? Further, the present emphasis of Langer cannot be said to give us a clue to determine what art essentially is. On her own criterion, a measure of 'vital import' — that is, some relatedness to feeling, sense or consciousness — may be said to be present in the case of *every* work of art, good *or* bad. After all, ill-matched colours and indistinct vocal patterns also strike our senses definitely. And if Langer is forced, as she here is, to speak only of *successful* works; and if, what is more, in the region of visual art, such success — in respect of being expressive — is to be conceded (as by her) only to works which are *happily proportioned and beautiful*, the fact of conveying 'some [that is, any] mode of feeling, sense, emotion . . . ' ceases to be the hallmark of art.

Finally, I feel stumped by the words: *just as expressive*. Howsoever it may tickle the eye, how can a pot be said to be as (much) expressive as a love-sonnet? The former affects but one sense, namely, the eye; the latter provides impulse and material to the reader's imagination, besides catering for his feeling for shades of sound, sense, and rhythm. One could rejoin, as I mistakenly did in my earlier work, *Art and Philosophy*, that the words, *as expressive*, may be taken to mean not '*as much* expressive', but 'expressive *in the same way*'; that is, as Langer would like us to say, by means of the overall form of the work. But such a reply, I now realize, is prevented by such clear utterances of Langer as the following:

> . . . Because art is a symbolic presentation and not a copy of feeling, there can be *as much* knowledge of feeling projected into the timeless articulated form of a painting or a stained glass window, or a subtly proportioned Greek temple, as into the flowing forms of music, dance, or recitation.[208]

I do not, however, discount the possibility that what Langer has to say on the individual arts of music, rhythm, and dance may yet be true and instructive, on the whole. The chapters that follow should determine if this is really so.

---

208. Langer, *Feeling and Form*, p. 373; italics added.

2

Of Music

Langer and an Indian Genre

THE present chapter may well be regarded as the crux of the entire book. I say so because of three clear reasons. First, Langer herself attaches great importance to her theory of music. She believes that

> the analysis of musical significance in [her work] *Philosophy In a New Key* . . . [can furnish] a valid theory of significance [*for*] *all the arts*, not only the non-verbal and essentially non-representative art of music.[1]

The theory that ultimately emerges is that art is a symbolic projection of the forms of human feeling; and, in her view, the art of music may be valued as the pre-eminent vehicle of such projection because whereas forms of sentience themselves 'occur only in the course of nature' their incarnation in music can be repeated at will.[2] Second, her concept of 'commanding form' in music has enabled me to look at the concept of *rāga*, so vital for classical Indian music as a whole, in a quite new way. So I think it necessary to bring out what Langer really means by 'commanding form' in music. Thirdly, because I yet find her aesthetics of music questionable in some basic ways, specially when I look at it from the viewpoint of Hindustani music, I think it imperative to pay very close attention to her views on the subject as they appear in *Philosophy in a New Key*, *Feeling and Form*, and *Problems of Art*.[3]

---

1. Langer, *Feeling and Form*, pp. 24, 26; italics added.
2. *Ibid.*, p. 27.
3. Langer's other works are not so relevant to her aesthetics of music.

I propose to do the needful by discussing her key utterances and views on music, one by one. The task will involve not only an attempt to see what exactly the extracts could be taken to mean individually, but a reasoned account of how *I* react to them from my chosen point of view. I attach value to the viewpoint as well, for I have found that even such simple emphases of Langer as the one on the occurrent nature of music deliver a new meaning when I look at them in relation to Indian music.

I may now list and comment on some such aspects of Langer's thought as are, in my view, specially relevant to her aesthetics of music:

> 1. Music is an occurrent art; a musical work grows from the first imagination of its general movement to its complete, physical presentation, its *occurrence*.[4]

This is not a very helpful remark. It does nothing to show how, as an art, music is occurrent in a *special* sense, for the making of art is even generally a development of what is at first but vaguely imagined into a complete physical presentation that a work of art is. I wonder if the creation of a poem is ever the mere projection of a verbal complex already quite completed in the mind. Nor does the extract being discussed enable us to see how, as an occurrent art, music differs from dance which too culminates in physical presentation and 'occurrence' as a definite event on the stage. *I* would like to explain the occurrent character of music quite differently, say, as follows:

The occurrence of music is its presentation in terms of a recital which goes on for a while; and what we here contemplate is not a complete and settled object, but a process, an occurrence. We follow the music as it goes on making itself. This at once separates music from the other arts — barring dance and dramatic performance — where the works contemplated are already whole objects. Within this generally occurr*ent* or visibly dynamic form of music, however,

4. Langer, *Feeling and Form*, p.121.

occurrences may take place and strike the listener as distinct events. Here, in the region of Hindustani music, quite unpremeditated changes may have to be brought into music under the stress of audience-response — which is often quite explicit and audible — though, of course, without flouting the norms of *rāga* and *tāla*[5]. Further, an exceptionally talented musician — like Ustad Wilayat Khan, the *sitār* maestro — may at times feels inspired and be able to reveal and utilize the space for creative variations (called **जगह दिखाना या निकलना**, in Hindustani) in music's flowing form, by suddenly producing a quite unexpected melodic phrase within a narrow tonal range, though, of course, without violating (I repeat) any grammatical norm of music. The very unforeseen character of such improvisations invests them with an extra measure of discreteness and makes them appear as special occurrences to the *rasika*. I am not sure if, as Peirce and Hartshorne appear to believe, *all* contingency may be regarded as a creation or an 'additional definiteness *to enrich reality*'.[6] Uncongenial situations like the need for immediate and expensive surgery on a suddenly discovered tumour can hardly be said to *enrich* reality; for, though they are surely clear cases of emergency, they do not in any way adorn or improve reality. But the improvisations I have just spoken of do not only look quite unexpected to the listener, but are acclaimed as an unquestionable index of the musician's creative power.

I here feel impelled to cite one glorious instance of an improvisation which may not only be regarded as a very special occurrence — in fact, the only one of its kind in my fifty years' experience as a listener — but also as an unmistakable sign of a singer's creative power to transfigure a patently dissonant element into the material of music, as well as of the inherent accommodativeness of a *rāga*:

More than forty-six years ago, during the second recital of Ustad Bade Ghulam Ali (in the Khadi Exhibition Music Festival, Ramlila Ground, Delhi, 1954), suddenly the whistle

---

5. A *rāga* is, roughly, a melody-type; and *tāla* is rhythm.

6. L.E. Hahn (ed.), *The Philosophy of Charles Hartshorne*, p. 38.

of a railway engine broke out from somewhere behind the stage and threatened to break the spell of the maestro's mellifluous *bhairavī* with its ugly discordance. The Ustad, however, took it as a challenge. He promptly let his voice ascend meteorically to the *tāra saptak,* merge into and linger for a moment at what was sheer noise to us; and then, with that high note as a base, executed a beautiful descending pattern which quite cancelled the otherness of the shrill sound and made it appear as an integral accent in the beauty of the *tāna.*[7] To conclude, though all music is occurrent in character, Hindustani music can also be *a locus of special occurrences.*

I do not, however, wish to suggest that Langer is not alive to the generally dynamic character of music. She sure is; see, for instance, the following:

> 2. The direct experience of passage, as it occurs in each individual life is, of course, something actual, just as actual as the progress of the clock . . . ; and like all actuality it is only in part perceived, and its fragmentary data are supplemented by practical knowledge and ideas from other realms of thought altogether. Yet it is the model for the virtual time created in music. There we have its image, completely articulated and pure; every kind of tension transformed into musical tension, every qualitative content into musical quality, every extraneous element replaced by musical elements. The primary illusion of music is the sonorous image of *passage,* abstracted from actuality to become free and plastic and entirely perceptible.[8]

This is, in my view, an important passage, and I think it necessary to explain and examine it in terms of individual points:

A. First, though it is (according to Langer) essentially a non-representational art, music is not quite

7. This para is a slightly altered extract from my article "Ustad Bade Ghulam Ali Khan", *The Hindustan Times,* New Delhi, 19.8.1956. *Bhairavī,* I may add, is perhaps our best *rāga* (or *rāginī*) from the viewpoint of room for creative variations. A *tāna* is a pattern of notes; *tār saptak* is the upper register.

8. Langer, *Feeling and Form,* p. 113; italics added.

unrelated to life. As it appears leisurely or nimble in the form of passage, the time that we sense in music is a reflex of the art's flowing form; and this flow or passage, which we can all easily identify as such, is an abstraction from real life. In music, however, it does not remain what it is as an object of our everyday experience. True, we do have a direct feel of temporal passage in daily life, at times; but whatever be the form of its occurrence, the tedious waiting for a friend whose arrival may be overdue, or the excited hastening to reach the place of work in time, it is always admixed with the thought of some practical purpose and some awareness of factors that make the actual situation. In other words, the experience of passage in life is never quite 'pure'. In music, on the other hand, there is no situation or purpose except the context or completion of a phrase; and the tensions — say, of waiting, sudden hurrying, or of mere suspense — are all projected in terms of tonal passages, modulation, and abidance. What is more, the discreteness provided by the individual character of notes and beats lends a thorough articulateness to passages in music. In our experience of passage in real life, on the other hand, discreteness is sensed (say) only when we watch the hands of a clock, mind the hurrying steps, or distinguish road signs on the way. To conclude, passage in music is perceived clearly and quite without any admixture, so to say. And because of this purity or freedom from 'extraneous' elements, the passage in question lends itself freely to regulation by the composer or the performing musician. This is what Langer means by the following words: 'abstracted from actuality to become free and *entirely perceptible*'. The last two words, it is obvious, only mean 'perceptible all along, not fitfully'; and, of course, they cannot be interpreted as *merely* perceptible, for (as we know) good music is that which also engages our feelings and fancy.

B. Second, passage in music (we are told) is *the primary illusion* of this art. According to Langer, every art has its own primary illusion, that is, something which 'is always created' by it, such as 'appearance of movement' in the case of music.

> Music flows; a melody moves; a succession of tones is heard as a progression . . . we hear marching, flowing or driving progressive motion.[9]

Here, however, it is important to note what Langer really means. Her meaning only is that movement is *the essential and dominant* appearance of music, not that it is the *only* possible appearance in this art. True, the primary illusion of an art is what is *always created* by it; but in occurrent arts like music and dance, what is created may not be present or visible *all along*. Langer herself admits the possible presence of a secondary illusion (or appearance) in music, namely, space;[10] and of the element of *sustained rest*.[11]

All these appearances, and some additional ones, are to be found in Hindustani music too. Thus, *passage* is here the dominant look in the up-and-down patterns (or *tānas*) executed by the *khyāl*-singer, and in the gradual, stepwise build-up of *ālāpa* by an exponent of the *dhruvapad* form of our vocal music. But there are many moments in our music (as contemplated) where the dominant look is not at all that of passage, but of stability and restfulness. Thus, where the *ṭhekā* or rhythm-cycle is correctly played, we admire its having been properly *established*. As for *ālāpa* of the *dhruvapad* variety, its *net* impression is that of a revelation of the aesthetical potential of a *rāga*, and surely not one of its ascent and descent across the notes it comprises. Even in the case of (*vilambit*) *sthāyī-antarā* interlacement

9. Langer, *Problems of Art*, pp. 36-7.
10. Langer, *Feeling and Form*, p. 117.
11. *Ibid*, p. 108.

in *khyāl*-style, if the composition is well-formed and properly projected by the vocalist, the *rasika* is struck not so much by the dynamics of singing as by the evocation of (what may be called) a self-completing form *which soon comes to appear as resting on its own self,* partly because its first segment (or the *sthāyī*) is sung more than once, and partly because it is framed in a steadily played rhythm-*cycle*. What adds to *the unified look* of the entire singing is the fact that every detail or passage of the music conforms with a particular *rāga* or melodic plan.[12] Langer, we may note, speaks of the commanding form of *individual* musical works. But in the case of Hindustani music (or of Indian music, generally) any one *rāga* can be the commanding form of numberless compositions; and because it thus permits an infinite amount of creative variety, it may well be said to be *fecund,* as Langer understands the word in the context of music.[13] But, I must add, this form is not only fecund, but importantly *restrictive.*[14] It is so in at least two clear ways: first, the details of singing are not to be allowed to deviate (at any point) from the determinate character of the *rāga* chosen; and second, the melodic identity of the *rāga* — say, *bhūpālī* — has to be kept all along distinct by eschewing trespass into the domain of other kindred *rāgas*, like *deskār* and *śuddha kalyāṇ*. This is why good Hindustani music often impresses the discriminating listener with its accuracy of *rāga*-rendering. But the main point which I wish to press here, as a *protest* against Langer's basic thesis being discussed, is quite different. I believe that the primary illusion of our music is not 'the sonorous image of passage' but the semblance of a vital and determinate melodic whole which reveals its aesthetical potential in ever more various ways, yet without ever allowing an overstepping of its bounds, and without, of course, itself appearing as the *agent* of self-revelation, the projection of creative possibilities in a *rāga* being obviously the work of the performing musician. To say so is clearly in line with Langer's view that the commanding form is both

12. A fuller interpretation of *rāga* occurs later in this chapter.

13. Langer, *Feeling and Form*, p. 123.

14. I here diverge a little from Langer's view that the commanding form 'is *not essentially restrictive*' Ibid.

fecund and restrictive. But, I ask, if the commanding form is, in fact, seen to be *fecund*, do we not get committed to the view that the primary 'illusion' of music is that of a potent and fertile matrix rather than that of mere melodic passage? At this stage, however, I cannot answer the question quite definitely. I must first explain, as I indeed propose to do later in this chapter, what a *rāga* really is; and must also consider some other, more definite utterances of Langer on the subject. Perhaps the most categorical of these runs as follows:

> 3. The *purpose* of all musical labor, in thought or in physical activity, is to create and develop the illusion of flowing time in its passage, in audible *passage* filled with motion that is just as illusory as the time it is measuring.[15]

Now, to begin with the very opening of the above extract, the word *purpose* may be taken to mean what is aimed at directly *or* as a desirable sequel, such as (in the case of a musical performance) eventual applause from the listeners or critics who publish their write-ups in daily papers. Further, in so far as Langer here speaks of the purpose *of all musical labour*, whatever this objective be, it has to be relevant to every kind of (Hindustani) music. But then this objective cannot be the traditionally cherished, metaphysical (and typically Indian) one of spiritual liberation, for the ends of our music *as it flourishes today* are in fact all quite mundane. Finally, whose judgment on the point at issue is to be taken as authentic? Of the musician himself or of the *rasika*, the discriminating listener? Music critics whose write-ups on music recitals appear fairly regularly in the press, and the professional aesthetician — who may all be genuinely interested in the art — can also claim to be heard. Above all, there may well be someone who has somehow been able to combine in himself the individual functions of the different kinds of music-lovers we have just distinguished.[16] Of all these people, *whose* judgement may be

15. *Ibid.*, p., 120; italics added.

16. Such a 'combination' is rare, but by no means impossible; and I may here refer to my own case. My present work is obviously an essay in aesthetics. I can humbly claim to be a *rasika* too, with over fifty years' →

said to support Langer's thesis that the basic purpose of all music-making is to create and develop the audible illusion of *flowing* time? Let us reflect on this question, once again from our chosen viewpoint of Hindustani music.

As for our performing musicians, they would all say in one voice that their overtopping purpose, as they set out to sing (or play), is just to project the *rāga* or *bandish* chosen to the best of their ability in the way they have been trained to sing (or play), and of course all along in conformity with the demands of the *rāga* and *tāla* chosen. The suggestion that what they are really going to do (as they perform) will be simply the creation of a sonorous illusion of *flowing* time, would bewilder even those of them who can be induced to reflect a little on music and are open to discussion. The *rasika* too would insist that what he really wants is a melodious presentation of *ālāpa, bandish,* and *tānas,* along with an unflagging observance of the norms of *rāga* and *tāla.* As a devoted listener myself, I too have never seen any *rasika* admiring a performance on the ground that it was an exquisite evocation of a temporal illusion. Maybe our *rasika*s cannot do the kind of analytic thinking that Langer, as an aesthetician, would like them to do. But the professional critic too, who is generally good at analysis and has a fair understanding of the basic concepts of music, would say essentially the same thing as the *rasika*s in respect of what he expects of a good music recital. To turn now to the aesthetician as a philosopher of music, we may not expect him to focus on individual recitals; for his primary task is to reflect on concepts and problems relating to the art, and perhaps also to advance a theory of music, like that of Langer we are currently discussing. But what is the *ultimate* ground of the aesthetician's cogitation? Obviously it is, first (his or her) personal experience of listening to music; and second, the language that the musicians, critics, and *rasika*s generally use in talking about the art. Now, I have not been able to lay

---

→ experience as a keen listener at concerts of classical music; and I have also worked as 'a music critic' (in the 1950s) for *The Hindustan Times,* a leading national daily of India. I still cover important music functions for *Śruti* (Madras), India's leading music and dance magazine.

hands on any account of Langer's own experiences as a listener; but as a student of aesthetics and as a lover of music myself, I find absolutely no warrant for Langer's view as to the basic 'purpose of all musical labour'. The *language* that is commonly used by people in India in talking about music focuses rather on the following:

> unremitting tunefulness; steadiness in respect of *laya* or aesthetic pace; orderly unfoldment of the canvas of the *rāga* chosen; fluency of *taans* 'without any deviation from the proper locus of constituent *swaras*, and also without any bedimming of their individual distinctness'; 'precision and intricacy of design';[17] 'the wide sweep of . . . [a] mellifluous voice . . . [that] attains the *taar pancham* as slickly as it descends affably to a reverberating *Shadja* and even achieves shapely *gamak* effects in that region;[18] manifestness of 'all the *svara*-links in the sequences'; and the melody. . . [making] aesthetical sense . . . its treatment [giving] a sense of organic unity and orderliness.[19]

I have indeed gone through a considerable amount of critical writing on music without ever finding even a covert suggestion of the view that music is a distinctive art essentially because it creates *an illusion of flowing time* in terms of tones and their collocations. On the other hand, I repeat, our music-talk abounds in words and phrases that signify a semblance of repose and fixedness or of a welcome melodic ambience, such as the following: "वाह कैसा ठेका क़ायम किया है" ।; "कैसा चैन और इत्मीनान है इनकी गायकी में"; "क्या कहने इस आलाप के — सारे हॉल में राग छा गया है।" Even where we admire the amazing fluency of the *atidrut* (extra-fast) *tānas* of a *khyāl*-singer like the late Ustad Bade Ghulam Khan, the focus of our attention is on the rapidity (and yet clarity) *of patterns*, and not at all on any semblance of *the lapse of time* creatively evoked. And where

---

17. S.K. Saxena's write-up "Newcomers Outshine the Ustāds" in *The Asian Age*, New Delhi of 28.4.1995.

18. Prakash Wadhera, India's leading critic of Hindustani music today, in his write-up, 'Donning the Mantle of Bade Ghulam Ali Khan' in *The Hindu* of 12.5.1995.

19. Prakash Wadhera's write-up 'In the footsteps of Malikarjuna Mansoor' in *The Hindu* of 5.5.1995.

we contemplate a *vilambit sthāyī* as sung by a vocalist like the late Ustad Ameer Khan, our feeling is not that a kind of 'creatively induced' time is *passing* slowly, but only that a composition is seeking to so establish itself that, on the one hand, the singer is enabled to imbue himself with its growing form; and, on the other hand, a kind of melodic form is created for the *rasika* to contemplate, enter into, and grow one with. The overall effect is indeed one of attunement with the breathing melodic form, and not of being a witness to an illusory temporal passage.

I find it difficult to abstain from suspecting that the main reason why Langer speaks of a sonant illusion of *flowing* time as the overtopping creative purpose of music is that this particular thesis enables her to relate music to the *forms* of feeling which too, as she distinguishes them, involve a *passage* from one state to another cognate one. Even in respect of feeling in general, we have seen, Langer holds that it is not merely a state but a *process*, and may have not only successive phases, but general simultaneous developments.[20] But, quite apart from my surmise, were any discriminating *rasika*, critic, or practitioner of Hindustani music persuaded to advance a general theory of the art — say, by seizing some feature which all its forms could be said to share — he would readily answer that music, as it is known to him, is essentially an attempt to bring out the infinite creative possibilities that are implicit in, and are yet determined by the individual nature of a *rāga*. He is not likely to pinpoint flow or progression as the basic creative fruit of music; and his (positive) answer, I may add, would square with a basic truth of creation in art which Ducasse puts thus:

> Art . . . actually begins only when the [imposed] limitations are not only understood and accepted, but are perceived as definite and positive opportunities for free spontaneous self-expression. . . . Without walls, one is indeed free, — to spread oneself out thin. With walls, a dam or a channel is created which permits one's energy to accumulate pressure or to

20. Langer, *Feeling and Form*, p. 230.

concentrate in a given direction.[21]

What *this* extract says, and not the symbolic projection of 'forms of feeling' of which Langer speaks, could be said to be generally true of *every* art. Indian music, in particular, is demonstrably an attempt to utilize, ever more variously, the infinite room for creation of melodic figures and forms that is immanent in every *rāga*, though all *rāga*s are not equally accommodative in this sense, some of them — like *hindol, jayat kalyāṇa*, and *mālaśrī* — being relatively संकड़े or incapacious for *phirat* or freely varying configuration of notes. But then I must explain what a *rāga* really is, not merely because it is a pivotal concept of Indian music, but because its watchful unfoldment has a far greater title to be regarded as the basic purpose of (Indian) music than the creation of any illusion of time or passage.

However, before I begin discussing what a *rāga* really is I think it necessary to make some prefatory remarks:

Rāga in Indian music

I do not wish to say that the definition of Indian music I have just suggested covers *every* kind of music. My purpose is only to show that *Langer's* definition of music does not hold true of *our* music. Further, I propose to do a little more thinking by way of vindicating my view that *rāga* may well be regarded as the 'commanding form' of our music. What is more, in so far as I am going to put forth a quite new definition of *rāga*, and wish at the same time to save my venture from appearing dogmatic, one-sided or bizarre, I have, on the one hand, to begin by paying due attention to some of our more important traditional definitions of *rāga*; and, on the other hand, to discuss the concept in question not only from the viewpoints of

---

21. C.J. Ducasse, *The Philosophy of Art*, pp. 38-9. Also see the following from Langer's *Feeling and Form*: "A perfectly free imagination suffers from the very lack of pressure; it is in the vague and growing state that precedes the conception of the total form. The great moment of creation is the recognition of the matrix, for in this lie all the motives for the specific work." p. 123.

creation and contemplation, but from that of critical evaluation as well — because the critic too is concerned with the concept of *rāga* quite as seriously as the musician and the *rasika*. I also hope to show, at some length, that it is not proper for a musician to confine himself to the grammatical identity of a *rāga*, and that he has to actualise its aesthetical potential too.[22]

But, of course, as I set out to do some fresh thinking on *rāga*, I must not ignore the fact that we have a whole traditional philosophy of music; and that, what is more, our theorists have always been concerned with the key question of etymology as well. So these two frames of reference have also to be borne in mind. I do not, however, suggest that our ancient works on music have been indifferent to the plurality of viewpoints from which this glorious art of *svara* and *laya* may be looked at. Yet I see it clearly that quite a few utterances which have been commonly regarded as whole definitions of *rāga* are, in fact, but aspectual characterizations of it from different standpoints.

The beginning may be made from the etymological point of view. But a note of caution must be sounded here. Just as the verbal meaning of an ethical concept like *ahimsā* is not identical with its significance as revealed by its gradual practice in everyday conduct, so the verbal meaning of *rāga* is transcended, though not quite left out, by what it appears in the full and methodical practice of music. This will, however, become clear only as we proceed.

The literal meaning of *rāga* is well-known. Coming from the root *rañj*, the word means 'that which charms or colours the mind'. But at this point a difficulty makes itself felt, and it would help if I put it pointedly, say, as follows:

A *rāga* is essential to all Indian classical music. But, at the same time, the ultimate aim of our music has been said to be

22. For some clear arguments in favour of this emphasis, see my essay "The Concept of *Rāga*: An Essay in understanding" first published in *Sruti* (Madras), Issue 80, May 1991, and reprinted in *Sangeet Natak*, journal of Sangeet Natak Akademi, Numbers, 101-2, July-December 1991, pp. 32-44.

liberation, and not mere entertainment.[23] How, then, can its mere *charm or pleasing* quality be regarded as the dominant mark of a *rāga* which serves as the necessary melodic matrix of all our classical music? Would not a merely etymological conception of *rāga* clash with our view of the ultimate goal of music which even today we are unwilling to give up totally, if only as a credo? Or could it be that a *rāga* pleases the listeners or colours their minds in a way which at once facilitates, though it may not guarantee, their upward growth and ultimate liberation?

At present I have to leave such questions open. But I cannot wholly ignore them; for, they are going to help the course of my thinking. I even feel impelled to mark another difficulty. It relates to the following 'definition' which looks at *rāga* from the etymological point of view:

a. इत्येवं रागशब्दस्य व्युत्पत्तिरभिधीयते।
रञ्जनाज्जायते रागो व्युत्पत्तिः समुदाहृतः।।[24]

The meaning is here clear. Etymologically, the word *rāga* means that which entertains people. But, one may contend, what charms us, and can even leave a more or less permanent impression on our minds, may only be the effective enactment of a love scene on the stage. Yet no one would regard such a presentation as *rāga*. How, then, can its ability to please us be regarded as a *distinguishing* characteristic of *rāga*?

It seems to me that the 'definition' just cited pinpoints but a single necessary mark of a *rāga*, and does not specify anything which could be said to be *uniquely* relevant to *rāga*. We must, of course, admit that whatever be its specific nature — and whoever be the artist presenting it — a *rāga*, if it is music at all, must (also) please the listeners. But here, again, a difficulty faces us. Is a *rāga* required to please everyone, *or* only the *rasika*s, that is, listeners who are conversant with the proper technique and aesthetics of the *rāga* in question? This question,

23, The reference, here, is to the Sanskrit aphorism: *muktidāyakam na/tu/ rañjakam*, *Sangeet Ratnakara*.

24. Mātanaga Muni, *Bṛhaddeśī*, śloka 283, p. 29.

again, I may not answer right now, though it *is* important. I want it to serve as a continuing theoretical irritant, hoping that it might lead us on to some more comprehensive definitions of *rāga*, such as the following:

b. योऽसौ ध्वनिविशेषस्तु स्वरवर्णविभूषितः
रञ्जको जनचित्तानां स च राग उदाहृतः[25]

c. स्वरवर्णविशेषेण ध्वनिभेदेन वा पुनः।
रञ्जयते येन यः कश्चित्, स रागः सम्मतः सताम्।[26]

d. ग्रहांशौ तारमन्द्रौ च न्यासोपन्यास एव च।
अल्पत्वं च बहुत्वं च षाडवौडविते तथा।।[27]

The meaning of definitions *b.* and *c.* is almost identical. They simply say that a *rāga* is a distinct complex of some specific *svaras*, and that it entertains people. The fourth definition, *d.*, on the other hand, lists the elements which go to make a *rāga*. This diversity of approach need not surprise us. What a thing appears to be or to do is obviously different from how, or as a consequence of what, it comes into being; and the two must be distinguished. This is indeed done by our theorists even in respect of *rasa*. Thus, phenomenologically, or as a matter of experience, *rasa* is said to be *svātma parāmarśa svātma viśrānti*; and, from the genetic point of view, it is said to emerge as a result of the integration of the three constituents of *vibhāva*, *anubhāva* and *vyabhicārī bhāva*, as working upon a *sthāyī bhāva*.[28]

However, my main purpose here is to pay a little close attention to the second and third definitions without, of course, forgetting the requisite comprehensiveness of concern. Quite generally, our music has been said to be *nāda sādhanā* or a disciplined and discriminating fellowship with *the world of sound* so as to come closer to the ultimate goal of life. But this, in turn, demands that we pay sustained attention to the world

---

25. Mātanaga Muni, *Bṛhaddeśī*, śloka 281.

26. *Ibid.*, śloka 280.

27. Bharata's *Nāṭya-śāstra*, ed. Pandit Kedarnath, śloka 74, chapter 28.

28. For a detailed discussion of the concept of *rasa*, see my essay "The Rasa Theory", Appendix II in my book: *Swinging Syllables: Aesthetics of Kathak Dance*, pp. 178-94.

in question. Nothing, however, can become an effective object of attention unless it combines within itself some differences in a more or less orderly and interesting way. This is exactly what the definitions in question suggest. A *rāga* is a distinct, but just as necessarily a pleasing combination of some select *svaras*; and, as thus regarded, it can draw and hold the attention of listeners with the definiteness of a physical object; hence, the importance of the two words, *dhvani* and *rañjana,* which our first two definitions share.

Indeed, the two most obvious ideas in the definitions that we have picked for attention are, first, that the material of *rāga* is *dhvani* (or sound); and, second, that (in principle) the *rāga* pervades or suffuses the minds of the listeners. Now, interestingness or charm in the way of a winsome and pervasive influence is not the same thing as mere momentary appeal. And, as we all know, the charm of a *rāga* is not just a peck of delight, as is sometimes the very first sip of a rare blend of wine or tea. Rather, it is seen to abide, if only for an hour or so. This is, however, possible not only because the *svara*s are (by definition) sweet, but because they make an integrated complex of inner differences. How otherwise could they grip our attention, I repeat, instead of attracting it for a mere moment?

Incidentally, it is interesting to see how it is distinctive of sound to meet the requirement of a complex singleness. Smells of different kinds can, of course, be presented to a person one after the other, and they may also quickly remind him of various delicacies; but they do not (as a rule) make a single object. On the other hand, as in the case of the *svara*s (or notes) of a *rāga,* different sounds can easily make for a complex that is perceived as a single and undivided unity. In other words, discrimination, or the perception of differences and relations, is easily possible in the region of sound. The fact indeed is that, however intense be the spellbinding quality of the beauty of a *rāga* as it unfolds its canvas ever more fully, our response here is never quite without discernment.

This is true even of the musician at work. He is, of course, quite conversant with the grammatical form of the *rāga* before he sets out to translate it into actual singing; and, as the music develops and takes effect, his mind may well come to be suffused with the unitary form of the *rāga* being sung. But this too is just as true that in thus experiencing the bliss of music he cannot, even for a moment, slacken his attention in respect of keeping the character of the *rāga* (being treated) quite distinct from that of its aesthetic neighbours. In other words, the pervasive charm of a *rāga* is always a little intellectual too, if subduedly.

One should indeed not underestimate the role of intelligence in the creation and contemplation of music. Even the *rasika*'s experience, as he feels captivated by a *rāga*'s variform beauty, is no mere abandonment to a quite nebulous relish, as when we give ourselves up to the taste of a richly spiced delicacy the constituent flavours of which we may not be able to distinguish. What he, the *rasika*, focuses on in listening to music is not only a *rāga*'s sensuous sweetness, but its calculated arrangements, specially those which project the 'approach phrase' or heighten the requisite dominance of the *vādī-samvādī*[29] relation.

Here it can, of course, be contended that the field of the eye — that is, outer space — also easily admits of the perception of relations and distinctions both within and between objects. But to this our rejoinder would be that the medium of sound, as music utilizes it, is possessed of a remarkable *extra* element. What we have in this art is not mere sound, but the *passage* of sound, say, from one note to another, *and at a particular pace*. In other words, the sound is here at once a rhythmic advance; and in so far as movement or flux seems to be very essence of life as lived, the regulated passage of music is at once a locus of lifelike appeal. Indeed, whereas things and spaces in the outer world compel attention only if they are big or in some way extraordinary, in the region of music, on the other hand, even a brief and tender glide may coerce attention, and

29. *Vādī* is the dominant note of a *rāga*; *saṁvādī* is the *svara* which is taken to add noticeably to the effect of the *vādī*. *Saṁvād* is the relation of aesthetic accordance.

continue to haunt the listeners' imagination for quite some time. And because, as already pointed out, the various *svaras* are easily perceived as distinct, though their grammatical character may be discernible only to the *rasika*, the rhythmical advance of the *rāga* depends more on our following, or moving along with *its* form than on its being able to move us into sympathy. And as we grow in the art of being at one with the flowing fabric of a *rāga*, it soon becomes obvious that its spell-binding quality is not the instant appeal of a single *svara*, nor even the merely *additive* effect of many *svaras*, but the emergent charm of the individual *svaras* as they *act upon one another* in respect of temporal order and sensuous quality.

This is why a *rāga* can easily become an object of aesthetic contemplation. As sung or played, a *rāga* is obviously not a mere concept, but the source of a directed, yet rich and free experience; and this experience is in part made possible by the very inherent possibilities of sound. Here, because of their relevance to the point I am seeking to make, the following remarks of George Santayana may be cited from his well-known work, *The Sense of Beauty*:

> . . . Sounds are also measurable in their own category; they have comparable pitches and durations, and definite and recognisable combinations of those sensuous elements are as truly objects as chairs and tables. Not that a musical composition exists in any mystical way, as a portion of the music of the spheres, which no one is hearing; but that, for a critical philosophy, visible objects are also nothing but possibilities of sensation. The real world is merely the shadow of that assurance of eventual experience which accompanies sanity. This objectivity can accrue to any mental figment that has enough cohesion, content, and individuality to be describable and recognisable, and these qualities belong no less to audible than to spatial ideas.[30]

I may here point out that its overall unity and inner diversity are both alike essential for an object if it is to compel our attention. Form in art is always the unity of a manifold. Here,

---

30. George Santayana, *The Sense of Beauty*, p. 44.

again, I think it necessary to quote Santayana:

> . . . A form is an aggregation, it must have elements, and the manner in which the elements are combined constitutes the character of the form. A perfectly simple perception, in which there was no consciousness of the distinction and relation of parts would not be a perception of form, it would be a sensation.[31]

The interesting quality of the form of a *rāga*, however, is due not only to its overall unity and inner diversity, but also to the intrinsic charm of its elements. A *rāga* comprises *svaras*; and a *svara*, by definition, is something which holds sway over the listener by virtue of its own intrinsic character (*svameva rājate*). This prepares the way to a discussion of the individual meanings of the key-words that the definitions we have picked for attention comprise.

To begin with, the definition that a *svara* is something charming by itself requires that in actual music it should sound sweet to the ear. In the definitions we are discussing, however, what is spoken of is not *svara* alone, but *svara-varṇa vibhūṣitaḥ*. And this seems unavoidable. We cannot confine ourselves to the thought that a *rāga* is *dhvani viśeṣastu* or a distinct sound. It is true that every *rāga* has a distinct individuality perceivable by the ear. But even two *noises* can be utterly unlike each other. The noise produced by the impact of some china cups as they fall on the floor is obviously different from the roar of an aeroplane engine. Yet neither of them can be said to be a *rāga*. The *śloka*, therefore, adds that a *rāga* is only such a distinct sound as is embellished with *svara-varṇa*.

The word *varṇa*, however, poses a problem and calls for some close thinking. What does it really mean? It has been freely taken to signify *sthāyī*, *ārohī*, *avarohī* and *sañcārī*. But, in so interpreting *varṇa* what is ignored is the fact that the word here seems to qualify, *svara*, not *rāga*. In other words, the definitions [(b) & (c)] speak of the *varṇa* of *svara*, not of *rāga*. The full exposition of a *rāga* may well be said to include *sthāyī*,

31. George Santayana, *The Sense of Beauty*, p. 61.

ārohī, avarohī, and *sañcārī.* Even the bare indication of the character of a *rāga* to a pupil may be said to emphasise *āroha* and *avaroha,* besides of course, the *vādī-saṁvādī.* But how can we, and do we ever, speak of the *āroha* and *avaroha* or *sañcārī* of a *svara*? It just does not make sense to speak thus, and in ordinary musical discourse no one really speaks thus. So I suggest that the word *svara-varṇa,* or rather *varṇa,* has to be interpreted differently.

Now, some of the important meanings of the word which immediately appear relevant to our purpose may be listed thus: (a) a musical sound or note; (b) sound, vowel, syllables; (c) class, kind, sort; (d) outward appearance, exterior form and shape; (e) lustre, beauty or complexion; (f) character or quality. But, if *varṇa* is taken to mean (a), it would just be a meaningless repetition, for the word *svara* already conveys the meaning of sound. Nor would (b) add anything significant to the meaning of *svara.* As for (c) and (d), they do not even throw a hint as to the expressive or aesthetic character of *svaras.* Notes may indeed be classified as *śuddh* and *komal* (flat). But, this does not at all cover the possibility that a *svara* may seem to be yearning or majestically self-assertive. And if we speak of the outward appearance or exterior of a *svara,* the awkward question will arise as to what could possibly be the interior of a *svara.* Nor does it seem natural to speak of the form or shape of a *svara.* We are thus left with but one option, that is, to interpret *varṇa* as character or quality. And this indeed seems to be the intended and *desirable* meaning of the word in the definitions being discussed. I say desirable too, because if the word *varṇa* is taken in the sense of character or quality it would cover, if but generally, all that is said in the fourth definition (d) which is commonly regarded as an exhaustive listing of the essential features of a *rāga* (or *jāti*); and would also go well with our traditional conception of the ultimate aim of music. But, I must explain why I say so.

The quality or character of a note is what distinguishes it from other notes. Now, this distinguishing feature of a *svara* may be any one of the following: its being a prominent point of repeated return and a moment of repose (*vādī* or *aṁśa*), its placement in *mandra*, *madhya* or *tāra* (*tāra-mandrau*); its terminal character, either as the destiny (*nyāsa*), or as the beginning of a musical passage (*graha*); its being infrequent and brief or recurrent and prolonged (*alpatva* and *bahutva*); or, above all, its appearing to be tender or energetic, luminous or faint, richly sensuous or a little otherworldly. In other words, if we interpret *svara-varṇa* as the character or quality of a *svara*, provision will at once be made not only for the grammatical exposition of the nature of a *rāga*, but also for the aesthetic, ethical and even spiritual suggestiveness of *svara*s which can in no way be ignored if we really mean to hold on to the traditional Indian conception of the ultimate goal of music.

What is more, even the pictorial representation of the nature of a *rāga* would gain some warrant from our interpretation of *svara-varṇa* as the quality of *svara*. It is true that one admitted meaning of the word *varṇa* is good colour or complexion. Nor can we deny that it may, in a sense, be meaningful to speak of the colour of notes. If we are allowed to speak of the rhythm of colours, as we obviously are, how can one object to the idea that a note may seem to be *colourless* or *colourful*? There is even some scientific basis for speaking of colours and notes in the same breath. A sound is sweet in itself — or is a musical note — only if

> the pulsations of the air by which it is produced recur at regular intervals. If there is no regular recurrence of waves, it is a noise. The rapidity of these regular beats determines the pitch of tones.[32]

Now, from this point of view, there seems to be a clear affinity between colours and tones; and 'we need not be surprised that the high rate of vibration which yields a sharp note to the ear should involve somewhat the same feeling that is produced by the high rate of vibration which, to the eye, yields a violet colour.'[33] Our traditional musicology seems to favour the affinity we are talking of. Thus, the absence of *pañcam* from

---

32. George Santayana, *The Sense of Beauty*, p. 45.

33. *Ibid.*, p. 47.

rāga lalita is explained on the ground that in so far as the *colour* of this note is that of *bright sunshine*, it cannot be given a place in a *rāga* which is meant for *early morning*. Further, in our everyday talk about music we often admire a particular singer's *akāra* as being रौशन or bright and luminous, and the *tānas* of a master musician of old may be acclaimed on the ground that at the *tāra ṣaḍja*, instead of appearing cramped or colourless, they would seem to sparkle and bloom in the way of an *anār*, a cracker that is used in fireworks.

But, noteworthy though they all are, facts such as these do not throw any doubt on our interpretation of *varṇa* as quality, because a *svara*'s appearing bright or effulgent is no less a quality of it than, say, its basic requisite sweetness.

However, in spite of all that may be said in favour of our interpretation, a final question is still possible. It may be agreed that a note can appear as possessed of different qualities; and that, for example, *śuddha r̥ṣabha* generally expresses strength and self-assertion,[34] just as, along with the basic *sa*, the *pañcam* of *rāga Rāmakalī* (as *vādī, saṁvādī*) suggests activity. But, one may ask, is *every* listener expected to perceive these qualities of *svaras*? If not, how are we to explain the words *rañjako janacittānām* ('appealing to the mind of people in general')? This question has to be answered with care. I choose to do it thus:

The qualities of *svaras* may be classified as immediate and mediate. The immediate or primary quality of a *svara* — 'primary', because it is implicit in the very definition of a musical note — is its sweetness. Other qualities, such as the seeming tenderness or dignity of a *svara*, may be said to be mediate in the sense that their perception depends on, or is the response of a cultivated taste. It is obvious that many more people — that is, even (superficial) *kanarasiyās*,[35] as distinguished from genuine *rasikas* — may be expected to perceive the basic or immediate quality, as against the mediate ones.

---

34. Swami Prajnananda, *A Historical Study of Indian Music*, p. 135.

35. A *kanarasiyā* is one who values music simply because it can tickle the ear.

In principle, everybody *can* perceive even the 'mediate' qualities provided he trains himself suitably, that is, if he becomes a *rasika*. But, as a matter of fact, everybody does not seem to be capable of perceiving perhaps even the most obvious qualities of *svara.* Some training of the ear, along with some acquaintance with the particular form or tradition of the music attended to, seems to be necessary for perceiving even the intrinsic, requisite sweetness of individual notes. Therefore, the words *janacittānām* cannot be taken to mean 'the mind of *every* individual'. I suggest that the word *jana* here simply means 'people *collectively*'.[36] In other words, the delight which is evoked by a *rāga*, as a complex of *svara*s of specific qualities, is not a private, but a shareable experience. This is indeed the point in Bharata's view that, like the eye, the ear too is an aesthetic sense. I here feel tempted to make an additional remark by way of bringing out the meaning of *janacittānām*. In so far as, in contrast to (say) works of literary art, music can appeal even to the lowly and the unlettered because of its basic sweetness, it may be acknowledged as an art of the people.

It would, however, be wrong to underestimate the aesthetic sensitiveness of the average man by supposing that he can respond *only* to the obvious physical sweetness of music. He can also be readily affected by the progression and descension of a *rāga* without, of course, distinguishing its constituent *svara*s from the viewpoint of musical grammar. The up-and-down contour of music is, in fact, a very easily noticeable feature. Again, hardly anyone can fail to be struck by such features as the width and majesty of a vocalist's *akāra*, the depth of the *vīṇā* tones in the *mandra* (or bass), or the quiver of emotion in a female singer's projection of the *antarā*[37] of a *bhajan* (devotional song) set in a *rāga*. It has even been noticed that listeners who are quite unfamiliar with the grammar of a *rāga* respond with the appropriate emotions of

36. Monier-Williams, *A Sanskrit-English Dictionary*, p. 572.

37. An *antarā* is the counterpart of *sthāyī*, the first line of the song. It is distinguished by the fact that it builds upon the higher notes of the scale. Together, the two make a complete composition.

wonder and awe to moments of exceptional spaciousness and grandeur in *ālāpa* of the *dhruvapad* manner.

Indeed, though music is intrinsically the most abstract of all the arts because it does not directly refer to anything in the outer world, it can as easily project and provide an objective image of an emotion as an actual situation of joy, sorrow or love. This is why our *rāgas* are so eminently relevant to all intense occasions — to prayer and partings, and to the festivity of a marriage or childbirth. What is more, there is another subtler reason because of which our *rāgas* can readily appeal to the common man without, of course, his being able to see this reason or to identify the nature of the *rāga*. The droop of despair, the surge of vitality and hope, nimbleness and cheer, the act of sharing or dividing in equal halves — these are all very familiar experiences of life; and they all freely appear in our *rāga*-music which builds as much upon variations of aesthetic pace as upon combinations of notes in the three registers.

All this has to be kept in mind in determining what a *rāga* really is. We have also to provide not only for the element of truth contained in the definitions already cited, but for the individuality of those persons who make or relish music, as also for the possibility that our traditional conception of the final goal of music may, after all, be tenable. Therefore, I propose to define a *rāga* as follows:

> A *rāga* is a specific melodic form which serves to permit and determine, as a matrix, the creation and contemplation of music on the basis of the quality, emphases and relatedness of tones and rhythmic abidance or passage, possibly with an eye to evoking the appropriate *rasa* (in some cases), and inevitably in accordance with one's individual capacities for technical grasp and aesthetic sensitiveness.

The meaning of this definition of *rāga* may now be brought out by commenting on its key ideas.

To begin with, a *rāga* is a specific melodic form. This means, first, that a *rāga* is a form, or an integration of its constituent *svaras*. It is an integration — not a mere putting together — of notes because, though none of them can be allowed to suffer in respect of grammatical accuracy and sweetness, they are all, in general, to be so built upon that they may not seem to usurp the requisite aesthetic dominace of the *vādī-saṁvādī* relation. It is indeed important to remember that a *rāga* is not an integration of its *svara*s in the sense of attaching *equal* importance to the different *svara*s that go to make it. It is common knowledge that some of these notes are to be given lesser emphasis (*alpatva*) than others. No note can of course be allowed to appear quite indistinct or even a little off-key; but, on the other hand, emphasis cannot be equally distributed over every *svara* of the *rāga*. In other words, the *rāga*-form is a unity of *regulated* emphases. It is not to be regarded as a rosary of even beads; and where a fluent *tāna* seems to treat every note evenly, the question may indeed be put if it is able to preserve the character of the *rāga*.

Secondly, the suggestion that a *rāga* is a *melodic* form means that its different *svara*s follow a before-after order. This order in the region of music is necessarily a series of the higher and the lower; therefore, progression and descension or *āroha* and *avaroha*, are integral movements in the being of a *rāga*.

Thirdly, by saying that a *rāga* is a specific melodic form we also mean that every *rāga* has a distinct and identifiable perceptual character. It strikes the ear differently from another *rāga*. But in so far as two different *rāga*s may employ exactly the same notes, if in different ways, the perception of the precise character of a *rāga* may call for a finely trained ear and discriminating attention on the part of the *rasika*. In other words, a *rāga* as heard is not passively perceived, but is at once some exercise in discernment on the part of the listener.

Further, I have chosen to speak of a *rāga* as a *matrix* of melody, and not as a melodic *type*. A type is the concept of a class. It certainly covers or is applicable to all things of the same kind; but it does not make or enter into the substance of what it covers. The concept-word *daśehrī* is certainly no part of the pulp of the (kind of) luscious mangoes it signifies. But a *rāga*, on the other hand, is the substance or material of the whole recital which unfolds and animates it. It has been freely regarded, I know, as a melodic *type* because many compositions can be created in the same *rāga*. But my point is that these compositions are also made out of, and bring out the nature the same *rāga*. Therefore, a *rāga* may be said to be a matrix in the sense of being a ground-mass which is at once the necessary and pervasive condition, the material, and the regulative and individuating principle, of a total musical performance. Further, though it is true that whatever is seen to appear in the treatment of a *rāga* must not transgress its grammatical character, and that one cannot here draw upon anything which lies beyond the limits of the chosen *rāga*, yet, within these ultimate limits, there is so much room for the creation of ever newer beauty and effects that all our musicians till today, along with their entire repertoire of compositions, cannot be said to have exhausted the aesthetic possibilities of even a single *rāga*. From this point of view, a *rāga* is infinite and exhaustless in spite of its being *saguṇa* or possessed of a specific individuality.

It is also necessary to see, at some length, how the *rāga*-matrix functions. An analogy would here help. Just as the bed and banks of a river facilitate, determine and contain the seamless flow of its waters, similarly, by virtue of its compass and character, a *rāga* provides both freedom and direction to the contemplation and creation of music. Again like the river bed which leaves the waters free to ripple or to eddy, or to simply flow noiselessly, a *rāga* too, apart from the norm of accordance with its grammatical structure and the classical idiom generally, offers infinite freedom for musical expression and embellishment. But, of course, the analogy is by no means absolute. The bed of the river is clearly not a constituent of its billows and ripples; but a *rāga*, on the other hand, by virtue of the *svara*s it comprises and builds upon, is the very material of a recital which brings out its specific melodic character and aesthetic potential.

But, one may press the point, how in detail does a *rāga* do what it does? The answer can only be, by working on 'the quality, emphases and relatedness of tones and rhythmic abidance or passage'. But to say so is to mean a great deal, and the implications must be distinguished. A *svara*'s quality may be taken to cover the following: its being high or low, by virtue of its placement in the *mandra, madhya* or *tāra saptak*; its fineness or amplitude, and tangentiality or penetratingness, which mean how slight or steadfast is the abidance of voice at a particular *svara*; and, above all, its being conducive to some affective semblance, say, of gaiety or of a sad and yearning intenseness. Variations of aesthetic pace can also lend a look of repose or impatience to tones or tonal passages; but their effect is also freely that of abandon, easy confluence, decorativeness and winsome grouping. The words 'relatedness of tones' (*upanyāsa*)[38] require some separate comment. They may be taken to cover the various formal graces — such as *sūta, mīṇḍ, gamak* and *lahak* — for which our music is known, and which mostly embrace more notes than one.

It is by bearing all this in mind, along with the apt choice of words and their proper articulation in the case of vocal music — excluding, of course, *ālāpa* of the *dhruvapad* manner which does not use language — that a musician can make a *rāga* evoke or project its appropriate *rasa*. But this *rasa*, be it noted, is no mere emotion conveyed *by*, or expressed *through* the form of the *rāga*; it is the feeling appearance *of* the total *rāga*-form itself as conjured up by the musician, provided this form has been evoked by means of an apt selection of the elements and their proper integration. The language used in a specific composition set in a *rāga-tāla* frame is, of course, no integral part of the *rāga-tāla* combine, but it can surely be made to help or prevent the emergence of the requisite emotive character of the *rāga*. Another noteworthy point is that the filling of decorative frills and regular patterns that a recital normally comprises is never to the allowed to bedim or disrupt the unity of *rāga*-form. This, in turn, would demand (in the case of a *khyāl*[39] recital) that the *sthāyī*,[40] which is supposed to

38. Monier-Williams, *A Sanskrit-English Dictionary*, p. 201.

39. *Khyāl* is the more popular form of north Indian vocal music. It is commonly believed to offer greater scope for imaginative and decorative work than *dhruvapad*.

40. *Sthāyī* is generally regarded as the first line of a song. In actual singing, however, it also serves as the stable ground against which the decorative and variform quality of the patterns is highlighted.

clearly embody the *rāga*-form in its aspect of unity and identity, be projected after every brief bout of pattern-weaving; and that the eminence of *vādī* and *saṁvādī* be kept clear even during the execution of fluent *tānas*. In the case of *dhruvapad*-singing the analogous requirement would be that hectic and random *layakārī*[41] is not allowed to dissipate the singleness of the composition, meaningfulness of its text, and the requisite charm of the *rāga*-form.

It is important to see how the various elements of our present-day classical music contribute differently to the evocation of the full aesthetic form of a *rāga*. *Ālāpa* of the older kind brings out the spaciousness, repose and dignity that are implicit in a *rāga*; and, what is more, even its power to elevate and encompass us in the way of a rarefied atmosphere. A good *bandish*,[42] be it a *khyāl* or *dhruvapad* one, projects the *rāga* as a single and identifiable wholeness. The *tāna*s of the *khyāl*-singer manifest how a *rāga* is as open to a close and varied filling of vivacious and decorative patterns as to the reposeful stretches of *ālāpa*. In other words, as the dominant form of our music, a *rāga* is neither a mere arrangement of *āroha* and *avaroha*, and of *vādī* and *saṁvādī*, nor a skeletal fixture to which the music has only to conform, but a rich and integrated wholeness of implicit depth, accommodativeness, repose and vitality, and variform expressiveness. That is why our master musicians freely speak of a *rāga*'s *personality*. Indeed, just as a man's personality is an actualisation of his determinate potentialities, so is the full-blown form of a *rāga* a realisation of its aesthetic potential within the limits, and on the basis of its grammatical structure. In thus interpreting *rāga*-form I am

---

41. *Layakārī* in *Sangeet* is a performer's attempt to explore evermore the creative possibilities inherent in *laya* or aesthetic pace — which, as measured with the help of beats, is rhythm — by resorting to: changes in tempo, manner of flow, and syllables filling; proper segmentation of *bols* or mnemonic syllables and their bunches; and regulation of emphases in such a way that the relation of the rhythmic variations to the basic pace may also remain perceivable.

42. *Bandish* is a rhythmically organised composition which clearly embodies a *rāga* and a *tāla*. Its two essential complementary segments are *sthāyī* and *antarā*, — I mean in the region of *khyāl*-singing.

not only encouraged by Aristotle's view that an immanent form

> explains a thing's development, [that] it is the intelligible structure that a thing has when fully developed, and [that] the growth of the thing is [to be] regarded as a striving to make actual its form,[43]

but also by the evidence of our actual musical practice and discourse.

Yet it would be of help if we argued why the form of a *rāga* cannot be regarded as the grammatical skeleton of *āroha-avaroha* and *vādī-saṁvādī*, etc. The point may be brought out as follows:

Every *rāga* is supposed to evoke a *rasa*; but the mere indication of *āroha-avaroha* and *vādī-saṁvādī* is never taken to be capable of evoking *rasa*. *Lakṣaṇa gīta*s admittedly reveal the grammatical identity of a *rāga*, but never its aesthetic form or personality. Further, to say that a *rāga* entertains people at large and suffuses their minds with its colour naturally means that it is developed and treated for a sufficient length of time, and in such a way that its hidden beauty may be brought out. Otherwise, how would it keep the listeners interested? What is more, if a *rāga* is a *dhvani viśeṣa*, it must appear as a distinct individuality. This, in turn, generally requires that the *rāga* be given the form of a composition with the aid of words and rhythm. But, if this is done, we clearly go beyond a mere indication of *āroha-avaroha*, *vādī-saṁvādī*, because rhythm and words are now brought in.

But, one may here wonder, what then shall we say of *dhruvapad ālāpa*? Does it not bring out the *rāga-rūpa*? It certainly does; but, as it is here brought out, the *rāga*-form cannot be said to interest *people at large easily* — a fact which lends some point to our earlier suggestion that a *rāga* is not supposed to actually interest everyone. Nor can the form of a *rāga* be identified with its appearance as embodied in a rhythmically organized composition; for here, though the *rāga*'s identity is

43. Antony Flew, *A Dictionary of Philosophy*, p. 123.

clearly indicated, its dimensions — that is, its depth and compass, and the possibility it provides for ever newer creation — are never brought out, because in most cases the *tāra* and the *mandra*, and so quite a few qualities of *svaras*, are not quite exploited here. It may be noted that *āroha-avaroha / vādī-saṁvādī*, and the *bandish* are already prefixed — and are merely given to, or found by the artist — at the very outset. The overall form of the *rāga*, on the other hand, is to be brought out or evoked by realising the various qualities of the notes and the possible (and permissible) diversity of their relations in different *saptaks* (registers) and at varying pace. The *rāga* thus comes to reveal its (virtual) vitality and depth, its heavenward reaches, its freedom of operation within the embrace of a determinate musical complex, and perhaps also its ability to serve as the locus of different emotions. This is why, I repeat, the more insightful of our older musicians prefer to think of a *rāga* as a living something.

A *rāga* is a living form not merely in the sense which Susanne Langer gives to such form — that is, a kind of organism in respect of the 'life' of which we cannot determine the exact individual contribution of each organ (or element)[44] — but essentially because (as Langer herself would like to add) it reveals the dynamic features of life, say, animation and repose, and varying and regulated pursuit of an end, here the evocation of *rasa* or disinterested delight.

To conclude, the *rāga*-form is a distinct and identifiable melodic wholeness. It is not a limited shape or a mere outline. It is what or how the grammatical character of a *rāga* comes to appear as a result of the musician's realization of the creative possibilities that it offers. The *rasika* and the critic have to follow this process of effectuation and to gather its successive moments through a constructive use of their sympathetic imagination.

Yet, in so far as the *rāga*-form is not the only content of a classical music recital, no *rāga*, as projected in music, has a rigidly identical look for every musician, critic, or *rasika*. Our

44. Langer, *Problems of Art*, pp. 134-5.

capacities and preferences differ; and so whereas a *khyāliyā* (or *khyāl*-singer) may look upon a *rāga* as a chartered region of freedom for the creation of ever newer compositions and *tāna*s, the *ālāpiyā* may think of it as an immense, if determinate, compass for evoking effects of depth and grandeur, sublimity and seamlessness. The *rasika* or the critic too, depending on whether he inclines more to grammar and musicology or to aesthetic relish, may look upon a *rāga* as an adroit manipulation of some specific *svara*s or as the potent locus or spring of a particular *rasa*.

Composition in music

Rāga may, therefore, quite properly be regarded as the matrix of all creation in the region of Hindustani music. Here, it is also the very first appearance of form. Composition or *bandish,* though undoubtedly of great value, emerges thereafter. But which of the two, *bandish* (composition) or *rāga,* may be regarded as (what Langer calls) the commanding form of music? To answer the question in its fullness we have first to consider Langer's view of composition. She says:

> The essence of all composition . . . is the semblance of organic movement, the illusion of an indivisible whole.[45]

This, I believe, is true of composition (or *bandish*) in every sub-type of Hindustani classical music, be it *dhruvapad*, *dhamār*, *khyāl* or *tarānā*. But before I illustrate the truth with reference to actual compositions in these musical forms, I think it necessary to make some explanatory comments on the extract cited, largely as Langer would like us to do:

Organic movement may be taken to mean processes which keep an organism alive, such as breathing and heartbeat. According to Langer, such movement may also be said to be rhythmic because it shows the very essence of rhythm, that is, 'the preparation of a new event by the ending of a previous one'.[46] I may add that one of the processes which keep an

45. Langer, *Feeling and Form*, p. 126.

46. *Ibid.*

organism alive is its capacity for a measure of self-repair, say, after injury. But, of course, all these processes are found in music only as semblance, and not as literal fact. There is no actual motion in music as art. There is no path to be traversed, and nothing changes places. The indivisible quality of a music composition is also a sheer appearance. Vital processes show actual functional continuity. The release of one breath is in fact 'synchronous with the growth of the need for the next'; and the diastole actually prepares the systole, and vice versa.[47] On the other hand, the singing of a music composition cannot be literally breathless; and, to speak quite generally, music is the art of blending sounding notes with pauses of silence in a measured way.

But, if only as semblance, (a) how exactly does a composition (in Hindustani music) come to wear a look of 'organic movement', and (b) how does it appear to be 'an indivisible whole'? This dual question, we may note, is not as difficult as it might appear to be; for the 'appearances' it distinguishes are not really two. But let me explain. If the context of the extract being discussed is duly taken into account, 'organic movement' would mean vital activity, of which the 'characteristic principle . . . is rhythm'; and rhythm, signifies (for Langer) 'the preparation of a new event by the ending of a previous one' *or* continuity (or undividedness) of movement, so that whatever is marked by organic movement necessarily appears be an indivisible whole so long as it lasts. The question, therefore, gets reduced to the following simple form. How does a composition appear to be single and undivided? Now, bearing a good *khyāl sthāyī* in mind, I may distinguish the following factors or devices that make for the appearance in question:

Where the filling of words is not coextensive with the full stretch of the flowing form of *sthāyī*, the empty (or wordless) spaces may be filled with mere continuities of musical utterance employing the, आ, ई, ए forms of *akāra*. This device, called *kanbharanā*, has been quite popular in our traditional *gharānās*.

47. Langer, *Feeling and Form*, p. 127.

Where this device is *not* made use of, as in the singing of the late Kumar Gandharva (till before the closing chapter of his life), the semblance of the unity of the basic line (or *sthāyī*) can be created by a joint operation of the following: such a definite and emphatic singing of individual verbal segments that their impact may persist even when the singing is suspended (for a while); the *rasika*'s familiarity with the *rāga*-form which enables him *to look for specific svaras* in intervals of silence, and to prevent by this act of imagining the *sthāyī* from appearing broken; and, above all, the *sthāyī*'s inevitable self-completion at the *sama* of the *rhythm*-cycle, thereby acquiring a cyclic — and so an unbroken — look itself.

Vital or organic activity, however, is not merely undivided; it is often automotive as felt. Thus, when a person takes a decision and promptly carries it out aright, the entire course of action is not only undivided but is tinged with a sense of agency and self-effort. Now, even this feeling of self-activation, oriented activity, and attainment can appear, as semblance, in a good *bandish* (or composition). Indeed, there are quite a few *sthāyīs* which are so structured *and sung* that, from a particular point in their rhythmically set flow they appear to gather themselves, so to say, to move towards the *sama*; and to get at it with split second accuracy. My reference, here, is to what is called *āmad*, a dynamic structural feature (of the first line of a *bandish*) which I have elsewhere defined as

> that identifiable section of the flowing form of a *sthāyī* or *gat*, in and through which the flow seems to activate and regulate itself perceptibly at a particular point of the rhythm-cycle, and therefrom to move towards, and . . . [to get at] the *sama* in a well-designed way; which attainment at once seems to be a self-completion of the entire *bandish* as a dynamic design.[48]

---

48. S.K. Saxena: "The Fabric of Aamad: A study of Form and Flow in Hindustani Music", a paper presented to the Seminar on Science and Music organised by Sangeet Natak Adademi from March 27 to March 30, 1970; and published in *Sangeet Natak*, No. 16, April-June 70, pp. 38-44. My compositions presented on the occasion, by way of illustrating this definition of *āmad*, are now a part of the Akademi tape recordings: 742-784.

From the viewpoint of this excellence, I may add, a distinction has to be made between the *singer*'s effort and ability to arrive at the *sama* correctly and the *sthāyī*'s own appearing to move towards and attain the focal beat. The latter is always a more satisfying appearance, aesthetically.

Musical elements and acts in life

There is indeed no doubt that a good *sthāyī* strikes a knowledgeable listener as a dynamic, self-completing whole; and so some thought may here be given to Langer's following remark:

> Artists . . . choose the most telling metaphors . . . Especially musicians are ready to simply indentify . . . turns of phrase [that] support the finding that the dynamic structure of elements in art is cognate to that of acts in physical organisms.[49]

Now, what could Langer possibly mean by 'the dynamic stucture of elements'? Not merely that there is (virtual) movement in almost every element of music, but that just as every act in life is motivated by, and can *motivate* a great number of other acts, so 'every [artistic] elment seems to emanate from the context in which it exists. . . Whichever [element] one attends to *carves out* a context that is *indispensable to its existence*'.[50] In other words, both (life-acts and elements of music) are 'internally' related. But this internality is clearly *dynamic,* partly because of the occurrent character of music. The *dynamic internality* (or unity) of a work of art is further secured by the fact that the pattern of relations is here dialectical — in the sense that the consummation of one phase at once paves the way to another. To sum up, the full meaning of the dynamic structure of elements is that they not only determine each other actively, but — as constituting phases (or stages) — *take time* in building up the fabric of music. This fact, I admit, provides some warrant to Langer's basic thesis that time is the *primary illusion* of music, though it still remains

49. Langer, *Mind — An Essay on Human Feeling,* vol. I, pp. 202.

50. *Ibid.*, p. 204; emphasis added.

open to question if the evocation of this semblance is the art's *overtopping purpose*.

We may focus now on Langer's reference to musicians in the extract being discussed. By saying that they easily 'choose the most telling metaphors . . . [and] turns of phrase' that favour her view — namely, that the dynamic structure of elements in art is similar to that of acts in physical organism — Langer may be taken to mean that musicians in general tend to speak roughly as follows:

> This note or phrase *demands* that what comes next should be this or that particular one.

But, I contend, 'the most telling phrases' that *our* musicians *generally* use in respect of a recital do not relate to what Langer speaks of as the dynamic internality of elements. They are, as a rule, of the following kind: कितना चैन है गाने में (how tranquil is the singing); तानें तैयार हैं, और सुर में भी (the patterns are fluent and melodious too); गाना दिलकश है (the singing touches the heart).

My feeling is that if Langer is keen, as she obviously is, to emphasize the internality in question, it is essentially because she wishes to build up support for her thesis that the art symbol is an organic unity, and that it partakes of the character of life, and so is a living form, if only as a semblance.

Objectivity of composition (or bandish)

But there *is* an emphasis in her theory of music which I readily accept. It is her insistence that the basic composition in objective in character:

> The matrix, in music the fundamental movement of melody . . . is born of the composer's thought and feeling, but as soon as he recognises it as an individual symbol and sets forth its outline it becomes the expression of an impersonal idea . . . the objective form . . . has . . . [been] created,[51]

51. Langer, *Feeling and Form*, p. 123.

> . . . The composition . . . exists, as something that could be committed to writing or to memory and that might be performed by another person.[52]

Now, this is all quite in line with the theory and practice of music in our *gharānās*. Here, compositions are freely passed on from father to son; and the latter takes delight in singing a composition strictly according to its original form without incurring from *rasikas* the charge of imitativeness. What is more, not merely individual compositions, but whole styles of singing may be replicated by pupils or 'grandpupils'. In such cases, if the replication is satisfying in itself, the singer does not make himself liable to the charge of mere mimicking — not at least at the hands of unbiased *rasikas*.[53]

Here, I may add, it would help us to remember the distinc-

---

52. Langer, *Feeling and Form*, p. 120

53. To illustrate, Madhup Mudgal's presentation of *bhajans*, all duly set in *rāga* and *tāla*, from Delhi Doordarshan II (on April 12, 1995, incidental to the official mourning observed for the death of Sri Moraraji Desai) appeared to have captured almost everything about the style of his mentor, the unforgettable Kumar Gandharva; but not for a moment could I think of denigrating the present performer as a mere imitator — so satisfying was the singing because of the power, inwardness, and elevating quality which one commonly associates which the music of Kumar Gandharva.

    Similarly, Ajoy Chakraborty's performance at the Shriram Shankarlal Music Festival (Bharatiya Kala Kendra, New Delhi April 13-16, 1995) was almost a photocopy of the late Ustad Bade Ghulam Ali, the father of Chakraborty's own teacher, Ustad Munnawar Ali Khan. But the critical reactions which the recital elicited were in no way derogatory; rather, they were full of praise. Here are some samples:

    (a) *Donning the Mantle of Bade Ghulam Ali Khan* — Ajoy Chakraborty is something of a miracle of natural gifts and tireless self-culture . . . [He set] the air waves over Delhi into [aesthetic] commotion with his tremendous voice, artistry, and the compelling passion of his music in his debut at the . . . Festival . . . on the third day (Prakash Wadhera in *The Hindu* of 12.5.1995).

    (b) Ajoy Chakraborty deserves not only acclaim, but our gratitude for preserving, to a nicety, the glorious *gāyakī* of Ustad Bade Ghulam Ali Khan. I cannot think of any technical or aesthetic excellence of the late maestro which could be said to be missing from Chakraborty's recital . . . (S.K. Saxena in *The Asian Age* of 28.4.1995).

tion between the attitude of a *rasika* and that of a mere critic. If the former feels delighted by the intrinsic charm of what meets his ear presently, the extra information — or his own reminiscence — that the music which he is now listening to is very similar to what he has heard in the past, will not dampen his immediate interest, for it is the present which occupies the focus of his attention at the moment.[54] He knows that adherence to, and preservation of the style of a master is surely not as easy a matter as copying a map with the help of a translucent paper. One has to master an eminent artist's technique and the specific functioning of his imagination; and this surely calls for rigorous training and self-discipline, in addition to long closeness to the teacher and one's own native talent. Be that as it may, if the traditional classical music of (north) India flourishes even today it is largely because of the *gharānā*s where the pupil of a master, pretty often the latter's own son, is not only not averse to following the way of the teacher, but is positively expected to do so, faithfully.

'Commanding form' — composition or rāga?

We may now turn again to the question which we posed before setting out to discuss Langer's thesis that 'the purpose of all musical labour . . . is to create [the illusion of] an audible passage filled with motion . . .'. Is there anything in Hindustani music which could be called 'commanding form' in Langer's sense? Her view is that the composition is the commanding form because it is this 'essential musical form' which determines 'the whole subsequent process of invention and elaboration'. She adds that this 'general Gestalt' has to be 'found' by the composer, as a result of 'conception' that takes place essentially in his mind, and that the recognition of its being the essential form is 'more or less sudden'.

Now, what Langer speaks of as 'composition' is *bandish* in

54. To illustrate, the singing of Pandit Bhim Sen Joshi today is in no way markedly different from what it was five or ten years back. But did any critic — who actually heard the maestro's recital at the Sriram Shankar Lal Music Festival of 1995 — complain of his being tied down to the set idiom of his past performances?

the region of Hindustani music. A *bandish* is a complex of tones as framed in a dual *rāga-tāla* setting. In the region of *khyāl*, which is the more popular form of classical Hindustani vocal music today, a *bandish* is generally taken to mean a *sthāyī* and its *antarā*. But it is doubtful if a *bandish* could be regarded as the commanding form of a whole recital. The *barhat*[55] that may follow the initial singing of *sthāyī-antarā* is not directly determined by, but only follows the singing in question. That which determines *barhat* is rather the need to vivify *swara* and *rāga*. The *tāna*s that come even later have to meet the following additional norms: clarity and beauty — at times with intricacy of design; distinctness of constitutent notes, without any interruption in the flow of the pattern; and a more or less determinate relatedness to the chosen pace of the rhythm-cycle. Very rarely, if ever, can the form of *sthāyī-antarā* be said to *determine* the extent or design of *tāna*s. The *sthāyī* only *serves* as a kind of steadfast ground against which the *tānas* appear as patterns and no mere collocations. It is indeed with a view to evoking this dual appearance that a good singer returns to the *sthāyī* after executing two or three *tāna*s, instead of reeling off *tāna* after *tāna* and delaying a return to *sthāyī* overmuch. Of course, even during the weaving of patterns the vocalist does not forget the form of the basic composition; but here this composition (or the *sthāyī*) is not borne in mind *as consciously and ceaselessly* as the grammatical (and aesthetic) character of the *rāga*.

It is indeed the norm of fidelity to *rāga* that determines every moment of our classical music; and, besides the argument outlined above, the following too (from Langer's *Feeling and Form*) may be taken to support my view that *rāga* alone can be regarded as the commanding form of Indian music:

> Perhaps the most striking thing about . . . [musical form] is . . . [its] objective character. . . . Once a matrix of musical thought, a 'commanding form' has been grasped by one's artistic imagination, it assumes a peculiarly impersonal status, like

55. *Barhat* is leisurely ascent, generally towards the key notes of the *rāga*, which makes the melody look deep and spacious.

> . . . something 'given'. Great musicians have spoken of the musical 'idea' with an unmistakable feeling of moral obligation towards it, a sense of responsibility for its development and perfection.[56]

Two main points have been made in the above:

First, once it 'has been grasped by one's artistic imagination', a commanding form in music appears to have an impersonal, objective status. Second, when it has thus come to assume an objective or impersonal status, the commanding form in music does not *remain* a mere 'given' something, but *operates* as a norm or regulative principle of the musician's entire artistic activity.

Both these points call for some comment. However, before I set out to reflect on them from the angle of Hindustani music, a distinction may be made, in the light of Langer's own writings, between *musical form taken generally* and what she chooses to characterize as the *commanding form in music*. Where she speaks of musical form as articulate, what she has in mind is but a general feature of *all* music. But where, as in the extract being discussed, she says that the 'commanding form' in music, in a way, enjoins the musician to work for its 'development and perfection' the reference is clearly to a special kind of form which — without, of course, being taken to fall outside the overall form of music — must be credited with a measure of plastic stress. Now, what is that in Hindustani music which could fairly be said to be its commanding form *in Langer's sense?* Obviously, it cannot be the *sthāyī* of a composition, be a *khyāl* or a *dhruvapad*: for, whereas the commanding form is something which (according to Langer) the musician is required to develop and perfect, a *sthāyī* has only to be sung strictly in line with its prefixed structure, and 'established', so to say, as the ground of further singing, by being steadily projected more than once. A *rāga*, on the other hand, has got to be developed and perfected in the sense that the room which it offers for unfoldment, tonal patterns — and production of various effects — must be turned to good

56. Langer, *Feeling and Form*, p. 131.

account.[57] Further, the more sensitive of our musicians indeed look upon *rāga* not merely as an objective framework into which the recital has to be somehow fitted, but as a living being with a personality of its own, so that any deviation from its form is taken to be as condemnable as the mutilation of a person's limbs (अंग भंग करना). Therefore, I conclude, so far as our music is concerned, only *rāga* can claim to be the commanding form in Langer's sense.

But, one may ask, can a *rāga* be said to be a *form* at all? I think we have to say, yes. Some common meanings of the word form are shape, a mode of arrangement, system. Now, a *rāga* may well be credited with a shape, for it *is* possessed of a distinct sensible appearance which is identifiable as such by the trained listener's *ear*. This ease of recognition follows from both the 'what' and 'how' of notes, that is, from what precise *svaras* a *rāga* comprises and from how exactly they are to be sung (or played). Thus, *kedāra* and *lalita* owe their identity, in part, to the use of two adjacent *madhyams*; and yet are distinguished *from each other* by marking the manner and setting of their individual appearances in the melody. The *r̥ṣabha* of *purīya* is quickly accomplished, and may even appear a little coy. In *rāga sohnī*, on the other hand, it is (as placed in the *tāra*) steadfast and a little plaintive. Further, the *svaras* in a *rāga* do not make a mere series; an essential *relation* or linkage of two or more *svaras* often provides the core of a *rāga*. Two clear examples are the linkage of *pa* and *ga* in *bhūpālī* and the sweep that unites *dhaivata* with *r̥ṣabha* in *rāga śrī*. In other words, a *rāga* is an orderly arrangement, and no random aggregation of *svaras*. So, to conclude, it may well be said to be the commanding *form* of Indian music.

It should now be clear that form *as composition* is not the earliest appearance of form in Indian music. *Rāga* is the basic form; form as composition arises only later; and this is why every composition (or *bandish*) has to be *in* (conformity with) a *rāga*. A composition is a form which results from the

---

57. It may be noted that Langer too speaks of the 'objectivity *and potency* of the commanding form'.

disposition of *rāga-svaras* in a rhythm-cycle in such a way that the resulting complex may appear to be a self-completing melodic whole, and not what it seems to be in its basic notational form, that is, an open-ended arrangement (so to say) of some specific *svaras* which, though not internally diffuse, *does not yet appear to gather itself*[58] *and to complete its flow at any focal point*, say, the *sama* of a rhythm-cycle. Indeed, though (as we have argued) it may well be said to be a form, a *rāga* is not as such a composition. The latter is created by a maestro, an Ustad or a Paṇḍit; a *rāga*, on the other hand, is mostly given to him as the matrix of many possible compositions. It is a norm which the music has to agree with; and its aesthetic potential may have to be patiently brought out, as is done by the *ālāpiyās*. A composition, oppositively, has to be sung (or played) — or 'established'— in the required manner. It sure *embodies* a *rāga*; but it cannot be said to aim at *unfolding the full aesthetic canvas* of the *rāga* chosen.

Is full-blown ālāpa a 'form'?

But, one may ask, when the aesthetic richness and creative range of a *rāga* have been duly brought out, say, by an expert *ālāpīyā*, can it (the *rāga*) be said to be (or to have) a form? The answer would depend (I repeat) on what precise meaning we here give to the word *form, and* on what exactly we intend to focus on, — on *ālāpa* simply as it now appears to contemplation, immediately after its completion, as the net impact of the entire singing, *or* as this crowning impression taken along with some recollection of *how* this impact has (ultimately) come to acquire the look that it now wears. Turning to *form*, it is obvious that the word cannot here be taken to mean (outward) *appearance* — a perfectly legitimate meaning of *form*; for *the completed ālāpa* is unquestionably an appearance to the listener's ear which may keep dwelling, for a while, on the music that has just ceased to be; and it would, therefore, be pointless to wonder if it is a form in the sense of *appearance*. The wonder would become a genuine question only if *form* is taken to signify harmony or orderly arrangement. But in this sense of the word

58. As in the classical songs called *lakṣaṇa-gītas*.

we may well ascribe *form* to full-blown *ālāpa* whether we think of its net impact alone, or also (in a measure) of the process of its growth. For the latter (or the unfoldment of *rāga*) is, as a rule, noticeably orderly; *and* the impact is unified and intense.

All this talk about commanding form, however, is hardly of any interest to the average *rasika*. What he would like us to focus on is the relation of music to feeling, — a relation which is widely accepted; and it is this relation which we may now seek to understand in the light of Langer's writings. Her view on the subject is important not only because its positive emphases seem to be original on the whole, but because her refutation of some widely accepted views of the music-feeling relation appears to be well grounded.

Langer on music and feeling

Langer opposes the widely held view which regards music as the *language* of feeling. But the opposition is not overdone. She, in fact, takes pains to emphasize a point of similarity too between music and language: 'Music, like language, is an articulate form'.[59] Indeed, a music composition or *bandish* is not a fuzzy mass. The *svaras* that go to make it are always distinguishable (in principle); and a *rasika* can register their discreteness without losing hold of the flowing, undivided form in which they nestle.

Langer is, however, more explicit in the way she *distinguishes* music from language. The elements of language are words; and, quite apart from the way they are put together to make a sentence, they have their own independent meanings fixed by convention. The 'parts' of music, on the other hand, have no independent meanings. This emphasis, I realize, collides with the traditional Indian view, according to which some individual *svaras* can be said to possess a measure of intrinsic and determinate suggestiveness. *Śuddha ṛṣabha*, for example, is believed to look strong and assertive. But I find it difficult to speak for this view. To my mind, what a note suggests is not any inherent 'look' or significance, but what it

---

59. Langer, *Feeling and Form*, p. 31.

comes to be invested with because of several factors such as the following: its brevity or abidance, the volume of the voice which articulates it, and the relatedness of the *svara* in question with the *svara*s which precede and follow it, and by virtue of which it may appear to mark the rise or close of a passage. Langer too believes that music 'lacks one of the basic characteristics of language — fixed association, and therewith a single, unequivocal reference';[60] that, strictly speaking, music is 'not a language, because it has no vocabulary'; and that, therefore, to speak of this art as the *language* of feeling is improper.

Nor can music be regarded as a direct self-expression of feeling. Here, too, Langer's manner is guarded. She takes due notice of the prevalence of the view she is going to challenge before she sets out to develop her protest. For clarity, the two sides of the matter may be outlined and discussed separately.

The view that the 'performer' transmits the feelings of the master, the composer, to a sympathetic audience

> is widely accepted by musicians and philosophers alike . . . from Rousseau to Kierkegaard and Croce among philosophers . . . [; and] among musicians themselves — composers, conductors, and performers — we find the belief very widely disseminated that music is an emotional catharsis, that its essence is self-expression . . . [.] Beethoven, Schumann, Liszt . . . have all left us testimonials to that effect.[61]

Here, however, I think it necessary to invite attention to a detail which Langer should perhaps have noticed for a fairer interpretation of what she regards as the bases of the theory under review. Other utterances which she cites in this context do not all suggest that it is the composer's *present* feeling which finds expression in his music. Thus, see the following:

> We may rest assured that (whatever feelings a composer

60. Langer, *Feeling and Form*, p. 31.

61. Langer, *Philosophy in a New Key*, p. 215.

> may convey) he will not express these sentiments with authority unless he *has experienced* them at some given moment of his existence.[62]

> In the case of a theme which Beethoven used *ten years after* he had first jotted it down[63] . . . it is probable that such a theme, translating an impression of keenest sorrow, came to him during a day of suffering.[64]

It would here be reasonable to assume that an interval of time separated the actual *impression* of the (feelings or) sorrow in question from its translation into the corresponding theme. So Langer is not quite justified in remarking, immediately in the wake of the second quotation, that the self-expression theory which — as interpreted by Carnap — classes music with "such expressions as 'oh-oh', or at a higher level, lyrical verses", is the most popular doctrine of the significance and function of music.[65] Exclamations like 'oh-oh' express a *present* feeling. In the extracts on music I have just cited, on the other hand, there is no definite suggestion that what musical expression gives vent to is an *immediate* feeling.

But quite apart from this matter of detail, the belief that music is nothing but a direct expression of one's present feelings could surely be opposed, as Langer does, in the following way:

> *Sheer* self-expression requires no artistic form. The [actual] history of music, [on the other hand] has been a history of more and more integrated, disciplined, and articulated forms.[66]

So music cannot be regarded as mere self-expression.

---

62. Cited by Langer, from an essay by Henri Prunieres, in *Philosophy in a New Key*, p. 215; italics added.
63. *Ibid.*, italics added.
64. *Ibid.*
65. *Ibid.*, pp. 215-16.
66. *Ibid.*, p. 216; italics added. As I cite them here, the words that make the extract differ (in order) from the way they occur in the book referred to.

But here, again, I suspect a tendency to slur over the evidence of fact. The view of music that Langer here seeks to demolish, has its ever been actually put forth? It is no doubt true even of Indian music that its history is a succession of newer ways of organizing melody and rhythm, though it would be clearly wrong to suggest that forms which appeared later in the evolution of music in India — say, *khyāl* and *ṭhumrī* — are more 'integrated and disciplined' — than the earlier ones of *dhruvapad* and *dhamār*. But has our music — or, I venture to ask, *any other music claiming to be art* — ever been regarded as *sheer* self-expression? What *is* such expression any way? Langer answers this question by citing the following (illustrative) cases of emotional behaviour:

> a lynching-party howling round the gallows-tree, a woman wringing her hands over a sick child, a lover who has just rescued his sweetheart in an accident and stands trembling, sweating, and perhaps laughing and crying with emotion . . .[67]

But, one may ask, how exactly do such cases illustrate *sheer* self-expression? The changes of bodily behaviour they involve are neither unrelated mutually nor to the objective situation. The relation is, in fact, determinate both ways. It cannot be wantonly altered, it being generally impossible, for instance, for the woman in question to wear a gentle smile, or for the lover to appear quite unruffled and relaxed *immediately* after the hectic act of rescue. In other words, the bodily behaviour is not 'sheer' in the sense of being utterly random and disorganised; were it so, it would be unintelligible to outsiders. What can be fairly said only is that, in the cases in question, the *pattern* of bodily behaviour itself or its relation to the outer situation is *not established by the individual involved by means of patient and self-critical effort*. The suggestion, I may add, is supported by Langer's own following remark:

> Verbal responses like 'Ah!', 'Oh-oh!' are *not creations*, but speech-habits . . . [68]

---

67. Langer, *Philosophy in a New Key*, p. 216.

68. *Ibid.*, pp. 216-17; italics added.

But with regard to a music composition, does (not merely *can*) any one say that it comes into being as a mere matter of habit and not as the result of creative effort? Even those Hindustani musicians — like Ustad Abdul Karim Khan and Pandit Omkarnath Thakur — who were known for the emotional quality of their music, would never concede that in actual singing they cared only for feeling, because in all classical Indian music *rāga* (and *tāla*) have to be kept in mind all along; and these two concepts, as we know, signify *forms* of melody and rhythm.

In fine, though it may be doubted if music has ever been regarded as sheer self-expression *as Langer understands it*, her insistence that music is importantly a matter of form, and never — where it *is* art — a mere discharge of feeling, is quite warranted. Langer admits that in playing music one can relieve one's feelings at the keyboard; but she hastens to add that such a possible catharsis is not the 'primary function' of music as art.[69]

Now, I find it easy to buttress this emphasis of Langer with a simple argument. Were music essentially the discharge of a presently felt emotion, and were its (seeming) expressiveness simply the outer side, so to say, of a corresponding inner experience, the changing 'moods' of music, which can follow each other quite rapidly, would call for a similar fickleness in the mind of the musician at work; but if the inconstancy happens to grip him in fact, it would ruin the self-possession that is needed for good performance. But no such discomposure is, in fact, experienced by a Hindustani vocalist as he switches over, say, from a wistful *jogiyā* composition in *vilambit laya* to a *drut tarānā* in the virile *rāga adānā.* It is indeed necessary to distinguish, as Langer does, the direct self-expression of a feeling from its artistic evocation.[70]

Further, the *self*-expression theory of music cannot account for the fact that there is no limit to what or how much this art can express.

---

69. Langer, *Philosophy in a New Key*, p. 217.

70. *Ibid.*, p. 221.

(Here, as I develop the argument, the factual basis is provided by some remarks of Langer, but their use as material for a possible objection to the theory in question is my doing.) Did music express only the immediate or general life-feelings *of the musician or the composer*, its expressiveness could not go beyond the limits of merely individual experience. The fact, on the other hand, is that music is often seen to surpass these personal limits. There is indeed eminent truth in the following words of Langer:

> (Music) bespeaks . . . (the composer's) imagination of feelings rather than his own emotional state, and expresses what he *knows about* the so-called 'inner life'; *and this may exceed his personal case*, because music is a symbolic form to him through which he may *learn* as well as utter ideas of human sensibility.[71]

> Even the artist need not have experienced in actual life every emotion that he can express. It may be through *manipulation of his created elements* that he discovers *new possibilities of feeling, strange moods, perhaps greater concentrations of passion* than his own temperament could ever produce, or than his fortunes have yet called forth. For, although a work of art reveals the character of subjectivity, it is itself objective; its purpose is to objectify the life of feeling. As an abstracted form it can be handled quite apart from its sources and yield dynamic patterns that surprise even the artist.[72]

It has not been easy for me to see how what is said in the above extracts could in fact be true; and I think it necessary, partly by way of reassuring myself, to explain as follows the passages cited, strictly in the light of both my own experience as a listener and my intimate talks with some master vocalists.

Where the music is really good, the overall affective look of a complete recital is never quite foreknown to a classical singer. That is why a full-blown exposition of *ālāpa* (in the *dhruvapad* manner) often tends to leave the singer feeling not only somewhat tired (yet deeply satisfied), but a little subdued

71. Langer, *Feeling and Form*, p. 28. Here, only the first emphasis is original.
72. *Ibid*., p. 374; all emphases are mine.

at the vast musical canvas of depth, repose, and dignity he has been able to evoke.

Sometimes, as the singing is about to begin, the very tuning of the *tānpūrā* may be so immaculate, and it may generate such a luminous and resonant sound of an important note — say, the note, *gandhār* in the case of *rāga hindol* — that along with (the *sa* and) his own awakening sense of the form of the *rāga*, the vocalist may straightaway feel upswayed into a mood of high seriousness, and be thereby enabled to invest the very start of his singing with an air of meditative stillness — and reverential access to *svaras* — of which (effects and attitudes) he was probably not thinking at all when he had just entered the stage after the compere's announcement of the bare name of the *rāga* to be rendered, and which (maybe) he has never *so clearly* experienced in actual life.

Nor is there anything surprising about such emergence (in art) of new and complex feelings. If reflection on some old ideas, now taken as one, can release a sudden, new insight, and if (for a beginner in geometry) a square comes to appear evenly and pleasingly self-divided the moment its two opposite corners are linked by a diagonal, why should it strain our credence to suppose that listening to a winsome musical note, and the contemplation of the whole-form (or *rāga*) that is itself embracive of that note, may unite to generate a quite distinctive mood? It is indeed the clear evidence of actual music that a specific tonal or rhythmic arrangement can make for the evocation of a feeling that has never before been a clear content of one's everyday experience.

But, to lend added support to the point I am seeking to make, I deem it here necessary to cite, as illustration, a composition of my own — the following *tarānā*, set to a cycle of 11 beats in *rāga sohnī*:

1	2	3	4	5	6	7	8	9	10	11
						मं-	मं,मंध	गग	[ध]मंध	निसां
						ताऽ	दा,रेऽ	ऽत	दारे	दानी
रेंनि,सां-	निध	निध	मंग	मंग	रेसा	मं-	मं,मंध	गग	[ध]मंध	निसां
दीऽ,ऽम	तदा	ऽरे	तद	रेदा	ऽनी	ताऽ	दा,रेऽ	ऽत	दारे	दानी
×			२		०		३			
	मंग,	ग[ध]मं	-मं	ध,मंध	[ध]सां	सां,मंध	[ध]सां	सां	सांसां	गंमं
	याऽ	ली,आ	ऽली	आ,लीऽ	अल	ला,ऽऽ	मौऽ	लाऽ	सब	कोऽ
गंरें	सां-	नि--सां	ध--नि	मं-मंध	गग	[रे]मंग	रेसा	-ग	[ध]मंध	निसां
सांऽ	इ ऽ	दाऽऽऽ	ताऽऽऽ	कऽरीऽ	ऽम	ताऽ	दारे	ऽत	दारे	दानी
×			२		०		३			

Now, before I turn to focus attention, as I want to, on a specific detail of this composition, let me make it clear that in the course of daily living I have never had the experience of dwelling upon *the benevolence of a person in a moment of felt acknowledgment, humility, surrender, and concomitant assurance of security*. But as I turn to sing the composition myself, with the requisite measure of attunement with the import of the text, melodic order, and the precise character of passage across the constituent *svaras*, I find that in the act of completing the *antarā* — beginning with याली, आली, and ending with the words: दाता करीम — the descending phrase तअदरे, (follwing करीम), if sung in a gently relaxed manner, adds to the feeling implicit in, and evoked by *the word* करीम (meaning 'merciful, here used with reference to God visualized as the supreme giver or दाता); and in so far as the word comes to rest, momentarily, at *ga*, a pretty low note in the scale, the entire utterance comes to wear the look of the complex experience I have put in italicized words, and even tends to imbue me with it, in a measure. The *recognition* of the complex character of the feeling that the music thus acquires may well be done, as I do now, with the help of elements drawn from my actual experience; but its being presented to me, *as a whole and as an object for contemplation*, is a quite new occurrence.

It should now be easy to see the point in Susanne Langer's

emphasis that, as a work of art, a music composition (or recital) is objective in the sense that its materials and elements are handled quite freely by the composer, though also — and importantly — in accordance with their own character; and that the world of melody and rhythm is intrinsically so open to the imaginative creation of ever new 'dynamic patterns' that the total music may *add to,* instead of merely projecting the musician's knowledge of felt life.

The following words of Mrs. Campbell-Fischer, which Langer cites with obvious approval, are no mere rhetoric:

> An artist . . . may go beyond the felt thing . . . In what actual person have we ever experienced the inevitability of passionate pattern that Oedipus or Lear present to us? . . . If I could be as sad as certain passages in Mozart, my glory would be greater than it is. . . . The fact that I know as much as I do of the essence of pathos comes from meeting with such music. . . . My grasp of the essence of sadness . . . comes not from moments in which I have been sad, but from moments when I have sadness before me released from entanglements with contingency. We . . . do not put or read into . . . [great works of art] some petty emotion we ourselves have experienced and can readily name. Rather we learn from them what an emotional reality of greatest stretch can be . . . or the calm, the spirit of eternal rest, that comes to birth in an Egyptian statue . . . — such are the emotions unnamed perhaps, but expressible and realisable in art. Those, and not personal emotional excitements, are what great artists give.[73]

Further, if *self*-expression is really the basic aim of music, only the composer (or performer) can be given the right to evaluate his works.[74] But this is obviously not supported by the practice of criticism. What is more, critical evaluation calls for a clear, discursive understanding of concepts and criteria, which in turn demands a good deal of analytic thinking; and our artists, as a rule, have neither the desire nor perhaps the ability to resort to such thinking.

---

73. Langer, *Mind — An Essay on Human Feeling,* vol. I, p. 88.
74. Langer, *Feeling and Form,* p. 18.

Finally, if not the direct *self*-expression of feeling, could the *evocation* of some feeling or emotion in the listeners be said to be the essence of music? Here, too, Langer's answer is in the negative; and she seems to be pretty definite about it, for it opens the following passage which may well be regarded as a succinct account of her entire conception of the relation of music to feeling:

> The function of music is *not* stimulation of feeling, but expression of it; and furthermore, *not* the symptomatic expression of feelings that beset the composer, but a symbolic expression of the forms of sentience as he understands them. It bespeaks his imagination of feeling rather than his emotional state, and expresses what he *knows about* the so-called inner life. . . .[75]

Now, of all that Langer says in the above extract, the most easily acceptable is her opening remark. Indeed, music as art cannot be said to stimulate our feelings as directly as an unconfined snake often strikes fear in us, or as a child's first sight of a rainbow makes its heart 'leap up' in wonder and delight. On the other hand, it is common knowledge that good music sometimes moves us very deeply and elicits spontaneous applause because it appeals to the heart and not to the ear alone. Yet its ability to affect our feelings or to appear as express*ing* some emotion cannot be regarded as the *essence* of music. What, then, are we to say (on the whole) of the relation of feeling to art (including music) to feeling? I think the following extract from an essay by John Hospers suggests a fair answer from the viewpoint, we may say, of knowledgeable lovers of music:

> I want art to provide me a pipeline to the life of feeling; I want art to move me, not merely to titillate my senses or inform my intellect; I want . . . to derive from it a memorable emotional experience — or at the very least, to provide me with some new insight into the life of feeling, as a novel may do even if it may not particularly move me, emotionally. But I would resist the tendency to say there is just one function of art, to be expressive or revelatory of some aspect of feeling.

75. Langer, *Feeling and Form*, p. 28; first two emphases added.

> I will take Mondrian for what he gives, and Tolstoy for what he gives, and not demand the same of every artist. Phrases such as '*the* function of . . .' are, I fear, usually preludes to a mistake.[76]

Three distinct points are made in the above; and all of them, I believe, are supportable by a careful look at Hindustani music. First, due attention to different kinds of art recalcitrates the possibility of there being just one blanket definition of art. Even emotive expressiveness, which often distinguishes music at its best, cannot be said to be essential to this art. Second, art which has something to do with feeling as well is prefer*able* — and is in fact, generally preferr*ed* — to art which only titillates the senses or informs the intellect. Thirdly, art which provides 'a memorable emotional experience' may be ranked higher than art which only provides 'some new insight into the life of feeling', may be without actually moving the contemplator. As we shall see a little later, Langer too believes that it is an important function of music to provide an insight into the life of feeling; but her overall view of the music-feeling relation also emphasizes the concepts of symbolic projection and forms of feeling or sentience. So the attempt to consider the views of Hospers from the angle of Hindustani music — and as providing a criticism of Langer's view — may not be made immediately, but only during the course of our study of her *complete* philosophy of music to which I now turn. As I proceed, my starting-point will be the extract from *Feeling and Form* cited (on the previous page) before the personal predilection of Hospers; but for fullness of treatment, some other extracts from Langer's writings will also have to be considered.

The great office of music?

Now, where Langer begins by speaking of the 'function' (or 'the great office') of music, what she means is the ultimate or essential purpose, *not the immediate concern* of this art; for she does not, in this context, make any mention of what *every*

76. Hospers, 'Hartshorne's Aesthetics', in *The Philosophy of Charles Hartshorne*, pp. 128-9.

composer — that is, the creator of any kind of composition, vocal or instrumental — is direcly required to do, namely, dealing creatively with the materials of music. To compose is necessarily, if not merely, to form or arrange; or to produce something by putting the given material in an orderly way. In the case of music the material which is requisite in every case of composition is *svara*s or tones. Words and beat-measured rhythm are also necessary for *most* sub-types of our music, that is barring *ālāpa* of the *dhruvapad* manner which is done quite without the aid of language and drumming. As for compositions which use language — say, our *khyāl*s and *dhruvapads* — some of them may be able to project, at places, the rise and fall of feeling, say, in the form of a devout yearning for God, or as a soulful longing for the vagrant beloved. But this is only a contingent appearance in our music. In the case of quite a few such *tarānās*, for instance, which use only mnemonic syllables and no language at all, there is no trace of any form of feeling. Such compositions may well be sung — as, I remember, they surely were by the late maestro Pandit Vinayak Rao Patwardhan — also at hectic speed. But, first, such accelerated singing cannot be said to be a necessary part of the composer's intention; and second, the singing in such cases usually ends at a point of climactic pace, not as reposeful subsidence, thus failing to correspond with that 'form of feeling' which Langer would perhaps like to put as terrific excitement *and emerging calm*. The plain truth is that a considerable amount of our music does not reveal any 'form of feeling', and is admired solely because of its sweetness, clarity of utterance, and design. Langer's positive thesis that music is, if indirectly, an expression of felt life is indeed not warranted by the actual practice of Hindustani music. The primary concern of a vocalist as he sings a *dhamār* is with adroit and variform treatment of the rhythm chosen, — besides, of course, due attention to the requirements of *bandish*, *svara* and *rāga*; and if he uses imagination, as he surely does, it is only in the act of creating ever new segments and patterns of rhythm, *and* in yet attaining to the focal beat of the rhythm-cycle with split second accuracy, rather than in projecting any *'forms* of feeling' of which, we may safely assume, he himself has no idea at all.

Langer, however, insists that

> [The] great office of music is to organise our conception of feeling into more than an occasional awareness of emotional storm, i.e., to give us an insight into what may truly be called the 'life of feeling', or subjective unity of experience; and this it does by the same principle that organises physical existence into a biological design — rhythm.[77]

What this extract means may be simply put thus:

Ordinarily, we take 'feeling' to mean emotions which we experience but fitfully and as states of mental agitation. Music, on the other hand, projects a semblance not merely of these episodic affective states, but of that wider *unity of felt life* which is, by and large, equable and which includes — but is by no means confined to — to emotions, like joy and sorrow, that make its inner emphases of heightened awareness. And in the region of melody, the unity in question appears not as an inert, uniform continuity, but as the dynamic, organic unity of *rhythm*, — that is, as revealing how one distinct moment or state of feeling at once paves the way to the next.

Let us now see if all this is defensible. First, what are we to understand by an organized conception of emotional (or subjective) life? An answer to this question is implicit in Langer's own following words:

> A succession of emotions that have no reference to each other do not constitute an 'emotional life', any more than a discontinuous and independent functioning of organs collected under one skin would be a physical 'life'.[78]

In other words, if (as Langer believes) 'the great office of music' is 'to organise our conception of feeling', it should make us see how the different emotions are interrelated. Further, this 'seeing' is not to be taken as superficial notice, but as *insight*. *Insight*, as 'the aim of art', is understanding of the essential life of feeling.

---

77. Langer, *Feeling and Form*, p. 126.

78. *Ibid*.

> But all understanding requires abstraction. . . . Anything *about* reality, that is to be expressed and conveyed, must be abstracted *from* reality. . . . What we understand, we conceive, and conception always involves formulation, presentation, and therefore abstraction.[79]

So when music is said to make us see, for instance, how joy is related to sorrow, the suggestion is not that what is projected is a replica of our *real life experiences* of the two emotions — which may include, respectively, some reference to a specific festive occasion, or to an estrangement from a dear one — but only their general (abstracted) features, say, the felt enlivenment and expansiveness of joy or the droop of spirit in sorrow.

All this is clearly admissible. But, what Langer says in the two extracts we have cited on the previous page is not merely that music projects the general features of emotions like joy end sorrow *separately*, but that it also makes us see how one emotion makes for and so is related to the others. Now, this emphasis on relatedness may be questioned; for it is simply not warranted by the evidence of actual (Hindustani) music. A good exposition of *rāga pūriyā* in terms of an aptly worded composition may well be able to create a semblance of *viyoga-śṛṅgāra* (or the grief of separation in love); but it cannot, without giving place to a quite different composition — say, a lively *dhamār* in *rāga hindol* — show a shift to the quite opposite emotion of *saṁyoga-śṛṅgāra* or the joy of reunion in love. Of course, in the region of our dances, where expression of emotions (as *nṛtya*) is a far more binding requirement than in the case of music, we may well be presented with a string of different emotions — say, in numbers like *navarasa-mālikā*. But even here we only *see that* one *rasa* is *followed by* another, may be without disturbing our relish; we do not *understand how an emotion directly* (*or necessarily*) *makes for the one that follows it.*

To redeem the balance, however, I must here admit that so far as the *expression* of emotions (as against an intelligible projection of their *interrelations*) is concerned, music *can be* an

79. Langer, *Problems of Art*, p. 93.

excellent vehicle, much better than ordinary language, as Langer would like to add. An instance would here help. Take the case of an experience of intense grief coming as a sequel to the sudden death of a loved one. It occurs, so to say, in the form of billows of sorrow that seem to well up and subside. The matter can surely be put in terms of words, as I am doing now. But no mere description in language as ordinarily used — that is, leaving out the way *a poet* may avail of words — can make one contemplate the rise and fall of poignant feeling as directly and convincingly as, say, the opening passages of *ālāpa* in *rāgas* like *pūriyā, jogiyā* and *sohnī* on the *vichittra vīṇā*. If we *speak* of the rise and fall of sad, intense feeling, because of the very *discursive* or before-after order of words as here used, the *cohesive* quality of the experience in question (or the sad intenseness of feeling as appearing incarnated in — and not merely as language makes it appear, that is, as related to, and so distinguishable from — the swell or subsidence of musical passages) is at once missed. On the other hand, the music I speak of here does not in any way loosen the singleness of the 'pattern of sentience' which (as Langer would say) it projects as semblance. Here, indeed, the significance (or expressiveness) of music is not 'logically discriminated' [or actively distinguished] but 'is felt [or intuitively seized] as a quality rather than recognised as a function.[80]

The crux of Langer's view

But the basic thesis of Langer, that music is necessarily a symbolic projection of the forms of feeling or sentience, is to me questionable. I propose to show this by paying close attention to some such expressions of her view as have not been considered fully or at all so far.

Take, for instance, the following passages which cover, if in brief, almost all the main points in Langer's philosophy of music:

> Music is 'significant form', and its significance is that of a symbol, a highly articulated sensuous object, which by

80. Langer, *Feeling and Form*, p. 32.

virtue of its dynamic structure can express the forms of vital experience which language is peculiarly unfit to convey. Feeling, life, motion and emotion constitute its import. . . . The basic concept [here] is the articulate but non-discursive form having import without conventional reference, and therefore presenting itself not as a symbol in the ordinary sense, but as a 'significant form', in which the factor of significance is not logically discriminated, but is felt as a quality rather than recognised as a function.[81]

If music has any significance; . . . [it has it] symbolically. [It is not usually] . . . the cause or the cure of feelings, but their *logical expression; . . . .*[82]

The tonal structures we call 'music' bear a close *logical similarity* to the *forms of human feeling* — forms of *growth and of attenuation, flowing and stowing, conflict and resolution, speed, arrest, terrific excitement, calm, or subtle activation and dreamy lapses* — not joy or sorrow perhaps, but the poignancy of either and both — the greatness and brevity and eternal passing of everything vitally felt. Such is the pattern, or logical form, of sentience; and the pattern of music is that same form *worked out* in *pure,* measured sound *and silence.* Music is a tonal analogue of emotive life.[83]

The essence of music . . . [is] a motion of *forms* that are not visible, but are given to the ear instead of the eye. . . . But in their motion nothing is removed. The realm in which tonal entities move is a realm of pure duration. . . . This duration . . . though it is an image of what might be called 'lived' or experienced time . . . is [yet] something radically different from the time in which our public and practical life proceeds. . . . [It] is measurable only in terms of sensibilities, tensions, and emotions; and it has not merely a different measure, but an altogether different structure from practical or scientific time.[84]

With an eye to clarity of treatment, I may now cull the main

---

81. Langer, *Feeling and Form*, p. 32.
82. Langer, *Philosophy in a New Key*, p. 218.
83. Langer, *Feeling and Form*, p. 27; all italics added.
84. *Ibid.*, pp. 107, 109.

points contained in the above extracts:

(*a*) Music is essentially a matter of *significant form*.

(*b*) The form (of music) is articulate, yet non-discursive; and the significance of this art is that of a symbol, not of a sign, symptom or stimulus.

(*c*) But, as a symbol, music is a 'sensuous object', and so quite different from language which is essentially an object of understanding.

(*d*) To the question, *what* is the significance (or import) of music, our answer may be: 'feeling, life, motion and emotion'.

(*e*) But *this* significance (of music), though it is symbolic (or semantic), is not logically discriminated; it is felt as a quality rather than recognised as a function. Here, a distinction has to be borne in mind. The way we *seize* the meaning of music is logical intuition; but the way feelings are *expressed* in music is 'logical'.

(*f*) Finally, music is essentially a matter of sonant forms that [appear to] move — in pure duration; and it is indeed its 'dynamic' tonal structures — which 'bear a close logical similarity to the forms of feeling' or 'vital experience' — that enable it to express our subjective life.

The points listed above do not include those which, though they occur in the four extracts cited on pp. 158-59, have already been discussed earlier.

Now, to turn to (*a*), we may focus on but one question. Why does Langer think it necessary to speak of *significance* in music? Why does she not prefer to discuss, say, the question of the beautiful in music? (Other cognate issues, namely, Langer's view of form, and of how musical form becomes significant, have already been attended to.) Here, as I set out to outline her argument by way of answering the questions posed, my reference will be mainly to *Philosophy in a New Key* (chapter VIII) where her aesthetics of music makes it first appearance, and to chapter III of *Feeling and Form* which explicitly approves of the thinking already done on the subject in the former work.

Langer begins by saying that the well-known thesis of Clive Bell and Roger Fry — the view that " 'Significant Form' is the one quality common to all works of visual art" — may be fairly extended to cover all art; for 'there is a strong tendency today to treat art as a significant phenomenon rather than as a pleasurable experience, a gratification of the senses'.[85] And it is easy to argue for this tendency. First, were art simply 'a direct sensuous pleasure' everybody could have appreciated 'great art', exactly as we all effortlessly enjoy 'cake or cocktails'. The fact, on the other hand, is that the 'uneducated masses' reveal a 'striking indifference . . . to artistic values', in spite of the fact that today they have a relatively easy access to the masterpieces of art (say, in galleries). Second, our leading artists of the day in all fields — 'in literature, music and the plastic arts' — do not seek mainly to cater to our senses, but to stimulate understanding. The use of 'ugliness' as an element of artistic expressiveness is quite common today. Music composers freely build upon dissonance which does not by itself fascinate the ear; and painters too include in their work figures (and shapes) that cannot be said to tickle the eye, Goya's *The Colossus* and Daumier's *The Witnesses* being two of the many obvious instances of the point. Picasso's *Guernica* is 'the mirror-image of a world of atrocity and bestiality from which it is man's duty to emerge';[86] and Osborne is surely justified in saying that to "apply the word 'pleasant' . . . [to it or to] Goya's *Disasters of War*, [would strike] one as wantonly irrelevant".[87] Thirdly, modern art freely uses symbols which are not to be sensed, but decoded, so to say. Therefore, art is not, in essence, a vehicle of direct sensuous pleasure. Rather,

---

85. Langer, *Philosophy in a New Key*, p. 205.
86. P. Daix, *Picasso*, p. 166.
87. H. Osborne, *The Art of Appreciation*, p. 41.

it is its significant form which lends to it its distinctive character, and separates it from everyday objects.

But what are we to understand by 'significant form'? For Bell, *form* means such a combination of lines and colours as is able to excite our aesthetic emotions, quite independently of the work's representational content; and Fry regards form — say, as found in a beautiful pot — as the 'harmony of line and texture, and color'.[88] Langer too, we have seen, looks on form as 'a whole resulting from the relation of mutually dependent factors . . . or more precisely, the way that whole is put together.[89] But, how is music (or any art) *significant*? Or what does it *mean*? We cannot accept the psychologists' answer that a work of art is significant as a 'symbol of loved objects, mainly, of course, of a forbidden nature' and, therefore, kept hidden in the unconscious; for it does not give us a criterion of artistic *excellence*. To explain *how*, or because of which particular drive, all art comes into being is one thing; to argue *why* this particular work is superior to that one (as art), is quite another.

Shall we then say that art is significant by virtue of its representational content, that is, because it makes us a little better aware of the intrinsic character of things, events and situations of everyday life? No, here too we cannot nod, because of at least three reasons. First, it is always a 'hopelessly entangled' task to determine what precise objects are represented by a work *and* to balance this exterior interest with attention to 'the visual or verbal structures' that we directly contemplate. Second, the representational theory of artistic significance does not fit music which is an essentially non-representational art. (It is true that, as in the singing of *dhruvapadiyās* and *khyāl*-singers like Pandit Jasraj, quite a few meaningful words may be there in the basic segments of the composition, say, *sthāyī* and *antarā*. But in neither case does the singer seek to make us really focus on facts meant by the words. Nor are we here required to judge the quality of music *mainly* by the criterion of due adaptation of the very manner

88. Langer, *Philosophy in a New Key*, p. 205.

89. Langer, *Problems of Art*, p. 16.

of singing to the meaning of words). Thirdly, it is the clear evidence of proper art contemplation and aesthetic experience that 'artistic meaning belongs to [though it cannot be said to be confined to] the sensuous construct as such; [and that] this alone is beautiful, and contains all that contributes to its beauty'.[90]

But, to confine ourselves to the work of art itself, could we say that it is its form alone — or its abstractable *design* — which makes a work significant? Here, again, we cannot answer affirmatively; for 'in poetry pure design is non-existent, and in the plastic arts it has played but a minor role until very recent times'.[91] The truth (according to Langer) is that the whole 'sensuous percept itself apart from what it ostensibly represents' is the locus of artistic meaning. From this point of view, musical works may be said to be meaningful in a way which is typical of all art.[92]

At the same time, we have to be clear about the *specific* way in which musical form becomes significant. Langer rightly says that music does not acquire meaning in the way of a sentence, the meaning of which is a mere sum of the independent, conventionally fixed meanings of the words it comprises. Whatever be the significance of a musical passage — say, its appearing markedly tender or majestic — it arises from the way the notes are put together, or (as Langer would say) from musical *form*; and, *I* would add, *from the way they are played or sung*. But, be it noted, this disposition of notes does not leave them as they are in their individual character. In our everyday use of language the order of words does not generally bring about any change in their individual meanings. The latter sure add up to the final meaning; but, in the process, they do not themselves undergo any change. In music, on the other hand, putting any two notes together is at once to make them look higher or lower, and so to invest them with a character which they do not originally possess in their

90. Langer, *Philosophy in a New Key*, p. 208.

91. *Ibid.*, pp. 208-9.

92. *Ibid.*, p. 209.

individual capacity. From this simple matter of detail it is an easy road to see the truth of Langer's remark that in musical form 'the sensuous character of each element is affected by its function in the complex whole'. In music, indeed, the ordering of notes is an *interplay* of elements. It is importantly in this sense that musical form is compact or non-discursive and becomes significant.

But if significance in music arises from its very form, that is, internally from the interplay of notes and not from any reference to things outside, two conclusions may be taken to follow: first, musical form must be said to be significant in itself; and, second, the significance in question cannot be said to be *meaning* as we commonly understand the word, that is, as verbal or conventionally appended to words, instead of being intrinsic to them. It is, in the main, its internality or deep embedment in its locus that prompts Langer to speak of the 'meaning' of music as its *import*,[93] though as (a kind of) meaning it is also (meant to be) conveyed . . . [or] made amenable to our understanding.[94]

Here, however, a note of caution is essential. The view that musical form is significant in itself should not be taken to suggest that it is similar to a self-complete, coherent fabric of *ideas*. Langer insists that musical form is 'a highly articulated *sensuous* object'. If this be true, and I see no reason to doubt it, seizing the significance of music cannot be utterly unlike perceiving the distinctive character of a physical object.

I have so far been using the words, *significance* and *meaning* interchangeably; but, as I now propose to argue, this assumed equivalence calls for some reflection. The commonly acknowledged meanings of *significance* are meaning, import, purpose, signification; and consequence, importance, impressiveness, relevance. Langer chooses to take 'significance' as *meaning*, and straightaway sets out to explain how exactly music could be said to be meaningful. Had she chosen to interpret *significance* as general importance (or consequence, value) the

93. Langer, *Problems of Art*, pp. 129, 134.

94. *Ibid.*, p. 60.

rasika could have easily explained that (for him) the value of music lies primarily in its ability to provide melodic *beauty* to the discerning ear, — a view which I propose to put forth and defend a little later. Instead, Langer takes significance (of music) in the *semantic* sense; and in so far as semantics is the science of the meaning of words which are mostly symbols, she is at once faced with the dual task of showing that music is meaningful *symbolically* and yet 'incommensurable' with language, because (besides other differences discussed earlier) whereas we can replace a set of words with a synonymous one from another language without any change or loss of meaning, *two different* music compositions (or works of art, quite generally) cannot have or express the *same* artistic meaning.

So, to separate art from language indeed makes sense. One may also accept, I repeat, Langer's negative thesis that the purpose of music is not to evoke emotions in the listener. There is indeed a good deal of Hindustani music which does not evoke any specific emotion in us, which we yet find generally agreeable, and admire simply because of its tunefulness, design, or fluency with clarity. Nor is it difficult to defend, we have seen, the view that music cannot be regarded as an expression or a symptom of the musician's own present emotions. Indeed, in essence, this art is neither the cause (evocator) of feelings nor their cure, say, by providing relief through discharge of repressed desires and impulses. But, I suggest, though all these negative emphases may be accepted, it would yet remain possible, with due reason, to disagree with Langer's positive thesis that the only important way to explain the significance that we find in music is to say that this art is a symbolic projection of the forms of feeling. I must, however, explain why I say so.

The value of music

An important argument that Langer advances in support of her basic thesis runs as follows:

> If music, patterned sound, had no other office than to

> stimulate and soothe our nerves, pleasing our ears as well-combined foods please our palates, it might be highly popular, but never culturally important. . . . Our interest in music arises from its intimate relation to the all-important life of feeling . . . to the pattern of sentience — the pattern of life itself, as it is felt and directly known.[95]

Here, the suggestion is that the only essential way in which music can be 'culturally important' is by projecting, and giving us an insight into, the life of feeling. But this is clearly open to question. How many lovers of the art would agree that music is good and culturally important *primarily* because it relates to feeling *in the way Langer thinks it does*? I am sure, very few. But most of us would readily accept Santayana's view that, being both evocative and expressive of emotional experience, music is 'appropriate to all intense occasions; we dance, pray and mourn to music'.[96]

This art is indeed more integral to an average man's way of life than any other art. Besides, music benefits those *rasika*s too who attend concerts more or less regularly, say, by generating in them a feeling of fellowship, and by making them see how a quite non-utilitarian concern with a created world of sound and silence can also be a locus of deep and suffusive delight. And, to speak quite generally, even a passing respite from the tensions of daily life is good for our mental health.

Here, it would be relevant to point out that Langer speaks of 'significance *in* music' not of the significance *of* music. The

---

95. Langer, *Feeling and Form*, pp. 28, 31.

96. G. Santayana, *The Life of Reason*, p. 319.

Langer could here rejoin that Santayana's remark only proves her point. Music is relevent to all 'intense occasions' precisely because it provides tonal analogues of the forms of the feelings that distinguish such occasions. Now, this may well be conceded. But it can still be contended that *all* music does not relate to the occasions in question; and that where it does not do so — as when, in a session of music, a vocalist aims only at singing very tunefully and correctly all along — the music may not show any semblance to what Langer speaks of as *forms* of feeling, and yet be culturally important because it gives the listeners a feeling of fellowship by letting them share a delightful aesthetic experience and some respite from everyday worries.

first way of putting the matter requires us to determine what is there *in music itself* which could be said to make the art significant, that is, worthy of consideration or important and and distinctive as an art; the second may be taken to enjoin that we discuss such questions as how music is *related and helpful to* our living in general and how it is important *for* those who create and contemplate music. The two ways are, of course, not unrelated to each other. As pointed out earlier, the very inherent power of music to express and evoke emotions at once makes it relevant to the *rasika* and to our life in general. But because Langer speaks of significance *in* music, we may focus on what makes the art intrinsically important. Further, in so far as she does not do so expressly, *we* may consider the significance of music not only from the viewpoint of the composer and the *rasika*, but from that of the performer too.

Now, to begin from the (Hindustani) composer's point of view, music is important to him because it gives him limitless freedom to create melodic forms which appear to be self-complete or even self-complet*ing* and which at once incarnate and articulate the *rāga* and the *tāla* in which they are framed. What the composer is here keen about is the form — that is, the inner unity and outer wholeness — of the composition (that is, the *sthāyī-antarā* complex) and proper projection of the *rāga-tāla* chosen. He is not at all concerned with — and may even be taken to be unaware of — what Langer speaks of as 'forms of feeling'. Differences in composition arise only from the style of the particular *gharānā* to which the composer belongs, and from his individual conception of the beauty of a *bandish.* They may also issue from the composer's view as to the role of words in a composition. Quite a few traditional composers prefer to eschew fullness of language and use words only to relieve, so to say, the flow of pure music. In every case, what the composer uses in creating a *bandish* is mainly his sense of musical form and not his *knowledge* of the life of feeling.

In some cases, the performing artist — say, a vocalist — may well be able to invest the composition with a tinge of feeling. But if this really happens, it will be the performer's doing in the main, and far less frequently the fulfilment of some inherent demand of the composition itself. So far as the *performer* — say, a singer — is concerned, music is of value to him, first, because it enables him to experience the delight or satisfaction of being able to perform an activity which he loves and has been trained for; and, second, because it is his chosen way of pleasing people and winning recognition. As for the *rasika*, music is important primarily because it can release him, for a while, from the yoke of everyday concerns and facilitate indwelling in the fascinating world of melody and rhythm. An occasional glimpse of feeling in the music may well move him deeply and elicit his spontaneous applause; but this is not what he expects all good music to provide unremittingly. His basic requirements rather are unfaltering sweetness of tone and steadiness of *laya* or aesthetic pace, and watchful adherence to the grammatical character of the *rāga* chosen for treatment.

Even apart from this variform evidence (seemingly unfavourable to Langer) from the regions of musical creation and contemplation, the orderly, audible and articulate world of melody and rhythm seems to be quite other than, if not intractably disjoined from, the seeming welter and formlessness of our subjective life. What could, then, be the possible ground of the relation which Langer envisages between the two worlds? She would say: it is, first, the imperfectly realised truth that the life of feeling is not formless; and, second, the fact that "the tonal structures we call 'music' bear a close logical similarity to the forms of human feeling . . ." [point (f)] on p. 160.

Tonal structures and 'forms of feeling'

Let us now see if these two emphases can bear scrutiny.

We may begin by reflecting on the key concepts involved: structure or pattern, logical similarity, and forms of human feeling; and then turn to see how, if at all, the tonal structures of music may be said to bear 'a close logical similarity to the forms of human feeling'. Now, as for the words, *structure* and *pattern*, they may both be taken to mean *arrangement.* Arrangement is disposition or ordering — as distinguished from mere lumpiness. It is necessarily a relatedness of distinct or distinguishable parts, aspects, or details. As for *logical* similarity, we have to interpret it essentially on the basis of what Langer generally means by the word *logical*. Now, where she speaks of *logical* intuition what she has avowedly in mind is the immediate perception of such *relations* as similarity, difference, relevance, congruity, and opposition.[97] Again, by *logical form* Langer requires us to understand a whole resulting from the *relation* of 'mutually dependent factors, or *more precisely*, the way that whole is put together'.[98] To put it simply, logical form is to be taken as the way in which the constituent factors of a whole are interrelated. It is, of course, not the same thing as material shape which is the most obvious meaning of *form*. Yet, the logical meaning of *form* is pretty close to its 'commonest, popular meaning', that is, 'just the shape of a thing'.[99] This may be brought out by reflecting on an example from everyday life which Langer herself uses.[100]

Suppose, while shopping, a person likes the shape of a particular lampshade, but not its size and colour; and so asks the shopkeeper to show him another piece *of the same shape*, but in a smaller size and lighter colour. The shopkeeper will easily understand what the customer wants, and may readily produce another piece of the desired character; but the understanding in question is possible only because both are able to abstract the concept of the shape in question from its embodiment in the first lampshade, and to find it incarnate in the second one. Neither person, here, has to *try* to make the abstraction in question; it takes place effortlessly. But, what is this shape as abstracted and rediscovered intuitively? It 'itself is not another thing';[101] it is rather a concept,[102] a more or less determinate understanding of 'the [similar] inter-relations

97. Langer, *Problems of Art*, p. 166.
98. *Ibid.*, p. 16.
99. *Ibid.*, p. 15.
100. *Ibid.*, p. 16.
101. *Ibid.*, p. 19.
102. *Ibid.*

among . . . [the] . . . various dimensions' of the two pieces. At the same time, it is not an *abstract* concept like 'abandon' or 'serenity'; for it signifies a relatedness between parts or details which are all quite *perceptible*. Yet this unique relatedness is to be called *logical* because it is not merely *seen* in the two lampshades severally, but is *apprehended* as something which is shared by them — partly by means of an act of abstraction which is, however, intuitive, not deliberate. Logical similarity may, therefore, be taken to mean similarity of (relational) structure.

It is important to mark that the forms of feeling of which Langer speaks also appear to have a relational form; for this is how she puts them: rise and fall ('growth', 'attenuation'), speed and coming to a halt ('arrest'), and 'calm' as opposed to 'terrific excitement' or to 'subtle activation'. Even 'poignancy' — of joy and sorrow — may be said to be relational in the sense that whatever is poignant is not only felt acutely, but *also* for only a brief while. My suggestion, here, is warranted by the following words in the last of the three extracts from which I culled points for individual study; 'poignancy . . . [that is,] the greatness *and brevity and eternal passing* of everything vitally felt'.

But, to turn now to the crucial question, how, (if at all) can music be said to work out, 'in *pure*, measured sound and silence', the pattern 'or logical forms of sentience', or the 'forms of human feeling'? Nobody will object to the suggestion that music builds upon 'sound and silence' in a measured way. But if the word 'pure' be taken to stand for wordless music, which can be singing too, as borne out by *ālāpa* of the *dhruvapad* manner (and by *many* of our *tarānās*)[103] — and, in the context of the specific art being discussed, I am not able to give any other, more essential meaning to' purity' — could we justifiably say that *all* such instrumental music as is commonly recognised as classical art projects what Langer calls the forms of feeling? I find it difficult to say *yes*; and what here prevents me from

103. Some *tarānās* use some words as well; hence, my words: 'many (not all) of our *tarānās*'.

giving an affirmative answer is my personal experience of listening to a fair amount of our classical music. But let me illustrate. As a *sitār* maestro, the late Mushtaq Ali Khan was an acknowledged representative of the famous Senia *gharānā*.[104] But even the most careful study of his way of playing the basic composition (or *gat*) could not reveal any trace of the rise and fall of feeling, or of calm as alternating with — or as simply capping — phrases of terrific excitement.[105]

But at this point it could perhaps be argued on behalf of Langer that the run of a *gat*[106] comes to a momentary pause at the *sama*;[107] and that the entire composition may, therefore, be said to project a semblance of the opposition (or relational form) of speed and arrest. But to this my rejoinder would readily be that, in the case of a *gat*, neither technically nor phenomenologically, can one speak of the *sama* as a point of *arrest*. From the viewpoint of musical grammar, the *sama* is the focal beat where one *āvṛtti* (or round) of rhythm not merely ends but, until the very final playing of the *gat*, another also begins there and then; and phenomenologically, if the *gat* is played with the requisite measure of structural unity and fluency, the *sama* appears to be the destiny, rather than an abrupt cessation (or *arrest*) of a seemingly self-propelling flow. Again, in the case of *tarānā* singing — which builds more upon mnemonic syllables than on words — the accepted criteria of evaluation *and* the singer's own cherished ideals are clarity, fluency, and tunefulness of utterance, as against emotive expressiveness, besides of course due observance of the requirements of *rāga* and *tāla*. Nobody here expects the singer to project any emotion. Langer may here point out that 'feeling'

---

104. A *gharānā* is a distinct school of music. Its core is generally provided by a single family. *Rasika*s identify a *gharānā* by marking its distinctive style. The maestro I here speak of was also a winner of the prestigious Sangeet Natak Akademi award for classical instrumental (Hindustani) music. He got the Award in 1968.

105. I say so after listening, very carefully, to quite a few of his recitals.

106. A *gat* is the basic composition in north Indian classical instrumental music.

107. *Sama* is the focal beat of a rhythm-cycle.

need not be identified with emotion, and that what *she* means by this word is not mere emotion but everything that may be felt.[108] But if we accept this extension of meaning, another problem would arise. On a slightly chilly morning the weather may well be felt as pleasant; but would it make sense to say that the experience in question involves an alternation of growth and attenuation, or of conflict and resolution? I do not deny that a clear semblance of what Langer speaks of as 'forms of feeling' can at times be evoked in music; and that such creative evocation is one of the accepted marks of excellence in music. But, however admirable it be, what is but episodic in music cannot be regarded as the very essence of this art. And to speak of art quite generally, there *are* some works, I repeat, that do not touch the 'life of feeling' at all.[109]

Nor can I accept the suggestion that sentience is always to be found in the form of a *pattern*. A sudden fright may for long abide in sentience *as a mere lump*, so to say; and where, because of an abrupt and passing lapse of memory, a young man delivering his first prepared speech experiences (at once) both an impulse to sink through the floor *and* an urge to somehow recall the missing words, the experience — as it directly feels and not as it is later analysed — cannot be said to be relational in form.

Cases of sentience *sans* pattern are, in fact, pretty easy to cite. Langer insists that even such cases of feeling as 'warmth, pinprick, ache, effort, and relaxation . . . have charateristic forms'.[110] But a pinprick generally lasts for a mere moment; and a headache may persist for quite sometime as simply a dull, inert pressure on the crown of head. In neither case is it possible to trace the presence of any *form of feeling*, because — upon her own view — a form is necessarily a complex of some details; and here, in the two instances of sentience we have taken, no details are distinguished.

---

108. Langer, *Problems of Art*, p. 15.

109. The reference, here, is to the essay, 'Hartshorne's Aesthetics', by Hospers, in *The Philosophy of Charles Hartshorne*, p. 128.

110. Langer, *Philosophical Sketches*, p. 16.

Is music essentially non-representational?

It would here be instructive to consider, first, why Langer puts so much emphasis on the tonal *structures* of music, as against its numberless *qualities* and its power to project verbal meaning; and, second, if this emphasis is justified. The basic reason seems to be that music is for her a non-representational art. But, I contend, if this view is accepted unreservedly, *all* singing that uses words will have to be ranked lower than instrumental music, because in music, as in everyday life, language is freely used to refer to facts, situations and happenings, and not only for expressing feelings and thoughts. From the traditional *Indian* point of view, on the other hand, vocal music is superior to instrumental (or pure) music, partly — yet importantly — because by using words set to music, which helps *attunement* by virtue of its tonal sweetness, one can easily imbue oneself with elevating thoughts and emotions, and so perhaps come a little closer to music's exalted purpose, that is, liberation of the spirit. This indeed is why, in India, great value is attached to *ārādhanātmaka dhruvapad*s and to *kīrtan* of the Sikh *rāgī*s.

Yet one cannot say, categorically, that meaningful language plays an equally vital role in every form of Hindustani classical vocal music. Where, for instance, the text of a *khyāl* speaks of the bridegroom who has come to wed a charming maiden,[111] neither the singer nor the *rasika* is expected to visualize the details of the situation meant by the words. Here, it would indeed be enough if the text in question evokes a gently festive mood. But in the case of *dhruvapad*s and *kīrtan* that I speak of, one is required to understand in detail the meaning of the text, and to even visualize the word-bound feelings and images. The need is perhaps more clearly seen in the singing of *kīrtan*. But let me explain why I say so.

The *dhruvapad*s I have mentioned are, of course, frankly

---

111. The reference, here, is to a composition in *rāga devagiri* the *sthāyī* of which runs thus: 'बना ब्याहन आयो, नीकी बनी के कारण'. It is a part of the repertoire of Professor L.K. Pandit, the present doyen of *khyāl gāyakī* of Gwalior *gharānā*.

devotional. Their aim is, on the one hand, to saturate the singer's mind with thoughts relating to prayer and devotion; and, on the other hand, to work up (for the *rasika*), a tranquil atmosphere. Improvisation, therefore, is here minimal. But there are quite a few such the *dhruvapads* too as speak only of valorous deeds and other purely secular matters, such as the delight of a *guru* on getting a good pupil. The music of the Sikh *rāgīs*, on the other hand, is (as a whole) all along devotional, though it too employs the *dhruvapad* form. It is further distinguished by a remarkable kind of composition in its repertoire, namely, *parhtāla*. A composition of this kind comprises some distinct segments of song set in *different* rhythm-cycles. And there is, I guess, a definite logic behind this structural device in the case of at least some *parhtālas*; and I may put it thus:

If, after a leisurely and more or less serene mention of God's many attributes, the text of the song suddenly changes into a joyous listing of the many ways in which His devotees have been helped in the past, would not the very principle of the integration of verbal meaning and pace of singing demand a ready, but well-managed shift, say, from the reposeful *savārī tāla* of 15 beats to *druta ektāla* comprising a rapid string of only 12 beats?[112] The aim of this thorough integration of the elements of music, I may add, is also to help the singer attune his mind better with the lofty import of the song.

Of course, the metaphysical view of the supreme end of music cannot be expected to find favour with aestheticians today. But singing which uses language can assist what Langer calls projection of the forms of feeling not only by virtue of the *meaning* of words utilised, but also because of the modulation of voice (as अकार, इकार, उकार) involved in the very utterance (Hindu, Urdu) words. To illustrate, where the text of a composition represents a devotee as yearning for the descent of His grace — say, in terms of the following words: दाता करम

112. This idea struck me after listening to the singing of the leading Sikh *rāgī* of today, Sardar Avatar Singh, at his residence (in South Extension, New Delhi) on 3.5.1995.

कीजे – the openness of the first word as pronounced (and sung as an ascent) may provide a foil to the 'closed' utterance of कीजे as a descending passage, and so strike us as a slight semblance of the surge and subsidence of a yearning. Langer herself seems to be quite alive to the value of the phonetic, as distinguished from the semantic aspect of words in music. Thus, see the following:

> Long or short vowels, open-mouthed and closed-mouthed ones, sharp or soft consonants, syllabic accents, and such formal similarities as alliteration, rhyme, and rhythmic analogy, which are rarely noted in talking, tend to be conspicuous. All these factors serve to shift interest from the literal content of words, the thing said, to the tonal form, the thing sung. Enunciation, originally intended to create words, now creates sonorities that are valued as ends rather than means. . . .[113]

Now, all that this extract says is seen to be true in the region of Hindustani music. But here, in the light of my experience as a *rasika* and critic, I would like to add that in a good composition the choice of words having a specific formal character *and of the way in which they are disposed* has to be made in such a way that, first, the form of the flow of music may not only be left undisturbed, but beautified; and, second, that all the formal factors involved may accord with, or even serve to project, the ideal and emotive significance of the words used. Let me bring out the point I am trying to make with the help of an example:

There is a *dhruvapad* song, set in *rāga bhairav*, which opens thus: हरि को नाम सुमिरन करो, सकल ताप नाम हरत

('Recite the Name of Hari, the Lord; this recitation relieves all suffering'). The notational form of this opening segment of the composition is as follows:

---

113. Langer, *Feeling and Form*, p. 142.

ध्रुपद (ध्रुवपद) राग – भैरव ताल – चौताल

A.	१	२	३	४	५	६	७	८	६	१०	११	१२
	सा	साध़	ध़	ध़	प	प	ग	म	रेग	ग	रे	सा
	ह	रिऽ	को	ना	ऽ	म	सु	मि	रऽ	न	क	रो
B.	सा	ध़	ध़	ध	सा	सा	ग	म	म	रे	रे	सा
	स	क	ल	ता	ऽ	प	ना	ऽ	म	ह	र	त

Here, we may note, it is A. which provides the opening line of the song. B. is the second segment; it builds upon lower notes of the scale, not going beyond *ma*. Yet it is this that I wish to focus on. Here, the *ordering* of the following words: नाम हरत is noteworthy. The open-mouthed utterance of नाम enables the singing to ascend as an unshackled meander, adding a little formal majesty to what the word signifies, that is, the Name of the Lord; and the *descent* which the word हरत describes provides a welcome parallel to the idea of *relieving* pain. On the other hand, if the two words are made to exchange places in the structural order — that is, if हरत is sung as an ascent (आरोह) and नाम as a descent (अवरोह) — there would, of course, be no loss of verbal meaning; but, aesthetically, the singing would suffer in two clear ways. First, the impact of the consonant र (in हरत) will tend to ruffle the flow of the ascent; and second, the singing of the word हरत as an *ascent* will clash with what it is supposed to mean in conjunction with the preceding words, that is, 'relieves pain', because the *removal* of pain is never visualised as an *ascent*. But the crucial point to be noted here is that if the words in question are sung in the proper order in relation to each other, and also — as the structure of the composition, in fact, demands — after the first line, हरि को नाम सुमिरन करो, the entire verbal complex as sung may well tend to imbue the mind of the singer with thoughts of faith in recitation of the Name and in God's redressive benevolence.

Music, pure duration, and 'lived' time

The ordering of *words* as agreeing with the flow of a particular *musical passage* is, however, a clear instance of the forming that distinguishes music; and it is surely proper to hold, as Langer does, that music is essentially (if not merely) a matter of moving *forms*. But what Langer says more in this context — about pure duration, in particular — provokes the following questions:

> What does it mean to say that musical forms move in *pure duration* which is none the less an image of lived time?
>
> Does it (yet) make sense to say that this duration is different in both measure and structure from 'lived' and scientific time?

Now, both questions may be answered by reflecting on the nature of movement in music and on the meaning of pure duration. Movement is here clearly virtual, a mere semblance or appearance. Actual movement involves a given path and something that traverses the path. In music, on the other hand, there is neither any set, given path nor any thing or person on the move. True, in actual singing, the voice may be said *to move across* a scale or a melodic plan (or *rāga*); but as a guide to music, and as providing some extent in a way, the virtual distance covered is never regarded as even or rough, or measurable in the way real paths are. Nor is an ascent (or *āroha*) in music the climb of an altitude. Notes or *svaras*, of course, appear to be high or low. But such differences are here marked by the ear, and not by any measuring rod or tape. Just as clear is the fact that notes and beats either occur at the same time *or* as a sequence. So the order may be said to be closer to time than to space in appearance. But the 'time' in which music may be said move is 'virtual' or pure duration. In so far as it is marked by simultaneity, abidance, and succession, it may well be regarded, as Langer says, as the image of 'lived' or experienced time; but its content is provided by tonal passages and rhythmic turns, not by actual happenings; and, therefore, because it is quite without the variegated filling of life — and because it builds upon nothing but sonant passages — the time that we see in music may be said to be 'pure'. Its otherness from the time that we experience in life is further argued by the fact that whereas the latter (or 'lived' time) is measured by clocks and passages in terms of equidistant ticks, the proper duration of a single *svara* or the right pace of a musical passage is determined by sensing, respectively, if the duration of the note in question gratifies the ear, and if the aesthetic pace of the passage allows the listener enough time to develop the requisite measure of deference, so to say, in moving towards the pivotal note of a *rāga*, like *gandhār* in *rāga darbārī*. It should now be easy to see why Langer says that musical time is measurable 'only in terms of sensibilities, tensions, and emotions'. If it be contended, here, that the beats in a rhythm-cycle occur at *mathematically* equal intervals, our answer would be that the precise pace at which they have *all* to move is yet determined by the musician's own judging if it suits the particular composition he is going to sing or play.

But the pivotal emphasis in Langer's theory of music — namely, her suggestion that music may be regarded as symbolic in significance — is, in my view, questionable; and it is this that I now propose to show at some length. I shall focus, in this context, on three main points; first, what may truly be regarded as the symbolic import of music ; second, the seizure of musical meaning by way of feeling, or as an act of intuition; and thirdly, music as a sensuous object in spite of its being symbolic in significance.

Is the import of music symbolic?

Now, as for the (symbolic) import of music, Langer believes it is provided by the following 'feeling, life, motion and emotion'.[114] She is, I may add, as emphatic on the manifestly dynamic look of music as about her thesis that what is expressed by this art is the pattern of our subjective life. Created or virtual motion, she believes,

> is the essence of music; a motion of forms that are not visible, but are given to the ear instead of the eye.[115]

---

114. Langer, *Feeling and Form*, p. 32.

115. *Ibid.*, p. 107.

The following utterance of hers is even more illustrative of the point I am seeking to make:

> Music flows: a melody moves; a succession of tones is heard as a progression . . . we hear marching, flowing or driving progressive motion.[116]

Its up-and-down contour, or the *āroha-avaroha* movement, is probably the only feature of music which strikes even the lay listeners. But, I ask, if motion in music is so apparent, how can it be said to be the import *of a symbol*, for the seizure of symbolic significance always calls for some effort or training on the part of the contemplator? Langer herself says:

> . . . sensitivity to the rightness and necessity of . . . musical forms is apt to be more . . . sure in persons of some artistic *training* than in those who have only a bowing acquaintance with the arts.[117]

Here, I realise, some attempt to meet my protest can perhaps be made by appealing to Langer's view that music is a presentational and not a discursive symbol. But to this I would rejoin that what she means by the presentational character of a symbol only is that the meaning here seems to inhere in, instead of being merely indicated by the symbol, *not* that the meaning of such a symbol is accessible to one and all. To speak generally, whatever be the region in which a symbol occurs, the arts or everyday discourse, its meaning or import (as a symbol) can never be *identified* with its merely sensuous appearance. Justice, for example, is not itself an evenly balanced pair of scales; nor is the meaning of a word identical with its appearance to the ear or the eye. Langer herself says that the symbol of sentience (here, music) is not the mere arrangement of tones, but *something new which emerges* from this arrangement.[118] But if that is so, one who perceives movement in music (only) as the before-after occurrence of notes cannot be said to be seizing the meaning of music *as art*,

116. Langer, *Problems of Art*, pp. 36-7.
117. Langer, *Feeling and Form*, p. 40; italics added.
118. *Ibid.*

because he does not attain to that emergent something which symbolizes sentience in Langer's view. I, therefore, repeat that just because it is directly accessible to one and all, *motion* in music cannot be regarded as the *symbolic* import of this art.

Intuitive seizure of music's import

But, other than motion, whatever be the import or significance of music, the way we seize it in actual contemplation is not that of logical discrimination, but an act of *intuition*. According to Langer, we have seen, it is *felt as a quality rather than recognised as a function*.[119] But for a clear understanding of this emphasis, as related to the other key concepts in Langer's view of music, we have to consider the words cited (in italics) in the light of their context in the text. They make the close of the first of the four extracts we have already cited (on pp. 158-59), — I mean those from which we culled points for individual discussion. It would help us here to recall the points made in that extract:

1. The basic concept of the 'special' theory of music, (first suggested in *Philosophy in a New Key* and approved and developed in *Feeling and Form*) is that of a form which is articulate, yet *not* discursive.

2. Such form has 'import without conventional reference', and so it cannot be called symbolic in the ordinary sense. It is not significant in the way of language. In other words, what it signifies is not *thought* to be meant by it, but is only *felt* as its inherent quality. Now, point (1.) is likely to appear questionable to many. How can an articulate form — that is, a relatedness of distinct or distinguish*able* details — be also *non*-discursive? Langer, I may add, also speaks of musical form, pretty freely, as logical (or relational). But a relation must relate at least two distinct terms; and if this is so, are we not compelled to say that a form which is relational as articulate — that is, as composed of recognisably distinct parts or details — cannot be *non*-discursive too?

Here, however, an answer may be developed by focusing

119. Langer, *Feeling and Form*, p. 32.

on the word *discursive*. Of all its various senses, *diffuse* seems to be the apt meaning in the present context; for that which Langer expressly opposes to artistic form is language *as ordinarily used*, and such language may well be said to be diffuse in the sense that the set, conventional meaning of the words it uses remains unaffected and unchanged. They are only juxtaposed, so to say; and the whole that they make is therefore loose, and no interplay of elements. The form of music, on the other hand, is not diffuse, *and so not discursive*. It *is* articulate, for the notes and beats that go to make it are (by and large) distinct, or at least distinguish*able*; but none of them can be said to have a set, independent meaning, much less to retain it in the flowing fabric of music. To say so is in no way discordant with the truth of relations. Of course, a relation cannot be except as a linkage between (at least) two *distinct* terms; but this admission does not bind us to say that in entering a relation the terms cannot both incur changes and yet remain distinct. What can tend to vitiate our thinking here is the image of two clear, but inert points linked by a straight line. But even a casual look at *human* relations in actual life is enough to make us see the truth and to vindicate the point I am seeking to make. The birth of a child transforms a couple into parents; the emergent relation does not let the two remain what they were before the happy event; but they sure do not become indistinguishable. So, I conclude, there is no oddity in Langer's view that the form of music is both articulate and *non-discursive*.

It is indeed the evidence of fact that, as in the case of a properly structured *bandish*, musical form is, on the one hand, not diffuse, but intense and coherent; and, on the other hand, not so dense as to look a mere lumpy mass. Further, as we noted in the first chapter, the *drut tāna* (or pacy pattern) of a *khyāl*-singer is, in principle, a compact knitwork of *svaras* that neither seem to be suppressed in, nor to jut out of the melodic run. Yet, if articulateness be taken to mean simply *the clarity of closely put individual notes*, a composition (or *bandish*) in Hindustani music cannot be said to be articulate *all along*, though it may, as a whole, be quite articulate in the other sense of being expressive (or revelatory) of the specific character of the chosen *rāga*. To lovers of Hindustani music it is a known fact that the कसी हुई (tight or unified) look of a good *sthāyī* often arises importantly, if not exclusively, from the use of little *mīṇḍs* (or glides), and that a glide does not *reveal* the notes it comprises as distinctly perceived — as distinguished from being (ideally) understandable — accents in the flow. The point may be clarified by considering those moments where *gāyakī* (or the idiom of singing) follows the *bīna aṅg* or the dominantly liquid manner of *vīṇā*- playing.[120] In respect of such passages, though a *rasika*'s निगाह (or trained intelligence) can surely apprehend *what* notes are being used, it is impossible *to point out* exactly where one note ends and the next one begins, except, of course, in the case of the opening and terminal *svaras*. And yet it is in such passages, *very satisfying* to the knowledgeable, that *the specific nature of a* rāga *as an organic unity is revealed.* The *vādī-saṁvādī* relation or the approach-phrase (पकड़ की तान) may well facilitate identification of the *rāga* being sung (or played); but the mere notice of such marks is as far removed from seeing a *rāga*'s whole-form as focusing on a mole — which may well help us in identifying a man — from a comprehensive awareness of what kind of a person he is. I may also here point to the difference between *our* being enabled to identify a *rāga* and a *rāga* revealing itself by means of its own inner dynamics.

But, to be sure, the 'liquid' passages I speak of are themselves parts of the total musical form; and, as wholes, they are also perceived (by the *rasika*) as quite distinct. So Langer's view that musical form is articulate in the sense that 'its internal structure is *given to our perception*',[121] has to be taken with two reservations. First, we have to remember that the structure in question is open to perception only in principle; that is, it *can be* perceived only by the knowledgeable. It is surely not (in fact) open to one and all. Second, the 'structure' has here to

120. I got this idea while listening (on phone) to a mellow, flowing *tāna* in *rāga hindol* during the course of a casual talk with Prof. L.K. Pandit on 5.1.1997.

121. Langer, *Feeling and Form*, p. 33.

be taken not only as the relation between individual notes, but between the different elements as well, some of which may not *project* the *svaras* they comprise.

It is also important to understand how the significance of (articulate) musical form may be simply felt, instead of being understood as the form's reference to something beyond its bounds. A simple example should here serve. When we are struck by the innocent look of a child, we neither miss any of its facial features nor confound them; yet we seize the 'innocence' directly and intuitively, and not by adding up the individual contribution of the different features to the overall look of innocence. The seizure of 'meaning' is here intuitive or non-analytical, but its 'expression', though unwilled, is the working of a collocation of details or features, and may, therefore, be said to be relational.

Symbols in art, like the lotus or the lily in a poem or painting, may well have to be *interpreted* as signifying — or functioning as symbols of — say, the purity of detachment or chastity. But the significance or character of music — its appearing to wear, we may say, a look of majesty or tenderness — does not have to be construed as something related to, and so incidentally distinguished from the music. It is indeed true that no logical discrimination is involved in seizing the import of music.

But, then, how is music's 'sensuous' form symbolic?

But, I ask, if this is so — and if, as Langer insists, musical form is a 'sensuous object' — why not say simply that the significance in question is a phenomenal *quality* of music, the semblance it wears — say, of robustness, gentility, or emotive expressiveness — by virtue of its own inner organisation? Why should we at all speak of the meaning of music as *the import of a symbol*? Here, again, the example I have already used should help. Where we feel fascinated by the 'cup of wonder' in an innocent-looking child's eyes, do we ever say (or think) that the visage, as it looks, symbolises the qualities in question? Here, in fact, were someone to ask us how exactly the perceived qualities are related to the face, we would never say they are symbolised by the face; we would prefer to say, quite naturally, that they are simply the clear look or expression of the face at the moment. Similarly, as really experienced, the sadness of (sad) music is inseparable from the music itself; in actual listening one does not even distinguish the two; so it would be better to speak of it as a (creatively evoked) felt *quality* of music than as its the *meaning* or *significance*. A quality may be said to be rooted in its bearer, if not entirely. A symbol only *means* what it signifies; the relation, here, is but ideal. So if, as Langer insists, " 'artistic meaning' *belongs to the sensuous construct* . . . [which] alone *is beautiful*, and contains all that contributes to its beauty",[122] the aesthetic character of a piece of music should be said to be its manifest quality, and not its meaning. Langer herself, we have seen, says that whatever it precisely be, the significance of music is felt as a *quality*.[123] A symbol is understood as having a meaning; and the act of understanding at once distinguishes, if not always clearly, the meaning from that which has it. A quality, contrarily, is sensed or intuited; and when it is actually sensed, it is not distinguished from the object to which it belongs.

An alternative: the beautiful in music

Further, and now I venture to suggest an alternative to Langer's view, where this quality is winsome, it may be said to be the *beauty* of the piece. Why I prefer the question, what is *beauty* in music, to the one that looks for 'significance in music' may now be explained. It is, of course, not easy to say what beauty really is. A widely accepted view is: beauty is a blend of unity and diversity. Another identifies beauty with expressiveness.[124] But neither of these answers is quite beyond question. A single, sweet *svara*, touched as a mere point, is

122. Langer, *Philosophy in a New Key*, p. 208; italics added.

123. Langer, *Feeling and Form*, p. 32.

124. L.A. Reid, *A Study in Aesthetics*, 43, 197.

often applauded as an accent of beauty; but it does not show any inner differences.[125] And, to take another instance, though it was surely a thing of beauty — because of its 'pulpy luminosity' and utter freedom from roughness, inner or edgewise — the *akāra* of the late Ustad Bade Ghulam Ali Khan could not be said to be essentially *expressive*. My own view is that *attractiveness, rather than expressiveness,* is an essential element of beauty. It would make perfect sense if I said that a *tāna* is beautiful because it is shapely, articulate, tuneful, and so admirable, *though it does not express any feeling*; but it would be meaningless if I said that the object before me is beautiful, *but I do not feel drawn towards it*. Proper integration of details or elements and expressiveness are, of course, potent factors that can make one feel drawn towards an object and so invest it with a touch of beauty; but they cannot be regarded as *essential* to beauty. Attractiveness, on the other hand, is always a key component of beauty, whatever be the particular locus of this value, — a figure, a work of art, or even a disciplined, self-effacing whole life of commitment. As compared to this point of very wide relevance, the thought that my proposal makes the nexus of beauty and love appear quite natural is but of secondary value.

As for the use of dissonance in music, I do not think our music needs it; and I can argue for my view. Why is the effective incorporation of 'the ugly' in music to be taken as a progressive step? Obviously, because of two reasons. First, it serves as a clear index of the composer's creative ability; and second, it is also a proof of the fact that music brooks no limits. But such reasoning can hardly be taken to make any point against Indian classical music which does not make use of dissonance even

125. See, here, the following:

"In some aesthetic objects the element of diversity appears to be almost absent, yet we may attribute to the object a high degree of aesthetic value. May not a diamond or a ruby be beautiful — but where is its complexity? Certain arias by Handel and Mozart consist of just a few tones; they are as simple as if any child could have written them, yet they are enduringly moving and memorable". Hospers: 'Hartshorne's Aesthetics', in *The Philosophy of Charles Hartshorne*, p. 128.

today. My argument, here, is not merely that the uniqueness of the art-forms of a particular culture has to be respected; and that, therefore, from the fact that dissonance is freely used in Western music it does not follow that Indian music too should fall in line. I would rather emphasize the point that the composer's creative competence and music's own limitless range — as indicated today in the West by incorporation of dissonance — are already both visible in our *rāga*-music. Every *rāga* permits an endless number of compositions; and our masters of music, therefore, choose to exercise their creative power in exploiting this intrinsic roominess of *rāga*s rather than in making use of dissonance.

'Illusions' in music and its 'great office'

No one who knows Indian music will question this. Yet the chapter cannot be allowed to end here, for our focus is on Langer; and in respect of *her* aesthetics of music, and of art in general, two points still remain to be clarified. First, what Langer speaks of as the primary illusion of music is not identical with what is (for her) the 'great office' of this art. This is an important distinction which is not always kept in mind. Secondly, Langer would like us to mark that though audible *passage* is the primary illusion of music, like any other work of art, a good music recital too can appear to be *substantial and individual* as well, though, of course, not in the way of articles and persons. Now, in respect of the first point, it is important to see the full significance of Langer's emphasis that time is the *primary illusion* of music.[126] In so far as it is an 'illusion', the time that we find in music is not the time of everyday life, but virtual time, — that is, just a semblance or created appearance of time. Langer takes pains to heighten the difference between musical time and lived time. But, on the other hand, because time (according to her) is the *primary* illusion of music, and because *such* an illusion (again, in her view) is all along present in the art which it distinguishes, the creation and development of 'the illusion of flowing time in its passage' may well be said to be the essential or necessary 'purpose of

126. Langer, *Mind — An Essay on Human Feeling*, vol. I, p. 201.

all musical labour, in thought or in physical activity'.[127] However, an essential pupose may not be a crowning one as well. Thus, though it is clearly an indispensable human purpose to make life liveable, the getting of a good dwelling and proper nourishment is obviously not our destiny. Similarly, though (in Langer's view) music just cannot be what it is without creating the illusion of flowing time, its 'great office' — that is, the purpose which makes music akin to all the other arts in respect of essential significance — is (for Langer) its ability to organise our conception of feeling into more than an occasional awareness of emotional storm, i.e., to give us an insight into what may truly be called 'the life of feeling', or the subjective unity of emperience.[128] *Every* work of art, according to Langer, 'presents *feeling* . . . [in the sense of] everything that can be felt, for our contemplation. . . . What is artistically good is whatever articulates and presents feeling *to our understanding*'.[129] True, like any other art, music (again, according to Langer) creates analogues of felt life; or, music does sound 'as feelings feel'.[130] But its creation is not a slavish and meaningless replication of the given; it serves the signal purpose of enabling us to *understand* the life of feeling.

Here, however, two questions would seem natural. How exactly does music achieve its 'great office'? And what is that kind of *understanding* which this particular art (or art in general) may be said to provide? Langer's answer to the first question is: by means of rhythm; that is, by so organising its (musical) content that the ending of one event may at once seem to be 'the preparation of a new' one.[131] And so she would like to settle the second question by saying that the insight which music provides is not the analytic understanding *why* one detail of music follows another, but the contemplative awareness *that* the sequence is there *and seems orderly*. What art enables us

127. Langer, *Feeling and Form*, p. 120.

128. *Ibid.*, p. 126.

129. Langer, *Problems of Art*, p. 25.

130. *Ibid.*, p. 26.

131. Langer, *Feeling and Form*, p. 126.

to do is to contemplate or follow intelligibly the course of 'the life of feeling' which, though it is commonly experienced, is not, as a rule, made an object of explicit attention. It is surely the evidence of actual musical listening that, provided our attitude is that of a *rasika,* we follow the run and the articulated details of the music discriminately. And such following may well be said to be *understanding* in the basic sense of grasping with the mind, as distinguished from mere listening on the one hand, and from deciphering the meaning of written or spoken word, on the other. In contemplating music, as we know, a *rasika* is clearly and directly aware of the distinct character of the elements and structure of the *rāga* and *tāla* built upon. This indeed is why the slightest deviation from their grammatical character strikes and even hurts him, so to say.

Music's substantial qualities

Yet the way I have so far presented Langer's aesthetics of music is open to a misunderstanding. The chapter opened with an account of her view that *passage* is the primary illusion of music; and in the para that precedes the present one I have just spoken of following the *run* of music. All this is likely to make us believe that music, according to Langer, is *nothing but* sonorous and orderly *flow*. This, however, is not the truth; and to redeem the balance I may now bring out how, in Langer's view, the qualities of substantiality, depth, unity, individuality or uniqueness, and the concept of organic or living form can all be said to relate to a musical work just as fairly as to creations in other arts; and how, even like emotion, all these qualities are here yet only virtual or created semblances. The point may be brought out as follows, essentially (but not entirely) in Langer's own way:

A substance is something that exists and is the bearer of qualities. It can be handled *and* its qualities make it useful. Poems and musical compositions are not handled and used the way things are. They are meant to be contemplated, understood, and relished. So (according to Langer) what makes a work of art appear substantial is only its '*semblance* of qualitative continua',[132] and complexity or 'interplay of identity and diversity of forms'. This is surely borne out by a careful look at Hindustani music. A good recital — say, by a vocalist like Pandit Bhimsen Joshi — *appears* substantial because of its rich filling of multiform *tāna*s (or patterns), all throwing into bolder relief the *sthāyī*'s steadfastness by virtue of their fluency and sweep. Yet, it is obvious, the singing is not substantial in the way of things which are solid and occupy measurable space. Depth too is a mere semblance here, evoked (in the main) again by the fullness of melodic content, steadiness of the *adagio ṭhekā*, and the *heightened* sedateness of the changeless *sthāyī* because of its interplay with winged configurations (or *tāna*s) of varying hue. It is surely not depth in the literal sense — depth as the state of being quite far from the surface. The look of *unity* is provided by the qualitative singleness of the *rāga* which characterises every exposition of our classical music. But the *singing* which projects the *rāga* and unfolds its distinctive character is never actually breathless. It is not merely that it cannot be so because of the physical limitations of the singer; rather, some actual discontinuity is desirable, because quite essential for aesthetic contemplation. *Tādātmya*, which the Indian theory of *rāsa* emphasises, is neither the inert coincidence of two points, nor akin to the seamless run of two parallel tracks, but (very clearly, in the case of music) a blend of recall, anticipation and filling-in along with keen attention to what is immediately presented to the ear (or to the eye or understanding in the case of other arts); and all these processes, which are involved in — and are vitally constitutive of — aesthetic contemplation, call for frequent, and regulated, yet *literal* breaks in the course of music. Even in daily life, I may add, we savour the bygones and 'pine for what is not' mostly in moments of silence; and in listening to music, as the vocalist relieves the singing of a *sthāyī* with intervening pauses of silence, allowing the *ṭhekā* to go on unimpeded, the *rasika* not only remembers but internalises the preceding phrase, and actively — and more or less determinately because of the foreknown form of the *rāga* — visualises the note or phrase to

132. Langer, *Mind — An Essay on Human Feeling*, vol. I, p. 206.

follow, deepening at once his own awareness of the aesthetic pace as marked by the drummer. Without these ideal acts on his part, the *rasika* will only have some impressions, not what Dewey calls 'an experience', the 'having' of which is no mere openness to an outer, orderly happening, but also *the owning of it all by the self.*

Nor is the unity of a recital *simple*. It is rather the result of a complex interplay of elements; and in *this* sense a 'living' or dynamic unity. I may explain the matter thus, largely in the way of Langer. When what meets the ear is the *antarā*, the *sthāyī* recedes into the margin of consciousness, so to say; but the latter, the opening line, is yet quietly remembered as the basic segment to which the *antarā* provides a clear counterpart. And even where a *tāna* (or pattern) characterised by intense inner filling (or 'over-determination') itself hastens the recession of other elements into the region of implicit awareness by virtue of its own quickening or gripping power (cathexsis),[133] the *rasika* surely does not forget the particular *rāga* the constituent *svaras* of which are only configured by the pattern in question, so that it (or the *tāna*) may at once be said to be within, *and* to vivify, the ambit or aesthetic potential of the *rāga*. The actual experience of listening to Hindustani music certainly bears out Langer's following remark:

> A good work of art presents itself as a matrix, from which all its sensuously given articulations are derived, while others which do not appear are none the less felt to lie somehow in limbo.[134]

The unity of musical form — illustrated

To make it a little clearer how exactly the form or unity of a musical work is a complex interplay of diverse elements, I may here analyse a composition sung by Ustad Iqbal Ahmed Khan, the present of doyen of the Delhi *gharānā* when his music was recorded by me for the Archives at the Sangeet Natak

133. Langer, *Mind — An Essay on Human Feeling*, p. 208.

134. *Ibid.*, p. 209.

Akademi.[135] The number I have in mind is the opening *khyāl*, 'जगत सपना री आली, काहे करत गुमान ('The world is ephemeral as a dream, dear friend. Why should you be proud — of what you are and what you have'?) in *rāga komala ṛṣabha āsāvarī*, set to *ekatāla* of 12 beats, and a well-known creation of the legendary composer, Sadārang. The *rāga* chosen is commonly regarded as fit to be sung in the morning, because it can serve as a good medium for the evocation of thoughts and images relating to religious elevation and detachment. Therefore, the moment the name of the *rāga* was divulged by the singer himself, fore-knowledge of its distinctive expressional character made *rasika*s in the studio look forward to effects of a particular kind. (This initial orientation of attention, we may note, facilitates the establishment of *tādātmya* — or imaginative identification with the aesthetic object — very clearly in the case of Indian music.) The notational form of the first line of the composition in question is as follows:

राग – कोमल श्रृषभ आसावरी

सारेमपध़,	(प)म	(ग)	रे रे	सा	रेनि़	सा(ग)रे	सा	नि़	ध़	ध़
जSSSS	SS	ग	S S	त	SS	सप	S	ना	S	S
सा सा।	ध़ ग	रे रे	म	(पम)ग	रे रे	सा।				
SS।	री S	S S	S	आ	S S	ली।				
सा	S	रे ग	रे सारे	(प)म	म	(म)प	S			
क	S	S S	र त	का	S S	हे	S			
सा	S	सारेमपध़	(धप)म	(पम)ग	ग	रे रे	सा	सा		
गु	S	मा SSSS	S S	S	S	S S	न	S		

Now, the singing of the very opening segment, जगत सपना री आली not only met the expectation, but gripped our attention, what by the flowing, mellifluous quality of singing and what by a deft employment of the principle of sound-sense harmony, — two admirable features, I may add, of Iqbal Ahmed's way of singing generally. But as it actually appears

135. On 22.4.1996, to be precise.

in the recording I am referring to, the principle in question is not a matter of simple one-one correspondence of individual melodic phrases with details of verbal meaning — as when the (Hindi equivalents of the) words, *thundering clouds*, may be sung vigorously in terms of the formal grace, *gamak* (as commonly understood) — but is essentially quite indirect. Some glimpses of obvious represen-tation are undoubtedly there. Thus, the opening ascent-descent passage, which projects the word *jagat* (world), may be said to signify the *whole* world in so far as it (the passage) both takes off from, and returns to the tonic. Further, the word *sapnā* (dream) is sung in terms of a *descending* passage which ends at the note ध in the *mandra;* and this (downward) manner may be taken to suggest the essential evanescence of a dream, just as the interrogative काहे (why) rightly consum-mates an *ascending* passage at प. But the quintessential *meaning* of the text — that is, the ephemerality of the world — appears as a *collected* look in the singing of the word गुमान, where the ध gently swinging towards the प — appears (but only appears) to lose colour in the process, just as the up-and-down and mellow flow of the melody looks like the quiet, running sadness accompanying contemplation of the fickleness of all that is. In short, if the singing in question impressed us as a compact wholeness, as it certainly did,[136] it was primarily becasue it was an exquisite integration of semantic values with some musical excellences such as mellowness and a flowing manner of utterance and an apt employment of ascending and descending passages.

Identical gestalts with unlike expressiveness

There is, however, a subtler way too in which the interplay of identity and diversity in 'the dialectical structure of the art symbol' can be brought out. Langer puts it thus:

> Especially the use of exactly the same gestalt in expressions of diametrically opposite feelings or impulses is a ready means of projecting that total qualitative dimension which

136. Be it noted that I am here speaking only of the opening stages of the recital in question.

> separates yet links its extreme degrees. The explicit image is of two particulars, but the whole gamut is implicitly presented so that they seem like selective realizations springing out of a matrix or body of potentialities.[137]

Now, luckily, I find it possible to illustrate how the same gestalt may be used to convey quite unlike, if not exactly 'opposite feelings or impulses'. There is a *dhruvapad* composition, set in *sūla tāla* and *bhairava rāga* the full text of which runs thus:

स्थायी :	प्रथम नाम लेत; शिव, शिव, शिव
अन्तरा :	विषयन को गरल साधो, नीलकंठ महादेव;
	ताप त्रिविध गुणातीत, देवन को देव, प्रथम. . .
आभोग :	डमरू तें नाद प्रगटे, आदि रूप सूत्रा निकसे ताल-अर्थ भेद उपजे
	शीश धरी गंगे, गंगे, गंगे; प्रथम. . .

The grammatical plan of this composition is as follows:

राग – भैरव ताल – सूल ताल

स्थाई

1	2	3	4	5	6	7	8	9	10
									नि़
									प्र
रे̱	-	सा	[ग]रे̱	ग	म	[ग]रे̱	-	सा	-
थ	ऽ	म	ना	ऽ	म	ले	ऽ	त	ऽ
×		०		२		३		०	
म	-	म	प	-	ध̱	[ध]नि	-	-	[सां]नि
शि	ऽ	व	शि	ऽ	व	शि	ऽ	ऽ	ऽ
×		०		२		३		०	
ध̱	-	प	-	[सा]ध̱	-	-	ध̱प	प	-
व	ऽ	ऽ	ऽ	शि	ऽ	ऽ	ऽऽ	व	ऽ
×		०		२		३		०	
म	-	रे̱म	-	-	मग	रे̱	-	सा	नि़
ऽ	ऽ	शिऽ	ऽ	ऽ	ऽऽ	व	ऽ	ऽ	प्र
×		०		२		३		०	

137. Langer, *Mind — An Essay on Human Feeling*, vol. I, p. 206.

अन्तरा

1	2	3	4	5	6	7	8	9	10
				म	म	प	प	[नि]धु	-
				वि	ष	य	न	को	ऽ
[नि]धु	[नि]धु	[नि]धु	धुसां	-	सां	सां	रें	रें	रें
ग	र	ल	साऽ	ऽ	धो	नी	ऽ	ल	क
-	रें	सां	रेंमं	–गं	रें	-	सां	नि	-
ण	ठ	म	हाऽ	ऽऽ	दे	ऽ	व	ता	ऽ
सां	रें	नि	सां	नि	धु	नि	धु	प	प
प	त्रि	वि	ध	गु	णा	ऽ	ती	ऽ	त
म	-	प	प	[ध]रें	-	सां	-	सां	नि़
दे	ऽ	व	न	को	ऽ	दे	ऽ	व	प्रं
×		०		२		३		०	

आभोग़

1	2	3	4	5	6	7	8	9	10
								म	प
								ड	म
ध	सां	-	[नि]धु	-	म	-	म	[ग]रें	[गा]रें
ऽ	रू	ऽ	से	ऽ	ना	ऽ	द	प्र	ग
सा	रें	रें	-	रें	रें	-	रें	रें	मंगं
टे	ऽ	आ	ऽ	दि	रू	ऽ	प	सू	ऽऽ
गंरें	रेंसां	सां	सां	सां	-	सां	सां	नि	सां
त्रऽ	निऽ	क	से	ता	ऽ	ल	अ	र	थ
धु	-	प	प	प	प	म	-	म	म
भे	ऽ	द	उ	प	जे	शी	ऽ	श	ध
प	धु	धु	सां	-	-	सां	सांनि	धु	-
री	ऽ	गं	ऽ	ऽ	ऽ	गे	ऽऽ	गं	ऽ
-	-	म	मग	रे	-	-	-	सा	नि़
ऽ	ऽ	गे	ऽऽ	गं	ऽ	ऽ	ऽ	गे	प्र
×		०		२		३		०	

Here, the opening line runs as follows: प्रथम नामलेत placing the *sama* at the letter थ which projects the *komal ṛṣabh*. It is an invocatory *dhruvapad* eulogising Lord Śiva and the value of the recitation of His Name. But what relates to the point I wish to clarify is the fact that in singing the following verbal complex: देवन को देव (after गुणातीत) the words को देव are first placed as रेंसां in the *tāra saptak,* to suggest *the thought of Lord Śiva's surpassing or transcendent divinity;* and that, immediately afterwards, exactly the same gestalt of *svaras* is used in singing the first word प्रथम, by way of returning to the *sama* at थ in *madhya saptak,* and evoking *the quite* different semblance of finding a haven, so to say, in recitation of the Holy Name.

What is more, the two figurations, though they are quite removed from each other by virtue of being located in different scales, do not in any way ruffle the oneness of the composition to which they belong, first, because of their parallel notational order; and second, because *this order* projects the character of the selfsame *rāga*. The look of the *rāga* — aided by the ceaseless nimble round of the rhythm-cycle (*sūla tāla*), keeps the 'qualitative dimension' of the composition unimpaired. What *strikes us* (or appears as 'the explicit image') is, of course, the distinctness of the two individual figurations, but they are quietly taken to articulate or spring out of the same matrix which, in the case of Indian music, may be taken as the composition set in a particular *rāga*. This also makes the total composition (in a *rāga*) appear not only as a settled matrix, but as a 'body of potentialities', exactly as a little peaceableness and a rising impulse to do one's best can both characterise the same living body at the same time.

Yet a musical work is not literally a body. If, in the region of Hindustani music, a *bandish* in *madhya laya jhap tāla* appears to be swinging, the swing is obviously not that of a suspended seat which can accommodate a person and which oscillates in actual space (or a झूला), but only of an ordering of tones and beats the measured repetition of which is accessible only to (or in) musical intelligence.

How is a work 'individual'?

A work's appearing *individual* too is not the same as a man's seeming to be so. Ordinarily, as signifying uniqueness, the character of individuality is taken as a work's being quite different from others. But, in actual fact — that is, as an object of aesthetic contemplation — a beautiful work may so impress us as to appear quite unique, though a cool and objective (or critical) look at it may later reveal that it is very similar to some other works. (Conversely, a table that we use everyday, but which is, on the whole, quite *unlike* many others of the same shape, may yet be dismissed as a mere oddity, instead of being *acclaimed* as unique). The uniqueness of a work of art is really a matter of its being internally rich, winsome in details, properly organised, and therefore striking; and there is indeed eminent sense in Langer's following remark:

> The individuality of a work of art is not a factual condition but a quality, as virtual as all other artistic qualities. It is the semblance of organism that creates the apparent uniqueness of a piece. The work seems unique when it is 'alive', i.e., expressive.[138]

What needs some comment here is only the close of the extract cited. For Langer, a work of art is essentially expressive in the basic sense that it is expressive of the *organic character* of life, and may *therefore* be said to be 'alive'. This may be questioned, for 'life' and 'organic character' can both be interpreted variously. But the other emphasis, that a work's individuality is a virtual quality, can be easily verified in the light of our experience of listening to Hindustani music. The several expositions of a particular *rāga* — projecting, may be, the same composition by an eminent Hindustani musician on different occasions — may not show any marked differences; yet each recital may appear unique because of its compelling appeal arising, in the main, from its integrated quality, besides of course its meticulous conformity with the technical requirements of, say, *rāga*, *tāla* and *svara*.

Artistic form as vital, organic

I may turn now to the one remaining question. How can artistic form be likened to vital or organic form. Langer answers this question variously, in terms of remarks which are not equally convincing. To provide a balanced account of the matter I think it necessary to pick for reflection some such utterances

138. Langer, *Mind — An Essay on Human Feeling*, Vol. I, p. 209.

from her works as appear acceptable, on the whole.

Consider, to begin with, the following:

> In a work of art, however modest, *the peculiar character of life* is always reflected in the fact that it has no parts which keep their *qualitative identity* in isolation.[139]

> Elements in art have not the character of things, but of acts . . . not acts in the dramatic sense nor . . . [as] moral acts . . . [but as units] of activity . . . [we may say; so,] once an element is created, it influences the entire work.[140]

I may now explain the above in terms of individual points:

First, 'the peculiar character (or the essence) of life, according to Langer, is not movement, [141] but interrelation of the contents of awareness, experience and behaviour. When a person is suddenly lifted from moroseness into cheer by the fleeting thought of something pleasant to be done a moment later, there is no movement (as ordinarily understood) but only a change caused by the openness of a present mental state to the influx of some new thought; and the change certainly makes the person involved feel alive. Movement, for Langer, is just a requisite of the primary illusion *of music*, that is, time.[142]

Second, it is to be noted that Langer here speaks of qualitative, not of *numerical*, identity. A man's getting up in the morning is, of course, likely to remain always the *first* thing that he does in the day; but its qualitative identity — that is, how it really feels to arise after a night's rest will in every case be determined by, and often vary in accordance with how he has slept in the night and what he is looking forward to in the day. A similar interdependence distinguishes the 'parts' of music which may be actual or virtual. The individual *svaras* and their combinations are all actual parts.

---

139. Langer, *Mind — An Essay on Human Feeling*, Vol. I., p. 200; emphases added.

140. *Ibid.*, p. 202.

141. Here Langer disagrees with Ernst Toch. *Ibid.*, 201.

142. Langer, *Mind — An Essay on Human Feeling*, Vol. I., p. 201.

But the elements which may be created by such combinations — or by figures — are *virtual* constituents. As for the 'actual' parts of music, it is easy to show how they are all inseparable from the whole. Taken in the abstract, or as merely notated, *svaras* that make a *rāga* are the mere *material* of music. As used in a composition, played or sung, they are all *parts*. But here, in actual music, a *re* is inseparable from *sa* and *ga*; and all these notes are related to the *bandish* too. When they combine to *create* semblances — that is, something which is here not to be found as it may actually occur in real life, say, ascent and descent, robustness and gentility of touch, or advance and recoil — they are elements; and they are 'inalienable from the whole'.

Thirdly, and this is a clear index of the complexity of interrelationship that holds the details of a musical work as one,

> no analysis can uncover a simple and direct relation of an element to the work as a whole. Its relations are with other elements, and are internal to these and to itself, that is, constitutive of the elements which are related. One may trace the relations of an element in many directions. . . [But] one . . . [can never] trace the relations of an element . . . to a limit . . .[143]

This, I believe, can be easily illustrated.

In a music recital every element *is* of course related to the entire work, but it is not related to the latter directly. Its character as an element is related to, and determined by, other elements that precede and follow it. For instance, the appearance that the *sthāyī* has come to 'establish' itself arises partly from a steadfast playing of the 'accompanying' *ṭhekā*; it is vivified by its contrast with the *antarā*; and is further heightened when it recurs after the execution of one or two fluent *tānas*, whereupon it comes to appear as the anchor of the entire singing..It is in this way of unceasing relatedness and transformation in appearance that the *sthāyī* is related to

143. Langer, *Mind — An Essay on Human Feeling*, Vol.I, p. 200.

the whole work. What is more, in so far as the variety of *tānas* is, in principle, limitless — in respect of pace, intonation, and configuration — the ways too in which the first line will 'appear' cannot be limited. Even that segment of the *sthāyī*, which is known as **पकड़ की तान** or *āmad* can serve as an illustration of the point just made. It freely assumes *different* appearances because of its varying relation, say, to the focal beat and *tānas*. As it arises and moves towards the *sama*, it appears as the take-off of an oriented segment, quite clearly if it runs as an ascent; but when it attains to the *sama*, it strikes us as the due completion of the passage known as *sthāyī*. Further, when it reappears, say, after a spell of *drut* pattern-weaving, it tends to look like an overall slowing of music, though there is no actual deceleration of the basic pace as marked by the drummer. The point which Langer here emphasizes is that *art* may be said to express the character of *life* primarily because both are marked by an extreme internality of relations (respectively) between the 'act-like' elements and everyday acts.[144]

Here, of course, a question may be put. Does music, like all the other arts, express the 'forms of feeling' (as is Langer's dominant view) *or* 'the character of life'? However, the question, it appears, admits of a ready answer; and one could put it thus:

The 'or' in the question is perhaps improper. Nothing compels us to choose the concept of 'forms of feeling' and to reject the concept of 'character of life'. For if, as Langer suggests, the 'character of life' be taken to mean that nothing in life retains its identity in absolute isolation, 'forms of feeling' may also be said to partake of the character of life in so far as they too are indivisible from the rest of life. After all, forms of feeling, like 'rise and fall' and 'flowing and stowing' do not occur in isolation. They are forms of joy or sorrow, or of anger or hatred. The surge and subsidence of sorrow is felt as something quite distinct from our experience of the rise and ebb of happy feeling; that is, in either case what Langer calls

144. Langer, *Mind — An Essay on Human Feeling*, Vol.I, p. 202.

'a form of feeling' is necessarily coloured by its wider affective context.

Art-elements and life-acts anew

What I have just spoken of is a familiar experience. But the *parallel* which Langer draws between elements and acts has to be brought out at some length. Her argument, here, is that

> [Just as] every act is motivated by a complex of past and/or concomitant acts, and motivates a great number of other acts, among which there are usually some that belong to its own motivating context[145] . . . [similarly] once an element is created it influences the entire work;[146] [and this is why] turns of phrase . . . [chosen by musicians and *rasikas*] . . . support the finding that the dynamic structure of elements in art is cognate to that of acts in physical organisms. . . .
>
> [Further,] all distinguishable aspects of the created work . . . have formal properties which, in nature, characterise acts . . . [namely], inviolability, fusibility, . . . the revivable retention of past phases in succeeding ones . . . [and quite importantly] the relationship of elements to the whole, which is very complex, so that it is ordinarily not possible to designate it as a single relation.
>
> [What is more,] every element seems to emanate from the context in which it exists. . . [This is true of every created element, such as] tension, gestalt, contrast, accent, rhythm or any that one may select . . . whichever one attends to carves out a context that is indispensable to its existence. This is, of course, a manifestation of the internality of relations *among created forms* [emphasis added], which is a principle of art, not of life. But it parallels a biological condition: [namely, the determination of present acts by past ones, and the former's influence in shaping the acts to come].[147]

There is a good deal in Langer's above-mentioned views that

145. Langer, *Mind — An Essay on Human Feeling*, Vol.I, p. 204.

146. *Ibid.*, p. 202.

147. *Ibid.*, p. 204.

calls for some explanation and is perhaps also open to some criticism. Both ends may be met by reflecting as under:

(a) That acts may determine each other is easy to illustrate. The act of nodding (in agreement) expresses or is determined by an immediately preceding or concomitant act of understanding. But nodding as intelligent also facilitates or determines a further looking forward-to. However, as a getting set to listen to what the talker has to say, such a qualitatively identical orientation of attention has probably also determined the act of nodding itself. This is why it seems fair to say that 'an organism is made up of its own acts, and at the same time is the source of all its acts'.[148] Exactly in the same way, Langer would add, 'every element [in art] seems to emanate from the context in which it exists', and determines other acts.

To me, however, it seems a bit too sweeping to say that *every* act is determined by and itself (directly) determines some other acts. Take, for instance, the case of a man crying out of grief. It is clearly an act, but what precedes and accompanies it may be simply the experience of the emotion of grief, and no *act* as such, it being obvious that changes like those of blood pressure, heart-beat and fainting cannot be regarded as acts. Further, what follows the act of giving vent to grief may only be the torpor of exhaustion, and no act at all.

(b) To turn, now, to the art of music, its more important elements — all alike the result of creative handling — are admittedly tension, gestalt, contrast, accent, and rhythm. And these are all easily traceable in Hindustani music. Tension is here seen as the dynamic orientation of a tonal or rhythmic passage towards the *sama*, specially if the latter, the focal beat, is to occur at a higher note (say the *tāra sa* of the scale). Gestalt, as an organised whole or pattern, is present as in a shapely *sthāyī* or *tāna*. The element of contrast is provided, quite clearly, by a simple *āroha-avaroha tāna*. Accent may occur as emphasis on the point from where the passage to the *sama* begins or as an immaculate touch at the *tāra sa* as the end-point of a passage.

148. Langer, *Mind — An Essay on Human Feeling*, Vol.I., p. 204.

What Langer would like us to mark, however, is that the elements we have distinguished are all intimately related to their context. Now, in our music this context is both overall and implicit, and immediate and manifest. The twosome of the *rāga-tāla* chosen for treatment is context of the former kind; and notes that immediately precede and follow a *svara* or phrase, context of the latter kind. In fact, the character of every note arises from — and is perceived in relation to — the context of adjacent notes. One cannot just perceive a note as *ga* or *ma* unless it is necessarily, if quietly, adjudged in relation to its neighbours. The note itself may be said to *demand* this (implicit) relating, if it is to manifest its precise character accurately. This is what Langer probably means by saying that 'whichever [created element] one attends to *carves out* a context that is indispensable to its existence'[149] as something possessed of a distinct character. However, an element '*seems to emanate* [*manifestly*] *from* the context in which it exists' only where no moment of literal silence immediately precedes it *and* if the passage from the context to the element in question is marked by a slight and gradual rise in volume.

All this makes it clear that in a work of art (or of music) all the elements (or created forms) are held as one by internal relations, that is, by relations which not only fall between, but also (in a measure) make the terms.

(c) But there are other *specific* similarities as well between acts and 'all distinguishable aspects of the created work'[150]. . . [say, the] 'formal properties' of 'inviolability, fusibility . . . [and] the revivable retention of past phases in succeeding ones'.[151] An act is inviolable in the sense that, if normal living is to continue, it *should not* be cut away from other acts which precede or follow it. It is marked by fusibility in so far as one's past experience of performing a particular task may quietly melt into, and lend added efficiency to its present doing. Incidentally, all these formal properties are but

149. Langer, *Mind — An Essay on Human Feeling*, Vol.I, p. 204; emphasis added.

150. *Ibid.*

151. *Ibid.*

individual instances of the basic truth of 'internal' relatedness; and all of them are easily traceable in the region of music. No element, here, can afford to stray from the specific technical fabric of the *rāga*. In a *mīṇḍa* different notes are actually seen to melt into each other, producing a quite distinct effect; and, of course, the appearance or perception of a *sthāyī* or a pattern as an ordered unity is possible importantly because the *svaras* which are outgone by the flow are all retained in memory. However, the unity of elements in art is only similar to, not identical with, the unity of acts in life. The former alone is a singleness of *created forms*.

Yet a work of art's unity is *quite as deep* as of acts in life.

> [Whereas] a figure may be transposed, inverted, enlarged and if it is at all elaborate, even fragmented, the *elements* created by means of it cannot. They can only reflect each other, enhance or otherwise modify each other, even seem to spring from one another. Their indivisible and inexhaustible character, due to the internality of all their relations, is what makes them expressive of life, even more than the fact that they assure movement . . .[152]

Two points are here made: first, that elements in music are created by means of figures; and, second, that whereas a figure may be transposed, inverted, enlarged and fragmented, an element is open *not* to *such* changes, but to some quite different ones. What is possible in the case of elements is that they may reflect, enhance or otherwise modify each other, say, by providing a parallel or foil. But all this has to be clarified. I may do it thus:

A figure (in music) is a characteristic short pattern of notes — characteristic of the *rāga* chosen, *we* may say. In *rāga lalit*, for example, ग म मं is a clear figure. It admits of transposition, for it can be played or sung in different *saptaks*; it can be inverted too, as मं म ग. And the two dispositions of the figure sung as one, can also be enlarged, by linking them with the prefatory phrase, नि़ रे़ ग. Fragmentation too would here be

152. Langer, *Mind — An Essay on Human Feeling*, Vol.I, p. 201; emphasis added.

possible, for the three constituent notes may be played (or sung) as a succession of separate notes. But if it is made to create an element — say, the suggestion of such a liquid continuity embracing three quite adjacent notes as appears to rise and recede effortlessly — it would be indivisible, for the effort to divide would at once disrupt the continuity.

However, not merely the (created) element of *continuity*, but all other ones — such as those of restfulness or meteoric ascent, upgathering or droop, meander or vigorous projection — resist fragmentation. It may here be pointed out that what Langer denies to elements is only *fragmentation, not transposition, enlargement,* etc. The truth indeed is that the elements *we* have listed can all be created in different scales, and so transposed; and if, as Langer herself admits, they can enhance — that is, augment or reinforce — each other, they may also be said to admit of enlargement. What is more, if their character is 'inexhaustible' it is so, again in Langer's own view, because they are internally related to changes in context. In this respect too, the elements may be said to be open to enlargement.

But how exactly is the character of elements 'indivisible and inexhaustible' because of 'the internality of all their relations'? The question may be answered by referring to an instance of 'transformation' in music which I took in the first chapter, namely, the *tāra r̥ṣabha* (in *rāga sohnī*) so sung as to create a semblance of distance. However striking and undivided it may seem to be from the outside, the semblance in question is internally related — because it owes its distinctive character to at least three factors, say, the following: its placement in the *tāra*, its subtle regulation of the inequal abidance of voice at the two *svaras*, and, of course, the specific *rāga* which it vivifies. It is this inner relatedness which really *makes* the illusory element in question what it presently is. And it is indivisible in the sense that we cannot determine the precise contribution of each determinant to the whole semblance.

Dialectic, phase principle, and a work's unity

But, whatever we have said so far about the unity of a work of art does not exhaust Langer's thinking on the subject. She adds that

> the unity of a work of art . . . [though it] stems primarily from the interdependence of its elements . . . is further secured by . . . [the] dialectical pattern of their relations. The principle of dialectic [here] is a phase principle, the consummation of one phase is the preparation for another, which in its own consummation prepares its successor, often a replica of the predecessor.[153]

This, again, is rich in meaning which may be brought out thus:

The unity of a work of art is not readymade; it comes into being as the result of a creative process. This process is by no means random. It follows an intelligible order, a phase principle, as Langer would have us believe; and is in this sense dialectical. A phase is a distinct period or stage in a process of change or development; and the dialectic that both determines the growth of a work of art and unifies its different stages consists in this that, in its very consummation, a phase paves the way to the one that follows.

Here, with a view to providing a link between Langer's present emphasis and her other view, to be discussed a little later, that the *time* taken by the growth of an organism and its parts determines their *form* noticeably, I may point out that the concept of phase necessarily involves the idea of some abidance in time. A phase is not a mere moment; it is rather an identifiable portion of a process, flow, or growth of some sort; and it *retains* its character *for a while*.

Now, if they are thus interpreted, phases are clearly traceable in Hindustani music. Take, for instance, the case of a *vilambit sthāyī*. In respect of this detail of adagio singing the language that we commonly use for description is: *sthāyī jamānā* or *sthāyī-bharnā*. Now, the first end — that is, of making the line look 'established' — is achieved only if it is sung *more*

153. Langer, *Mind — An Essay on Human Feeling*, Vol. I., p. 204.

than once, and in a manifestly reposeful way. The other purpose, of making the *sthāyī* appear filled-up or unbroken on the inside, is served by using *mīṇḍs* and a dominantly *flowing* manner with a *lesiurely* look.[154] When this phase of singing is completed, or rather consummated, the *antarā* is called for; and the wholeness of *sthāyī-antarā* interlacement paves the way to subsequent stages of singing like *barhat* and *tānas*. Two or three *tānas*, again, call for a repeat of the *sthāyī*; and *vilambit* singing, as a whole, clears the ground for *drut* singing.

Further, the unity of a work is (for Langer) not only intense, but organic in a way. In this context, she builds upon some morphological studies of organisms which make it clear that

> the time element, which is implicit in the idea of *growth* can . . . very seldom . . . be wholly neglected in our consideration of form. [Not only does the whole organism grow at an] average or aggregate rate, [but there is] a *gradation* of rate from one part to another. [Further, the specific characteristics of each organ are determined by the rate at which it grows; and, what is more, if there is] the least change in the ratio, one to another, of these partial or localised rates of growth, . . . striking differences of form — [begin to manifest themselves].[155]

Now, it is easy to trace parallels of such facts in the region of our music. If a *vilambit* composition appears to unfold its form and to wear a tranquil look, it is primarily because of the pace at which it is sung. Just as clearly, a *drut* composition looks lively and compact in form — and so both engaging and easy to seize — because of its nimble gait. Further, if because of his penchant for fluent singing, a young vocalist does not give enough time to the *sthāyī-antarā* two-in-one of the *vilambit* composition, and switches over to a *drut* one a bit too early, the *form* of the slower composition will not appear to have been properly 'established'; and, correspondingly, the overall

154. The reference, here, is to my essay on Prof. L.K. Pandit, entitled 'The Master of Gwalior' in *The Pioneer* of 11.7. 1996.

155. Langer, *Mind — An Essay on Human Feeling*, Vol. I, p. 211. I may add that the extract, as cited here, diverges from the order of its words in the source.

structure of the whole recital will suffer, because the (imperfectly) accomplished relief of the *drut* composition against the *vilambit* one would lack the requisite sharpness. Quite generally, the form of any *bandish* flowers only at a specific pace, which is why every vocalist prefers only that *tablā* accompanist who is not merely generally conversant with the different rhythm-cycles, but is familiar with the precise pace demanded by the composition chosen for singing, by virtue of past experience of 'accompanying' the particular vocalist.

Virtual time (or growth) in music and in non-occurrent arts

At this point, however, two questions may be put. First, how is the pace or time I have just spoken of *virtual*, as it really is in music, according to Langer? Secondly, how is all this talk of growth in time relevant to, say, poetry, painting and sculpture, — that is, to arts which are not occurrent? Of these two questions, the first is quite to easy to answer, say, as follows. Whereas the pace at which the parts of an organism develop is *determined by nature*, the tempo of a musical passage is creatively *regulated by the musician himself*. Allied to this is the other difference that whereas changes in organic structure are *not intended* by any one, but simply appear along with the process (and pace) of growth, emergence of a particular kind of *form is consciously aimed at* by the musician in regulating the pace of music.

The second question has to be answered more carefully, specially in view of Langer's categorical emphasis that

> the semblance of constant becoming . . . belongs in some measure to *all* good art work and in a high degree to its really great products.[156]

How exactly is 'becoming' present in the plastic arts? A musical work is largely a matter of passages, leisurely or quick; and, what is more, we can easily distinguish the moment when a recital opens from its finale. So, though the (period of) time in

156. Langer, *Mind — An Essay on Human Feeling*, Vol. I, p. 212, Italics added.

which a recital completes itself is not the same as the time that we see *in* music, a temporal ingredient is here clearly present. On the other hand, a painting or a building is not ordinarily seen in the process of being made. So here a semblance of becoming has to be created quite without any actual temporal ingredient. How can this be done? It would not serve as an explanation to say that the suggestion of becoming arises (in the case of non-occurrent arts) from the time that *we* may take in *coming to see* the subtler details of a work; for (according to Langer) artistic import may well be seized by a *rasika* intuitively, that is, through the very first application of attention. Nor would it do to say that old figures — say, in a representational painting — may convey the feeling that someone *has advanced* in years, for a painting may be quite non-figurative. The true explanation, according to Langer, is the following:

> The sense of becoming, i.e., of process, is symbolically rendered very largely by gradients of apparent completeness among elements so related to each other that they possess a visual unity and make a forcible impression of evolution from the slightest to the richest articulation of volume, line, surface and implied inner tensities.[157]

(a) This extract, it is clear, is about the visual arts. But the emphasis it puts on gradients may be taken to relate to art in general. Langer, in fact, insists that 'gradients of all sorts . . . permeate (or run through) *all* artistic structure'. So, the word *gradient* has to be taken in a sense that may make it applicable to all the arts. Now, as acclivity or declivity — or as rise and (a kind of) slope — the word in question would appear to relate naturally to music *alone* which cannot work except through ascent and descent. So we have to take the word in question in the other sense of *stage* or *step* which, however, includes ascent and descent because they both are conducive to (and so are stages in) the development of a musical work.

(b) But what are the different kinds of gradients of which Langer speaks and which lend a semblance of growing

---

157. Langer, *Mind — An Essay on Human Feeling*, Vol. I, p. 212.

significance to a work in aesthetic contemplation? They are, in her view, grades 'of relative clarity, complexity, tempo, intensity of feeling, interest'. The most obvious gradients are, of course, the geometric ones. In a painting, for instance, the *central* position of a figure and the direction at it of the looks of other figures may *make for* the cohesiveness of the whole work quite visibly.

The other gradients we have listed can all be easily identified in the region of our music. *Tānas* of varying pace and complexity heighten each other's distinctness, and so make for the articulate richness of the whole recital. They also make the recital appear *to gain in musical filling*. Again, extra-fluent *tānas* may not be as clear in their *dānā* as the *madhya laya* ones; but the former may yet be of help in making the latter look a little more reposeful than they would on their own.

Intensity of feeling or interest may be manifest, as attunement with the act of singing, right at the beginning of a recital. The vocalist, here, may seem to breathe life into the very opening utterance. This is what Langer may be taken to mean by her remark that the 'promise' of the 'all-important character' of 'livingness' or expressiveness may sometimes be 'evident from the beginning'.[158]

But how are we to relate to the art of music Langer's emphasis that the semblance of becoming (or process) is created 'very largely by gradients *of apparent completeness*'? Again from the viewpoint of Hindustani music, I may answer the question thus:

The *sthāyī* appears to be a single, unified wholeness. But it is complete only *apparently*; for it 'demands' the *antarā*. One cannot go on repeating the *sthāyī* endlessly (It is, of course, possible to do it; but it cannot be done consistently with appeal. Incidentally, we have to remember that though she does not make it explicit, Langer's whole talk about gradients proceeds from the viewpoint of the *rasika*.) So, the *sthāyī* is a gradient, because it prepares the way to the *antarā*. Further, the *sthāyī*-

158. Langer, *Mind — An Essay on Human Feeling*, Vol. I, p. 209.

antarā complex twosome which emphasises *fixity and self-sameness of structure* calls for, or paves the way to, the *variety* of *tānas*.

After two or three *tānas*, when the vocalist returns to the *sthāyī*, though there is a clear change of pace and design, there is no suggestion of abruptness. As a return to a slower pace, the change may well be said to be a *descent* (or declivity); but because the leisureliness follows the pacy fluency of *tānas*, and also because the *sthāyī* is the line with which the singing began, the change feels like a home-coming, partly because the singer is thereby enabled to re-saturate himself with the pace of the rhythm and the form of the *rāga*; and the recital seems to continue growing, instead of being disrupted. The metaphor of growth here holds also because if the *vilambit khyāl* is not allowed to develop itself fully, and if the vocalist turns impatiently to *drut* — may be, with a view to please lay listeners who prefer the excitement of quick music — the entire recital will look stunted or ill developed.

But is all virtual motion in art 'growth'?

Yet I wonder if Langer's following remark can be seconded without reserve:

> *All* [apparent] *motion in art is growth* — not growth of something pictured, like a tree, but of lines and spaces.[159]

True, I have myself just indicated a way in which the metaphor of growth may relate, if indirectly, to a whole recital. Yet, in respect of an ongoing performance I have never heard any one say that it is *growing* well. The kinetic metaphors that we here use are quite different. We say: जम रहा है गाना; that is, the music is *taking* effect or is *coming* to establish itself. In the case of reposeful *ālāpa* in particular (specially as done by Dagar Brothers) we may well be struck by its look of stepwise progression (एक-एक सुर बढ़ना) in the initial stages;[160] but here

159. Langer, *Feeling and Form*, p. 64.

160. The reference, here, is to both pairs known as Dagar Brothers, 'Senior' and 'Junior'; that is, to Ustads Nasir Moinuddin, Aminuddin; and Zahiruddin and Faiyazuddin Dagar. Today, all these names are but cherished memories.

too we never say that *ālāpa* is *growing*.

Again, whereas it may well make sense to say, as Langer does, that an ornamental border seems to *grow*, the elements of our music hardly admit of such talk. A *tāna* may well appear to *move* up and down, and in a particular way. We may admire its clarity (of *dānā*), and its sweetness. But we never say: it appears to *grow*. It does seem to run its course, but not to *grow*. Of course, we freely speak of *barhat* in *khyāl*-singing, but this word too does not mean *growth*. It rather means a kind of reverential access, as if with unshod feet, to some *svara* or *svara-samūha* that is expected to bring out the distinctive nature of the *rāga* chosen unmistakably.

Substantive, 'bodily' character of the art symbol

But organic growth and unity are not the only semblances that Langer ascribes to a work of art. She insists that

> (a) The work as a whole . . . has more than unity; [and that] it has a substantive character which is, of course, wholly illusory[161] . . . [or] the illusion of bodily existence.[162]

She also explains that what

> (b) gives the art symbol its semblance of bodily existence is . . . [a host of] technical devices . . . the most essential [of which] is the interaction of the primary illusion with the highly variable secondary illusions. . . .[163]

Now, neither extract is likely to seem intelligible, much less acceptable, to the average lover of music, or of art in general; and so I think it necessary to explain and discuss them as follows:

A. To begin with, it is difficult to see how the concept of *substantive character* can be readily identified, as Langer seems to do, with that of *bodily existence*. As used in the two extracts

---

161. Langer, *Mind — An Essay on Human Feeling*, vol. I, p. 205.

162. *Ibid.*, p. 207.

163. *Ibid.*, pp. 206-7. Here, again, I diverge from the order of words cited from the way they occur in the work referred to.

just cited, the word *bodily* is an adjective; and, as such, it can only be taken to mean: belonging or relating to the body. But if we take the word thus, we cannot help objecting to Langer's easy passage from one word to the other. To speak of *the substantive character* of an object may simply mean that it has it own independent, distinct, and significant appearance, but not necessarily in the way of a body. A *rāga*, for example, may well be said to have the kind of character we are talking of, just because it is a clearly identifiable and integrated complex of some specific *svaras*; strikes the ear in a way which is quite different from the impact of other *rāgas*; and admits of *figurations* which are (in principle) numberless, — because of which openness it may well be said to be *rich in its content of creative possibilities* and so significant, even as a book is taken to be substantial because it teems with serious reflections. The figurations I speak of may evoke various effects, such as those of repose and excitement, upsurge and recoil, yearning and fulfilment, or of sheer expansiveness (विस्तार). Some individual *svaras* and phrases may even seem to throb with emotion. It is because of all this, as also because of its integrated unity that our veteran *rasikas* and musicians freely speak of the personality of a *rāga*. Where the grammatical character of a *rāga* is infringed, our complaint often is that the *rāga* has been 'polluted' (भ्रष्ट कर दिया गया है); or that it has been 'dismembered' (उसके अंग भंग कर दिए गए हैं). But, though the living and organic character of a *personality* is here surely meant, in no case it is suggested that the *rāga* in question exists in the way of a body. The concept of *bodily* existence is inseparable from the thought of occupancy in space; but no one speaks or even thinks of a *rāga* — or of a whole recital — as appearing to *occupy* space in the way of a body, as distinguished from *including* suggestion of space *in* quite a few of its figurations. I cannot help suspecting that because she is anxious to build up support for her view that art expresses how it really feels to live, Langer is a bit too quick in identifying suggestions of bulk and volume *in* art with the *overall* bulkiness of a body. The utterance of Samuel Johnson which she appears to take as some clear warrant for her view, namely the following:

> ... The sound of Homer's verses exhibits the idea of corporal bulk,[164]

only means that the sound in question, just an element *in* poetry, seems to have some bulk or volume, not that any whole poem seems to exist in the way of a body or as occupying space. And though it may well be true to say, as Langer does, that "the illusion of bodily existence is so strong that *some* writers on art sometimes designate [even] purely . . . audible forms as 'tangible' ",[165] if (as again Langer herself does)[166] the word 'tangible' be taken to mean 'imaginable', our protest here could be that whereas a body as imagined cannot be visualised except as *occupying* space, the act of imagining a musical figure is only to focus on how the constituent notes are disposed *in relation to each other*, and on the overall design of the figure, *not on how it is related as a whole to some surrounding space*.

B. The second point (b) may be discussed by reflecting on the following words of Langer herself:

> The most essential [of the devices] . . . which [seem to] give body to a composition [or make it appear substantial] . . . is the interaction of the primary illusion with the highly variable secondary illusions that arise and dissolve again, while it remains steady, complete and all but imperceptible because of its ubiquity. The fact that secondary illusions never present completely developed realms of virtual time, space, etc., makes their manifestions appear against the plenum of the entirely developed primary illusion which consequently seems like a negative background supplying their complementary forms; and since secondary illusions may be of many kinds, that background has to have a protean character, which gives it an air of indefinite potentiality.[167]

I may explain the passage thus, from my chosen viewpoint of (Hindustani) music:

---

164. Langer, *Mind — An Essay on Human Feeling*, Vol.I, p. 205; 2nd footnote.
165. *Ibid.*, p. 207.
166. *Ibid.*
167. *Ibid.*, p. 206.

The primary illusion of this art is (according to Langer) virtual time. Here, however, a question may be put. The primary illusion of an art is that which is present in that particular art always and everywhere. But from this point of view, as an Indian *rasika* would like to contend, may not *laya* (or aesthetic pace) rather than time (समय) be said to be the primary illusion of music? The doubt would seem natural to most of us. Yet *I* find it possible to argue in favour of Langer's view; and this is how I would like to reason:

Besides such non-aesthetic meanings as *mergence, dissolution* (प्रलय) or *absorption, laya* in actual music signifies गति or *pravāha,* a (seeming) passage *from one point or svara* or *svara-samūha* — or from one *mātrā* — to another. This is indeed the meaning when we speak of *vilambit* or *drut laya*. In this specific sense *laya* cannot be said to be present at *every* point of music. Thus, where a *svara* — say, the *tāra sa* — is not sung long enough (and where our complaint, in a little crude, but meaningful Hindustani, could be: 'सुर का पेट तो भरा ही नहीं',[168] *duration or abidance* in time is sensed as being too short, but there is no feeling of *passage* at all.

I may here suggest that the right equivalent for Langer's *virtual time* seems to be aesthetic *duration,* not aesthetic *pace.* The word *pace* means: a step, gait, rate of walking, rate of speed in movement or work. Its necessary meaning is *movement,* which is not there in the case (I just now took) of a single note as held on to. Duration, on the other hand, means both (mere) *continuance* in time and time indefinitely. The concept of time arises from change as experienced and observed. As such, it is quite applicable to the experienced flow of music from one note or phrase to another, or of rhythm from one *mātrā* or *vibhāg* to the following one. What is more, clearly unlike the word *laya,* time covers the idea of simultaneity too. It is just as sensible to speak of two athletes breasting the tape at the same point of time (where they actually do so) as of both the drummer and the main performer arriving at the *sama* in perfect simultaneity. So, as a thoroughly

168. This is the language of the late Ustad Chand Khan known as the leading vocalist of Delhi *gharānā* of *khyāl gāyakī* in independent India.

pervasive character of music, *time* may be preferred to *laya*. The point of the protest, that *rasikas* speak of *laya* rather than of time in respect of music, may be tempered by reminding ourselves that Langer regards only *virtual* time, not time *as such* as the primary illusion of music.

As for the secondary illusions of music, some easily identifiable ones are the following: depth and height, surge and subsidence, power and softness, or directed endeavour. Now, the primary illusion (or time) 'remains steady and complete'. It never snaps; after all, music is never to be found quite without duration and pace, slow or brisk. So the primary illusion, here, may be said to be *complete* in the sense that it remains whole and undivided. On the other hand, the 'illusions' we have listed as 'secondary' are all alike fickle; they arise and dissolve. But precisely because of their episodic and variable character, they attract attention. Contrarily, the primary illusion remains almost imperceptible, just because it is present always and everywhere. It is like the quiet air all around us which we notice only when it becomes a draught or acquires a smell. Yet the primary illusion is unquestionably important. It can assume various forms (in the shape of secondary illusions), and so it may be said to be protean in character. It is also a plenum in the sense that it teems with creative possibilities; and Langer rightly emphasises its 'indefinite potentiality'. By contrast, secondary illusions — like rise and fall, ascent and descent, fleeting and abiding appearance — are all specific and limited, though they may well be said to complement each other. Yet, in so far as it is only the secondary illusions which mostly draw attention, the primary illusion is not seen to create them. So it may be regarded as only a *negative* background which just permits the play of secondary illusions.

But how exactly does music acquire a look of *bodily existence* by virtue of the interplay it provides of its primary and secondary illusions? Langer's answer, here, may be briefly put thus:

The essence of bodily existence is an *indefinite potentiality* 'which feeds the continuous burgeoning of life'. It is *the living body* which enables one to perform ever newer acts which make the content of life. It indeed appears to be 'an ever new constellation of possibilities' of action. Now, the same may be said of the primary illusion of music. It admits of ever more various secondary illusions. They all seem to emerge from 'a common core', revealing *its* vitality, so to say; and it is this interaction of the primary and secondary illusions that gives body to a composition[169] and makes 'the work as a whole' appear as a complex of 'figurations and rhythms' arising from an *identical* centre,[170] and so body-like, in so far as a body too serves as the *common* source of numberless actions.

At this point, however, the following comments may be made, strictly in the light of what Hindustani music is and how we react to it:

First, it is common to see our veteran *rasika*s remarking that any rhythm-*cycle* or *rāga* admits of numberless figurations; but such '*indefinite* potentiality' is, as a rule, *not* ascribed to *laya* or duration (or time), though it is surely a known fact that *laya* admits of quite a few (yet not indefinite) variations of pace, such as *vilambit*, *drut*, and *atidrut*, or in the form of *jāti*s. Second, the Indian *rasika* is also likely to protest that where she speaks of the semblance of bodily existence as resulting from the interaction of the primary and secondary illusions, Langer is not quite justified in ascribing the appearance in question indiscriminately to both a composition and the musical 'work as a whole'.[171] For the *rasika*, and also for the Hindustani musician, a *composition* is a *bandish* or *cheez*, that is, the *sthāyī-antarā* pair; and whereas a complete recital (or the whole musical work) may well be said to acquire, with some show of reason, a semblance of bodily or rather vital existence from the interplay it provides of the primary illusion (of *laya* or time) and the various figurations (secondary illusions), a good *sthāyī-antarā* pair strikes us as a well-knit self-completing whole, or as having a distinct, likeable form, but surely not as something that exists in the way of a body.

169. Langer, *Mind — An Essay on Human Feeling*, vol. I, p. 206.

170. *Ibid.*

171. Langer, *Mind — An Essay on Human Feeling*, Vol.I, p. 205.

3

Imaging Time in Music

Langer and Hindustani Rhythm

Introductory

IN the preceding chapter I have freely used the following terms interchangeably: *composition, bandish, sthāyī*. But this is not quite proper, and I now think it necessary to make up for the lapse by making some distinctions in this context. Speaking quite generally, to compose is to set in order or at rest. In literature and music, in particular, the word is taken to mean the act of creating. Its wider meaning, relevant to all the arts, is 'to dispose artistically', that is, with an eye to producing an orderly whole that may be beautiful and (/or) expressive, inviting and helpful to percipience, or striking or informative in some integrated way, and in the imaginative mode. The two meanings of 'to compose' that are specially relevant to music are 'to create' and 'to dispose artistically'. If not quite sharply, the two may be distinguished, because whereas 'to create' is commonly taken to mean the process of bringing something *new* into being, disposition of details in the way of art signifies, in the main, some *winsome* arrangement which can, of course, take numberless forms. Such arrangement, which may tickle sense or our feeling for design, is a norm for the *khyāl*-singer's *tāna*s as well; and so it would be wrong to suggest that *sthāyī* is the only appearance of *composition* in Hindustani music. Indeed, one cannot restrict the word *composition* to mean nothing but *sthāyī*. Yet, be it noted, if *composition* is taken in the sense of 'setting in order' or 'disposing artistically' — and, what is more, if the latter concept is interpreted as integration of *all* the constituents of a work of art — a *sthāyī* must be regarded as composition in a richer sense than a mere *tāna*. It is true that a *tāna* is not expected to stray from the *rāga* being presented; and that it is also required, though it may not always able to observe, a more or less determinate relation to the basic rhythm as marked by the drummer. Yet it cannot be said to concretise or explicate the *rāga* or the *tāla* as identifiably as is done by a *sthāyī*. The reason is that, quite unlike many *tāna*-s, a *sthāyī* is (as a rule) framed visibly, as a self-completing passage, *in a round of the rhythm-cycle*, besides, of course, keeping to the distinctive emphases and चलन or specific manner of interlinking notes required by the *rāga* chosen. Rhythm is indeed a vital component of musical structure, and an important source of its overall appeal. So it should be interesting to see how Langer's view of rhythm relates to the practice of Hinustani music.

Langer's explicit view is that like every other art rhythm too is *a symbolic projection of life as felt*. But this is very likely to look odd to many; for, specially in India where solo expositions of rhythm by seasoned drummers are still welcome to trained audiences, this art is ordinarily taken to be appealing *in itself*, and not by virtue of any relatedness to objects or happenings in the everyday world or to contents of inner, personal life. Yet, because she nowhere speaks of rhythm as an *imitation* of some detail of life, and distinguishes *symbolic projection*, her own preferred concept for relating art to feeling, pretty sharply from direct representation, Langer's entire thinking on the subject calls for a careful study before any judgment is passed on its net value. One may even say that her view of rhythm is distinctive not only because of its positive emphases, but also by virtue of the way she opposes the commonly accepted notions of this art. However, the angle from which I propose to consider her account cannot be very wide; it has to be specific, or that of *Hindustani* (or north Indian) rhythm; for only with this genre of rhythm can I claim to be truly familiar and still actively concerned.[1] This is going to be

1. I say so because only on November 26 and 27, 1996, I recorded a fairly analytical discussion on, and exposition of the art of *tablā*-rhythm for →

a clear limitation of this chapter; but it is luckily set off, if in part, by the fact that quite a few concepts and general features of Hindustani rhythm are also to be found in the way the art is understood and practised in south India.

I also feel encouraged by the fact that — though, of course, in its own way — Hindustani rhythm utilises almost all the individual appearances of rhythm in the various arts; and that this is easy to illustrate. In music, in its basic form of virtual time, rhythm appears as regulation of abidance at some chosen notes, as also by way of a quick or leisurely passage across different *svaras*; in poetry, as arrangement of words into a more or less regular sequence of stressed/unstressed or long and short syllables; and in painting, sculpture and architecture, in the following diverse ways: harmonious or balanced employment of lines, colours, figures and volumes; interactive sequences of massess and voids; and adroit alternation of light with shade. Now, temporal analogues of these devices are all clearly seen in our art of rhythm. Variations of pace and accent; alternation of brief and crisp segments of syllables with those that seem to elongate themselves majestically; and a deft punctuation of collocated *bols* with pauses that do not divide the pattern, but only idealise its unity by prompting the *rasika* (and the drummer himself) to visualise where exactly the (sounding) playing is to resume, — these are all common features of our experience of listening to a recital of rhythm. But the *overriding* features that determine our rhythm as norms are not the ones that Langer emphasises, namely, 'mutual conditioning' and the build-up and release of tension; I would rather pick articulate form, *regulated pace*, and accentuation as the main determinants of creative work in our rhythm. By 'articulate', I here mean 'relatedness of syllables which yet retain a measure of clear self-existence'; and by 'regulated',

→ our national archives, and on behalf of Sangeet Natak Akademi, New Delhi. The *tablā* maestro who played and was 'interviewed' on this occasion was Sudhir Kumar Saxena, a retired Professor of *tablā* from the College of Performing Arts, Baroda University. He was ably assisted by his leading pupil, Madhukar N. Gurav who provided longer pieces of illustrative playing.

not all along changeless, but only 'actively controlled with an eye to fitness and clarity of both form and flow'.

However, before I turn to bring out the differences that separate Langer's view of rhythm from the way this art is practised in the field of Hindustani music, it would obviously help if the essentials of Hindustani rhythm are outlined quite simply. Incidentally, if it be taken to mean a measured and organised number of *mātrās* (or beats) — (that is, a *tāla*) — *rhythm* is not really the fundamental temporal concept of Indian music; that place can be given only to *laya*. *Laya* is aesthetic pace or duration which may either be regulated (measured and identified) with the help of beats including some accented ones; or, as in the case of *ālāpa* by a *dhruvapad*-singer, only by his individual aesthetic sense, and with an eye to some specific effect or proper unfoldment of the *rāga* chosen for treatment. So to speak of *laya* is, however, a bit too succinct; and I think it needful to clarify what I have just said.

First, *laya* signifies not only the pace at which the musician moves from one note or rhythmic syllable (or segment) to another, but the length of time (or duration) he invests in singing a *svara*, or melodic phrase, or in playing a bunch of *bols* (or syllables) of rhythm. As sheer pace, *laya* has to keep itself steadfast, unwavering; that is, unless the drummer himself intends to quicken or decelerate it, the present tempo should not undergo any change. But expressly it can surely be made to move leisurely (*vilambit* or adagio), nimbly (*drut* or allegro), or very fast (that is, *atidrut*). Yet, once any one of these paces has been taken, it has to be kept as such, quite without wavering for some time, that is, until a further change is wilfully desired. So, to use a concept suggested by Langer, '*vilambit*', '*drut*', and '*atidrut*' are *phases* in the flowing fabric of *laya*, not mere steps to be climbed without a break in an ever upward motion, as we do while negotiating a staircase.

As duration in the form of *abidance*, rather than as pace of *passage*, *laya* contributes to the quality of music in quite a few striking ways. If the singer just marks the *tāra ṣaḍja* (upper tonic) gently and tunefully, but for *a mere moment*, the note may seem to twinkle as a star; and if he lets his voice tarry at the note in question majestically in a sweet, steadfast and full-throated *akāra*, it may look like a column of radiance. Further, how long the singer dwells at a particular note is, in general, also a vital determinant of the grammatical rightness of the *rāga* being sung. A prolonged utterance of *ṛṣabha* in *rāga pūriyā*, and a mere touch at the same note (in *tāra saptak*) in *rāga sohnī* would both be violations of the set character of the two *rāgas*.

If it be contended, here, that whatever I have just said about *laya* does not relate to rhythm as such, and so is irrelevant to the subject of this chapter, my answer would be threefold. First, even if it is taken in the familiar sense of regular recurrence of beats, rhythm would not be itself if the beats it comprises do not follow one another at *even* pace. In other words, *laya* is the requisite underrunning evenness of rhythm; and, therefore, to talk of *laya* is in no way to abjure, but only to refer to the very essence of rhythm. Second, in *dhruvapad*-singing which is a venerable, if not very popular form of classical Hindustani music today, the traditionally accepted forms of *rhythmic* variations, such as *ārh*, *kuvārh* which do not (in principle) cause any violence to the verbal meaning of the composition, are called types of *laya*, not of *tāla* or rhythm. Thirdly, *laya* not only signifies something which is the very essence of rhythm (that is, as evenness of pace) but relates to a distinct and important temporal idiom to which the word rhythm or *tāla* is generally not applied. My reference, here, is to *jāti*. We commonly speak of *jāti*s of *laya*, not of *jāti*s of rhythm or *tāla*.

A *jāti* is simply a distinct kind of *flow*, distinguished by the number of beats it comprises and the location of its emphases. *Tāla* or rhythm, on the other hand, is (in Hindustani music) necessarily a *cycle* with a focal beat, called the *sama*. It sets out from and lapses back to the first beat, making this beat appear central and itself as completing a round. No such focus or cyclic quality is to be seen in a *jāti*.

But there is one other important difference too between *laya* and *tāla* (or rhythm). The beats of a *rhythm*-cycle, and the strokes that make the regular patterns played across and ultimately within the cycle, are all roughly similar in sound to the *bols* — or utterable syllables, may be a single letter or bunch of letters, but all alike meaningless — that may be said to name the elements of drumming. This is why whatever is played at the drums, be it a cycle or a rhythmic pattern, is foreknown to the drummer and can be recited by him. The only exception to this parity of playing and openness to recitation is provided by those improvised flourishes with which a seasoned drummer may choose to relieve his set playing. All this relates only to rhythm, not to *laya* as such. However, the point to be noted here is that Hindustani rhythm as actually played (as a solo recital) is subject to a double orientation. It has to arrive at the *sama* recurringly, and with split second accuracy; *and* it has to conform to the design and details of the pattern (or the cycle) as remembered and recitable. In other words, it is all along an intentional blend of overt act and parallel ideation.

To conclude, the place of rhythm in Hindustani music is multirole. It makes for determinateness of the pace of singing or playing, and for variety in the look of notes or phrases as they appear to contemplation; helps in accuracy of *rāga*-rendering through *laya* as extent of abidance at some notes; makes the basic composition appear self-complet*ing*; and serves (in its cyclic form) as the ground of numberless collocations of *svara* and changes of pace, thereby making them appear orderly or patterns, and not mere variations. *Rhythm in Indian music is surely not a mere paving of the way for what is to come.*

The autonomy of (Hindustani) rhythm

But, one may ask, is it proper to focus on rhythm *as such* in the face of contemporary practice of looking on it as essentially a support for music? Can rhythm fairly claim to be an independent art? My answer is, yes; but I know many would here hesitate to agree with me. For, even in India today rhythm is presented and admired mostly as 'accompaniment'; and a lay listener would perhaps question the view that rhythm is autonomous. But, I may point out, it is also a fact that in our main music conferences even today a *solo* rhythmic recital may well be the main draw of an entire session of music.[2] In fact, in India it has ever been so. Sculpture, in the West, had to shake off subservience to architecture. Painting too had to win its freedom from representation. In the case of our rhythm, on the other hand, it is the *heightened* emphasis on *accompaniment* that may be said to be a recent development. The primal, if not the full test of the skill of a drummer for us has ever been his capacity for effective *solo* playing.

The musicologist may protest by pointing to our well-known integrative word: *sangeet*. It certainly covers both music (vocal, instrumental) and dance, and *does not omit rhythm*. How then is rhythm independent? My reply here is that if the same word is used for many things, they are not thereby prevented from functioning severally. To illustrate, though they all come under *sangeet*, there is, in fact, no dancing or drumming with *ālāpa* of the *dhruvapad*-singer, nor any singing with the *taṭkār*[3] of a Kathak dancer; and, so far as rhythm is concerned, it is not only true to *say* that it can be independent, but quite easy to *explain* this possibility.

The cyclic quality of our basic rhythm (or the *ṭhekā*)[4] at once favours the suggestion of wholeness. If the unique manner of the cycle has been properly 'established';[5] if, what is more, the accents neither seem to tug the flow nor appear blurred in its running unity; and if the playing is also possessed of a measure of euphonic charm, — say, by virtue of the proper tuning of the right drum, and also because of the 'blended' use of the two drums that the *tablā* comprises[6] —

2. Thus, in accordance with the convention that the most eminent artist is to perform last of all in a session of music, Ustad Zakir Hussain's *tablā* recital was the concluding item of the Shriram Shankarlal Music Festival, April 13-16, 1996.

3. *Tatkār* is a display of pure footwork in Kathak dance. It is generally presented as the closing number of a full recital.

4. *Ṭhekā* is the rhythm-cycle as drummed.

5. This is English word for what we mean by क़ायम करना.

6. *Tablā* is the more popular drum in the region of north Indian or Hindustani music. It comprises two pieces, literally called according to the way they are put in relation to the drummer's own position, — the 'left' and the 'right' ones (दाँयाँ-बाँयाँ).

the rhythm as heard can not only appear to run because of its own *inner impetus*, but hold our attention, happily, in utter abstraction from everyday concerns. It is indeed quite easy for a duly played cycle to wear the look of what Dewey calls 'an experience', that is, *an* experience which appears to stand out as a distinct wholeness.[7]

But the independence of rhythm as an art can be argued also by appealing to aesthetic theory. Langer proposes that an art may be taken to be autonomous if it is seen to have its own materials, its 'peculiar primary creation', and its own creative principles.[8] Our rhythm, I believe, meets all these requirements adequately; but the point obviously calls for some explanation in detail.

A. Consider, to begin with, *the material of rhythm.* It is doubtless distinctive; what it comprises is mere letters or meaningless bunchess of letters, like *tā, dhā, tin, dhin* (ता, धा, तिन, धिन); and the drummer's task is to produce their rough parallels on the drums. As thus replicated, they do not appear unmusical to the ear; but they mark but one or two notes of the scale. Their function is to make us identify the actual sounds produced, and their beauty arises as much from the design of their collocation as from their clear, but mellow execution.

Now, it is possible to hold that because of this uniqueness of its material, rhythm is not only distinctive, but *important* among the arts. One may here build upon Herbert Read's way of arguing for the pre-eminence of *music*:

> . . . almost in music alone, it is possible for the artist to appeal to his audience directly, without the intervention of a medium of communication in common use for other purposes. The architect must express himself in buildings which have utilitarian purpose. The poet must use words which are bandied about in the daily give-and-take of conversation.[9]

7. A much better illustration of the point in question would, however, be a *quāyedā*; for this pattern has a far richer structure than a mere cycle.
8. Langer, *Problems of Art*, pp. 78-9.
9. Herbert Read's essay, 'A Definition of Art', in *Aesthetics and the Arts*, p. 4.

But if, as argued in the above extract, the rank of an art is to be judged by considering if its medium is *not at all* used for 'other (non-aesthetic) purposes', rhythm, I believe, should be given a place higher than music; for, whereas musical notes are in fact sweetly employed, say, by some hawkers in their typical cries, or by some bells to chime the hour pleasantly — purposes which are both clearly utilitarian — the mnemonic syllables (or *bol*s) of rhythm are never employed for any non-aesthetic purpose.

Nor do they refer to anything external. A good rhythmic recital is quite non-representational. Yet, because of the excellence of its own inner organisation and articulateness, it can be so absorbing that it may induce in knowledgeable listeners a state of self-forgetfulness and attune them in *tādāmya*[10] with the variform, winged beauty of rhythm. Of course, if he so decides, the drummer *can* produce syllables that *resemble* everyday sounds and familiar happenings, such as the movement and noise of a train as it steams out and gathers speed; but whenever this is attempted, those who know the *art* of rhythm only feel amused. Our rhythm is indeed very true to the ideal of 'pure' art.

Here, I may add, it would be wrong to contend that rhythm, *as played*, represents or 'imitates' syllables *as recited* or contemplated; and that rhythm is, therefore, not free from subservience to the external. For, merely as it occurs in speech, writing or thought, a *bol* (of rhythm) is nothing self-complete. It is meant to be played, and it just receives the supplement it intrinsically needs when it is reproduced on the drums. Therefore, when they are played, the *bol*s may not be said to be imitated by, but only to consummate themselves in living rhythm, so to say.

B. Nor can rhythm be said to lack a 'primary creation' of its own. Such 'creation', here, is *an automatic and articulate symmetry of pure pace*. It is *primary* because, as Langer would

10. *Tādātmya* is imaginative self-identification with the essence of the other.

like us to say, it is always created in an exposition of rhythm.[11] The other keywords in my formulation of rhythm's primary creation may be explained as follows:

By 'symmetry' I mean beauty of form. Everything in the region of rhythm is indeed required to seem well organised and shapely. This is true of both the basic rhythm-cycle and the patterns that are woven across and (ultimately) within it. As for the epithet *articulate*, I think it is truer of our rhythm than of any other art. Langer emphasises the term in the context of music. I recall that 'a composition', according to her, 'is not merely produced by mixture like a new colour made by mixing paints but is articulated, i.e., its internal structure is given to our perception'. Here, the parts, she adds, 'maintain some degree of separate existence'.[12] But, as I have already argued in the preceding chapter, this is not categorically true of form as it obtains in Hindustani *music*, where it is often *mīṇḍs* or glides that serve to bring out the organic form of the *rāga* and of the composition chosen. The notes which a *mīṇḍ* comprises are just not seen to have a measure of *separate* existence, though they sure remain distinguish*able* to the discriminating ear. Further, in *ālāpa* on the *vīṇā* an important aesthetic excellence is often a winsome stilling of individual notes into, rather than affirming their separateness from, their immediate neighbours in the *rāga* or tonal arrangement.[13]

In the region of rhythm, on the other hand, articulation is always a key requirement. Here, even in the case of such patterns as a *relā* or a *rau*, which are all meant to be presented at quick pace, we insist on the clarity of syllables, — consistently, of course, with the requisite measure of fluency. The ideal indeed is to see that the *bol*s are 'cut out' so as to keep off fuzziness. This detail of manner is called *bol kāṭnā*; and

11. Langer, *Problems of Art*, p. 35.

12. Langer, *Feeling and Form*, p. 31.

13. The reference, here, is to my remarks on *ālāpa* in *rāga eman kalyāṇa* by the *vīṇā* maestro, Pandit Gopal Krishna, in my write-up, 'Ustads pay brilliant homage to Dagars', on the 11th Dhrupad Samāroha (Kamani Auditorium, New Delhi, March 18-20, 1995), published in *The Asian Age*, New Delhi, of March 24, 1995.

playing which quite meets this requirement is called *khuśkhat* (खुशख़त) by some. The syllable *'dir, dir'*, as played at a fast pace, may seem to be an exception to this general rule; but it is not really so; for, the effect aimed at is one of *tremulous* fluency, *and the palpitation is not to be allowed to get quite eclipsed in the flow*. This, indeed, is why the old masters would be averse, as a rule, to playing at hectic speed[14] where the syllables are bedimmed and come to appear as a mere flowing lump.

Its *automotive* character is another important feature of rhythm. What I mean by this emphasis is not merely that rhythm *somehow* appears to be self-propelling, but that the length or brevity of the very first syllable or beat as played or recited[15] — or its own temporal extent — directly determines whether the entire subsequent playing is to be leisurely or brisk. In *parhant* (or recitation of *bols*) it is in fact quite easy to see the point that if one utters the first beat slowly — in the manner of a drawl — the entire subsequent counting has to be just as leisurely; and that if the same beat is then spoken sharply and briefly, the following beats too have to be quickened correspondingly. I wonder if we can anywhere find a more obvious instance of determination of the whole-form by the character of a part. And this is, I may add, a *clearer* indication of the 'autonomous form' of rhythm than Langer's following remark on some records of African music in which the constructive power of the drum is paramount:

> . . . Anyone familiar with many works of that sort would probably feel their structure and mood almost from the opening beat.[16]

C. The automotive symmetry of pure pace is, however, not the only 'illusion' that distinguishes rhythm. It evokes

14. An oft quoted example of such masters is the late Ustad Natthu Khan of Delhi.

15. In the case of Indian rhythm, we may note, most of the sounds which the drummer produces, while playing, can be recited by him, as syllables or *bols*, the playing and the speaking being related by similarity of mere manner. Recitation of rhythmic syllables is, for us, an important part of the drummer's art.

16. Langer, *Feeling and Form*, p. 125.

some 'secondary illusions' too, as all 'advanced artistic creations' do, according to Langer.[17] But before an attempt is made to trace such illusions in the play of rhythm, it seems necessary to recall how exactly she distinguishes between primary and secondary illusions.

A primary illusion, she says, is not that which the artist makes *before* everything else, but that which comes with the very first moment of the act of creation. In painting, for instance, 'it comes *with* the lines and colours, [and] not before them'; further, it is '*always* created', like virtual space in painting.[18] What is more, this basic illusion 'remains steady, complete and all but imperceptible because of its ubiquity'.[19] Now, all this is clearly true of what I have spoken of as the primary illusion of rhythm. As already explained, the automotive symmetry of pace is the evenness or constancy of tempo as determined by the length or brevity of the very first rhythmic syllable as played or recited; and this evenness, I may add, gains an added look of symmetry from its being framed as a cycle — in the form of a *ṭhekā*. Further, the symmetry or temporal evenness in question arises *along with*, and surely not *before*, the playing of the first syllable. What is more, in so far as this evenness of *laya*, as kept and projected by the *ṭhekā*, persists as a largely visualised background throughout the recital — that is, even during the playing of patterns which may dominate attention because of their variform and striking design — it is only occasionally that the equable pace of the *ṭhekā* is *expressly* noticed, though the *rasika* surely remembers it all along, if not intently. Secondary illusions, on the other hand, 'arise and dissolve again'.[20] Two clear instances of such illusions are 'the sudden impression of colour in music, or of eloquence in the lines of a statue . . . [both making for] a sublimation of the expressive form'.[21]

17. Abridged edition of Langer's works by G.V.D. Heuvel, p. 94.
18. Langer, *Problems of Art*, p. 35.
19. Abridged edition of Langer's works, p. 82.
20. *Ibid.*
21. *Ibid.*, p. 94.

In the practice of rhythm too *such* illusions — or semblances which are quite unlike the look of a merely steady pace — freely arise. There *are* patterns that seem to make for, and to flower at the *sama*, and also such as appear to deviate designedly from the focal beat, without really losing sight of it.

These two 'illusions' may be called, respectively, the rhythm of orientation and the rhythm of intentional abandon or willed waywardness. They are 'illusions' in the sense that they only appear to be, but are surely not *actual* cases of goal-directed endeavour or wilful waywardness that impart a little zest or relaxation to daily living. Yet both are real features of our aesthetic experience of rhythm. For this reason, and also because they have been generally ignored by writers on rhythm,[22] not excepting Langer who too speaks *only* of the setting up and release of tensions — and of continuity and repetition — where she discusses rhythm,[23] I think it necessary to comment on them at some length:

THE RHYTHM OF ORIENTATION

When a drummer plays a well-designed pattern of *bols* it often happens that, from a particular point in its flowing yet articulate form, it appears to rouse and gather itself by way of reaching the *sama*, and finally climaxes at the focal beat in due fulfilment, so to say, of its own inner impulse. The *sama* here appears as the destiny of a clearly oriented rhythmic flow. I wonder if any other art can provide clearer instances of the linkage of a structural focus with its immediately preceding oriented context.

Here, it would be relevant to point out that, as is (according to Langer) requisite for any art that claims to be independent, rhythm too can be credited with some criteria that relate to it uniquely. One of the these is the drummer's capacity for a 'blended' employment of the two drums. The reference here is obviously to *tablā* which comprises two drums; but it needs

22. As by Frye, where he speaks of the various kinds of rhythm. See his *Anatomy of Criticsm*, pp. 251-81.

23. Langer, *Feeling And Form*, pp. 125-32.

some explanation. The point is that each drum has its own share to contribute to the total playing. The 'left' drum is meant to work up effects of a certain breathing continuity (called *sāns*), and of depth and inwardness; and the 'right' one contributes crispness, discreteness or clarity, a measure of tonal sweetness, and fluency. The requirement is that (at least) in the actual projection of the rhythm-cycle the use of the two drums is to be duly co-ordinated, so that the total playing may neither appear to be a mere succession of disconnected sounds, due to undue dominance of 'the right one', nor a mere booming loudness because of overmuch use of the left, but (positively) a mellow, flowing round wherein the details occur gently, without being blurred in resonances of 'the left'. Another requirement which relates to rhythm alone is the drummer's ability to come back to the *sama* with split second accuracy.

This (second) criterion, I believe, is more clearly usable than standards that relate to evaluation in the field of other arts. Two critics, equally competent and watchful, may find it difficult to decide whether a piece of music is properly structured or expressive. But two listeners, who have but a fair knowledge of rhythm, are almost bound to agree as to whether or not the drummer has reached the first beat accurately. For them it is as easy a matter as it is for us to mark that a person has arrived on the dot.

THE RHYTHM OF ABANDON

Some patterns are so knit and played that they end a little before or after the *sama*. The deviation is here willed; and is demanded by a little economy or ebullience of structure itself. Here, the *sama* as played is slightly overstepped or just not attained; but it is heightened in idea by the very design of refusing to end the playing exactly *at* the beat. A *part*[24] of this artifice may not seem new to those who are familiar, say, with the art of poetry. It is indeed common knowledge that

24. Why I here speak of only 'a *part* of this artifice' will be brought out in the para that follows the extract to be cited presently.

inspired artistic content may, so to say, spill over the bounds of prefixed extent, and thereby vivify 'form' as internal structure by its very incompliance. See, for instance, the following from an eminent writer on poetry:

> Form does not lie simply in the correct observance of rules. It lies in the struggle of certain living material to achieve itself within a pattern. The very refusal of a poet to sacrifice what he means to a perfectly correct rhyme, for example, can more powerfully suggest the rhyme than correctness itself would.[25]

But, I believe, it is not *so* easy to realise the other half of the matter, — that is, the truth that our awareness of 'form' may be heightened even by the act of falling a little daintily *short* of the normal stretch, in intentional response to the structural demand of a specially designed pattern. Yet this is exactly what is done by our patterns that are made to end a little before the *sama*.[26] As a rough parallel, one may perhaps here refer to a detail of Rodin's artistic practice. It is said that once he had succeeded in finding the precise kinetic touch in a figure or bust, he would often stop and leave, say, the hands or feet literally unfinished; and yet without any harm to the seeming self-completeness of the works as contemplated, may be because of the operation of the Gestalt law of coercive design.

THE RHYTHM OF SIMULTANEITY

But a better known rhythm — and surely easier to follow — is that of simultaneity. I have here in mind the kind of rhythm that *distinguishes* the drummer's art of providing 'accompaniment' to the main performer, say, a *sitār* player. This is the rhythm of similarity, or parallel flow, and of coextension and unitive advent. The reference is to a very skilful kind of *sangat* (or 'accompaniment'). Where the music seeks to dally with rhythm, the drummer may seize forthwith the manner (*andāz*) of the *sitārist*; and, without ever slackening his hold over the

25. Stephen Spender, *World within World*, pp. 313-14.
26. Such rhythmic patterns are called *anāgat*.

cycle, may so adapt his own playing to that of the main performer that the two flowing forms may seem to be a quite free confluence, and finish at the *sama* with well-nigh perfect simultaneity. Here, *what* syllables the drummer plays is not the basic thing; and what counts, I repeat, is only his unerring grasp and replication of the *manner* of the music. The instant of jointly reaching the *sama* satisfies not in detachedness, but largely because it consummates a flowing *design*; and the net effect, because of confluent form and rhythmic turns, is one of intertwining.[27]

This rhythm too, I may add, is nameable as a 'secondary illusion', — an 'illusion' because the drumming in such cases is not *strictly* simultaneous with the playing of the main performer. The drummer often lags a little, but the lag, where it occurs, is so slight that it hardly strikes us, and the semblance of conjoint run is not at all ruffled. And, of course, as is all along implicit in Langer's talk about the virtual in art, the semblance of simultaneity is here created artistically; and its perception is at once some notice of design or manner. In everyday cases, on the other hand, simultaneity is rarely brought about intentionally. It just happens as when two runners breast the tape at exactly the same moment. What is more, in such cases we are here struck essentially by the moment of simultaneous occurrence, not by the approach that leads upto it.

CREATIVE DEVICES

Rhythm may also be said to have its own '*principles of constructing* its final creations';[28] and, in the context of Hindustani rhythm, these 'creations' may be taken to mean not merely

27. The Hindustani word, here is लिपटना. The other kind, which is easier and more current today, is quite different. Here, the drummer reproduces the rhythmic parallel after the *sitārist* has finished the pattern and has begun playing the basic *gat* (composition) again. But this, I believe, is closer to solo playing than to *saṅgat* which literally means 'accompaniment', and not mere following or reproduction.

28. Langer, *Problems of Art*, p. 79.

the basic structure of a pattern, but the variations it permits. The point may be illustrated by considering the case of what is called *quāyedā* by our *tablā*-players.

A *quāyedā* truly is what it means as a word — a very methodical composition in respect of both conception and practice. First, it is named after the main *bol* (or syllable) which occurs freely and prominently in its individual structure. Second, though every *quāyedā* admits of a fair number of variations — which is why the legendary Ustad Natthu Khan of Delhi could develop a single such pattern into an hour-long recital — such freedom is by no means absolute. No *palṭā* (or improvisation) can include a syllable (*bol*) which does not figure in the basic composition. Thirdly, the variations must follow a particular sequence. The first variant has to build upon the opening *bol* of the composition; the next one, upon the second *bol;* and so on. What is more, the terminal syllables of the two segments (of the basic composition) have to rhyme, without being identical. Thus, if the last *bol* of the first segment in *tinākinā*, the *bol* which closes the second segment has to be *dhināginā*. This technical device is called *quāfiyā radeef*, and is roughly comparable to end-rhymes in poetry.[29] If it be objected, here, that if everything is so prefixed in the playing of a *quāyedā*, it cannot really provide for creativity, the answer would be, first, that though every variation has to open with a specific *bol*, what exactly the alteration is going to be in respect of pace and order of syllables, without incorporating any such *bol* as is alien to the basic structure of the *quāyedā*, surely calls for some independent, if disciplined thinking on the drummer's part; and, second, that in the art of solo drumming improvisation cannot be rated higher than design and clarity in the actual playing of syllables.[30]

I may add that in the making of Hindustani rhythm one also finds a free use of the Gestalt laws of perception, such as

---

29. Whatever I have said about *quāyedā* in this para has been taken from my 'recorded' discussion with Prof. Sudhir Kumar Saxena referred to in NOTE 1.

30. This has sure been a continued emphasis of our *tablā* maestros of old.

those of figure and ground and common destiny. But what I wish to focus on, in this context, is another constructional device which is at once basic to, and perhaps distinctive of the Indian art of rhythm.[31] This is the act of so filling a stretch of some beats, or the duration *between* two separate beats, with orderly bunches of *bol*s that the playing gets invested with the *spatial suggestions of teeming, or appearing crowded or even overflowing* with them. A syllable so inserted may even come to look as a wedge holding the neighbouring ones apart. On the whole, the richer and the more orderly the placement of *bol*s within a narrow interval of time, the greater is the title of the drummer to acclaim, provided, of course, the *bol*s are also neatly and truly played. From the viewpoint of this particular feature of the drummer's craft, our rhythm may well be regarded as an *aesthetic demonstration of the divisibility of time.*

Langer on Rhythm

Now that enough has been said by way of arguing that even from the viewpoint of Langer's conception of what makes an art autonomous, Hindustani rhythm may be regarded as an independent art too, and that it is therefore proper to consider our rhythm in relation to Langer's aesthetics, I may now proceed to consider what exactly *she* has to say on the subject.

A. NEGATIVE EMPHASES

To begin with her negative emphases in respect of rhythm, they may be briefly put as follows, along with some argument from my side:

> It is commonly believed in scientific thinking that the essential character of rhythm is the repetition of any distinct, recognisable event at equal intervals of time, i.e., that is, rhythm is periodic repetition. But, in fact, not all rhythmic repetitions are strictly periodic. There may even be rhythmic sequences of events which are not really repetitive; for instance, a performer of 'modern dance' rarely repeats a

---

31. Not only in the region of solo *tablā* playing, but in that of Kathak dance.

> movement, yet every least motion of the dance has to be rhythmic.'[32]

in the sense, we may add, that in the economy of the whole number every step or bestirring of the limbs leads to, or makes for the one that follows.[33]

Recurrence of identical units at equal intervals is, of course, what we commonly understand by rhythm — at least in the case of drumming which builds upon beats or *mātrās*. But such periodic repetition cannot be taken as the *essence* of rhythmicity taken generally, though it may well be regarded as a key structural principle of music. Consider, for instance, the ticking of a clock. It is repetitious and regular; and the ticks are mostly identical. But it cannot be regarded as rhythmic in itself. Why *I* say so (supporting Langer) can be brought out with the help of two simple examples. If fifty stone slabs, all similar in shape and size, are put up on the roadside at equal distance from one another, we may well be struck by the appearance of order and similarity, but nobody will call the entire arrangement rhythmic. Even regularity of succession *in time* may not be said to be the essence of rhythm. Day and night follow each other with unfailing regularity, but nobody takes this alternation as a case of creative rhythm. The point really is that in cases of mere regularity of succession — that is, where there is no dynamic interplay of elements or processes — the mind must enter into, and do some active ordering in respect of *what is presented to it* before the presentation can come to appear and be regarded as rhythmic. Thus, if in the process of counting, one chooses to group every four adjacent numbers ideally as one, and then utters the opening number of every segment a little emphatically, the process will at once come to wear the look of rhythm. So there *is* truth in Langer's remark that the ticks of a clock come to appear rhythmic only when 'the human mind organises them into a temporal form'.[34] By

32. Langer, *Mind: An Essay on Human Feeling*, Vol.I, p. 323.
33. "Rhythmic concatenation . . . [is] a sequence wherein the subsiding phase, or cadence, of one act (or similar element) is the up-take for its successor" Langer, *Mind: An Essay on Human Feeling*, Vol.I, p. 323.
34. Langer, *Feeling and Form*, p. 126.

themselves, indeed, features like similarity and repetition are not enough to produce the appearance of rhythmicity.

Nor are these features *always* there in what seems to be rhythmic. Consider, for example, the case of a talk that impresses the listeners with its rhythmic quality. Obviously, it cannot be a succession of segments of equal extent, all comprising words of similar sounds. In such cases, the pace is indeed not even all along. Nor are the sounds, extent, and meaning of the words used similar. The truth here rather is that phrases, emphases, and even single pauses are all so organised that the present utterance (or pause) makes us look forward to *what is to come next*; and that the complex of succeeding words satisfies the expectation.

Take, again, a matter that relates to rhythm as it permeates the 'pure' patterns of Kathak dance. In collocations of *bols* that begin, thus: तक्थरि। तक्थरि। कुकुथरि। कुकुथरि। तक्धलांग। तक्धलांग। (in *tritāla*) we sure have both identity of syllables and equality of extent (of rhythmic phrases), but neither of them is so visibly there in patterns that run thus: (again, in *tritāla*):

धिननन नागेतिट क्ड़धेतधातिट घेघेतिट घेघे(ना)तिट गद्दीधिड़ान नागोतिट किड़ान।
9 12 13 1 5 12
तकिटतकिटधातिटधिटतिरान ऽधातिटधिटतिरानऽधातिटधिटातिरान (सम)
13 1 5 9 13 16

Here the syllables क्ड़धेतधातिट, which serve as a kind of wedge between the adjoining bunches of *bols*, appear to move quicker than the rest; and the bracketed ना before तिट seems a whit more restful in pace. Nor is the order of syllables importantly similar or repetitive, the opening धिननन occurring only once in the entire pattern. But what *is* invariably present in every rhythmic pattern is that, by virtue of its own pace, the very opening syllable generates in our minds the expectation that, by and large, a definite tempo will be kept, and that occasional increase or deceleration of pace will be duly redeemed, so as to save it from appearing as a positive infringement of the basic, overall requirement, namely, *laya* or evenness of pace. Where the reparation is not duly done, rhythm disappears forthwith.

B. LANGER'S POSITIVE VIEWS

The way is now paved to consider langer's positive account of rhythm. Here, perhaps the most striking detail is her thesis is that rhythm is 'related to *function* rather than to time'.[35] Function, as we know, is a (potential) activity appropriate to a person or thing. An activity is a happening or an event. As a process in time, it has a beginning and an end; and a 'rhythmic pattern arises whenever the completion of one distinct event appears as the beginning of another'.[36] Langer is indeed emphatic on this point. In *Feeling and Form* she openly declares that the *essence* of rhythm is the preparation of a new event by the ending of a previous one.[37] Can we illustrate this emphasis? Langer is convinced, we can; and she here lists quite a few instances:

> The classic example is the swinging of a pendulum. The momentum of its drop drives the weight upward in the opposite direction, and builds up the potential energy that will bring it down again; so the first swing prepares the second; the second swing was actually begun in the first one, and similarly, after that, each swing is prepared by the one before. The result is a rhythmic series.
>
> Or, consider the breaking of waves in a steady surf on a beach; the momentum of the water drives it up the beach, until that momentum is spent, and the slant of the shore causes the water to run seaward again; but the piling of the second, incoming wave is also sucking back the spent water, and making its return a downward rush, that stops the bottom part of the new wave and causes it to break over itself. Here, again, is a rhythmic pattern. The completion of each breaker's history is already the beginning of the next one's.
>
> In a living organism . . . the most obvious rhythmic processes are, of course, heartbeat and breath. In the heart, every systole starts a diastole, and vice versa. . . . In breathing, . . . as the

35. Langer, *Problems of Art*, p. 50.
36. *Ibid.*, p. 51.
37. Langer, *Feeling and Form*, p. 126.

> oxygen of a breath is used up, it builds up the imperative need of oxygen that is really the beginning of the new breath. This sort of mutual conditioning is the law of organic function. . . . In every cell, the very process of its oxidation — its burning away, breaking down — is the condition that has already started the chemical change which builds up its characteristic substance again. . . . [Rhythm is really] a functional involvement of successive events . . . [and] periodic rhythms [are only] a special sort [of rhythm].[38]

Now, I have nothing to say about the first two examples. But, in the third extract, Langer's account of instances from *organic* life appears to contain some clear errors. Where she characterises the swinging of a pendulum and of 'the breaking of waves in a steady surf on a beach' as rhythmic, her meaning professedly is that each movement is not only prepared by the one before, but makes for the one that follows. This is also why, in her view, hearbeat is a rhythmic process; 'every systole starts a diastole, and vice versa'. But, we may note, though the two physiological events are definitely cyclic in recurrence, so that the one necessarily starts after (or before) the other, neither can be said to give rise to the other *straight-away*. Systole and diastole are quite disparate haemodynamic events; the former is a positive action brought about by the pacemaker and the latter is a rather passive, relaxed state of the heart. Each one of them *ends* before the other one begins; so neither can be said to start the other directly. What is more, according to clinical pathology of the heart, there may even be a very brief interval between systole and diastole of auricles and ventricles, — a kind of refractory period during which the heart remains quite still. If this period is prolonged beyond a certain point, the stillness can even be felt as a sinking sensation of the heart.

Again, it is *not* the consumption (or being 'used up') of the oxygen *of a breath* that 'builds up the imperative need of oxygen that is really the beginning of a new breath'. The need in question relates rather to the metabolic requirements of the body cells and tissues; and, though it is undeniably imperative,

38. Langer, *Problems of Art*, pp. 51-52.

the need varies from time to time. Langer's explanation of the way the two breaths are related is further invalidated by a simple, verifiable fact. As in a heart attack or cerebral stroke, a dying tissue may simply perish *after consuming* the last available amount of oxygen *without* creating any need for a fresh supply of the life-giving gas.

It is also wrong to speak of the oxidation or 'burning away, breaking down' *of cells*. Only the nutrients in a cell — such as carbohydrates, fats, and protein — are burnt out, the first two completely, and the third one partly, to yield energy for cellular activity. Cells and their structural contents (organelles) certainly age and eventually die, but they are never oxidised or burnt away in the sense of getting metabolised. Incidentally, the term *oxidation* is used only for chemicals (and biochemicals). Finally, it is too sweeping to speak of '*mutual* conditioning [as] *the law* of organic function'. A major process like secretion of enzymes (and hormones) operates only as a *one-sided response*, so to say, to a need. Unlike the heartbeat, it does not work ceaselessly. The sight or smell of food may well bring about a secretion of saliva containing an enzyme, but the secretion in question does not obviously bring about the presence of food. Again, there is nothing rhythmic — in the sense of 'mutual conditioning' — about the working of brain and organs of sense-perception. When a person wishes to raise his hand, a motor impulse from the brain/spinal cord may readily bring about the desired movement; but all this is occasional, not periodic in a regular way. And, to be sure, the raised hand may not directly cause any further motor impulse. Barring, of course, the heart, most of the bodily organs — like the liver, stomach and kidney — work by way of unidirectional response to some need or stimulus, and not as a mutual conditioning of stimulus and response.[39]

However, inaccuracies such as these need not disturb us; for what Langer here wishes to emphasise — namely, the point that rhythm is importantly, if not exclusively, 'a functional

39. Here, in pointing out all these inaccuracies in Langer's view, I have been helped by my son, Dr. P. Kumar, a Reader in the Deptt. of Zoology, Hans Raj College, University of Delhi.

involvement of successive events'[40] — is surely relevant to a considerable amount of art; and so we cannot ignore it. Even in drumming, practised in India (I repeat) also as an independent art, the completion of one rhythmic phrase is freely seen to make for what follows, quite directly. Langer's overall writing on rhythm, however, makes some other points as well; and to make our study of the matter adequate to her total view, we may discuss them all individually, along with some recall, where necessary, of what we have already noted.

I. (a) Rhythm is essentially a matter of function, not of time. In organic life, as also in nature, rhythm is to be found as the 'mutual conditioning'[41] of processes, movements, or events; *or* as (b) 'the preparation of a new event by the ending of a previous one'.[42] The mind too, "even in its highest operations . . . follows the organic rhythm which is the source of vital unity: the building up of a new dynamic *Gestalt* in the very process of a former one's passing away".[43]

Now, the reason why rhythm cannot be regarded as, in essence, a matter of periodic succession has already been discussed earlier. But a little clarification is surely demanded by some other points in (a part of) Langer's veiw just stated. Is (a) the *mutual* conditioning of processes exactly the same thing as (b) 'the preparation of a new event by the ending of a previous one'? We can hardly say, yes. For, whereas (a) may well be regarded as signifying a kind of cyclic rhythm — a clear instance, here, being the twosome of inhalation and exhalation which determine *each other* — (b) can be merely serial and ever onward, that is, quite without a determination of the antecedent by the successor. Which of the two may be said to be Langer's overtopping emphasis? I cannot say, *mutual* conditioning, specially if we look at the matter from the viewpoint of rhythm as it appears *in the arts*. Langer, I believe, opts for the 'serial' view where she says that everything that

40. Langer, *Problems of Art*, p. 52.

41. *Ibid.*

42. Langer, *Feeling and Form*, p. 126.

43. *Ibid.*, p. 128.

prepares a future creates rhythm';[44] that the rhythm of destiny is the feeling or appearance that the future is already an entity 'embryonic in the present'[45] — which is obviously quite different from the thought that the future too *determines* the present; and that the tragic rhythm is '*the deathward advance of* . . . [our] individual lives . . . which has a series of stations that are *not repeated*: growth, maturity, decline'. Tragedy, she adds, 'is a cadential [not cyclic] form. Its crisis is always the turn towards an absolute close'.[46] In all such cases the rhythm involved is clearly not cyclic. The difference is heightened by what Langer has to say on rhythm as dialectic. Where, as in the case of repetitive playing of a rhythm-cycle, the successor is 'a replica of the predecessor', which is 'often' [but not necessarily] the case;[47] and where '*each* element in spending itself prepares and initiates its own converse', such as a rise making for a fall, or suction pressing for expulsion — rhythm may be said to be a dialectic.[48] This means that, according to Langer, cyclic or dialectic rhythm represents only a form of rhythm, and not its very essence.

But, to turn anew to the opening formulation (in I. p. 240) of the points being discussed, how can *the higher workings of mind* be said to bear out Langer's basic thesis in respect of rhythm? I may answer thus, largely following Langer's own line of thinking:

Suppose, after a look at works of art which are commonly admired because they seem to move us readily — to tears or laughter, or to open acclamation — we arrive at the unifying view that art is the powerful expression or transmission *and evocation of emotions*. Suppose, further, that thereafter our attention is invited to acknowledged works of art which are *non*-representational in character and which, like the whole of our classical instrumental music, charm us essentially by

44. Langer, *Feeling and Form*, p. 129.

45. *Ibid.*, p. 311.

46. *Ibid.*, p. 351.

47. Langer, *Mind — An Essay on Human Feeling*, vol. I, p. 204.

48. *Ibid.*

virtue of their formal organisation or some other striking quality — such as sparkling fluency, clarity of utterance or steadfastness in *vilambit* playing or observance of *laya* (or even pace) generally. Attention to such cases may well impel us to reject our first generalisation about art. But in the very dissolution of this *gestalt* (or whole-view) we may be moving towards an alternative view, say, the view that art is 'expressive' in the sense of giving utterance not only to the commonly recognised emotions of joy and sorrow, fear and jealousy, but even to such details of felt life as excitement, vitality, languor, and repose; or to a third simpler view that, quite without any essential relatedness to human emotions, art is just the creative aesthetic embodiment of some meaning which emerges only when the work is completed.

It must, however, be added that trasition to 'alternative views' will actually take place not automatically, but only if *we* try to remove, by means of more careful thinking, our dissatisfaction with the first view. The 'highest symbolic operations' of which Langer speaks in this context have all to be kept up *by us*; but, of course, because of its very felt quality, the (unsatisfactory) *gestalt* of the first view may also be said to press for its own transcendence by a more adequate view, and so to generate a kind of tension, as Langer would like us to say.

(II) Rhythms like the one of self-correcting, evermore embracive thinking that we just visualised are, however, not the 'fundamental' ones. The latter, according to Langer, are those processes of mutual conditioning that regulate organic function; they may be called 'fundamental' or 'major' because if they are 'greatly disturbed, or suspended for more than a few seconds, the organism collapses, life stops'.[49] It is because of the ceaseless operation of these basic rhythms that life, as the process of remaining active and suffering diverse experiences, feels one and undivided.[50] This unity does not stand in need of any proof; for it is felt, and feeling is 'the sense of life

49. Langer, *Problems of Art*, pp. 52-3.

50. *Ibid.*, p. 50.

itself. . . the realization in direct [experience] of what sets organic nature apart from inorganic'.[51] But in the higher organisms, 'secondary rhythms [also] develop; [these are] specialised responses to the surrounding world, tensions and their resolutions within the system; emotions, desires, attentive perception, and action'.[52] In organic life at the lower level, three of the many *subsidiary* rhythms that Langer takes pains to distinguish are those of *successive individuations*,[53] *contraction and expansion* and *induction and inhibition*.[54] She points to these three kinds of rhythm where she speaks of some cases of colonies of coelenterates, mutilated organisms, and organs or cell types. But in so far as her ultimate aim in citing such instances is to show that it is the symbolic projection of these very rhythms of life that makes *art* significant, it would be quite proper if, instead of dwelling upon details of the cases referred to, we straightaway turned to see if *the three rhythms we have just spoken of* are to be found in the region of art as well.

Now, I see it clearly that they all operate in rhythm considered as a distinct art in itself. But the rhythm of successive individuations — which, in the case of some coelenterates, is *necessary to preserve the life of the stock*[55] — is important quite differently in the art of drumming; here it often brings out the room that the ambit of a single rhythm-cycle offers for endless creative work, so impressively indeed in the case of a top class drummer that he is himself awestruck, at times, by the illimitableness in question; and, therefore, generally prefers to focus, in his solo playing, essentially on *one* tāla *throughtout his career*![56] The patterns woven across the rhythm-cycle — and also, in a way, *within* it, for they have (as a rule) to end at *its*

51. Langer, *Feeling and Form*, pp. 327-28.
52. Langer, *Problems of Art*, p. 53.
53. Langer, *Mind — An Essay on Human Feeling*, vol. I, p. 341.
54. Abridged edition of Langer's works by H.V.D. Heuvel, p. 125.
55. Langer, *Mind — An Essay on Human Feeling*, vol. I, p. 341.
56. Roughly the same infiniteness of aesthetic potential may be seen by a great vocalist in the ambit of a single major *rāga*.

focal beat — are all 'individual' in the sense that they appear to be *self-complete and are no mere fragments*; and in case the form of the cycle has been properly established at the very outset, they strike us as its own individuations, and not as merely imposed on it, because they all appear to *rasika*s as welling up from within its intrinsic, determinate pace and compass. Here, however, I may also refer to a detail of Hindustani rhythm which may seem to — but does not really — counteract what I have just said about the individuality or wholeness of patterns. What is called a *tukrhā* in the region of *tablā*-playing is admittedly an extraction (as a rule) from some elaborate collocation of *pakhāwaj*[57] *bols*; but it is yet saved from appearing fragmentary by adding to it, as a suffix, a *tiyā* or threefold rhythmic phrase which generally suggests completion.[58]

The rhythm of contraction and expansion too is to be freely seen in the practice of Hindustani rhythm. To illustrate, I may turn again to the following *anāgat* pattern which has already been used earlier for a different purpose:

घिननन नागेतिट क्ड़धेतधातिट घेघेतिट घेघे(ना)तिट गद्दीघिड़ान नागेतिट किड़ान।
9 12 13 1 5 12
तकिट तकिटधातिट घिटतिरान ऽधातिटघिटतिरानऽधातिटघिटतिरान सम।।
13 1 5 9 13 16

Here the *bols*: क्ड़धेतधातिट show a little contraction; for, धातिट comes after क्ड़धेत very quickly, almost impatiemtly. On the other hand, the relatively sedate नातिट, घिड़ान and किड़ान (the bracketed ना, in particular) look like a little loosening or of expanision of syllabic filling.

To turn, in the end, to the rhythm of induction and inhibition, it may be said to operate in the rhythm-cycle itself; and this, as follows: The *ṭhekā* (or the cycle as played) *induces* the grounding of the basic pace by virtue of the temporal

---

57. *Pakhāwaj* is big, one-piece drum; so quite different from the *tablā*. It produces deeper sonant effects than the latter, and is the right kind of drum to provide rhythmic accompaniment to the *dhruvapad-dhamār* forms of Hindustani classical vocal music.

58. That is, in the way of a correct arrival at the *sama*, the focal beat of the rhythm-cycle.

character of its very first beat. But, at the same time, it may also be said to inhibit, first, its own run by coming back to that beat, the *sama*; and secondly, the course of the patterns too in a measure, because they are (as a rule) required to end (ultimately) at *its* focal beat, failing which they fall into immediate error.

(c) Such (secondary) rhythms are quite various, and are often the explicit objects of attention as we contemplate art. But, according to Langer, reflection on art itself requires us to pay due heed to rhythms in *life* as well; for it is, she believes, only by projecting these rhythms that art acquires its distinctive significance. Now, 'life' may be taken in two basic senses: first as 'the characteristic functioning of organisms', or as what is 'opposed to death'; and, secondly, as what happens, or as 'what the organism encounters and has to contend with'.[59] In both these senses, life may be said to be characterised by rhythm. Indeed, besides the fundamental rhythms of organic function that we have already spoken of, the rhythm that may be regarded as basic to man's *existence* as an animal is

> the strain of maintaining a vital balance amid the alien and impartial chances of the world, complicated and heightened by passional desires. The pure sense of life springs from that basic rhythm, and varies from the composed well-being of sleep to the intensity of spasm, rage, or ecstasy. . . .[60] As comedy presents the vital rhythm of self-consummation. . . . [The tragic rhythm is] the deathward advance of . . . [our] individual lives . . . [a passage] towards an absolute close. This form reflects the basic structure of personal life, and therewith of feeling when life is viewed as a whole.[61]

(d) Now, what really concerns us here, in respect of Langer's views given above, is not the validity of the way she relates tragedy and comedy to human life, but how exactly the diverse instances she cites of organic function, man's

59. Langer, *Feeling and Form*, p. 214.

60. *Ibid.*, p. 330.

61. *Ibid.*, p. 351.

existence, and the literary genres of tragedy and comedy can all be said to be cases of rhythm. This, in turn, demands that we reconsider the basic question. What exactly is rhythm, in life and in art? Here, two of Langer's unambiguous answers that we have already touched are as follows:

> (*a′*) The essence of rhythm is the preparation of a new event by the ending of a previous one.[62]
>
> (*b′*) The essence of rhythm is the alternation of tensions building up to a new crisis, and ebbing away in a graduated course of relaxation whereby a new build-up of tension is prepared and driven to the next crisis, which necessitates the next cadence.[63]

Now, either definition assumes that rhythm is matter of function (see: 'building up' 'preparation of' in the two definitions just cited). This is, in fact, a view which Langer freely repeats in her works. But if this emphasis is agreed to, how can one speak of the (literally moveless) rhythm of colours in a painting? This, however, is not the only point that I wish to press against the definitions. My protest is fuller, and I put it thus:

The first definition, claiming (like the second) to seize the essence of rhythm, does not use the word *tension* at all. Therefore, it may be said to be quite relevant to the cases of rhythm as *mutual conditioning* which Langer cites in *Problems of Art* — say, 'the swinging of a pendulum' and 'the breaking of waves in a steady surf on a beach' — in respect of which she herself uses the word *momentum*, not *tension*. And the preference is warranted; for, *none* of the more widely acknowledged meanings of *tension*, namely, the following:

> stretching, a pulling strain, stretched or strained state, strain generally, (or, formerly, pressure in gases or vapour), a state of barely suppressed emotion, as excitement, suspense, anxiety or hostility,

---

62. Langer, *Feeling and Form*, p. 126.

63. Langer, *Mind: An Essay on Human Feeling*, vol. I, p. 324.

is really applicable to the cases of mutual conditioning just listed. But, if this is so, if no tension may be said to there in instances of rhythm which Langer here cites, how can *(b')* which defines rhythm in terms of *tension* be said to hold?

Further, if [as *(b')* requires us to do] rhythm be defined as a *cycle* (see 'alternation') of 'tension-crisis-ebbing away (or cadence)-another tension-crisis-cadence', and so on, how can the deathward (or towards a *final* or *'absolute* close')[64] advance of individual lives be regarded as making for tragic *rhythm*? The second definition *(b')* is indeed not true to the practice of Hindustani rhythm. Here, so far as the *ṭhekā* is concerned, there is (ordinarily) no building up of a tension, nor any 'ebbing away in a graduated course of relaxation. . . .' Artistic form is here secured only by an evenness of pace and clear and 'blended' execution of the constituent syllables of the *ṭhekā*, besides, of course, a consistently accurate marking of the *sama*. The language in which a well played *ṭhekā* is commonly acclaimed is roughly as follows:

"वाह! क्या ठेका क़ायम किया है!; दाएं बाएं का वज़न भी बराबर है!"

In the first segment of applause, the reference is to evenness of pace; and in the second, to a skilfully balanced employment of the two drums. And, to turn to the various *patterns* in which a solo exposition of rhythm abounds, though some kind of tension may well seem to be built up, at times, in the manner of their gaining access to the *sama*, what follows the attainment of *sama* or completion of the patterns — is surely no 'ebbing away in a *graduated* course of relaxation', but a prompt return to the *ṭhekā* as it was before the pattern took off.

A few more details are suspect in Langer's view of rhythm, if we look at it all from the viewpoint of Hindustani rhythm. Traces of tension, I admit again, are surely to be found at places in our rhythm as practised and as contemplated. In fact, one important feature of our rhythmic system is that (as pointed out earlier) if we are used to contemplating rhythm as art, the pace at which the very first *bol* is played or uttered,

64. Langer, *Feeling and Form*, p. 351.

makes us *expect* — maybe, a little tensely, say, where the pace indicated is markedly slow — that the subsequent pace too will be leisurely according to the way the first *bol* has been projected. Further, though evenness of pace (or *laya*) is admittedly a basic requirement, what is admired as a mark of *special* technical excellence is not this steadiness in itself, but the ability to keep it even when the *sitār* or *sarod* player executes patterns of 'wanton heed and giddy cunning', or when the drummer himself plays a pattern which does not go haywire in *laya*, in spite of the incorporation of a phrase or syllable that deviates purposely from the basic *laya*. In either case, we may note, a kind of gentle *pull* is created, and even felt, between the normal tempo and the moments of wilful deviation. Yet it seems to me that the emphasis that Langer puts on the build-up and release of *tension* is a little overdone. When a *ṭhekā*, which is the ground of our rhythm, has been properly established as a measured extent of even and articulate pace, it seems to move on effortlessly — of its own impulse, so to say. Nor does the *rasika* here see any tension. Rather, in an *easy* exercise of imaginative sympathy, he just feels swayed and lulled into sweet acquiescence by the self-completing rhythmic flow. Our experience, here, is one of effortless following, not of any strain or pressure at all.

Consider, next, a detail of Langer's protest against the commonly held view that rhythm is a matter of periodic succession. As a rebuttal of this view, she points to a matter of fact. A tennis player's motions may well 'impress one as rhythmic — [even though] he does not repeat a single action'; and, what is more, he may well be less metrical in his step than 'a drunkard walking'.[65] Langer would like us to believe that in such cases we see rhythm only because every movement of the player at once paves the way to the next. But I do not think her reasoning here is supported by the evidence of fact. The most easily identified locus of rhythm in tennis is a long rally comprising (seemingly) effortless and flowing strokes unruffled by jerky movements. If a movement prepares the

---

65. Langer, *Problems of Art*, p. 50.

way to the next, *but with sudden and manifest effort* — say, by way of a leap to counter a lob, or as a dive for scooping a drop shot — the playing is likely to seem acrobatic rather than rhythmic, and if some may yet prefer to call it *rhythmic* it will only be if the return turns out to be a winner, in which case the appellation will relate to the adequacy of effort *as a whole* to attainment, and not really to the conduciveness of just *one step* to another.

And in the context of architecture and painting, the inaptness of Langer's view is perhaps even *more manifest*. No one can deny the presence of rhythm in every art. As Otto Baensch points out,

> rhythm not only dominates music and poetry, but also, in a wider sense, architecture, sculpture, and painting: the bigger part of a space is heavier than the smaller; one spatial form, whether linear or plane, weightier, more striking, or stronger in character than another; colours, also, are distinguished from various points of view by their greatly varied impressiveness. . . . If, therefore, we want to define rhythm in general, we have to say: rhythm is the alternation between heavy (stressed) and light (unstressed or less stressed) parts, in so far as it follows certain rules.[66]

Now, there is no doubt that we freely speak of the rhythm *of colours*. But, by and large, our meaning here simply is that they seem to go well together; and it would be very odd if, using Langer's language, some one chose to say that in the case in question every colour (as perceived) is *an event that paves the way to the next*.

I hasten to add, however, that the generalisation on rhythm by Otto Baensch (which I have just cited) itself seems questionable. It cannot be said to cover *every* instance of rhythm; and my argument here is as follows:

The basis of north Indian rhythm, we have seen, is the *ṭhekā* or the rhythm-cycle. The structure of this cycle is admittedly a blend of *khālī* and *bharī*, or the unstressed and

66. Langer (ed.), *Reflections on Art*, p. 26.

stressed beats, the *sama* being always the focal point of emphasis. But though this structure is, of course, the foundation on which the entire edifice of our rhythm stands, it is not aesthetically the most satisfying feature of the practice of this art. Much more admirable is the infinite variety of patterned ways in which a good drummer can gain the requisite access to the *sama*-point. Such access surely heightens the look of the *sama*-beat too, partly because it is reached with split second accuracy; but our delight here, we may note, relates to the whole manner of gaining access to the pivotal beat, instead of being confined to this beat as played; and the distribution of delight over that complete segment of the pattern where it appears to take a look at, and (so to say) to move towards the *sama* noticeably, is precisely what *is not* covered by the conception of rhythm as a mere balancing of stressed and unstressed beats. The same may be said of those brief passages where the pattern is made to *deviate* purposely, though for a very brief while, from the basic pace of the *ṭhekā* — only to repair to that pace unfalteringly.

What is rhythm: A proposal

To cover *every* instance of what strikes us as rhythmic in the creation and contemplation of art, *and* in everyday life, I think *we* could perhaps put forth the following definition of rhythm:

> Rhythm is such an order*ed* (or order*ly*) disposition of elements, acts, processes, events, or stages that, because of some specific factors, the mind feels (on the whole) happy — or in some way enlightened — in traversing it as an object of contemplation. The factors in question are mainly the following: regular recurrence, contrast and balance, mutual complementariness, directed attainment of an end, or the mind's own expectations generated by habituation, past training, or present interest.

We may now see if this definition covers our experience of rhythm and rhythmic quality in diverse areas of life and activity.

To begin with, notice may be taken of a possible distinction between the order*ed* and the order*ly* or between that which has been put in some order *by* human effort — as in the creation of a work of art — and that which is *originally given to us in an order*, like the sequence of seasons or the alternation of systole and diastole. The word *disposition*, as meaning arrangement, may be taken to signify not only sequence and juxtaposition but interplay; and so to cover not only the occurrent arts of music and dance, but literature, sculpture, painting and architecture. As for *contemplation*, it obviously stands for both *looking at* and *considering* attentively. 'Enlightenement', again, is to be taken in its usual senses of 'imparting knowledge or information to' and 'elevating by knowledge'. Discriminating awareness of the regular and repeated sequence of the various stages of human life not only informs us, but may even elevate us into a philosophical acceptance, of the inevitability of decay and death. These stages may be said to provide a kind of rhythm not only because of the constancy of the order in which they occur, but because, as Langer would say, the very tapering of one stage is at once a making for the emergence of the next.

How our definition appears to cover every feature of our practice *of rhythm as a distinct art* may be brought out next — at some length, say, as follows:

The shapely passage of a pattern towards the *sama* of the *ṭhekā* is covered by 'directed attainment of an end'; and the momentary passages of wilful straying from — and prompt reparatory return to — the basic pace, by the following words in our definition: *mutual complementariness*. And, of course, we feel gratified in either case, as we follow the turns and passages of rhythm.

The *felt agreeableness* as the mind traverses details of the object contemplated is, indeed, the essence of the matter here; otherwise they are not likely to appear as making a *rhythmic* whole or sequence. Where we speak of the rhythm of events, actual or as projected in a novel or film, our reference is to such likeable chains of events as are, on the whole, satisfying and/*or* in some way enlightening. A good instance of such a chain *in actual life* is provided by the following:

> the long incarceration of Nelson Mandela as the champion of South Africa's struggle for freedom from *apartheid*; his eventual release; repeated meetings with the country's President F.W. de Klerk; the holding of non-discriminatory, democratic elections; the President's magnanimous admission of defeat; the election of Mandela as the country's first black President; therefore, the establishment of black majority rule through negotiation; and a graceful acceptance of the right of the majority Black by the minority White.

Where the chain comprises events that are merely virtual, as is to be found in the unfoldment of plot in a novel or a play, it may put an edge on our awareness of a good deal of what we surely encounter in real life, but do not contemplate enough: say, the diversity of human nature, the interplay of situation and character, the havoc that may be caused by petty human foibles, and the (possible) ominousness of a present situation. The chain of *actual* events we have referred to (in the preccding para) is of course good warrant for Langer's view too; but just as clearly, it does not elude the grasp of the definition *we* have put forth. It is, in fact, duly covered by the following words in our definition: '*directed attainment* of an end'.

As for the 'several factors' that lend a little charm to the mind's passage across concatenated details or elements, and make it seem rhythmic, they are all at least as clearly at work in the practice of our rhythm as in the region of any other art. Thus, regular recurrence is visibly there in the beats that occur at equal intervals; and in being actually played on the drum (that is, as *bharī*) or as quietly affirmed in the mind (*khālī*), they not only provide a kind of balance by opposing each other, and so prevent an overplay of sound or silence, but necessitate attention to both overt playing and ideal attunement, again by virtue of their very opposition. It is also a noteworthy feature of the practice of Hindustani rhythm that whole bunches of mnemonic syllables (*bols*) often seem to be mutual complements in the sense that, besides being similar by virtue of covering an equal number of beats, the later bunch provides what the earlier one *lacks*, say, syllables having a subdued sound. Thus, in the following sequence: **तकिटतका**,

तिटकतागदिगिन whereas the first phrase has only one *bol* of closed sound (किट), the second has as many as three: तिट, गदि, गिन.

The *effective* working of all these factors, however, depends on the past training, habits of attention, and present interest of the contemplator. No detail of the practice of rhythm as a *flowing*, yet articulate form can be rightly perceived unless one is able to hold on to the basic pace of the *ṭhekā*; and this ability is not an instant acquisition, but the product of long training or habituation. It works necessarily, if subduedly, where what is contemplated is not merely the *ṭhekā* as such, but a full pattern that runs across and, on the whole, within the ambit of the *ṭhekā*. And where the pattern in question is exceptionally intricate — may be because of some moments of intentional deviation from the basic pace — intenseness of present attention is an indispensable requirement.

Three critical questions

But these explanatory comments on *our* definition of rhythm do not throw any light on a question that is often debated by aestheticians today. (1) Is the time (or its semblance) that we find in rhythm similar to, or different from time as we experience it in daily life? Nor has our discussion so far addressed the key question relating to Langer's aesthetics of rhythm. (2) How does she avail of the concept of rhythm in defending her thesis that all art is a symbolic projection *of felt life*? (3) And, finally, how does the concept in question facilitate interrelation of other concepts in her aesthetics of music and of art in general, — concepts like 'forms of feeling', composition and organic unity.

The second question may be taken up first, because of its greater relevance to an assessment of the crux of Langer's aesthetics. It calls for some critical attention to all the major arts. But, to keep our discussion within manageable limits — and also because it is *literature* which is commonly regarded as essentially *related to life* — we may here focus on drama, ignoring non-dramatic poetry which has already been touched on in the first chapter.

Now, turning to the two key concepts that figure in the second question — namely, *rhythm* and *life* — I find it necessary to give a clear, if brief, account of what Langer has to say about them, though it is bound to involve some repetition of the thinking we have already done. Rhythm, we have seen, can be cyclic — that is, a matter of mutual conditioning — *or* merely serial. A distinct form of the latter is what Langer, would like us to call, *cadential* rhythm. The word *cadence* admits of at least three clear meanings: the beat or measure of something rhythmic, a *fall* in the pitch of the voice at the end of a sentence, and the *close* of a musical phrase or section. Langer seems to take the word, quite generally, in the sense of a fall or close. I say so in view of her following remark:

> Unlike the simple metabolic process [which may be said to be cyclic], the deathward advance of . . . [our] individual lives has a series of stations that are *not repeated*; growth, maturity, decline. That is the tragic rhythm. Tragedy is a *cadential* form. Its crisis is always the turn toward *an absolute close*. This form reflects the basic structure of personal life. . .[67]

Now, a mere close as such cannot be said to be rhythmic. But where it comes as the end of a series of events or stages each of which appears to prepare the way to the next one, it may well be said to culminate a cadential rhythm. What is necessarily present in every kind of rhythm is (a) change, process flow and succession — besides, of course, (b) determination of that which follows by that which precedes. Strictly speaking, the 'stations' Langer distinguishes in our individual lives are not fixed positions, but phases, that is, stages in growth or development. But, be that as it may, according to Langer the two essentials we have distinguished hold of every instance of rhythmicity; where a process *is* rhythmic, 'the consummation of one phase is the preparation for another, which in its consummation prepares its successor'. . . .[68]

---

67. Langer, *Feeling and Form*, p. 351. Italics added.
68. Langer, *Mind: An Essay on Human Feeling*, p. 204.

Some attention may now be given to the other concept, *life*, as Langer understands it. Here, for the sake of clarity, our treatment may be divided under two distinct heads:

1. Life as featuring rhythms
2. The pure sense of life

1. The rhythms that distinguish life are organic, emotional, mental; the rhythm of attention is an interesting link between them; and, taken together, they compose the dynamic pattern of feeling,[69] or how it actually feels to be alive. As mutual conditioning, we have seen, rhythm 'is the law of *organic* function'.[70] On the outside, the daily life of an individual shows the rhythm of vigorous activity and consequent languor, followed (as naturally) by sleep which, in turn, generally prepares one for another day of vigorous activity. *Emotional* rhythms are provided, say, by the dualities of excitement and depresssion, joy and sorrow, elation and frustration which are all cases of mutual conditioning in the sense that the more we yield to any one of the pair, the more liable we become to experience the other, if not quite readily. Attention connects them all in the sense that one is always more or less clearly aware of their character when they occur; but, we may note, attention is itself rhythmic in nature in so far as every act of intense concentration of attention presses for, and is followed by a state of felt relaxation which, however, may or may not be incidental to the attainment of a desired end.

2. By 'the *pure* sense of life' Langer means sensation, awareness, and expectation. These may be called 'pure' because they belong 'to *all* higher creatures'. The *personal* sense of life — that is, the realisation that one is a distinct self and possessed of a life that has a 'beginning, efflorescence, and end' — 'probably belongs only to human beings, and to them

---

69. 'Dynamic' *and very complex*, because "all sorts of processes may culminate in feeling with or without direct relation to each other . . ." *Ibid*. p, 67.

70. Langer, *Problems of Art*, p. 52. Italics added.

in varying measure'.[71] It is 'more elaborate and more integrated' than the pure sense of life. Yet both are alike 'fundamental forms of consciousness' that drama may be said to abstract from reality as its building material; and, speaking quite generally, they may be taken as one to make 'the sense of life'. This (total) sense is infinitely complex and 'variable in its possible expressions'. But it is by no means the feeling of a chaotic series of indeterminate elements; for, as that which distinguishes the animate from the inanimate, life is teleological, — a characteristic which manifests itself as 'self-preservation, self-restoration, functional tendency, purpose'. And, what is specially germane to our present purpose, all these manifestations involve rhythm as determination of what follows by that which comes earlier, often in the way of a need as itself pressing for a specific fulfilment. To illustrate,

> A tree . . . that is bereft of the sunshine it needs by the encroachment of other trees, tends to grow tall and thin until it can spread its own branches in the light. A fish that has most of its tail bitten off partly overcomes the disturbance of its locomotion patterns by growing new tissue, replacing some of the tail, and partly adapts to its new condition by modifying the normal uses of its fins, swimming effectively without trying to correct the list of its whole body in the water, as it did at first.[72]

In a much more complex and integrated way, human beings too manage to survive by regulating their efforts and attitudes to changing circumstances. This is the rhythm of adaptation. The challenge of new situations elicits new responses, because of the pressure of the instinct of self-preservation.

RHYTHM IN DRAMA

Now that Langer's basic views on both rhythm and life have been brought out, in order to see how (according to her) rhythm serves as a link between art and life, we may first state, in brief, how exactly she traces the presence of rhythm

71. Langer, *Feeling and Form*, p. 327.

72. *Ibid.*, p. 328.

in literary art, say, in drama.

An important, if general remark that she makes in this context is that

> a dramatic act is a commitment. It creates a situation in which the agent or agents must necessarily make a further move; that is, it motivates a subsequent act (or acts). The situation, which is the completion of a given act, is already the impetus to another — as, in running, the footfall that catches our weight at the end of one bound already sends us forward to land on the other foot.[73]

So, as determination of what is to come next by the present event, act or stage, rhythm may be said to be necessarily there in the art of drama. But some critical comments have to be made here. The word *act* in the extract cited is to be taken as something done or as a doing, *not* as a distict main section of a play; for there are one-act plays too, and *such* a play cannot obviously be said to make for something to follow. But then, if *act* is to be taken as a *doing*, what shall we say of those *speeches*, as by the Fool in Shakespeare's tragedies, which only throw into bolder relief the gloom or ominousness of the situational context in the play, instead of directly suggesting any further move?

RHYTHM AS A PAVING-THE-WAY-TO

Langer could possibly rejoin by suggesting that the very deepening of the character of the situation makes the reader *expect* something catastrophic to happen; and that, therefore, the speeches in question could well be said to create a rhythm. I make this suggestion because of the following emphatic utterance of hers:

> (a) Everything that prepares a future creates rhythm; (b) everything that begets or intensifies expectation, including the expectation of sheer continuity prepares the future; (c) and everything that fulfils the promised future, in ways foreseen or unforeseen, articulates the symbol of feeling.[74]

---

73. Langer, *Feeling and Form*, p. 355.

74. *Ibid.*, p. 129.

But one of the three points listed in the above extract, and distinguished by me as [(a),(b),(c),) is clearly questionable; and another, not readily clear. (a) is clearly too sweeping. Where excessive bleeding on his surgeon's table is seen *to lead* a patient straight to his death, no one will profess to see any rhythm in the situation, in spite of the fact that the flow in question is very likely to cause alarm, and apprehensive expectation of what is *to come*. So it is too much to say that *everything* that prepares a future creates rhythm. Further, the emphasis does not show any awareness of the truth that, speaking quite generally, rhythm involves *recurrence*. (b) may be allowed to pass; for to *expect* is necessarily to look forward to some future happening. But what does it mean to say (c) that *everything that fulfils the promised future . . . articulates the symbol of feeling*? To answer this question we have, first, to remind ourselves that by 'feeling' Langer means 'whatever is felt' — may be, the passage of 'lived time'; and, second, to consider the italicised words along with the following that the make their immediate sequel:

> Whatever the special mood of the [musical] piece, or its emotional import, the vital rhythm of subjective time (the lived time that Bergson adjures us to find in pure experience) permeates the complex, multi-dimensional, musical symbol as its internal logic, which relates music intimately and self-evidently to life.[75]

Now, looking at all these cited words as one — they, in fact, occur in the same para —'the symbol of feeling' may be equated with 'the musical piece', also because *all art* (according to Langer) is a symbolic projection of the forms of feeling. 'The vital rhythm of *subjective* time', of which she speaks here, may be taken to mean the rhythm or complementariness of need, expectation or effort, and fulfilment or attainment. This is indeed what lived (or felt) time really is. Clock time is unchangingly periodic; the ticks occur at equal intervals. But lived time, or time as experienced in actual life, seems to move slowly or quickly according as one's life is soured with

75. Langer, *Feeling and Form*, p. 129.

anguished waiting or enlivened with a series of happy events. As for the word 'articulates' (in 'articulates the symbol of feeling'), it may be taken to mean 'gives a clear appearance of elements that are distinct, though related in an orderly way'. Here I take my stand on Langer's explicit view that the *form* of music is *articulate* in so far as the elements which are here held as one retain a measure of self-existence in spite of the interlacement.[76]

The net meaning of the extracts we have picked for reflection could now be put thus. (a) Every *individual* phrase, accent or change of aesthetic pace (*laya*) which makes a *distinct* contribution to the emergence of the music's final form at once invests the piece with an *articulate* form. (b) Such a *form*, however, is no mere juxtaposition of parts, but an organic unity; and this is so because the whole is permeate with a rhythm in the sense that every part prepares the way, and makes us look forward to what is to come next. Both these points, I may add, are clearly borne out by even a casual look at the practice of Hindustani rhythm. Generally speaking, every beat, as marking and maintaining the even flow of aesthetic pace, makes us look forward to the next one at an equal interval of time; the next one, as it comes expectedly, not only relieves the gentle tension of looking-forward-to, but paves the way to yet another beat; and, what is more, far from disrupting the unity of the *laya*-flow, the plurality of beats only lends a look of articulate form to the total playing which, in turn, makes them all appear as gentle accents, and no protuberant wedges in the *laya*-flow.

Rhythm and 'life' in drama

To turn again to literature, we may now briefly outline Langer's views on how it is rhythm which enables tragedy and comedy to project a semblance of life. As forms of drama, both of course show the rhythm that has already been referred

76. "Music, like language, is an articulate form. Its parts not only fuse together to yield a greater entity, but in doing so they maintain some degreee of separate existence, and the sensuous character of each element is affected by its function in the complex whole." Langer, *Feeling and Form*, p. 31.

to, namely, the rhythm of an act as creating a situation which presses for 'a further move';[77] and so on, throughout the play. In life, on the other hand, if an individual's career is considered in relation to the totality of situations and happenings that fill it, two distinct kinds of rhythm may be distinguished: the rhythm of destiny and the rhythm of fortune. As rhythms, both signify a kind of dynamic relatedness; but whereas the rhythm of destiny or fate is the 'appearance that the future is already an entity, embryonic in (or determined by) the present',[78] 'the rhythm of fortune is that of 'vital continuity',[79] that is, the open and episodic rhythm of challenges or obstacles as making for appropriate, remedial action. Now, according to Langer, 'tragedy is the image of Fate, as comedy is of Fortune'.[80] Tragedy shows the largely inevitable rhythm of growth, efflorescence, and exhaustion. This is obviously quite similar to the rhythm of stages (of ageing) in real life. But comedy too may be said to project the motion and rhythm of daily living, — the rhythm of confronting and dealing with situations as they arise, off and on. But in neither case does the dramatist merely copy life; he has to organise and articulate a symbol for the 'sense of life'.[81] This, however, calls for some explanation.

Take tragedy, to begin with. Whereas in actual life something *singular* and menacing must happen *a little before* we become apprehensive as to what is imminent — as when the doctor's definitive diagnosis that the only earning head of the family is suffering from cancer at once makes us think of the ruin that awaits them all — in a play we are quickly presented with 'the whole [complex] set-up of human relationships and conflicting interests *long before* any abnormal event has occurred',[82] but in such an integrated and suggestive

77. Langer, *Feeling and Form*, p. 355.
78. *Ibid.*, p. 311.
79. *Ibid.*, p. 335.
80. *Ibid.*, p. 333.
81. *Ibid.*, p. 363.
82. *Ibid.*, p. 311.

manner that we *readily* perceive 'an ominons situation' and visualize that some far-reaching action must develop out of it. This creates the peculiar tension between the given present and its yet unrealised consequent, [or] form in suspense, [which is] the essential dramatic illusion. . . . [This *tension* is the *rhythm* of destiny. It does not imitate anything in life, but it surely resembles] 'an aspect of real experience . . . [something] which distinguishes human life from animal existence; the sense of past and future as parts of one continuum, and therefore of life as a single reality'.[83]

ART AND THE CHARACTER OF LIFE

This should not however make us believe that, as a dynamic relation, rhythm brings about a perceptible resemblance between life and drama *alone*. According to Langer, every work of art betrays this similitude. See, here, her following emphatic utterance.

> . . . All art has the character of *life*, because every work must have *organic* character and it usually makes sense to speak its *fundamental rhythm*.[84]

Now, partly because fundamental rhythm is here taken to be present not only in *life* but in art, and partly because Langer also introduces — elsewhere, but again in relation to art — the concept of *commanding form*, I think it necessary to make some explanatory remarks on the extract cited.

To begin with, 'life' is here to be taken *not* in the 'social' sense — that is, as 'what happens, (or) what the organism . . . encounters and has to contend with' but as 'the characteristic functioning of organism' or as what is 'opposed to death'.[85] With this specific meaning in mind, we may say that all art is organic in character — or is similar to life — because, very much like life, no work can be regarded as a mere summation of elements of determinate individual values. Langer's following remark is here very pertinent:

---

83. Langer, *Feeling and Form*, p. 311.

84. *Ibid.*, pp. 214.

> Who could say *how much* of a natural organism's life is in the lungs, how much in the legs, or how much more life would be added to us if we were given a lively tail to wave?[86]

The task here visualized is impossible; and, similarly, 'although it is possible to analyse *what* [or *how* the elements of a work of art] . . . contribute to the . . . [work], it is not possible to assign them any of its import *apart from the whole*'.[87] What a line contributes to a painting, a look of tension or of tranquillity, or of mere flow, can be determined only by noticing its position *in* the whole work; and, of course, the question, *how much* it contributes, would be quite out of order. "The essence of all composition . . . even purely percussive . . . is the semblance of organic movement [that is] the illusion of an indivisible whole".[88] Now, this is surely true of composition in the region of Hindustani rhythm. Like any vital, organic process — such as digestion or circulation of blood — the run of a rhythmic pattern is inseparable from, and is determined by many other factors or processes. Here, indeed, a pattern has to be so composed that (a) the *bol*s it integrates may, in fact, be *playable* in the same order in which they have been put together; (b) that the whole pattern may bear a determinate and identifiable relation to the basic pace as set and marked by the *ṭhekā*; (c) that the various segments of the pattern may appear to demand each other; and (d) finally, that the whole form may strike the knowedgeable listener as moving towards the focal beat as its destiny.

But though we may agree that, as a dynamic interplay of elements or processes, rhythm is to be found in works of art as well, before we finally accept the thesis that art projects the rhythms *of life*, we have to settle an important question of general significance. Can the analogues of a rhythm which has its locus is in a particular region of reality or experience

---

85. Langer, *Feeling and Form*, p. 120.

86. Langer, *Problems of Art*, p. 135.

87. *Ibid.*

88. *Ibid.*, p. 126.

be effectively projected in a quite different setting? Here, following Langer, we may at once say *yes*, and with due reason. When, for instance, we speak of the rise and fall of a stately life, we create *in language* an analogue of the rhythm which we often come across in inorganic nature — say, in the run of an undulating billow; and which may also be said to resemble the rhythm of the gentle swell and easing off of the chest in normal breathing. But if a brief linkage of words, which are admittedly symbols, can create an analogue of the rhythm of life, why should the elaborate structure of an art symbol be denied the power to project analogues of the complex rhythms of life?[89] The artist achieves this by exercising a common capacity with which he is very well equipped. Langer calls this capacity 'logical intuition'. As we noted in the first chapter, such intuition makes for the immediate recognition of such relational factors in experience as 'distinctness, similarity, congruence, relevance'.[90] It is this capacity which enables the artist to seize the equivalence between forms of felt life and certain artistic structures.

But does an artist actually do this, or are we merely supposing that he does so? Now, so far as I know, and I speak in the light of my close personal relations with them, our *tablā* or *pakhāwaj* drummers would simply feel bewildered if they are told that what they really do (when they play at their drums) is projection of some forms of feeling. They would hasten to add, in one voice, that they only try to play the *ṭhekā* and the various patterns according to established norms; and that their playing is determined not at all by the thought of expressing any feeling or its 'form', but by such basic requirements as are valued by all those who practise the art of rhythm, namely, the following: crystal-clear cutting of syllables that make the various patterns; due accentuation of some of the constituent *bols*; correct attainment of the *sama*, preferably in a well-designed way; methodical sequencing of patterns as

89. Langer, *Problems of Art*, p. 132-33.

90. *Ibid.*, p. 166.

they make a whole recital; and, of course, the ability to keep the basic *laya* from wobbling.[91]

To conclude, a close look at the art of Hindustani rhythm does not bear out Langer's basic thesis in respect of art taken generally. But what she says about the nature of *time* in rhythm seems fair to me. I hope to make this clear in my discussion of the following question.

IS TIME IN MUSIC UNIQUE?

What does Langer mean by saying, and how does she argue for the view, that the semblance of time (or rhythm) that we find in music is *virtual*? Both parts of the question admit of a definite answer which I may put as follows, at places with some comments of my own — with an eye to greater clarity:

Ordinarily, we experience time as a sequence or passage of states or happenings. 'Is', 'has been' and 'yet to come', — such are the words that we commonly use in respect of the temporal aspect of our everyday experience. More or less similarly, what enables music to present an auditory apparition of time is the (apparent) movement that we see in it. 'Music flows; a melody moves; a succession of tones is heard as a progression'.[92] But this movement of music, we may note, is *virtual*. It is quite different from the *actual* vibrations that cause the sounds that we hear. The motions of strings are 'extremely small, rapid, and repetitious'. They are as different from the movement of a simple melody towards its keynote (*vādī*) — or towards the focal beat of the cycle — as 'the spatial relations of pigments on a canvas' from 'the relations of sky and breakers in a seascape'. Surely,

> we do not hear vibratory motions in music, but large linear movements . . . rhythms that are not at all like physical

---

91. I may here cite the following from my write up, 'Ustads pay brilliant homage to Dagars', already referred to: "Most of those who provided 'accompaniment' (to the musicians) on the *pakhāwaj* . . . impressed one and all, by virtue of their fluency, clarity and steadfastness of playing.

92. Langer, *Problems of Art*, p. 36.

> oscillations. We hear marching, flowing, or driving progressive motion. Yet in a musical progression there is nothing that is displaced, that has gone from somewhere to somewhere else.[93]

Frets and keys which produce music are, of course, laid out in space; but *the music* which they produce cannot be said to occupy space. One cannot put any *thing* between two accents *of music*, as one can between any two points in actual space; and, in respect of vocal music, it would be clearly silly to say that the notes are spread out all over the vocal chords. Indeed, in a musical ascent or descent no actual thing is seen to traverse a moveless path. 'The listener (only) hears musical figures that move through a definite tonal range, from points of origin to points of relative rest'.[94] Musical movement may, therefore, be said to be illusory — in the sense of being different from movement of things in actual life, quite like 'volumes in pictorial space' which surely do not fill a room as chairs and tables do. Another very clear index of the difference between what we hear and follow in music and actual motion is provided by the fact that 'when a figure ascends to a resting tone' and we hear 'sustained rest' — that is, 'a changeless continuity in time' — 'the *actual* motion of the air is faster on that resting tone than anywhere else in the passage'.[95]

Now, as an evocation of this virtual movement, the *time* that we see in music is also *virtual* — not only because of its patent otherness from clock-time, but because it is a *created* analogue of time as lived and felt. Here, two clear differences are to be borne in mind: first, between clock-time and experienced time; second, between the latter (or lived time) and musical time, — a difference which is (for Langer) at once partly a relation of similitude or semblance as well. Clock time, that is, the time by which we regulate our daily work and appointments, is 'a simple one-dimensional trickle of successive

93. Langer, *Problems of Art*, p. 37
94. *Ibid.*, p. 38.
95. *Ibid.*, p. 39.

moments'.[96] It regulates our lives, to be sure; but it has no content of its own, and is rigidly set in its abstract, unvarying course. Lived time is very different. To read in a watch the exact moment of one's arrival is surely not the same thing as the felt moment of relief on having made it at last, without delay and after a long and arduous journey. Indeed, our direct experience of time has a felt quality, a

> sort of voluminousness and complexity and variability that make it utterly unlike metrical time. That is because . . . (it is) the passage of vital functions — somatic, emotional, and mental tensions, which have a characteristic pattern.[97]

When we notice the changing positions of the hands of a clock we do not experience, but only infer the passage of time. And this passage (as experienced), "involves more properties than 'length', or interval between selected moments"; it involves what may be called bulk or *volume,* a sense of being full on the inside.[98] The suggestion is warranted by such familiar turns of speech as 'a moment of destiny', 'a memorable occasion', or 'a hectic day at the office'. In such temporal experiences of daily life the 'volume' as felt is by no means simple, but is full of '*tensions* — physical, emotional, or intellectual',[99] tensions which may appear as impatience to do diverse jobs quickly; as subdued anxiety, maybe, in respect of challenges that a new responsibility brings to light; or as the dawning of a pregnant insight which, so to say, insists on being worked out straightaway.

This 'lived' time, however, differs not only from clock time, but from the time that we sense *in music* — or, as I would prefer to say, in the autonomous art of rhythm. Virtual time, or the time in which musical forms or rhythmic patterns move, is not a part of our everyday, actual time; *it rather tends to obliterate our sense of the latter,* at least for the duration of the

---

96. Langer, *Problems of Art*, p. 37.

97. *Ibid*.

98. Langer, *Feeling and Form*, p. 112.

99. *Ibid*.

music, provided the music is good. Again, what fills actual time is a shifting mass of everyday situations and activities. The content of musical time is, on the other hand, provided by orderly collocation of tones and rhythmic turns. Actual time is measured by clocks and watches; virtual time (in music), through *sensibilities, tensions, emotions*.[100] The former fact is common knowledge; but the latter too is pretty easy to illustrate with references to Hindustani music. For instance, if in spite of its tunefulness, the singing of the *tāra sā* does not satisfy him, a *rasika* — that is, a person of trained aesthetic *sensibility* — will tend to complain that the note has not been sung long enough, *without of course looking at his watch*. Again, in the case of *ālāpa* in *rāga pūriyā*, the note, *niṣad* (in the middle register) is said to have been given its due occupancy in time *only after* it has created in our minds a *tense* expectancy for the requisite supplement of a touch of *ṛṣabha* followed by *sā*, both in the *tāra saptak*. Finally, a *sthāyī* deserves to be called *vilambit* (or adagio) only if it *feels* tranquil to *rasika*s.

There is at least one other way to distinguish actual time from virtual time. The lattter, which is (according to Langer) the primary illusion of music, is entirely perceptible through hearing alone; we sense it *only* in the relations of tones to one another. The perception of actual time, on the other hand, depends on such motley objective factors as a clock, delay in the arrival of a friend, or a satisfying filling of the day with a quick succession of pleasing engagements. This is the point in Langer's following remark:

> Inward tensions and outward change, . . . clocks, daylight and routines and weariness furnish various incoherent temporal data, which we coordinate for practical purposes by letting the clock predominate.[101]

Yet, though (as we have seen) she does not in any way identify the two, Langer openly speaks of our everyday experience of the passage of time as providing a model for the virtual time

---

100. Langer, *Feeling and Form*, p. 109.

101. *Ibid.*, pp. 109-110.

created in music. See, here, the following:

> The direct experience of passage, as it occurs in each individual life is, of course, something *actual . . . yet it is the model for the virtual time created in music*. There we have its image, completely articulated and pure; every kind of tension *transformed* into musical tension, every qualitative content into musical quality, every extraneous factor replaced by musical elements.[102]

This is a significant utterance, and I think it necessary to make some explanatory comments on it, partly because it is likely to appear a little rhetorical to casual attention:

All that Langer here says by way of heightening the *difference* (too) between actual time and the virtual time of music admits of supportive illustration. Time in the art of rhythm — I prefer to speak of rhythm, I repeat, as an independent art, as against rhythm *in music*, because as a mere element of music rhythm is not able to manifest its full aesthetic potential — is surely 'pure' and 'completely articulated'. It is pure in the sense that it is quite free from the admixture of everyday happenings which variegates our experience of time in real life; and it is fully articulated in the sense that not only the syllables which make the *patterns* of rhythm, but the beats and segments (*vibhāgs*) which the basic *ṭhekā* comprises present the picture of (*laya-*) flow as *the underrunning unity of quite distinct accents*. The tensions which appear in configurations of rhythm are freely seen to assume the following diverse forms: a seemingly compulsive orientation of a patterned flow towards the *sama*; the aesthetic strain of having to hold on (inwardly) to the basic pace, even where the (overt) playing is made to stray for a while, purposely and as a mark of wilful abandon; and where the drummer has to provide accurate 'accompaniment' to a *sitār* (or *sarod*) player, including moments of conscious endeavour to replicate the latter's patterns faithfully, again *sans* loosening his grip on the present pace of the matrix (or the *ṭhekā*). All these 'tensions' in rhythm, I may add, have their rough parallels in daily life, say, in the form

102. Langer, *Feeling and Form*, p. 113.

of unremitting endeavour towards a goal, intentional abstention from indulgence in a friendly gathering of revellers, and meticulous description of the details of a complicated situation. Nor is it difficult to show how rhythm — or rhythm in music — transforms every qualitative content of everyday experience into rhythmic (musical) quality, or replaces every extraneous factor in everyday experience with a rhythmic (musical) element. We freely distinguish the course of daily living as leisurely or crowded with happenings; and the distinction can be just as easily made in the flowing form of music or of rhythm as patterned. And as approximate aesthetic parallels of seeming 'irrelevances' in everyday experience — such as the *protracted* waiting for the outcome of an ongoing surgical operation — rhythm may project expansive, winsome patterns which are richly inlaid with syllables; wind their way majestically through three segments of equal extent; and which ultimately complete themselves immaculately at the *sama*, which itself may be all along foreshadowed by the determinate relation which the pattterns appear to bear, as they flow, to the underrunning basic pace. But all these rough parallels, it is obvious, do nothing to bedim the *difference* between 'virtual' time (or rhythm in music) and time as experienced in daily life. The sense that a very busy day has passed very quickly is one thing; the notice of a nimble rhythmic pattern as a close collocation of winged *bols*, quite another.

Langer's view that time as sensed in music (or as rhythm) is *virtual* has, however, been questioned, as by Philip Alperson.[103] It is a reasoned protest, and so I think it necessary to consider if it could be fairly met by Langer. Alpersons's formulation *and* criticism of her conception of musical time as 'virtual' may, in brief, be put thus:

1. According to Langer, all music creates an order of virtual time, in which its sonorous forms move in relation to each other — always and only to each other,

---

103. In his essay '" Musical Time"' and Music as an "Art of Time, *The Journal of Aesthetics and Art Criticism*, summer 1980, pp. 407-17.

for nothing else exists there . . . music makes time audible, and its form and continuity sensible.[104]

2. Musical or virtual time is quite different from *clock-time* in two clear ways. First, whereas clock-time is an 'abstraction' (of 'pure sequence') from the 'direct experiences of time' — or a mere *concept*[105] — musical time is *perceptible*. Second, whereas clock-time is but a one-dimensional continuum — say, of 'before' and 'after' — musical time has more than one dimension; it has form and organisation, volume and distinguishable parts.[106]

3. On the other hand, no such clear differences may be said to separate musical time from *actual* (or lived) *time*. The truth rather is that, "musical duration is an image of what might be called 'lived' or 'experienced' time — the passage of life that we feel as expectations become 'now', and 'now' turns into unalterable fact. Such passage is measurable only in terms of sensibilities, tensions and emotions".[107]

4. But, and now Alperson turns to criticism, if this is so,[108] if the resemblance between the model and its image is so complete, wherein lies the difference? Langer does not specify . . . [any] difference. . . . [Could it not, then, be said that] the temporality of musical perception is simply another example of our direct, intuitive experience of all things temporal [?]. . . .[109] As an occurrence, . . . a piece of music is of a piece with all phenomena that occur in time: it has a determinate period of duration; an objective and irreversible time-order . . . [;] it calls upon the same faculties we employ

104. Langer, *Feeling and Form*, p. 109-110.

105. *Ibid.*, p. 111.

106. *Ibid.*, p. 116.

107. *Ibid.*, p. 109.

108. Alperson's essay, p. 413.

> in all time perception . . . [namely,] attention, memory . . . . apperception . . . [and] anticipation. [Indeed] . . . (for Alperson) the truth . . . seems to be that the temporal dimension of musical experience is *not* [*sui generis* or] fundamentally different from that of any other sort of temporal experience. [So] why say [at all] that "music creates an order of virtual time"?.[110]

The crux of Alperson's *protest*, it is clear, occurs in 4. But, I believe, the critical points it makes can all be met by Langer, squarely. To begin with, it is incorrect to say that Langer does not specify the difference between 'lived time' (or the 'model') and its image, that is, musical time. In fact, if 1. is taken along with some (other) utterances of Langer, at least two differences between the two orders of time would seem to be suggested by her, pretty clearly. Here are some such utterances:

> A′. The direct experience of passage [or lived or actual time] . . . is . . . like all actuality . . . *only in part* perceived, and its fragmentary data are supplemented by practical knowledge and ideas from other realms of thought altogether. *Yet* it is the model for the virtual time created in music. There we have its image, completely articulated and pure . . . [only] the sonorous image of passage, abstracted from actuality to become free and plastic and *entirely* perceptible.[111]

> B′. Virtual time [which music creates] is entirely perceptible, through the agency of a single sense — hearing. There is no supplementing of one sort of experience by another. . . . Music spreads out time for our direct and complete apprehension by letting our hearing monopolise it — organise, fill, and shape it, all alone.[112]

Now, a look at B′ (and at 1. in Alperson's formulation and criticism of Langer's view) makes it clear that, according to Langer, the virtual time which music creates is experienced only *through* the sense of hearing or by attending to sounding

---

109. Alperson's essay, p. 413.

110. *Ibid.*, pp. 412-14.

111. Langer, *Feeling and From*, p. 113.

112. *Ibid.*, pp. 109-110.

('sonorous') forms. But this at once suggests, though it does not quite project, a difference between virtual time *and lived time which is* freely marked by a 'supplementing of one sort of experience by another'. To illustrate, my experience of the present moment is a 'heterogeneous'[113] mix of some thinking incidental to writing, visual perception of the words being written, hearing of the birds' chirping from outside the window of my room, and some bodily sensations arising from being seated in a chair and from a shuffling of the forearm across the sheet of paper being used. One's experience of attending to music, on the other hand, comes essentially through listening to tones and passages as they rest or move up and down the scale. It is true, of course, that musical listening is *not merely a matter of hearing*; and that, for example, the evenness of pace *between* two adjacent beats has to be kept and followed *in idea*. But unless the beats are *drummed* — or in some other way so marked as to be easily perceived — the requirement of keeping to the pace and sensing that it is being properly done cannot be met.

Here, however, I feel compelled to qualify what I have just said, from the viewpoint of our rhythm *as an independent art*. Of *our* rhythm it is indeed very true that whole collocations of syllables — even the most intricate and elaborate patterns — can be rehearsed merely in the mind. Such subdued recitation may be well be said to involve some implicit speech, but there is no question of hearing here, because no sound is produced. But Langer and Alperson do not discuss rhythm as an independent art; and of rhythm or time as sensed *in music* it is certainly true that the sole agency of its experience is hearing which (I repeat) at once distinguishes it from lived time.

The second distinction that Langer draws between the two temporal orders is to be seen in A'. I may put it as follows:

Whereas the direct experience of the lapse or passage of time — or of lived time — is only *partly* provided by perception, music presents the passage in question in an *entirely* perceptible form. Perception may here be taken to signify immediate

113. Langer, *Feeling and Form*, p. 109.

experience; and the net meaning of the distinction suggested could be put quite simply. The passage of time is, of course, ceaseless; but, because we generally remain occupied in life's diverse activities, it is only dimly or fitfully that we remain or become conscious of the passage. Occasions that make it a distinct object of direct awareness, like a prolonged waiting for the delayed arrival of a friend, are infrequent; otherwise, in general, some practical knowledge — as of the fact that the milkman rings the door-bell at a particular hour — may make one aware, say, of how long one has been working at the study table. Similar awareness may also by provided by ideas from some altogether different 'realms of thought', as when a look at the many reports of his pathological tests makes a person aware of *the long course* of a disease he has been suffering from. On the other hand, when we listen to music, temporal features like the *meteoric* ascent of a *tāna*, the *leisurely flow* of a *ḍagar* passage, or the sweet and reposeful *abidance* of voice at the upper tonic are all *directly* presented to us.

Nor is it proper to argue that the two temporal orders, rhythmic and everyday, cannot be regarded as *dis*similar because the *same* mental acts or attitudes are involved in the way we experience them. Would it make sense to deny the distinctness of sweet from salted food on the ground that they are both known by tasting? It is, I would say, not *how* we experience them, but *what* exactly we experience *in* them that makes the two orders of time quite unlike each other.

The point becomes very clear if we consider it in the context of rhythm as an independent art. A *tablā* or *pakhāwaj* maestro dwells in the unique world of rhythm — comprising beats, *bols*, and their variform collocations — with as perfect a sense of encompassment as a mathematician in the company of symbols and formulae. And 'happenings' in the drummer's world can be quite out of the ordinary. Where, for instance, in the ordinary world do we produce beauty, as our drummers occasionally do, by deviating designedly from a set course of flow, with meaningless letters (or *bol*s) alone as the instruments of charm? Even generally, the time that *we* regulate and beautify cannot be the same as the one which is only *given to* *us* and is so often the locus of wayward and unforeseen events.

RHYTHM AND SOME OTHER CONCEPTS

Finally, by way of integrating some aspects of Langer's thought, we may discuss a broad question. How does the concept of rhythm provide a connecting-link between the concepts of, say, composition, organic unity, and 'forms of feeling' in Langer's aesthetics of music in particular and of art in general? Following the main tenor of her own thinking, I may answer the question thus:

For Langer, we have seen, the essence of rhythm lies in the preparing of a *new* event by the ending of a previous one. But here the word *new,* as distinguished in meaning from the merely *next,* suggests that the continuity implicit in (her view of) rhythm is not the undifferentiated sameness of an unbroken line. *Exact* repetition is not the *essence* of rhythm, though a measure of such repetition may well be found in many cases of rhythm. (All this can be easily verified by considering the patterns of Hindustani rhythm.) As Langer rightly points out, even in the case of bodily movements — say, like walking — a rhythmic look appears only when 'one can sense [in the movement contemplated, the different moments of] a beginning, intent, and consummation, and *see in the last stage of one [gesture] the condition and indeed the rise of another*.'[114] Continuity that is implicit in conduciveness of one detail to another indeed seems to be necessary for the appearance of rhythm. To illustrate, if on being asked to get into a car, an intoxicated person lifts his foot repeatedly, but in vain — because it misses the door of the vehicle — his movements will only be said to be random, and not rhythmic, even though they clearly involve some repetition. On the other hand, if (as in the game of cricket) a fielder keeps his eye on the ball aloft and a good way away, runs for it covering quite some distance, and brings off a last-minute catch by hurriedly adjusting his hands and stance suitably, the whole act may well be called rhythmic because,

---

114. Langer, *Feeling and Form*, p. 127.

though it hardly repeats any movement, it shows 'a beginning, intent, and consummation' quite clearly. Now, such conduciveness of one detail to another distinct one (or rhythm) is also an essential feature of what Langer means by *composition*. True, she speaks of composition, first, as merely 'the total Gestalt', and 'the fundamental form of the piece'; but in so far as she hastens to add that it is precisely this form which, once it has dawned upon the artist's mind, presses for development — and denies him freedom 'to wander irresponsibly from theme to theme, key to key, and mood to mood'[115] — the idea of interrelatedness of details is by no means left out.

Nor is it difficult to show how rhythm is related to the other key concepts of Langer's aesthetics, such as organic form and expression (of forms of feeling). I may do it, thus, largely by reflecting on what she has to say in *Feeling and Form*.

The creation of virtual time, or of a semblance of flowing time, is (we have seen) a necessary, though not the highest function of music.[116] Now, the chief way in which we experience time in daily life is as passage. Therefore, movement is essential for music too. But even movement is here 'virtual', that is, a mere semblance. What is seen to move up and down in music is only created *forms*. According to Langer, we may note, that which clearly distinguishes music from noise is no mere sensuous quality, but the play of forms. Noise is by no means intractably opposed to music. It may, in fact, furnish quite a few musical phenomena; 'hammers on anvils, rotary saws, dripping faucets are very apt to do so'.[117] But noise does not at all show what distinguishes music, that is, the seizure of a motif and its use 'either as a form to be developed, or as an element to be assimilated to a greater form'.[118]

Now, what we have just said can be easily related to Hindustani music. A motif is a melody, subject or concept, or a design, shape, or form not merely as such, but *as repeated or*

115. Langer, *Feeling and Form*, p. 121.

116. *Ibid.*, pp. 120, 126.

117. *Ibid.*, p. 126.

118. *Ibid.*

worked upon. A *rāga*, we have said, is a form; it may even be said to be, we argued, a *commanding* form. Music arises when either (a) the concept of a melody — that is, the *rāga* chosen — is itself developed in terms of (audible) tones, as in the case of *ālāpa* that precedes the singing of a *dhruvapad*; or is used (b) as the matrix or pervasive element of a *bandish* or composition. In either case, we may note, the *conduciveness* of one detail or phrase — that is, of a *svara* or *svara-samūha* — to another is a clear feature of the music. In both cases the quality in question is sensed and determined by means of the foreknown and prefixed — and all along quietly remembered — form of the *rāga*. In the case of a *bandish*, however, the conduciveness we are talking of is also determined, in respect of its run, by the rhythm-cycle chosen; that is, *svaras* have to follow each other, if but generally, not only according to the melodic scheme (or *rāga*), but in such a way that the *sama* may be duly attained. Even all along rhythm is clearly there, as a kind of paving-the-way-to what is to come.

It is indeed specially so in the case of the best known instance of composition in the region of Hindustani music, namely, a *sthāyī-antarā* unity. The more visibly a composi-tion appears *rhythmic* in the specific sense Langer gives to the word, the better it is said to be as a *bandish*, that is, as a distinct and cohesive incarnation of a particular *rāga* and *tāla*. Our words of acclaim here are: 'कैसी कसी हुई/गंठी हुई बन्दिश है!, And the norm that we here go by, if not quite knowingly, is not essentially different from what Langer appears to emphasise in the following:

> The essence of all composition . . . even purely percussive, if you will — is the semblance of *organic* movement, the illusion of an indivisible whole.[119]

The word *organic* here means *indivisible*,[120] and a good *bandish* can indeed be credited with this quality. We cannot account for its overall beauty by merely pointing to its rightness in

119. Langer, *Feeling and Form*, p. 126.

120. Langer, *Problems of Art*, p. 135.

respect of *svara, rāga,* and *tāla*. Sometimes it is the pauses which punctuate it, and its take-off from a quite unmarked point in the run of the *ṭhekā* (rhythm-cycle as drummed) which produce its distinctive charm. Such details can hardly be given an independent value, and this is one very clear reason why the aesthetic value of a musical composition just cannot be regarded as the mere sum of the value of its several moments.

So, in respect of what she says about the organic quality of a composition, we may concur with Langer unreservedly. But what are we to make of her following additional remarks:

> *Vital organisation* is the frame of all feeling, because feeling exists only in living organisms. . . . The most characteristic principle of *vital activity* is rhythm. . . . All life is rhythmic. . . . The highest *organic response* . . . [is] the emotional life of human beings. A succession of emotions that have no reference to each other do not constitute an 'emotional life'. . . . [The] rhythmic character of organism [that is, its indivisibility in the sense already explained] permeates music . . . [so, as an exercise of its 'great office, this art is able] to organise our conception of feeling into more than an occasional awareness of emotional storm . . . [or] to give us an insight into what may truly be called the 'life of feeling', or subjective unity of experience. . . .[121]

I may interpret the above as follows, with some such interpolations of my own as are likely to make Langer's meaning appear a little more plausible than it presently does.

The necessary setting or locus of feeling is a living organism. Only such an organism *feels*. But what makes and keeps it organised — and living — is rhythm, that is, the contribution or relatedness of one organic process (or activity) to another. This is quite manifest in the life of a human being which, however, requires (and provides) much more content to be organised than life at the level of lower animals. Our lives feel undivided in spite of their content of quite diverse actions and experiences. Here, however, the *highest* organic response, we may say, is evidenced by emotional life; for an emotional

121. Langer, *Feeling and Form*, p. 126.

response involves, first, a clear perception of the specific character of the object or situation faced; second, impulses to combat or shrink from, or to dwell with (or on) lingeringly; thirdly, a fuller involvement of integrated — and so more or less predictable — inner and outer bodily changes; and, above all, a deeper and more or less abiding awareness that the experience is one's own than the self-feeling involved in routine activity. It is precisely through *this* felt appropriation of experience by self that a man's joys and sorrows make his unique emotional life, and may make him look upon the whole course of his life as studded with satisfying achievements or as a long, wan barenness of unrelieved failure. The art of music shows a similar organic rhythm. On the one hand, the various 'forms' of life as felt — namely, the rise and subsidence of emotion; pursuit and recoil, or endeavour, attainment, satiety; integration and enlargement, as of ways of learning or human relations; or a rich single experience with some moments of bliss, — these are all quite available, as apt tonal analogues, in our experience of music. On the other hand, they all alike arise from the interplay of tones, phrases, and aesthetic pace. It is this dual integration that makes our listening to a good music recital (what Dewey would call) quite *an* experience. Above all, because of its generally articulate character, as also by virtue of its logic of creating and interlinking *forms* which draw and hold attention easily, music is able to project for discriminating following the 'forms' of lived experience, that is, their directly felt look, as distinguished from the diversity of *content* of actual experience which (in real life) takes attention away from the intimate *feel* of life. It is the forms in it which stamp music with the character of life as lived — though, of course, as a mere semblance, because things, persons, and actual situations are all here missing.

However, I find it difficult to accept all the points that the extract in question (p. 277) seeks to make. It declares that the 'great office' of art is to give us an insight into the 'life of feeling' or subjective *unity* of experience, and (/or) 'to *organise* our conception of feeling. Further, it regards 'the life of feeling' or man's 'emotional life' as an integration, and not as a mere succession of emotions. Now if, as is again suggested in the passage being discussed, to give an *insight* into the life of feeling is nothing less than to *organise* our conception of feeling', and if the life of feeling is already an interrelated complex of emotions, are we to believe that art enables us to *understand how exactly the various emotions are related to each other*? To say *yes* to this question would, in my view, be untrue to the evidence of fact. Every exponent of Hindustani classical music knows that the emotive look of *rāga adānā* is that of valour (*vīra rasa*) and that of the *rāga jogiyā*, pathetic (*karuṇa rasa*). But if he be asked as to *how* the two feelings, of valour and pathos, are related, he will only be able to say that they are quite unlike each other. Our classical dancers may be able to say a little more on the point; for the two shades of *śṛṅgāra rasa* — (roughly, the emotion of love with a sexual base), *viyoga* and *saṁyoga śṛṅgāra* (pathos of separation, and the bliss of reunion, *in love*) do have something visibly in common. But they (the dancers) too will be unable to *explain* how all the nine *rasa*s (*navarasa*s) interrelate, istead of merely following each other in the elaborate number known as *navarasa-mālikā*, though in actually dancing this number they may well be able to give vivid glimpses of *each rasa in its individual character*.

4

Magic in Movement

Langer and Kathak Dance

I SEEK in this chapter to consider Susanne K. Langer's views on dance, with special reference to Kathak[1] dance of India. I also hope to meet, or at least to mitigate, some common objections to her aesthetics of this particular art of magic in movement.

What is Kathak?

With a view to assist those who have never seen Kathak dance, I may begin with a simple account of what it really is.[2] It is, in the main, a solo dance. Further, barring the opening invocation (or *vandanā*)[3] every intraform[4] (or number) of the recital has to conform to a rhythm. Our rhythm is cyclic.[5] It not merely rises from, but reflows to the first beat, completing a round (*āvṛtti*) and thereby making the beat in question (called *sama*)

---

1. *Kathak* is one of the major styles of classical Indian dance. An exponent of this style is also called a *Kathak*.
2. This account is taken largely from my essay: 'Aesthetic Theory and Kathak Dance of India' published in the *Journal of the Indian Musicological Society*, vol. 10, No. 3 & 4, September-December, 1979, Baroda (India) pp. 5-19. The present chapter, however, contains many references to Kathak which are not to be found in the essay in question.
3. Which may be done as the dance-presentation of a Sanskrit text *without* rhythmic beats.
4. Or item. As to why *I* prefer the word *intraform* to *item*, see my article: 'Kathak — Some Terms and Distinctions' in *Sangeet Natak*, Jan.-March 1979, pp. 5-8.
5. I speak here of north Indian rhythm.

appear clearly central. The drummer (*tabla*[6]-player) keeps marking the cycle as long as the dancing lasts. The other key accompanist is an instrumentalist whose role is the ceaseless playing of a single musical line (*lahrā*). Both are required to retain the tempo chosen with absolute poise. In fact, it is they who make and keep the rhythm-cycle available and clear to the dancer. Yet their functions are not quite similar. The drummer is free — nay, he is often required — to duplicate, and sometimes share the rhythmic patterns which the dancer builds upon. The other accompanist's work is not so open to variety. His only task is to keep to the pace throughout, and to serve as an anchor to both the dancer and the drummer when they take in hand some filigree in rhythm.

The help of a singer too is often enlisted to facilitate *abhinaya* — or representation and expression — in thematic numbers. *His* basic function is to lend musical texts to the dancer for accordant treatment and projection through gestures and rhythmic turns and steps. All the participants must avoid involuntary lapses from the chosen pace. However, what holds the dancer *and the drummer* as one is not merely the canon of steadiness, but a distinctive detail of rhythm as vivified in all our classical dances; namely, the fretwork of *bol*s. Both, indeed, have to execute *bol*s or syllables of rhythm.

A *bol* is a mnemonic syllable. It is a letter or a tuft of letters (alike meaningless) roughly similar to the sounds produced by the impact of the dancer's feet on the floor, or by the drummer's varied handiwork on the drums. *Bol*s, therefore, help us name, identify, and even recite the details of rhythmic figures. The basic *bol*s of Kathak dance are: *tā, theyī, theyī, tat*: *ā, theyī, theyī tat* (ता थेई थेई तत, आ थेई थेई तत). But many other syllables, quite a few of them drawn from the various drums, bedeck the rhythmic arabesque created by the dancer. In the simple arrangements from which one starts, a *bol* is (so to say) the name of a beat; the two concur at the same rhythmic instant.

---

6. *Tablā* is the common drum used in north Indian classical music. It comprises two pieces, literally called as they are placed, — the left and the right ones.

But, it is important to mark, the *bols* are not merely required to seem clear and sweet to the ear — a demand that they meet *in dance* partly by means of the ankle-bells (घुंघरू) which every Kathak uses throughout the recital — but themselves have a varied euphonic character. Thus, a syllable like *trām* (त्राम) seems to sparkle (provided the *t* is kept soft as in Italian, and *r* is pronounced quite clearly, if wrongly according to English standards. Others like *dhaḍanna* (धड़न्न) have a weighty, elongate quality; and those that resemble *thowng* (थौंग), seem a little rounded.[7] *The percussive element in our dances is, therefore, not merely rhythmic but strikes the ear variably; and, to get fuller accordance with the auditory character of the syllables danced, the dancer has to modulate bodily bearing suitably, along with rhythmically apt footwork*. Thus, the main constituents of Kathak are: the body and its various parts (अंग, उपांग); musical text, to be represented or expressed (अभिनय); rhythm-cycle; and the variform syllables of rhythm. The ideal working of imagination and accordant dancing integrate all these diverse elements so thoroughly that, though they contribute to the wholeness of effect differently, a *rasika* does not ordinarily *distinguish* them.

What is the content of a Kathak recital as a work of art? It is today the opening invocation (or वन्दना) followed by *thāṭ* which is non-representational; some intraforms that are even more so, and of purely rhythmic charm (*nṛtta*); and a sprinkling of thematic compositions which are danced in accordance with the import — and sometimes even with the *manner* — of the text of the composition *as sung*. These compositions are often prefixed and traditional, and the ways they are set may themselves be distinct stylistic forms of music, such as *ṭhumrī*, *dhruvapad*, or *dhamār*. The import (or emotive character) of these classical compositions has to be expressed (or represented) by the dancer, providing the *nṛtya* aspect of his (or her) repertoire. Further, every intraform, following the *vandanā*, is required (as danced) to seem shapely to the eye,

7. Like the word 'owl' in the following line from 'The Eve of St. Agnes' (Keats): 'The *owl*, for all his feathers, was a-cold'.

and in line with the rhythm, which means that the *sama*,[8] or the focal beat of the rhythm-cycle has to be reached — and more or less *marked* — by the dancer with split second accuracy. Internally, no accent of rhythm or detail of movement is (in principle) merely slurred. Where these requirements are duly met, a Kathak recital seems inlaid with forms and intra-forms that are all complete on the outside *and internally articulate*. This double character is, as a rule, clear*er* when a competent dancer simply *recites* the patterns before presenting them as dance. An occasional use of such recitation (पढ़न्त) is an accepted part of Kathak dancing; and, if done within limits and properly, it can both appear as a locus of intrinsic charm *and* gently draw attention to the subtler details of dance, eliciting more discriminating reactions. More integral, however, to the intrinsic nature of dance are footwork and *aṅg* or the winsome adaptation of the body to such needs of dance as relate to rhythm and expression. A good Kathak dancer is mindful of both. The bulk of footwork is here done on flat feet (and the heels), though the sides and toes may also be used at times for the proper dancing of some specific syllables. Sustained footwork on the *toes* of both feet is, however, not done here. A display of pure footwork (or *tatkār*) is the common way[9] to end a Kathak recital.

I may now turn to discuss, in the context of Kathak dance as outlined above, some key aesthetical questions with special reference to Langer's views:

To begin with, why is dance regarded as an art at all? Langer's own view is that the question, why any *art* is regarded as such, is to be answered by considering what exactly it aims

8. For a fuller understanding of *bol*, *sama* and other main elements of our rhythm see my book: *The Winged Form — Aesthetical Essays on Hindustani Rhythm*, pp. 33-95.

9. Though not, in my view, the best way. Why I say so will be clear from my remarks, later in the essay, on *ṭhumrī bhāva-pradarśana*. In a paper presented to the Kathak Kendra Seminar of 1977 (New Delhi: March 10-12). I presented a new composition, *samāpan*, as possibly a better finale to a Kathak recital than the conventional *tatkār*.

at *creating*.[10] But, by way of enabling ourselves to see the *distinctive* character of her aesthetics of dance, we may first see how she opposes some common theories of this art. In doing so, however, our statement of *her* specific position may have to be supplemented with reference to others' views as well; and at places, with our own interpretative or critical comments.

Langer: The basic negations

(a) Is dance merely the 'gestural rendering of musical forms', that is, simply a case of dancing *the music itself*, as against merely dancing *to music*? No less a danseuse than Isadora Duncan has spoken of dance 'as the visible incarnation of music'. Langer, however, opposes the view; and a look at Kathak should quickly make it clear that her protest is justified.

There *is* an aspect of music — say, its rhythmic *flow* — which lends itself readily to parallel dancing; and this alone is of value in music for Isadora. But how can we ignore, and how can dance replicate that celestial sustainment of individual notes in music which suffuses the listening ear with sweetness? And how can the many subtle modulations of *akāra* (vocal tone) — say, as *ā, ē, ae* — be reproduced in dance? But, of course, one *can* pick music's balletic aspect for exclusive attention. This is, in fact, freely done by a Kathak dancer.

The *vādī* and *saṁvādī*, or the revelatory phrase (or the पकड़) of the *rāga* are not his concern. He cares mainly for the rhythmic aspect of the *lahrā-ṭhekā* twofold anchor, even though the *lahrā* may be set in a regular *rāga*. In other words, he keeps his eye essentially on the following: the general constancy (and sweetness) of the *lahrā*, so that his own concentration may be helped; the contour, or the up-and-down movement of the musical line, but this too as a passage that properly attains to — and generally also sets out from — the *sama* or the focal beat, rather than from the viewpoint of its formal graces, such as *khaṭkā* and *mīṇḍa*; and the steadiness of the *ṭhekā* as projecting

10. 'Creation', we may note, is (for Langer) a key aesthetic *concept*. Thus, see her book; *Problems of Art*, pp. 3, 4.

a particular rhythm. Where the drummer, as accompanist, not merely plays the basic cycle evenly, but seeks to duplicate the pattern being danced, the dancer is concerned essentially with the likeness of the way and extent of rhythm, and not so much with the individual character of the *bol*s interwoven. This is so specially where the *sangat* being provided by the drummer is extempore; in which circumstance he is not expected to be quite faithful to the distinction, say, between *tin* and *dhin* or between *tirkit* and *dhirkit.*

So, in respect of the music-dance relation, two points have to be borne in mind. First, dance does not seek to be quite similar to music; perfect likeness of the two is, in fact, impossible. Second, dancing (as Kathak) cannot yet be quite independent of the rhythmic aspect of its accompanying music. Further, the two arts are similar in respect of being occurrent in character. 'Just as music is made of sonorous forms succeeding each other in time, so is the dance made up of human forms in motion in space also succeeding each other in time'. Dance may even be said to need music in a vital way. It is indeed true that 'the division and structuration of time through sound is easier to achieve and more precise than that which is achieved with the aid of forms such as bodily movements'. But in the region of Kathak this particular need is met not so much by the *lahrā*, the musical line, as by the contemplation or recitation (*parhant*) of the *bol*s or mnemonic syllables that make the pattern being danced. And, to speak quite generally, dance may not be said to be inseparable from music. Jerome Robbins, we are told, created a silent, yet successful ballet. Such creative ventures are of course not possible in Kathak, because of its necessary use of ankle-bells that jingle at the slightest move. But the point is that these bells are important here not so much because of their musical sound, but because they mark the accents of rhythm *as built upon by the dancer*. For the 'pure' Kathak intra-forms, indeed, what is necessary is just a *lahrā* of sure (and sweet) step, and not elaborate music. *Jugalbandī* with musical instruments like *sitār* and *sarod*, I may add, is only a modern innovation, and surely not an original part of Kathak.

Further, though it is true that the word *sangīta* covers both dance and music, in practice the distinctness — nay, even separateness — *of training* in the two arts is quite manifest; and whereas 'dancers are not particularly discerning critics of music',[11] our musicians seldom make a perceptive audience for the Kathaks. Finally, though dancing *the music itself* may well be said to be present, at times, in such Kathak *abhinaya* as is done in close accordance with meaningful singing, the confluence in question can hardly be called an essential feature of this dance-form, because quite a few merely formal intra-forms are an integral part of dancing here, the commonest of these being *thāṭ*, *āmad*, and *tatkār*.

(b) Could we then regard dance as quite akin to the plastic arts — say, as just a spectacle of shifting pictures or animated design, or as a series of statues in motion? No; here, too, we must answer in the negative. It is true that the view in question has sometimes been held, as by Noverre.[12] And in the region of our own dances one could perhaps here point to *chinnhayātrā* of Assam.[13] But figures in a film or moving statues, though they can be clearly three-dimensional, are not really similar to the dancing figure. Movement, in the former case, affects (in the main) the mere outside of the whole figure or statue; in the latter case, on the other hand, it impregnates the entire figure, animating its inner parts. The intentional mobility of the face, eyes[14] and at times of even eyebrows, not to speak of the rhythmic movement of the feet and other parts of the body — is alone enough to mark off the dancing figure from a moving statue. *Langer's* protest, however, here is that in a movie, and more visibly in the case of a statue transported, we do *not* find that dynamic play of powers — comprising the upgathering and release, or emanation and ebb, of sheer movement — which constitutes the essence of a dance.

---

11. Langer, *Feeling and Form*, p. 171.
12. *Ibid.*, p. 172.
13. Mohan Khokar, *Traditions of Indian Classical Dance*, p. 149.
14. Such mobility is not ignored in film acting; but here the eyebrows, for instance, are *not* used in the way they may contribute to, say, *thāṭa* in Kathak.

(c) From this, however, we cannot lapse into the other extreme of believing that dance is merely a matter of rhythmic movement.[15] The rhythmic quality of military marches, though it is generally simple, cannot be denied. Yet nobody regards them as dance. Nor even the more skilled forms of bodily movement can be straightaway called dance. Consider acrobatics, for instance. Its principal aim is

> . . . not to create beauty but to give proof of skill, strength, suppleness. . . . The acrobatic dance, in which powerfully muscled men of Herculean strength throw female dancers . . . back and forth between them like a ball, has no relation at all with the art of the *porteur* whose object is not to display his personal strength but rather to show, if only through a simple effect of contrast, the grace of a female dancer whom he can set into motion merely by lending her the support of a finger.[16]

Where Kathak becomes mere acrobatics — as indeed it often does in long and involute *parans* — the dancing is generally dismissed by the knowledgeable as a display of mere virtuosity and as lacking in beauty and expressiveness.

Virtuosity, we may note, is overmuch emphasis on 'the means of execution as against perfection of the [whole] work'. The virtuoso seeks merely to show off — alas, too often in the region of Kathak — what *he* can do, much to the detriment of the charm of *dancing* as a whole.

> He does so not because the arabesque designed by his body will be beautiful but because the effort necessary to achieve it will be crowned with success. Hence the highest possible leaps, the interminably repeated pirouettes and other exploits of the same kind. . . .[17]

(d) Yet, in our recoil against emphasis on mere skill of rhythmic movement, we should not commit the mistake of regarding representation or 'expression' (in their common meanings) as the essence of dance, though we have doubtlessly a good deal

15. Langer, *Feeling and Form*, p. 172.
16. Gilson, *Form and Substances in the Arts*, p. 197.
17. *Ibid.*, p. 196.

of both in Kathak.

Some thought may here be given to the view that dance is really a dramatic art and that pantomime is the essence of dance. Cohen rightly explains why this view cannot be upheld.[18] Mime is movement which aims only at being meaningful.[19] When we fail to *understand* the movements of the mime we find no pleasure in its performance. In the region of dance, on the other hand, we *can* enjoy the performers' movements without feeling the need to define their meaning. This is clearly true of Kathak as *nṛtta*. Again, though here too the face has to seem not merely pleasant but as intelligently registering (or responding to)[20] the character and variations of rhythm, in mime the face plays a far *more important* part all along. Indeed, Indian classical dance can easily do *without the marked facial expression of any nameable emotion or idea*. Thus, in Chhau dance, where the mask is the focal point of the dance, the face — as covered with the mask — only 'wears a static expression' and *abhinaya* is really done with the help of 'the total body dynamics'.[21]

But a note of caution is here necessary, in respect of Kathak. Even where it eschews (like mime) spoken word of the ordinary kind, Kathak dance cannot be really called 'a dumb show'. I say so not merely because of the effective *parhant* which usually accompanies or punctuates the pure dance numbers, but essentially in view of the fact that the footfalls have here to 'express'[22] the rhythmic design of the pattern

18. S.J. Cohen, 'A Prolegomenon to an Aesthetics of Dance' in *Aesthetic Inquiry*, p. 274.

19. Mime is mimicry (or a play) without words. A pantomime too is essentially a dumb show; but it is a theatrical entertainment and may well involve dancing, songs of the day and some buffoonery. So they differ. But, because of their pronounced common interest in imitation, the differences are for our purpose immaterial.

20. The addition within brackets is justified by situations where the Kathak just waits to 'reproduce' a pattern being played by the drummer, may be as a kind of friendly challenge.

21. Mohan Khokar, *Traditions of Classical Indian Dance*, p. 133.

22. Such expression, be it noted, is no direct spilling of any actual feeling; it is a carefully organised *projection* of the rhythm.

being danced, by means of their deftly regulated sounding impact. The dancer here does not speak, but sure the accents of dancing do![23]

On the other hand, direct self-expression can hardly be regarded as the essence of dance. Yet, we may note, it is precisely in the literature of dance that the theory of art as direct self-expression is almost unanimously accepted;[24] and this is true, Langer adds, not only in respect of the primeval forms of this art, but in that of the modern ballet. Thus, see the following:

> . . . The dance of men is in its beginnings a pleasureable motor reaction, a game forcing excess energy into a rhythmic pattern.[25]

> [Ballet may defined as] the spontaneous expression of emotion through movement, refined and lifted to the highest plane.[26]

Now, Langer opposes such a view of dance by availing of the distinction that may be fairly drawn between dance as an art taken generally and the individual dances:

> . . . The really great experts — choreographers, dancers, aestheticians, and historians — although explicitly they assert the emotive-symptom thesis, implicitly contradict it when they talk about any particular dance or any specified process. No one, to my knowledge, has ever maintained that Pavlova's rendering of slowly ebbing life in 'The Dying Swan' was most successful when she actually felt faint and sick. . . .[27]

This is, to my mind, a very valid protest; and I find it easy to

---

23. I here recall the reaction of an American friend to a Kathak dance recital presented by me (at the Orientation Centre, School of Economic Growth, University of Delhi) more than 35 years ago: 'Good heavens! every beat speaks!'.
24. Langer, *Feeling and Form*, pp. 176-77.
25. *Ibid.*, p. 179.
26. *Ibid.*, p. 178.
27. *Ibid.*, p. 177.

buttress it with some argument of my own, warranted by the actual practice of Kathak dance in north India:

An important thematic (representational/expressional) number, here, is *navarasamālikā*, — a dance-presentation of the nine basic sentiments (conceived by the traditional Indian view) in the gathered form of a garland (*mālikā*). The complete number does not take more than ten to fifteen minutes, which means that the different sentiments — such as valour, love, and disgust as projected in dance — follow each other pretty rapidly. Now, were the danseuse (at work) to actually experience — as she is to be taken to, according to the self-expression theory — the quick changes of feeling herself, it would be impossible for her to remain unperturbed and retain the composure required to meet the demands of rhythm and the norm of adapting figural modulations properly to the shifting import of the text of the 'accompanying' song.

And where the dancing is 'pure' (or *nṛtta*) — that is, an aesthetic treatment of rhythm alone — and where, let us say, the rhythmic cycle chosen is a difficult one (like *savārī* of 15 beats), in the actual dancing of patterns (against or within the cycle) attention has to be kept glued at *their* design and extent rather than on anything relating to the self. Dancing, here, is not at all an act of *self*-expression, but the proper projection of a prefixed *form*. This is why most of the patterns (that is, barring the improvised ones) can be repeated on request. Even where a rhythmic improvisation is resorted to, the danseuse has to keep a very firm hold on the form of the basic rhythm as marked by the drummer. Similarly, if a pattern has to be 'thrown up', so to say, to the 'double' of its present pace, the form of the pattern, and also of the basic rhythm-cycle, has to be kept in mind undimmed, and all along.

Further, were dance necessarily an expression of the actual, specific feelings of the danseuse herself, it could not have been repeatable, for emotions cannot be aroused at will. The fact, on the other hand, is that dance *is* repeatable, for most of the numbers in our classical dances are prefixed — not merely in their own form, but in the dancer's memory. So this art cannot be regarded as, in essence, the mere outpouring of some present emotion. On the other hand, however, we have to reckon with the fact that Kathaks themselves are almost unanimous in holding that dance is direct self-expression. Our musicians and dancers indeed freely say that if *sangeet*[28] is not an outpouring of one's own heart, it is not art at all. Yet, and this is a fact which (we have seen) Langer herself emphasises in the context of Western dance, when *our* dancers talk of a *particular* number their language may not at all square with the direct self-expression theory. Thus, in the context of *thāṭa*, they speak of मिजाज़ बनाना, and not of giving vent to their present feeling. Allied to this detail is the fact that in the dancing of 'pure' or merely rhythmic numbers, whenever the basic *laya* of the drummer or the *lahrā* player wobbles, the dancer simply feels disturbed, instead of regretting the inability to express himself. And, to turn to the frankly expressional numbers, after the *successful* presentation of a *viyoga-śṛṅgāra* composition, the danseuse would only say that she enjoyed doing it, not that she is feeling relieved after weeping quiet tears.

But if this is so, why should *dancers* find it difficult to accept Langer's view that 'it is *imagined feeling* that governs the dance, not real emotional conditions'? Why are they, along with the common man, nearly unanimous in speaking of dance (taken generally) as direct self-expression? Here, Langer's answer, a part of which has been already given in the first chapter, could be put as follows:

First, the way the dancers think of dance is largely mythical. In other words, they do not distinguish between a fact, a *symbol*, and its import; and I can explain why I say so, with the help of a simple illustration from my own experience as a *rasika*. Once, in a brief bout of discussion with me on the occasion of a Kathak seminar, Birju Maharaj, the Kathak maestro, insisted on characterising *āmad* as that from which the dance really *begins*.[29] When I asked as to whether his

28. The Hindi word *Sangeet* (I repeat) covers not only music, both vocal and instrumental, but dance as well.

29. The reference here is to the Kathak Kendra (New Delhi) Seminar of 1976, — to the proceedings of the afternoon session of March 24, to be precise.

insistence meant that the preceding *thāṭa* and *vandanā* were not dance *at all*, he surely betrayed some uneasiness, but could not yet refrain from just repeating the emphasis. I later realised that, as an artist, he just could not make himself see the difference between the vibrant *aesthetic* character of *āmad* which provides *the first clear glimpse* of bodily vitality and self-opening of *aṅg* — as opposed to the more or less placid and self-gathering look of the preceding number, *thāṭa* — and dance's *actual* beginning at a define point of time. Merely to begin is one thing; coming to life, is quite another; and, as a moment, the latter can be easily more definite in impact. Incidentally, the openness of *aṅg* that distinguishes an *āmad* not only impresses the eye, but prepares the body for subsequent activity; and this may be said to bear out, if in part, the modern view that 'the concept of amplitude is the fine bridge between gymnastic performance and aesthetic movement'.[30] The same (understandable) inability to distinguish the artistically evoked from the actual and the directly sensed determines the Kathak's attitude to what his dancing may be said to express. As an artist, he finds the 'created' world quite as real as the world of daily happenings; and he is reluctant to see that the 'feeling' he puts into his work is merely the semblance (or a symbol) of feeling, and not an actual feeling that issues straight from his heart.

Secondly, we all find it difficult to distinguish 'a precisely *conceived* emotion that is formulated in a perceptible symbol [from] . . . a feeling or emotion *actually experienced* in response to real events'.[31] Yet, as we noted in the first chapter, the two *are* different. An actual feeling is a biological event; the concept of it, on the other hand, is a intellectual object. Nor is a feeling *perceived* from the outside necessarily identical with a feeling inwardly *experienced*. Thus, a *rasika* may not at all *feel* downcast himself when he *sees* the characteristic sadness of a *jogiyā*[32] rendering. Immediate, personal experience is surety not the only locus of emotion. Affects can also be quite imaginary.

30. Benjamin Lowe, *The Beauty of Sport*, p. 117.

31. Langer, *Feeling and Form*, p. 181.

32. My reference, here, is to *rāga 'jogiyā'*.

One often imagines what great fun would it be if he could somehow secure a cherished objective; and we do impute feelings to fictitious characters in literature.[33]

Thirdly, though the work of art — or, as Langer would say, 'the Art Symbol' — is not a thing (or is 'virtual'), its import may well 'refer us back to actuality'.[34] The meaning of the symbol is 'the reality which the artist has found in the world and of which he wants to give his fellow-men a clear conception'.[35] To illustrate, *tatkār* in (Kathak dance) is not as such a thing of daily life. But, what it projects — that is, a knitwork of diverse, yet regulated accents — becomes intelligible as such partly in the light of our actual experience of what is neat, orderly, and yet variegated. Indeed, the comprehension of the dynamic relations which make the fabric of dance starts 'from our actual *experience* of obstacle, conflict, victory or defeat'.[36] This, indeed, is why we tend to confuse the artistically projected with the actually experi-enced.

The truth, on the other hand, is that the Kathak's own overall *experience* of his dancing — as distinguished from the way he may *talk* about the art-form, quite generally and casually — does not warrant the view that what he does on the stage expresses his own present feeling. And, of course, he would himself object to the suggestion that the expression of feeling in his *abhinaya* is direct and unformed like a liquid percolating. What, however, *I* wish to contend here, following Langer, is that expressiveness in dance cannot even be regarded as the quality of an *ordered* projection of a *presently felt* emotion; and, my argument at this point would roughly run as under:

---

33. The 'feeling' of a *complete* work of art is, however, *not* imaginary. It is something 'that is revealed, articulated made manifest by the symbol'; Langer, *Feeling and Form*, p. 182.

34. *Ibid.*, p. 186.

35. *Ibid.*, p. 182.

36. *Ibid.*, p. 188.

A fair part of a common Kathak recital comprises pure dance (*nṛtta*). Here, there is no story to be told; and rhythmic trellis-work is the chief locus of beauty, though *aṅg*, of course, has also to be duly kept. In *nṛtta* the *artist* himself does not experience or express any particular feeling, though (because of their own inner arrangement) *the patterns he dances may well appear to be shy, frolicsome, or ebullient.*[37] What the dancer has to worry about in pure dance is only the accord of bodily movement with the sound, pace and extent of the matrix and filling of rhythm,[38] along with proper attainment of *sama*. As for numbers which are essentially expressional, projection of emotion is properly done only when there is no *actual* turbulence of feeling on the inside.[39]

Here, in passing, a point may be made in respect of the relative place of the thematic and formal elements in *Kathak* dance.[40] The word literally means a story-teller. But *in the order of actual instruction* it is the formal part that serves as the basis. Thus, the learner has to begin with proper hand movements (*hastachālan*); and clean, rhythmically apt and duly varying use of the two feet in *tatkār*. The third essential element which the dancer has to keep to is the twosome of the musical line (*lahrā*) and the cycle (as marked by the drummer). None of these elements is expressive of a feeling or in any way representational. In respect of bodily bearing too, the *basic* requirement here simply is that the figure should not appear

37. As to how this actually happens in rhythm, see my essay, 'Aesthetic Theory and Hindustani Rhythm' in *The British Journal of Aesthetics*, Summer 1976, vol. 16, No. 3.

38. The matrix is the basic rhythm-cycle (or *ṭhekā*) and the filling is provided by syllables inserted into the main segments of the cycle.

39. As Susanne Langer rightly insists, all composition requires a certain lucidity. This is one reason why she refuses to regard artistic expression as a direct spilling of some actual feeling. See her *Feeling and Form*, p. 28.

40. Like other major styles of classical Indian dance, Kathak has always been a blend of the formal and representational/expressional elements. But, I must add, though numbers of pure dance here abound, no intra-form in this dance is quite without the formal element of rhythm, barring the opening invocation in some cases.

too stiff, unsteady or awkward, and not that it has to represent an attitude or to manifest some emotion.

These elements, therefore, are all called 'pure'. But, I hasten to add, even the most unmixed of our 'pure' numbers are not meant for the senses alone. Everyone of them is (in our dances) rhythmically organised; and the appreciation of rhythm is never a matter of hearing alone. The right response here requires us to hold on to the flow of *laya* (or aesthetic pace) as an *ideal* grasp.[41] Yet, on the other hand, in spite of the presence of this non-sensuous element, the listener does not here visualise the form of any feeling.

(e) But if the essence of dance is to be found neither in music nor in bodily movement or expression alone, shall we say (with Gilson) that dance is an art of the whole man; and that its aim is 'to *impart* a formal beauty to . . . his body, soul or *to both taken together*'?[42]

I feel tempted to say, yes; specially in view of what is implicit in the words in italics. Mark that Gilson here speaks not of a body which is as such beautiful but of *imparting* a formal beauty to the body; or, to use Kathak parlance, of *cultivating proper aṅg*. Indeed, a figure which is not itself comely may yet appear winsome where the dancing is good. Gilson rightly contends:

> Certain (bodily) defects can even be advantageous provided they facilitate the effort and movement proper to the dance. A feminine dancer with a fairly small head on a fairly long neck, with legs and arms that are longer than the average can achieve effects that would be otherwise impossible. Here bodily movement outweighs bodily structure. The most beautiful Apollo must also be beautiful *in motion* if he wants to be a dancer. . . . Natural beauty doesn't harm; but it is

---

41. As I have said elsewhere, "the proper awareness of rhythm is, so to say, bifocal. Immediately, of course, we notice and follow the patterns presented directly. But this mere confluence . . . [will not be perceived rightly] if we loosen our hold on the underrunning *laya*". Saxena, *The Winged Form — Aesthetical Essays on Hindustani Rhythm*, p. 79.

42. Gilson, *Forms and Substances in the Arts*, p. 184.

> neither enough nor necessary. . . . Njinsky had a below average build. His Mongol type face was tied to his body by a very high and large neck. The muscles of his legs and those of his calves stretched the material of his trousers and gave him the appearance of having legs arched backward. His fingers were short and as though cut at the phalanges. In short, one would have found it hard to believe that this little monkey with sparse hair . . . was the idol of the public.[43]

Further, though it is difficult to see what Gilson really means by speaking of 'giving a formal beauty . . . *to the soul*', there is no doubt that dancing is not merely bodily movement, however rhythmic this movement be; and that — even if we ignore the importance of *abhinaya* in Kathak — the dancer has necessarily to exercise a kind 'of plastic imagination which enables [him] to see in his mind the exterior aspect of his body in each of its movements . . .'[44] Finally, it cannot be denied that aesthetically the most satisfying intra-forms of Kathak are those in which deep and variform expressiveness appears dovetailed with beautiful and duly rhythmic bodily movement.

In spite of all this, however, Gilson's final definition of dance as:

> the art which orders *the natural bodily movements* by imparting to them a form which is pleasing itself, independently of any other end,[45]

does not do justice to Kathak as a whole. It does not — and because of cultural disparity, it could not — take note of the rhythmic elements (and *bols*) of Kathak dance where, barring the *vandanā* which is sometimes done without the assistance of drumming, nothing is permitted to stray unwittingly from the set rhythmic flow. Indeed, where emphasis on the proper execution of syllables and on *rhythmic* accuracy (with variety) is so unremitting, it is clearly inadequate to speak only of *form* imparted to *natural bodily movements*, even if the form in question is taken to be pleasing to the eye.

---

43. Gilson, *Forms and Substances in the Arts*, p.190; Italics added.
44. *Ibid.*, p. 191.
45. *Ibid.*, p. 186; Italics added.

Langer's positive views

DANCE, ITS RICHNESS AND AUTONOMY

Our main concern, however, is with *Langer's* own positive views on dance. One of these, which is clearly tenable, may be put thus. The autonomy of dance is unquestionable, though it surely incorporates and builds upon material from quite a few other arts. To illustrate, 'story (often) runs through it like a thread [but] without linking it at all to literature'. In Kathak dance, a *kavitta* — like the one which opens as: दृगन मटकत, अंग फरकत ('the eyes ogle, and the limbs pulsate') — is often distinguished by a clear verbal theme; and quite a few images, like liquidity of eyes and bestirring of limbs, have to be truly represented, which means that mime too is here present. Yet dance remains distinct from both narrative literature and drama.[46] The net emphasis, here, is neither on story-telling or interplay of circumstance and character, nor on the proper integration of the main and subsidiary plots, but on beautiful and expressive postures and gestures; and, what is more, on rhythmic movement *which looks good to the eye*. Indeed, a (Kathak) dance is of value mainly because of its postural and kinetic qualities, — say, grace or majesty, effortlessness, and beaded appearance,[47] the last of these resulting as much from its setting in a rhythm-cycle as from the articulate character of the rhythmic patterns that go to make the total recital. Some of these points, however, call for individual comment.

1. To begin with, the value of the visual in dance can hardly be exaggerated. It is true that the dancer himself does not have visual impressions of the dancing *as a whole*; in fact, if it is a group dance, a single dancer may not even be able to see some other members of the group.[48] But,

> every dancer *sees* the dance sufficiently to let his imagination grasp it as a whole; and with his own body-feeling he understands the gestic forms, that are interwoven, basic

46. Langer, *Feeling and Form*, p. 204.
47. Our expression here is: 'दाना नज़र आना'.
48. Langer, *Feeling and Form*, p. 196.

> elements. He cannot see his own form as such, but knows his appearance — the lines described by his body are implied in the shifts of his vision, even if he is dancing alone, and guaranteed by the rhythmic play of his muscles, the freedom with which his impulses spend themselves in complete and intended movement.[49]

Further, though it *is* true that near darkness is sometimes introduced in a dance recital, this is done precisely for the sake of some specific *visual* effects, such as 'the blurring and melting of forms, [or] the mystery of black spaces'. Indeed, 'dance is essentially addressed to sight. [We] . . . know of no cult that practises dancing in total darkness, nor of any accomplished dancer who is blind'.[50] This, again, is why dance may be said to achieve its true creative aim when it is addressed to an audience, and becomes a *spectacle*. No merely bodily experience — be it muscular tension or the feeling of precarious balance — is enough to give form and continuity to the dance. 'Every such kinesthetic element must be replaced by visual . . . or histrionic elements to create [the dance] . . . for the audience'.[51] The propriety of *abhinaya* in Indian dances can be judged only by the onlooker; and, generally speaking, dance is, in the main, a dynamic *spectacle,* not mere activity. Here, movement itself is required to appear well-formed and bewitching *to the onlooker's eye*.

2. It would here be relevant to consider some questions regarding the dance-audience relation:

(a) There is, of course, no doubt as to the *formed* character of artistic expression.[52] Nobody consciously checks and regulates the movement of limbs while giving vent to a feeling *in everyday life*. But anyone who takes to Kathak — or to any other classical dance of India — has necessarily to carefully learn the varied employment of eye-brows, eyes, neck and

49. Langer, *Feeling and Form*, p. 197.

50. *Ibid.*, p. 196.

51. *Ibid.*, p. 199-200.

52. The work of art is, in Langer's view, an expressive *form*. Langer, *Problems of Art*, pp. 15, 133.

wrists in making the total dance effective; and the rhythm often moves in *patterns* which all have a discernible form. But does this formed quality of dance achieve its purpose when the onlooker merely *apprehends* it, or has it also to *infuse* him with the emotion that dancing (as thematic) may appear to express?

I believe apprehension is here enough,[53] though it may well be accompanied by a feeling of approval. The dancer does not *aim* at producing any specific emotion in those who watch him. He only expects them to follow and approve of what he presents as dance. This is partly borne out by the fact that a good Kathak dancer's grievance against lay audiences is not that they lack sympathetic feeling, but that they do not *understand* what he does on the stage. The word of complaint here used is generally *koorh* (कूड़) which means 'uninitiated or undiscriminating'. On the other hand, where dancing is expressional (*abhinaya*) and yet weak in appeal, the charge *of the rasika*s is not that the dance presented has failed *to imbue them* with a particular emotion, but that the portrayal of the emotional event or situation has not been *convincing*, partly because — say, due to his penchant for *fluent* rhythmic work — the dancer has not been able to treat the number with the requisite *poise* and inwardness.

(*b*) Again, does the fact that it is watched all along by the audience make dance occurrent in some *special* sense? The question is perhaps uniquely relevant to the (music and) dances of India, for they do not merely occur under, but are often (partly) determined in respect of both content and order by, the reactions of those who watch the performances. Here, however, I can deal with the matter only in the limited context of my concern with but one classical dance, that is, Kathak.

There is no doubt that, as a rule, the Kathak dancer expects and feels encouraged by the open applause of the audience

---

53. I agree that "in the dance situation it [is] surely sufficient that the audience *apprehend* what the dancer projects". M. Sirridge and A. Armelagos: "The In's and Out's of Dance: Expression as an Aspect of Style", *The Journal of Aesthetics and Art Criticism*, Fall 1977, p. 15; italics added.

after every intra-form, barring perhaps *vandanā* and *thāṭa*, that is, the invocatory item and the immediately following formal one. (I say *perhaps*, because where *vandanā* is rhythmically organised, besides being inlaid with beauteous postures, the audience may well admire it audibly. This can happen also where *thāṭa* is done with the requisite measure of grace, subtlety of movement and poise. Such opening excellences are, however, rare).[54] Therefore, if applause seems withheld for a bit too long, the dancer may well be abruptly impelled to enliven the pace of dancing, assuming — what *is* true — that quick (and reasonably accurate) footwork elicits readier response.

(*c*) But if it is done all along with an eye to applause from the audience, is not the dance likely to lose in aesthetic quality? To this my answer is divided. As he dances, the Kathak has to pay extremely close attention to three diverse factors: accuracy of movement in respect of fidelity to rhythm; the character of the syllables with which the figure must be made to accord as much as possible; and the overall likeableness of bodily bearing. So, *during* the dancing of a pattern, the movement or the dance itself has to be the dancer's only concern, and no separate thought is to be given to how the onlookers react. But *between* any two intra-forms, when the basic rhythm is generally heeded anew and patiently, some thought may well be given to changing (generally, quickening) the pace of dancing or the sequence of items so as to elicit positive response which seems essential to deepen the dancer's own immediate interest. The fact that there is commonly a brief suspension of dancing as such between every two intra-forms facilitates the needed attention to audience and to requisite adjustments in dance.

In practice, however, the average Kathak dancer of today abuses the facility and cares overmuch for the audience. He makes an express effort to invite our attention by telling us, a bit too frequently, about the subtlety or rarity of what *he* is

---

54. I have here in mind the finer movements of wrists and eyebrows; and a hardly perceptible, though surely intended, heaving of the chest.

going to present. This is why Kathak today is often quite without *the spellbinding quality* that should distinguish good dance. Our attention, here, is compelled to divide itself between what the Kathak *does* and what *he says* he is going to do. On the other hand, as Langer rightly suggests, in watching a good dance (knowledgeably) one does not notice the dancer *apart from* (his/her) movements.[55]

It is helpful, in this context, to mark what occasionally happens during our Kathak *rehearsals*. Here, there is no regular audience, nor any compere. The danseuse and her musicians all care for the dance alone. The result is that the glory *of dance, as against the dancer's own skill or charm*, is here sometimes better brought out than in an average stage performance. The entire team feels uplifted into dance contemplation and as sharing an act of making beauty.

This does not, however, mean that the presence of a gathering, and the dancer's awareness of it are in essence hostile to quality in dance. Nor do I agree with the view that a dancer who chooses 'to work only for intimate and initiated audiences' tends to ignore 'the demand to produce performances clearly and coherently enough structured for the impartial audience'.[56] And what I wish to question here is not merely the opposition suggested between being initiated and being impartial, but the very substance of the view; and this on the basis of the following well-known facts of Kathak practice:

When they can afford to let up on fees, Kathak dancers of stature indeed prefer to present their art to small, intimate and knowledgeable gatherings. Here they feel happy in being informal. This freedom from constraint of a kind can, of course, induce them to do a little more talking than the norm of compact presentation permits. But the feeling in question is a symptom of the faith that here they will get the kind of attention they need and deserve; and this confidence, in turn, produces a quality in dancing — an inward, yet manifest relish — which amply compensates for the defect of looseness caused

55. This point will be discussed later in this chapter.

56. "The In's and Out's of Dance", *op. cit.*, p. 17.

by intervening talk, and makes (on the whole) for recitals that leave one very deeply satisfied. The dance *within* the individual intra-forms is here so shapely and clear that the relative lack of cohesion *between* them — where the talking usually occurs — does nothing to detract from enjoyment.

What is more, there are quite a few subtle and dainty details of Kathak movements — say, in *thāṭa* and *ṭhumrī bhāvapradarśana*[57] — which just cannot be seen by the bulk of a *big* audience, that is, leaving out those who sit in the first few rows. This justifies dancing to small audiences of genuine *rasikas*; and, instead of lowering the quality, *such* performances only make it more accessible to perception and deserving of applause.

3. But whatever be the content that appears in (or enters) the 'illusory' world of dance, it suffers *radical artistic transformation*. Space is here plastic; time, as a rule, musical and (I would add) incarnate for vision, as also beaded (दानेदार) to the ear; actions are symbolic; and themes, pure fantasy.[58] All this, however, has to be brought out at some length:

(*a*) Just as 'spatial phenomena in music are more like plastic space than like the spaces of geometry or geography, so in dance both space and time, as they enter into the primary illusion . . . are always created elements, i.e., virtual forms'.[59] As geographical, space is static; it merely seems spread out, empty or occupied, even or uneven, proximate or recessive. Further, as we find it in the practical world, space 'has no shape [of its own]. . . . There are spatial relations [betwen things in space], but there is no concrete *totality* of space'.[60] In our everyday experience indeed, 'space itself is amorphous'; and in scientific thought [on the other hand] it is purely abstract,

---

57. *Ṭhumrī* is a light classical vocal form. Its theme is generally amorous. *Bhāva-pradarśana* here means varying expression and representation (in dance) of the emotive or merely descriptive import of the text of the vocal composition.

58. Langer, *Feeling and Form*, p. 204.

59. *Ibid.*, p. 197.

60. *Ibid.*, p. 71.

. . . a (mere) co-ordinate in mathematical functions. It is never an *entity*'.[61] Geometrical space is but a surface that is measured and outlined. It can of course take many shapes. But that which makes it significant is its measure or determinate quality; in itself, it is inert. In the art of music, on the other hand, space (or its semblance) is plastic; we see it being moulded in various ways, and producing many forms *and auditory* effects. Thus, in *rāga śrī* the ample 'space' between *komal r̥ṣabha* and *pañcam* can easily lend a slight, but clear sparkle to the second note, provided the latter is marked as a mere moment and quite without stiffness; and the much lesser 'space' between *komala r̥ṣabha* and *śuddha gandhāra* can be utilised in such a way — by employing a concave, leisurely and gentle glide — that the passage may come to appear imbued with a measure of tranquil inwardness.

Turning to space in *the primary illusion* of dance, which is (for Langer) that of *virtual power*, we find that whereas actual space confronts and *surrounds* us inertly — besides having the different attributes already referred to where we spoke of geographical space — the space that we see *in dance* appears as being sliced, carved out, encompassed and unfolded, always by means of rhythmic movement; and as thus assuming diverse forms, it all *confronts* us, besides lending various shapes to the dancing figure.

(*b*) Time, too, is utterly transformed in the art of dance. I have elsewhere brought out, at fair length, the differences between actual time and the 'virtual' time that we see in rhythm; and here I think it needful only to mark what separates the virtual time *in dance* from its presence *in pure rhythm*:

An emphatic footfall, a look that registers the advent of Kr̥ṣṇa, and an arm as completing a curve of *āliṅgan* (or embrace) — details such as these often occur at some particular beat; but here in Kathak, as in dance quite generally, they must all tickle the eye too, through deft figural adaptation. In solo drumming, on the other hand, the process and syllables of attaining to the *sama* produce a rather abstract delight as we

61. Langer, *Feeling and Form*, p. 72.

follow, mainly as a mental act, the shapely self-completion of patterns. Even where the dancing is an essay in pure rhythm — as in *tatkār* — the charm of the rhythmic lattice-work is inseparable from the winsome *and visible* nimbleness of footwork, so that the moment the feet begin to appear being merely tossed about, the charm of the footwork vanishes, in spite of all its rhythmic brilliance. Here it is, of course, also requisite that the footfalls seem winsome *to the ear*; but in meeting this demand, one cannot possibly ignore *aṅg*. And where the dancer is a really good one, the two demands are met quite effortlessly. The fact indeed is that the dancer whose *feet* seek to mark or execute the *bols* endearingly at once comes to wear a gentle, pleasing *look*.

Talking of footwork, I here feel impelled invite attention to a small, but significant matter of detail. It *is* true that the sounds generated by footwork in Kathak should seem, as a rule, similar to the varying auditory character of the *bols* being danced. But, though it may well be used as a criterion for assessing the overall value of a Kathak recital, the requirement of *actual* similitude is by no means unremitting. There is, in fact, a measure of clear freedom from it in the dancing of the basic *tatkār* itself. Here, the first segment of the basic *bols* required to tbe danced are as follows: ता थेई थेई तत but the dancing feet *do not really produce corresponding differences in sound*. Nor is any discordance here felt between the footfalls and accents of the (*tīnatāla*) *drumming*, though the syllables supposed to be provided by the latter are utterly different: say, नाधिनधिनना or धाधिनधिन धा. In other words, whatever be the requirements of Kathak *training*, so far as *watching* a recital is concerned, there *are* moments when footfalls are heard as merely marking the major beats, and not judged as *reproducing* the sound of the *bols* that, so to say, name the beats.

(c) Transformation of action is just as clear in Kathak. Action is here symbolic, not symptomatic. Rādhā's moods determining her varying behaviour with Kṛṣṇa are no actual states of the danseuse herself, though she has of course to *imagine* them. They project her conception of these states; and we understand them as such, ascribing them to the danseuse *only in so far as she represents Rādhā*.

(d) This at once gives us a clue to see how the themes in dance are pure fantasy or merely imaginary. They are so not because they are quite improbable — in fact, as we know, they are often drawn from actual life — but simply because they present the dancer's *imagination* of happenings which may be actual or possible, or merely mythical. The nine basic sentiments, which our dancers take pride in projecting, are a matter of everyday experience, though not as making a single series; the dancing of Śiva, on the other hand, can at best be imagined. Yet, *in dance* a *navarasamālikā* is as much a product of the artist's imagination as an essay in *Śiva-tāṇḍava*.

To conclude, in the art of dance all the materials are transformed into the virtual mode. This is indeed a clear emphasis in Langer's writing. She says:

> The entire world of dance . . . [is] a field of virtual powers — there are no actualities left in it at all, no untransformed materials. . . .[62]

But, I may add, this is but the statement of an ideal. It is only when 'the dance (is) in *its pristine strength*' (that it) is completely creative,[63] that is, a thoroughgoing transformation of all that it builds upon.

In other words, though *in principle* 'actualities' should utterly vanish in dance, in a presented recital they may well be manifest in some measure without necessarily detracting from the relish of the *rasika*. The two sides of the matter may now be explained, specially because the first of these is related to a common criticism of Langer which we shall consider later:

First, though the figure of the danseuse remains (visible) throughout the recital, if the dancing is good as art, the bodily postures or movements do not remain 'untransformed'; instead, they all along seem adapted to the needs of the total dance (or of a particular intra-form) as conceived. Thus, even where the accent is on footwork, as in *tatkār*, the upper part of

62. Langer, *Feeling and Form*, p. 187.
63. *Ibid.*, p. 197.

the body is not free to *sway disagreeably* with the passage of rhythm. Similarly, where a simple gesture of beckoning is made — as when the little Kṛṣṇa wants his playmates to look at a pitcher of butter he has at last espied — the movement, though momentary, is not only made to stand out more noticeably than it does in actual life, through a skilful subduing of the dance both a little before and after the gesture, but may even be deftly adapted to the rhythm, say, so as to mark an *unaccented* moment in the flowing cycle, which device may at once make the detail appear a little more *delightful* to the knowledgeable.

Secondly, though the ideal certainly is that space and time should 'disappear almost entirely in the dance illusion serving to beget the appearance of interacting powers rather than to be themselves apparent', in an actual recital moments of actual space and time keep appearing repeatedly, though such effects may 'almost immediately [be] merged again into the life of the dance'.[64] Thus, when the drummer has to tune the drums in the midst of a recital and the danseuse has to suspend dancing for a while, *and even appears* to be waiting to resume; or when, if the stage is uneven, the feet of the danseuse seem to be clearly probing for the right spot, we become aware of actual time and space. But these occasional intrusions of actualities are soon swallowed up in the life of the dance, and do not really ruffle the *rasika*'s delight, essentially because his attention is focused on what the danseuse creates, and not on what is merely given to her as the material of dance.

The way is now paved to a fuller study of the positive aspects of Langer's aesthetics of dance.

SOME OTHER EMPHASES

Gesture as the basic abstraction

What does a dancer create? Or, what *is* dance, considered as a distinct art? And what does it focus on — and appropriate from life as its basic building material, so to say? Or, in

64. Langer, *Feeling and Form*, p. 204.

Langer's language, what is the basic abstraction of dance? Now, to the first of these questions, Langer's answer is both definite and distinct. She is convinced that dance is essentially an apparition of virtual powers or a dynamic *image,* — a view which is perhaps not shared by any other aesthetician, and is even actively opposed by some philosophers of art, notably by L.A. Reid. And as for the basic abstraction of dance, it is (in Langer's view) *gesture*. Now, in so far as reflection on what an art is created *out of* may well be expected to give us some direct help us in understanding what exactly the creative effort *results in,* it would only be proper if we began by attending to Langer's emphasis that *gesture* is the basic abstraction of dance.

What, then, is gesture? As commonly regarded, a gesture is such an action, specially (but not necessarily) of the hands, as *is expressive of* some sentiment or passion, *or is intended to show* inclination or disposition. It may also be taken to mean some, but surely not all cases of sign or signal. What is, in my view, necessarily common to all gestures is the fact that they are (willed) human actions; and it is easy to see why I say so. Smoke is a *sign* of the presence of fire; but it is obviously not a gesture, because it is not the result of anyone's willing. On the other hand, if a wronged person, who is duly cognisant of what the wrong-doer has done, pardons the latter, the *act* of forgiving will at once be regarded as a noble *gesture* and as a *sign* of the pardoner's magnanimity. Similarly, a pistol shot which marks the beginning of a race is a mere signal, not a gesture, again because the shot as such cannot obviously be said *to will* the start of the race. But if, per some prior understanding, the starter makes the runners take off with a mere wave of his hand, the action will be both a signal *and* a gesture because of its intentional character.

Action, I repeat, is the keyword here; and, as is obvious, it is not mere movement. A meteor which is seen to *move* across the sky at terrific speed is not said to be *acting*. An action is a deed, something done *by a person*. As such, it comprises bodily movement *and* conscious willing. Blinking and the slight heaving of the chest that breathing involves are both bodily movements, to be sure; but they are not actions or gestures, because they are not consciously willed. However, we cannot say that all willed movements are gestures. Rubbing the skin when it itches intensely is often done with express vigour; but it is, so to say, a kind of self-enclosed action; and is *not meant to* indicate anything; so it is not said to be a gesture. A gesture must express or indicate something; *and* it must be willed to do so. Further, if we look at the matter in the context of our dances, a distinction has to be made between a gesture on the one hand, and a mere posture, on the other. *Tribhaṅgī*, which distinguishes quite a few of our classical dances, is only a posture, not a gesture, because it only *looks* curvaceous or beautiful, and cannot be said to *express* these qualities. It may well be said to *suggest* movement if we look at it a little analytically, for curves do appear *to flow*; but surely the danseuse does not *intend* the posture to convey any such suggestion to the onlooker. This is another reason why gestures cannot be identified with mere postures.

Nor is a gesture exactly the same thing as a *mudrā*. The latter always conveys some meaning, in many cases more than one; it formulates some thought for our contemplation, and so may well be said to be a symbol. Thus, in one of its many uses, the *patākā-mudrā* — along with an apt disposition of the whole figure — can make us *think* of a welcome being extended to someone. What is more, as is the clear evidence of our classical dances, a *mudrā* can easily appear bewitching to the eye as well, if only because it is not merely made with loving care, but is also projected a little. On the other hand, a gesture may work as a mere mark. Thus, the Kathak's nod at the *sama* is a gesture because it is both willed *and* indicative of the advent of the beat; but, as we know, nobody speaks of it as a *mudrā*. Again, a *mudrā* is distinguished by the fact that it is necessarily a making, specially in our dances. This is why whereas we speak of gestures as follows: 'इशारा देना या करना', in respect of *mudrās* we say, मुद्रा बनाना. In respect of *abhinaya* as it occurs in our dances (and drama), one can only wonder if it may be regarded as a fabric of gestures *through and through*; for the bodily changes that occur in what is called *sāttvika abhinaya*[65] though they are admittedly expressive of a present affective state, cannot be said to be *action*, because they are not directly willed.

So, on the whole, Langer appears to be right in saying that gesture is vital and deliberate movement; and that, to one who makes it, it is clearly known as kinetic experience or as action, though he also *sees* it (rather vaguely) as an effect. The external observer does not of course *experience* the movement in question in the same way; he *faces* it, instead of animating it; but, at the same time, he does not regard it as merely physical, but sees and understands it as vital movement, and so as having a subjective side too. An actual (or life-) gesture indeed always functions as a signal or symptom of our desires, intentions, feelings, expectations, and demands. Through skilful and elaborate combinations gestures can also *be made to* serve as a kind of language, as is done by the mute. But whether it is thus subordinated, intentionally, to the purpose of communication or not, a gesture in real life is always '*spontaneously* expressive, too, *by virtue of its own form*; it is free and big, or nervous and tight; quick or leisurely, etc., according to the psychological condition of the person who makes it'.[66] Langer adds that this self-*expressive* aspect of an actual gesture is similar to the tone of voice in speech. It is of help, as we know, in conveying one's meaning to others. But an actual gesture, however helpful it may be in daily life, is not in itself art. It is simply vital movement. It becomes a *dance*-gesture (or an artistic element) only when it is *imagined*, or brought to the mind quite apart from the demand of (actually present) situations which warrant it in real life. Only then it becomes 'a free symbolic form, which may be used to convey ideas of emotion . . . or . . . combined with . . . other

65. *Sāttvika* here means *truthful* or *genuine*. *Abhinaya* is acting as representational or expressive. So, taken together, the two words mean acting which expresses an actually experienced, *not merely imagined* feeling. Horripilation and pallor of skin may be said to make *sāttvika abhinaya*; for they may indicate, respectively, *actual* ecstatic joy or fright.

66. Langer, *Feeling and Form*, p. 175.

virtual gestures, to express either physical or mental tensions'.[67]

In everyday life, we have seen, a gesture is a *willed* expression or symptom of some actual mental state of the man who makes it.[68] It is indeed by so regarding his gestures that others are able to adjust their behaviour in relation to him. But a virtual (or dance) gesture is not a signal of what the dancing individual *himself* really wants or expects. It rather *means* (or conveys the idea of) wanting this or that; it is a *symbol* of the will. Langer insists that gestures in dance do not express the *dancer's* own personality, and that what they mean is just a part of the dance. And, it is obvious, we too (as *rasika*s) do not regard the dancer's gestures as indications of what he does or wants in his everyday capacity; indeed, we do not for a moment forget that what the gestures in question mean relates to the dance, and not to the person behind the dance. So, if they yet appear to express present emotions or attitudes, as they certainly do where the dancing is good, their 'spontaneously gestic character' — or their appearing to be directly expressive *of the dancer's own states* — must be said to be 'illusory'.[69] Here, I may add, a reference to what Langer says about the rainbow as a virtual image would help understanding. Surely we do *not* believe that the rainbow really hangs in the heavens, and that it could be taken down like a coat from the hanger; but, at the same time, we do not at all doubt its appearing-to-hang. In the same way, where *abhinaya* in dance is really good — and elicits remarks like the following: **कैसे डूबकर अभिनय करते हैं!** though we know that the emotions expressed are not the dancer's own present feelings, we also see it clearly that they *appear* to be experienced and not merely expressed or represented by the dancer; this is, in fact, what

67. Langer, *Feeling and Form*, p. 175.

68. The italicised word is here significant. A mere symptom is not (as such) a gesture. It becomes the latter only when the individual's will gets involved. Thus, trembling during sickness may be a *symptom* of malarial fever; but here it is not a gesture at all. It, however, becomes gestural in dance when it is deliberately included in a movement aiming at conveying fear.

69. The possibility that one *can* speak thus will be brought out later.

we mean when we admire a particular spell of *abhinaya* for its *intenseness*. And to speak of dance quite generally, — that is, of both expressional/representational and 'pure' dance — the vital force that it expresses is but seeming; that is, it is not the given energy of the dancer himself, but the power of the aesthetically created 'dance-personage'.[70]

In the light of the distinction just drawn between actual and virtual gestures, it would be instructive to look at what is called *thāṭa* in Kathak dance. Here, the nods (or some other movement) of the dancer, may well indicate his own actual acknowledgement of the location of important beats. But the other individual gestures which are uniquely relevant to Kathak dance — that is, those that involve regulated employment of the chest, and neck, etc., and are called *kasak-masak, dorā* — are meant to convey to the onlooker the general *idea* of the bestirring *of the dance*, or of its flowing or articulate form. They neither are nor are regarded as a direct expression of how the dancer himself is feeling at the moment. Throughout a dance recital, indeed, actual and virtual gestures go hand in hand; and careful thought is needed to distinguish the two.

But though the distinction is as such borne out by the evidence of Kathak, close attention to this dance-form may also prompt the average *rasika* to raise an objection to the thesis that *gesture* is the basic abstraction of the art of dance. Some point to this objection — which I propose to meet a little later — is lent by Langer's own insistence that "every dance which is to have balletic significance . . . is (for the dancer) necessarily ecstatic. It must take the dancer 'out of himself', say, by the merest suggestion of motion [or] by music at once monotonous and exciting".[71] This, I believe, is perfectly true. But that which is commonly seen to take a Kathak — and also his audience of genuine *rasika*s — quite out of concern with everyday life, and

70. Langer, *Feeling and Form*, p. 197.

71. *Ibid.*, p. 196. Langer is right in saying that 'in highly ecstatic performances the temporal autonomy of the dance does not require a very well-made musical fabric to emphasise and assure it'. *Ibid.*, pp. 198-199.

to trasplant them alike in the region of dance contemplation, is the very first one or two *auditions* of the *lahrā-ṭhekā* jointness which may appear 'monotonous' to those who are not able to visualise how the *dancer* reacts to it, and which are positively 'exciting' to the dancer himself, because they not only bestir his body to begin a dance-number, but at once transform his whole being, if only for the duration of the dance, into 'a dance-personage'. The basic unifying feature of this artistic twosome is a cyclic rhythm[72]; and *this rhythm* co-extends with the whole of dance, provided we leave out invocations (of the *ālāpa* manner) which are not so far regarded as really integral to a Kathak recital. It does not disappear even in *ṭhumrī bhāva-pradarśana* which is pre-eminently thematic and expressional in character. The *ṭhekā* (or the basic rhythm as played) persists here too; and, in respect of its repetitiveness, the first line of the song itself — though it *is* at times relieved by the *antarā* — may be said to resemble the *lahrā*. So, it may be contended (by the average *rasika*) that, if *the basic abstraction* be regarded as that without which — if only as a matrix or background — the dance just cannot begin and proceed, the *lahrā-ṭhekā* duet alone, in its aspect of rhythm, should be said to be basic. Kathak dance is indeed so dependent on the duet in question that the moment there is the slightest wobble in its rhythmic pace, the dancer feels it as a painful jab, so to say, and — if only for a while — the course of creation may be visibly disturbed.

Yet another objection may be put by Kathak *rasika*s to the thesis that gesture alone can be regarded as the basic abstraction of dance. To most of them the word 'gesture' is not usable at all in respect of *footwork* which plays such a vital part in Kathak; and so they would wonder if gesture can truly be

---

72. The twosome in question comprises a simple musical line and an equally easy-to-follow *ṭhekā*, both utterly devoid of variations; yet it at once lays down a vibrant foundation for creative work, quite removed from our daily concerns. I here feel impelled to cite the following remark of the late Sri Kundan Lal, a well-known teacher of Kathak of the Jaipur *gharānā*, when we were conducting the 1980 annual examinations of the Kathak Kendra (New Delhi): **'वाह! क्या ज़मीन क़ायम होती है!**

regarded as the basic abstraction of Kathak *as a whole*. They may even feel tempted to put forth the following argument. Unlike the use of *aṅg* and *upāṅgas* in expressional intra-forms, pure footwork (or *tatkār*) is not *called* gestural. On the other hand, movement *is* present in both *aṅg-bhāva* and *tatkār*. So, instead of gesture, vital rhythmic movement (**लयात्मक चेतन गति**) may be regarded as the basic abstraction of dance.

But, and now I turn to meet the objections I have posed provisionally, the following rejoinder may be given from the viewpoint of Langer's position:

Vital movement as such is not necessarily a part of dance *as art*. As he dances, the Kathak surely breathes, and breathing *is* vital movement; yet nobody refers to it while admiring the dance aesthetically. On the other hand, the moment such breathing *is made* gestural — as, for instance, in *thāṭa* where the intentional heaving of the chest may be made to signify the flow of *laya* — it becomes a part of the art of dance. And, turning to *tatkār*, why must we insist that it is *non*-gestural? It is true that, in *common* Kathak parlance, we speak only of *hand*-gestures, and not of a *footfall* as a gesture? But, if the *guru* wants the pupil to mark the *sama* of a particular *lāsya* pattern not broadly, but as a very slight, yet clear footfall, his language here is very likely to take the following, form: "**सम का *इशारा* ज़रा हल्का सा, नफ़ासत से दो, क्योंकि यह लास्य अंग का काम है**". But the moment this is done, *sama*, which is the pivot even in *tatkār*, is meant to be gestural; for, **इशारा** is *our* common word for 'gesture'.

Consider, again, the following words used in relation to footwork; *tatkār*, *bānt*, *larhī*. I believe they all alike signify movement that is gestural; for a gesture, as we noted at the very outset, not merely expresses sentiment or passion, but may aim at showing *inclination or disposition*. Now, it *is* the evidence of really good *tatkār* that its footfalls not merely mark the location of beats, but *express* the dancer's relish of, and attunement with the basic flow of rhythm and its variants. This, indeed, is how I would like to interpret Langer's emphasis that 'all dance motion is gestural'.

I may add that, according to our ancient texts, the positioning and movement of the feet are all part of *āṅgika abhinaya*; and can with ease be gestural. Should one still persist in refusing to see the gestic character of footwork, he will have to accept the impossible view that *tatkār* is mere movement of the feet, and that it signifies nothing and lacks all character. Further, I suggest that if the word *tat* be taken to mean 'that (which is the basis of rhythm)', *tatkār* may be regarded as an express objectification (or articulation) of *laya* (aesthetic pace); and that it is, therefore, improper to regard footwork in Kathak as quite non-gestural. In fact, like gestures generally, the footfalls invite attention to what one obviously wants to make known; and they furnish understanding — say, of the proper location and pace of the beats. As for the *lahrā-ṭhekā* confluence, it is not the basic abstraction *out of which* Kathak dance is made, but only, though importantly, the matrix *within which* the dancing proceeds; and even as a matrix it is not *uniquely* relevant to Kathak, for it is just as necessary for a solo *tablā* recital. My final argument in support of Langer's thesis is that quite a few of the predicates which are used in respect of *tatkār* are the same as we use in speaking of everyday gestures, namely, *clean, crisp, definite* or *indistinct,* and *playful.*

The dynamic image

Indeed, it is gesture, not the *lahrā-ṭhekā* confluence, that gives to dance its incarnate and visual, rather than its merely rhythmic character. And if, as I have just tried to argue, even *tatkār* may be regarded as a knitwork of gestures indicating the willed dispositions of beats *and* footfalls (पदचाप) — I distinguish the two because, where foot*work* is subtle in *tatkār,* the foot*falls* may be expressly deviated from the proper location of beats — it is gesture which may be said to create the 'complete and autonomous art' of dance as 'a realm of virtual powers *made visible*'.[73] Langer prefers this way of speaking about dance to the common ways in which we characterise our classical dance generally, that is, as a blend

73. Langer, *Feeling and Form,* pp. 192-193.

of *nṛtta* and *nṛtya*, or of *the pure* and *the representational*. The first two (Hindi) words only distinguish two aspects of our classical dance; they do not tell us what dance itself is; and the English (italicized) words listed are applicable, if not uniformly, also to painting and vocal music, and so do not give us any clue as to how dancing is *distinct* as an art. In Langer's view, the needed distinguishing can be done only if we address the question with which we opened this section, namely, what exactly dance may be said to create, in the main.

Langer's own answer to this question may not be given at once. It would help understanding to consider, first, how she focuses on the 'virtual' dynamics of dance. I may do it thus:

Dancing is activity which, on the one hand, *abstracts* the sense of vital power (the feeling of personal power and will) from the practical experiences in which that sense is usually 'an obscure factor'; and, on the other hand, *creates* the image of 'a world of vital forces *embodied or disembodied*'.[74] These *dance-forces* are quite other than the 'physically exerted power' that may be directly seen, say, in the actual running of a long and arduous race. Nor have they anything to do with the 'field of forces' of which physics speaks in a quite impersonal way. The dance forces are mere '*appearances* of influence and agency created by *virtual* gesture'; and are akin, in a measure, to 'the subjective experience of volition and free agency, and [what is more] of reluctance to alien, compelling wills'. Dance is a dynamic image, a symbol of the very 'consciousness of life, the sense of vital power, even of the power to [merely] receive impressions, apprehend the environment, and meet changes. . .'[75] The abstraction of this *sense of power* and its incarnations in the dance are no easy and direct acts; they take place through the adroit use of gestures, of course, in accordance with the dancer's own conception of the individual dance. Gesture, however, is not a mere *means* to abstract the sense of power in question, but is itself, as actively formed movement, a display of vital power. But in the region of the

74. Langer, *Feeling and Form*, p. 193.

75. *Ibid.*, p. 176.

art of dance, gesture is always virtual, that is, so long as the dance does not peter out into movement or stance of the everyday kind. And, therefore, just as gestures here only *appear* to be projections of the dancer's own feelings and thoughts, so also the complete dance just *seems* to be an expression of *his* (or her) vital powers. This mere semblance, or the dance's (only) appearing to be an expression of the dancer's own vital powers and present feeling is the primary illusion of this art, as against its secondary illusions.[76] What is projected by the gestures that make the dance is only the dancer's *imagination* of the feelings, ideas and situations that join to produce the total dance; and the dance itself, as a whole, projects only its *own* 'life' and power, not the vitality of the dancer himself. Dance may indeed be said to be *an apparition of 'virtual powers'*, that is, of powers that do not really relate directly to the dancer himself.

This basic thesis of Langer may now be explained and its implicit ideas brought out at some length:

To begin with, the dance (according to Langer) is an *apparition* not in the sense of a phantom or a ghost, but in the other, perfectly legitimate senses of an appearing or that which appears. A phantom is a *deceitful* appearance, an *immaterial* form, a show without reality. The word *ghost*, on the other hand, means not only a faint or false appearance, but a semblance, besides of course its spiritual connotations. Now, it is important to see what Langer does *not* mean by speaking of dance as an *apparition*. First, she does not mean that a dance is a mere spirit or quite immaterial or a disembodied soul. Such meanings are, in fact, incompatible with many of her explicit remarks on dance. Consider, for instance, the following:

> (*a*) The physical realities (of the dance) are given: place, gravity, muscular strength, muscular control, and secondary assets such as light, sound. . . . All these are actual. (*b*) But *in* the dance they disappear; (*c*) the more perfect the dance, the less we see its actualities. (*d*) What we see, hear, and feel are

---

76. The distinction here suggested will be brought out a little later.

> the virtual realities, the moving forces of the dance, the apparent centres of power and their emanations, their conflicts and resolutions, lift and decline, their rhythmic life. These are the elements of the created apparition, and are themselves not physically given, but artistically created.[77]

Now, (*a*) lists the 'physical realities' *of the dance*, its basic 'materials'. Without these given actualities, the dance just cannot be. How indeed can a dance come to be if there is no one, in flesh and blood, to occupy and traverse a solid floor? So if the actualities in question could be said to disappear, as indeed they are said to in the extract cited (*b*), it could only mean that they disappear *into*, or are thoroughly assimilated by, the dance, not that they vanish into thin air, leaving no trace behind. The actual physical basis — adequate lung power, for instance — is indeed so essential for the dance that if the dancer — say, a Kathak — appears to run out of breath, his completion of the pattern (being danced) at the *sama* where he is required to assume, for a moment, a perfectly moveless stance, will be adversely affected, detracting at once from the quality of dance. So, the (given) 'actualities' of dance, of which sheer physical stamina is clearly one, are (in principle) concurrent with the whole course of a dance recital; and far from disappearing totally, they do not admit of the slightest weakening, for they have to sustain the ongoing dance.

I am not only arguing on my own that the given, actual bases of dance do *not* and should not disappear. Langer's own writing, I believe, does not recalcitrate this negative emphasis; and I say so in spite of the following remark which has disturbed L.A. Reid, in particular: 'the *more* perfect the dance, the less we see its actualities'. But then I must explain what these words really mean:

One clear meaning is that, generally, the quality of a dance performance is but an approximation to, and not the actual attainment of perfection. Now, this is certainly true. Not only the *rasikas*, but good dancers themselves are rarely *quite*

77. Langer, *Problems of Art*, p. 6.

satisfied with the quality of the dance they are able to present on the stage. But the point to be noted here is that if the dancing is good, its very overall quality compels our notice, so to say, to slur over quite a few of its (non-aesthetic) actualities; *and* that, conversely, where the dancing is weak, we cannot help noticing them, often a little disapprovingly. Here, again, a look at Kathak dance is of help. One clear 'actuality' in a full-length presentation of dance is literal discontinuity, or some actual gaps of quiet *between* the different intra-forms. Such gaps or intervals can appear quite pronounced — and may even irritate us a little — where the music or the *laya* of the succeeding number is clearly different from that of the preceding one, and where the inner arrangement of individual numbers as danced does not quite merit the adjective *coercive,* as the Gestalt psychologists understand the word. But where the first few intra-forms have been danced properly, and so the *rasikas*' attention (more or less) captured, while presenting the numbers that follow, even if the dancer visibly wipes away beads of sweat from his face with a handkerchief — or beckons the *tablā*-player to alter the tempo slightly — both actual actions, obviously, and not really integral to dancing as art — the *rasika* will probably not be *struck* by them as unrelated to the making of art. But, and this is important, in suggesting (following Langer) that the actualities of dance may not be clearly seen or distinguished, it is in no way implied that the 'realities' which provide an actual basis to dance — or appear at times as its literal (not aesthetic) content — *disappear* at any point of the performance.

Here, incidentally, I think it necessary to make some additional remarks relating to the point at issue:

First, whether or not a dance is good, in what precise measure we notice its given actualities, and which ones of these are more likely to be noticed or ignored, — questions such as these cannot be settled *ab extra*. Much here depends not only on the character of the dance itself, but on the discrimination of the onlooker; and this indeed is why Indian aesthetics has always emphasised the role of the *rasika* or the trained contemplator. Langer does not make an explicit mention of this truth. But it is perhaps implicit in the general tenor of her writing on the subject, and I can argue for the assumption as follows. Langer takes pains to distinguish the given from the artistically created in dance, and insists that it is the dance-apparition thus created which is the real object of attention when we watch a dance. But in so far as the import or character of what is *artistically* created can be seized only by those onlookers who are conversant with the technique and aesthetics of the art, reference to the need for *trained* attention may well be said to be integral to her view.

I may add that, even apart from the actual situation of watching a dance, it is possible to bring out, if only generally, how the training of the onlooker relates to the perception of, or indifference to, the actualities of dance. The dress that a dancer generally wears — and it is more or less set for our classical dance — is clearly one of the given actualities of dance; the dancer's own figure — in some cases, corpulent — is another. But, as is well known to those who see Kathak frequently, even if he appears on the stage in a simple *kurtā* and *dhotī* or *pyjāmā* a (male) *guru*'s dancing can be so exquisite — and bewitching to a knowledgeable audience — that his being quite without *sartorial glamour* and *facial make-up*, as also his physical oddities, if any, may not be marked at all. The point is that the actualities we have referred to, though they are (as a rule) always there in the case of a stage performance, are not really integral to the dance. The *lahrā-ṭhekā* twosome, on the other hand, is much more essential for a Kathak recital. But, after the measured extent of the rhythm (लय का हल्का या दायरा, आवृत्ति) has been firmly established in the minds of the *rasikas* by the formed quality of the first few dance-numbers, even this twosome, though it would of course not disappear or become inaudible, may not remain the *express object of the rasikas' attention*, and in that sense go unnoticed as a separate something.

The way I have been arguing suggests that even the *lahrā-ṭhekā* pair is an actuality. It sure is; in fact, it strikes the ear repeatedly, throughout the course of the dance. But, as we know, it is not found readymade like the dancing floor, dress, and gravity. The drummer and the *lahrā*-player have to establish the twosome in question and to keep it on an even keel, sometimes with a little conscious effort, say, when the Kathak recites a pattern having some moments of intentional deviation from the basic *laya*, before replicating it with dancing feet. So we have to distinguish between actualities (or realities) that are *given* and the ones that are *artistically created*. Langer herself is careful to make the distinction. 'The *physical realities*' of dance, she says, 'are given . . . (But) what we see, hear, and feel (in watching a dance as art) are the *virtual realities* . . . not physically given, but artistically created'.[78] But, in respect of the latter (or virtual realities) one has to take care to see how exactly they are 'real' and how (yet) 'virtual'. A gesture that expresses, say, the anger of a maiden as she rejects her lover's advances is real in so far as it is a movement that is actually willed by the dancer. And, what is more, its *being formed* is meant to be seen by the onlookers; otherwise, the loving care that goes into the making of gestures — or of *mudrās* like *patākā*, *sūcī*, and *caturam* in the instance taken — would remain unnoticed, detracting from the visual locus of aesthetic delight. But, *as expressive* of the anger in question, it is *virtual* in the sense that the expressiveness, here, does not really — but only appears to — relate to the dancer's own present disposition or feeling. The danseuse is not rejecting anyone in her personal capacity; no approaches are in fact being made to her in her own life. The expression in question only projects what she *imagines*, not what she herself *experiences*. If she feels relieved after this particular detail of dancing, it will only be because she has been able to express what she wanted to, *in accordance with the needs of the dance*, and not because she has been able to rid herself of a nuisance in real life. Yet, if the dancing is good, the *rasikas*' immediate experience will not be ruffled by the sense of this distinction. Their acclaim will take the following form: 'How intense is her *abhinaya* here'. In such cases, our contemplation of the dance is surely not disturbed by the thought that the dancer is only enacting the emotive situation, and is not really experiencing it. As we have said

78. Langer, *Problems of Art*, p. 6.

earlier, the expression does appear to be anchored in her own personality — of course, without being truly so; and *to that extent*, that is, as a mere appearance, it is illusory. But, on the other hand, the appearance in question is *not illusory* in so far as it does not lead to any mistaken behaviour, as when the illusory perception of a rope as a snake may make us flee the spot in sheer fright. This is how I interpret Langer's emphasis that the 'forces' which a dance creates are meant and exist only 'for our perception',[79] and not (*we* may add) for any adaptative action. Nor should the conscious realisation, as is *my* state and emphasis at the moment, that the expressed emotion which appeared to give vent to a feeling of the danseuse herself was not really felt by her, encourage anyone to dismiss the expression in question as unreal, in the way we reject the initial perception of the 'snake' as unreal on coming to know that it is only a rope in reality.

The thing is that, though the presence of a lifelike quality may well prompt us to acclaim a work of art, its *overall value as art* does not depend on the measure of its approximation to real life. In this context, it seems necessary to mark the precise sense in which a work of art may be said to be *an image of life* in Langer's view. Largely because of its visual connotation, an image is commonly thought to be a copy or imitation of something actual. But the concept of imitation is just not applicable to a considerable amount of art. On what given object does one model a melody? And, to turn once again to Kathak dance, what can a *thāṭa* or *tatkār* — nay, the whole range of our *nṛtta* numbers — be said to copy? Nothing, obviously. So, Langer chooses to speak of a work of art as an *image* in some quite different senses of the word. For her an artistic creation is an image, first, in the sense of an apparition, like the rainbow, which in only meant to be seen (or contemplated), and not to be judged as real, unreal, or useful by everyday standards; and, secondly, in the sense of being a symbolic representation of felt life, in case we choose to take *image* as an image — of something or the other. The second

79. Langer, *Problems of Art*, p. 5.

aspect of Langer's view (justed stated) may be discussed later. As the basic emphasis of her total philosophy of art, it calls for some detailed reflection; so here I may say something only by way of explaining, a little more clearly than I have so far done, what Langer really means by speaking of a work or art as an apparition, that is, as a virtual entity. Her own account is here as follows:

> Anything that exists only for perception, and plays no ordinary, passive part in nature as common objects do, is a virtual entity. It is not unreal; where it confronts you, you really perceive it, you don't dream or imagine that you do. The image in a mirror is a virtual image. A rainbow is a virtual object. It seems to stand on the earth or in the clouds, but it really 'stands' nowhere; it is only visible, not tangible. Yet it is a real rainbow . . . for any normal eye looking at it from the right place. We don't just dream that we see it. If, however, we believe it to have the ordinary properties of a physical thing, we are mistaken; it is an appearance, a virtual object, a sun-created image. What dancers create is a dance; and a dance is an apparition of active powers, a *dynamic image*.[80]

This passage provides a succinct account of what Langer means by a virtual object or entity, and I think it necessary to give close attention to it, first, because it culminates in what may be regarded as her explicit definition of dance; and, secondly, because it does not clearly distinguish, but merely uses concepts like *common objects, virtual entity, appearance, object,* and *image*.

To speak generally, whatever is an appearance or an image is 'of' something or the other, in the sense of representing this other object, more or less direcly. The concept of 'object' itself is not *thus* relational, though it does quite freely imply relatedness to a *subject*. Langer takes pains to oppose the view that art is, in essence, a direct representation or imitation of given reality. So, where (as in the above passage and elsewhere) she speaks of dance as an *image* or appearance, she cannot be

80. Langer, *Problems of Art*, p. 5.

taken to mean that it represents whatever it does *directly*, as distinguished from indirect or symbolic representation (or expression). This indeed is why she freely speaks of what is created by art as *mere* or *pure* appearance; and, what is more, of dance as not merely a (dynamic) *image*, but as an *apparition* ('of active powers') which word may quite fairly be taken to mean 'that which appears' or a mere 'presence', as distinguished from a representation — of something else. The passage under review, I may add, underlines this emphasis on the independent, *objective* reality of art-creation, in spite of its being virtual. A virtual entity may be quite different from a common object; but, we are told, it is not (wholly) unreal; 'where it confronts you, you really perceive it, you don't dream or imagine that you do'. This is surely true of 'a rainbow in the sky'. It *is* a virtual object in the sense that it is not really what it appears to be, that is, as something hanging in the sky; but there is no doubt as to its being a distinct object for the eye.

But the *difference* between a virtual entity and common objects is, according to Langer, just as unmistakable. Things that we deal with in daily life are visible and tangible, and can be handled. They are usable too, because of their 'ordinary properties', say, shape, solidity, or commodiousness. On the other hand, a virtual entity like a rainbow, or (in Langer's view) a dance, is only meant to be perceived, that is, to be seen and not to be used. Further, though its ongoing course does occupy varying positions on the dancing floor, the total dance cannot be made to abide, like a thing, as the moveless occupant of a particular spot.

Here, in passing, I may also explain how exactly a dance is 'illusory' according to Langer. It is 'illusory' because it appears to be what it is really not, that is, a *direct* expression of the dancer's own energy and immediate feeling. And in so far as, because it is a virtual entity, it exists 'only for *perception*', so long as we keep watching a dance it is its (illusory) appearance that keeps our attention engaged. The *judgement* that the appearance — of the dance's being a self-revelation of the dancer himself — is illusory, has to be regarded as an utterance of subsequent thinking.

Finally, and with this we turn to Langer's definition of dance, we have to see how, as a virtual entity, dance is quite different from other such entities.

> We do not enjoy every virtual image, just because it is one. A mirage in the desert is intriguing chiefly because it is rare. A mirror image, being common, is not an object of wonder, and in itself, just as an image, [it] does not thrill us. But the dynamic image created in dancing . . . is more than a perceivable entity: . . . [it is it an] apparition, given to the eye, or to the ear and eye, *and through them to our whole responsive sensibility* . . . . [and] it strikes as something charged with feeling.[81]

We may add that whereas a rainbow and a mirror-image can only hold the eye for a while, good dance can not only people our imagination with images of beauty, but liberate it into some creative imagining on our own.

But, of course, our main task here is to see what Langer means by saying that a dance is an apparition of *virtual powers or forces*; or, more simply, a *dynamic image*. To begin with the first emphasis — as in the case of virtual objects or apparitions, so in respect of powers or forces — a distinction has to be made between what is and what *is not* the result of *artistic* creation. Langer speaks of the rainbow as 'a virtual object', but it is a 'sun-created' rather than an artistically created image. Similarly, the pull that a magnet may exercise on a piece of iron and the power that an athlete may reveal in making a record-breaking lift are both real, physical forces. But the forces that we see in a dance issue from the dancer's creative effort. He has, of course, to use his physical strength in making the movements that constitute the dance; but the power in question is used up and does not show directly in the dance. What we

> percieve most directly and convincingly [here are forces that] are created for our perception . . . a display of *interacting* forces . . . not the physical forces of the dancer's muscles . . . [forces] like the weight that tips a scale or the push that

81. Langer, *Problems of Art*, p. 6.

> topples a column of books, but purely apparent forces that seem to move the dance itself . . . [all] virtual realities, the moving forces of the dance, the *apparent centres of power and their emanations, their conflicts and resolutions, lift and decline, their rhythmic life.* These are the elements of the created apparition, and are themselves not physically given, but artistically created.[82]

The 'virtual' or artistically created realities that Langer here speaks of are by no means mythical, for they are all clearly visible in a good Kathak recital. Rhythmic segments comprising similar syllables and an equal number of beats, — and danced, in quick succession, on opposite sides, left and right, such as तक्थरि तक्थरि, कुकुथरि कुकुथरि, तक् धलांग तक् धलांग illustrate the interaction of balance. The beat, generally the *sama* — and sometimes a quite unsuspected moment *between* two adjacent beats — from where a pattern may be made to take off, both exemplify what Langer speaks of as 'apparent' (that is, artistically created) centres of power and their emanations. 'Conflicts and resolutions', both generally relating to rhythmic work in the case of Kathak, are visible where intricate patterns, first merely recited by the dancer to the simple but unwavering playing of the *ṭhekā* by the drummer — and projected as a kind of friendly challenge to the latter — are quickly replicated by the drummer *and* the dancer in happy unison. Further, subtly varying emphasis on footfalls that mark some successive syllables — so that whereas one segment appears to proclaim itself, the other seems merely to whisper — can make the dance impress us as a clear alternation of the rise and subsidence of its 'life'.

All these dynamic features, however, relate to *the dance* itself; and it is obvious they are all alike the result of the dancer's artistic skill. They sure do not reveal, I repeat, his physical strength as directly as the bulging muscles of an athlete betoken the power that he puts into the lifting of a heavy weight. The former or the dynamic features of dance are acclaimed in a good dance for their own grace, measure

---

82. Langer, *Problems of Art*, pp. 5-6.

and beauty; the latter (bulging muscles) are noticed but incidentally, the focus of public attention being on the success or failure of the attempted lift. Where the *dance* direcly shows some exertion on the *dancer's* part, as may easily happen if the Kathak chooses to dance an unduly long pattern — say, a लम्बछड़ परन — what we see is only some laboured gymnastics, not the art of dancing as a fabric of virtual passages that appear to be automotive.

But at this point two questions are likely to trouble a careful reader of Langer's writings. First, why does she often open the word *powers* with a capital letter and/or put it within inverted commas? And, second, is it proper to distinguish the dancer from the dance as sharply as she appears to? Now, for getting some clues to answer the first question we may reflect on the following from Langer's *Problems of Art* and *Feeling and Form*:

> (a) Two people in a *pas de deux* seem to magnetise each other; a group appears to be animated by one single spirit, one Power.[83]

> (b) (We may) think of the dance as apparition of interactive Powers . . . a purified and simplified aspect of the outer world, composed by the laws of the inner world to express its nature.[84]

> (c) The primary illusion of Dance is a virtual realm of Power — not actual, physically exerted Power, but appearances of influence and agency created by virtual gesture.[85]

> (d) The recognition of a true artistic illusion, a realm of 'Powers', wherein purely imaginary beings from whom the vital force emanates shape a whole world of dynamic forms . . . , lifts the concept of Dance out of all its theoretical entanglements with music . . . [and other arts].[86]

---

83. Langer, *Problems of Art*, p. 10.
84. *Ibid.*, p. 11.
85. Langer, *Feeling and Form*, p. 175.
86. *Ibid.*, p. 184.

> (e) . . . As a complete and autonomous art, [dance is] the creation and organisation of a realm of virtual Powers . . . [a play of Powers made visible.][87]
>
> (f) The entire world of dance . . . [is] a field of virtual powers — there are no actualities left in it at all, no untransformed materials, but only elements, living Beings, centers of force, and their interplay.[88]

None of these extracts is readily clear, but a little close thinking enables me to make the following points:

Though it is not easy to make them precise, the concepts of dance, power and being are all quite workable. We use them in everyday discourse, and they are fairly intelligible. What is more, where we wish to emphasise their general significance, and to distinguish them from the individual cases which instantiate them, we tend to hypostatise them, and so to capitalise their first letter in writing. This is why nobody is disturbed on seeing words like *beauty, love,* and *poesy* open with capital letters in the course of writing that is not merely prosaic and is charged with a faith in the wider reality of what the words in question signify. Therefore, it should not be difficult to see why *Power* and *Dance* begin with capital letters in the extracts cited above [(a)-(e)], though a more convincing argument here would be that great dancers themselves tend to look on the art of dance, to which they are committed, as being far more important than their own individual performances. But how are we to justify 'Beings' in (f)? *I* can offer only one explanation. The Beings that Langer here speaks of as 'living' are all 'virtual' (see 'virtual powers' in the opening segment of the extract in question); they are apparent — not physical or literal — 'centers of force and their interplay'. These 'beings', it is obvious, do not breathe and digest food as we do; so they are not beings in the literal sense; we do not deal with them as we deal with actual persons; and they do not change the course of actual events by radiating energy which too is only virtual here. But, at the

87. Langer, *Feeling and Form*, p. 187.

88. *Ibid.*

same time, they *appear* to radiate power and to influence each other. To illustrate, the beats in a rhythm-cycle are no mere inert marks, but *enable* the flow of *laya* to keep itself even; *and*, in doing so, they are themselves made to look as accents in — or as articulating — a flow, rather than as jabs that appear only to cut and divide.

Langer does not explain the point so simply. She appeals, instead, to what "Cassirer has termed 'the mythical consciousness' . . . [that is, the] telescoping of symbols and meaning, words (or symbols, generally) and world into one metaphysical entity".[89] However, this does not seem to collide with the way *I* have explained the matter. For, as a symbol of the articulation and evenness of the *laya*-flow, by apprehending which the Kathak regulates the course of dance-passages, the rhythmic beat is 'virtual', because artistically created; and it remains *un*distinguished from what it signifies (or its import) *in actual art contemplation*. What is more, the import itself, or the articulate and measured character of the aesthetic pace, is an experienced *fact* for the *rasika*; — and is *objectively measurable as even*, lending point to Langer's view that the import of the symbol 'refers us back to actuality'.[90]

Indeed, I have reason to accept her philosophical thesis that, structurally, the artistic consciousness is the same as the mythical consciousness. But quite apart from this emphasis of theory, the clear fact is that the more sensitive of our musicians and dancers tend to personify not only the art-form of their choice as a whole, but some individual notes and beats; and that, though to a philosophically trained person their utterances may well appear to be mythical, the artistes themselves would be reluctant to admit that 'artistic consciousness . . . is metaphorical from first to last'. In his informal discussions with me on the nature and significance of *ālāpa*, the late Ustad Rahimuddin Khan Dagar would often insist, with manifest feeling, that the notes which go to make a *rāga* are no mere points, but living entities. The unforgettable *khyāl*-singer,

89. Langer, *Feeling and Form*, p. 186.

90. *Ibid*.

Kumar Gandharva, is known to have admitted, at times, that *a note which had come to gain a specific character* because of the atmosphere created by prior singing, *demanded* irresistibly that *a grammatically forbidden* one be chosen next; and more recently, the Kathak maestro, Birju Maharaj, once made a very instructive remark which has impressed itself indelibly on my memory:

> I feel very happy and grateful to God at the thought that Dance has chosen to pick my body as a way to reveal its beauty, power, and richness.[91]

Should one here protest, as a man of robust common sense, that dance is not really a person; and that, therefore, it cannot be credited with the power to make choices, the ready answer could be that the contender has no idea of the objective, because regulative, status of the world in which a committed Kathak dwells — a world which is no less real to him, *as an artist*, than the world of everyday experience *to a householder in real life*.

The framework of personal experience and individual commitment, and its power to determine one's conception of reality, cannot be ignored. It may work not only in the direction of personifying concepts, but in that of enlarging the way we understand them. The man who is committed to the good life does not look on duty as mere regularity in going to the place of work, or on religion as simply a matter of reading the scriptures every morning. In the same way, the Kathak dancer may be led to make his understanding of words like *laya* and *cherh* (छेड़) ever more embracive by the very stress of his individual concern with his chosen art. Luckily, I find it possible to illustrate the points I am trying to make by narrating a personal experience.

On the second day of a Seminar (on classical dance) organised by the India International Centre, New Delhi, in the year 1994 (November 11-13) comprising 'encounters' in

---

91. The maestro made this remark as an introduction to his account of the Lucknow gharāna's contribution to Kathak, on March 30, while participating in the Kathak Kendra (New Delhi) seminar of 1978.

the form of question-answer sessions engaging three select scholars and three top exponents of Bharata Natyam, Kathak, and Odissi, when I prodded Birju Maharaj with the key question for discussion, namely, if creativity was compatible with fidelity to tradition, his eventual answer, though he did not pointedly put it thus, seemed to be that in so far as a Kathak, who is thoroughly imbued with the spirit of the art he cultivates, cannot help extending the meaning of the very words relating to it — so that they come to cover regions of life and experience which are commonly thought to be unrelated to dance — the question had to be answered with a definite *yes*. I construe his answer, thus, because of his insistence, fervently expressed by means of both gesture and speech, that *laya is* there even in everyday conversation and in such practical activities as the blacksmith's use of a hammer in beating out solid metal into, say, a piece of sheet-iron; and that what is signified by the word *cherh* — which occurs freely in our talk about Kṛṣṇa's छेड़-छाड़ with the *gopīs* and Rādhā — is clearly there even in the relation of a plectrum to a musical instrument, say, the *sitār* or the *sarod*. Subsequent reflection on such emphases of the maestro has enabled me to enlarge my own understanding of the words in question: of *laya* as that regulated movement which not only makes for beauty in dance, but for intelligibility in discourse, and effectiveness in everyday activity; and of *cherh* as the act of bestirring someone or something into some kind of response. Were someone to protest that such semantic extension does not square with the everyday use of words, the dancer may well succeed in finding some support for his attitude even in the region of popular discourse. For instance, is not a classical singer often seen to admonish his pupil gently with the words: 'तानपूरा ज़रा ध्यान से छेड़ो'? Further, does not the speech of a stammerer become unintelligble partly because it rushes and falters at random? And is it not a fact that a child enjoys learning verses or songs if they can be made to chime with rhythmic clapping? But the point to be noted here is that a good Kathak does not first consider such cases and *then* enlarge the meaning of the words we are talking about. Rather, he first realises, in the course of his own dancing, (a) the endless variety of ways in which a particular beat may be enlivened (or made manifest) by the feet or a nod of the head, or by the gentle upturn of a palm; or (b) the changing forms in which *laya* may be used to make for ever newer rhythmic turns, patterns and effects; and is then (c) effortlessly led on to see छेड़ and लय in regions that remain quite unrelated to the practice of Kathak for the average dancer. This is why a maestro sees nothing unnatural or forced about the semantic extension I have been talking about. I therefore conclude that when the Kathak tends to personify dance or speaks of the confrontation of *bol*s (बोलों की लड़न्त) we cannot fairly accuse of him of abusing language. *His* language and *his* way of interpreting concepts are both quite relevant to his personal communion with dance; and, as I propose to argue a little later, it is by realising the value of 'first order' aesthetic discourse that the seeming extravagance of quite a few of Langer's utterances on dance can be duly tempered.

But let me first dwell upon those points in the extracts cited [(a),(f) on pp. 327-28] which have not been addressed so far. Why does Langer speak of the (virtual) Power that seems to animate dance as something akin to *spirit* [see (a)]? The answer is that whereas the power of an external physical push generally does not enliven a man, though it may well make him fall to the ground, the power that we see in dance can appear to quicken not only the whole body (*aṅg*) but even the smallest bodily parts (*upāṅg*s), such as the eyeballs, with visible animation; and that such thorough enlivenment is similar to the way *spirit* is normally taken to make and keep the whole body alive.

This at once gives us a clue to improve our understanding of what Langer could possibly mean by 'interactive powers'. The eyes turning along with the sideway extension of arms; a gentle, but distinct nod of the head — or the mere upturn of the palm of a hand held a little away from the body — conjoining with a footfall to make the *sama*'s advent a little more articulate than it would be without the supportive *upāṅg*s; and, quite generally, but very importantly, the bodily bearing as according with the passage of rhythm or with the meaning of the text of a composition being sung for *abhinaya*, — these are all familiar instances of the interplay of elements which may here be called 'powers' (or forces), because they actively determine the form of numbers (in Kathak dance).

Tensions and other elements in dance

Such interaction, I may add, can also make for the various *tensions* which are, in Langer's view, essential for the establishment of the basic illusion that dance really is — that is, a play of *virtual* powers or forces. These tensions, she believes, are of three kinds: 'space tensions', 'body tensions' and "the less specific dance tensions created by music, light . . . poetic suggestion, and what not".[92] Here again, it is clear, some explaining is required. I may begin by making a distinction. As a creative device used by artists, tension is not the same as our becoming taut in real life; and I can bring out the difference by referring to a known detail of the practice of Kathak. Some real tension may be actually felt by a dancer when he has to wait for the recital to begin, or where he has to curb his known penchant for *drut* dancing during the course of presenting a *reposeful thāṭ* simply as an answer to the criticism that he just cannot dance in the *vilambit* idiom. But this actual tension cannot be allowed to appear as such in the dance that we *see*. If it shows itself, the number would lose its requisite look of peaceableness. Indeed, where a young dancer *appears* impatient to somehow get through an adagio piece, seasoned lovers of Kathak find it difficult to refrain from making the following remark: 'मिजाज़ में इत्मीनान नहीं है'।

But instances of *virtual* tension — which are meant for mere perception, and are no necessary source of any real discomfort — are far more numerous in Kathak. Thus, the two arms stretched out diagonally and firmly, though not too stiffly, are a clear case of *body* tension; they make the body *look* clearly stretched. But they are also an instance of *space* tension, for whereas the pointed fingers of the right hand held aloft suggest an ascent, those of the other hand invite the eye to a much lower level in space.

92. Langer, *Feeling and Form*, p. 186.

It is just as easy to see how music, light, and poetic suggestion create the *less specific* dance tensions. First, a steady and *vilambit lahrā*, quite without frills, can easily impart an *extra* look of fluency and rich inner filling to a pattern of close syllables danced at a *nimble* pace. The same principle of evoking a look of tension by means of contrast is freely at work in *ṭhumrī* dancing of the older kind. We see it where the *selfsame* first line of the song, sung all along steadily and quite without change, is made to oppose the *diversity* of ways in which its meaning or emotive import is brought out through *abhinaya*. Secondly, focused light on the feet during *tatkār* may heighten the nimbleness of footwork *as against* the (requisite) poise of the upper body. Thirdly, if the terminal phrase of a *lāsya aṅg* pattern is नैनबान ('the arrow of a furtive glance') the daintiness of wafting a mere hint of the *sama*, so to say, may be heightened by the sharp visual image which the word in question is likely to evoke in the *rasika* and which the dancer's own eyes may duly crystallise.

Besides these little pulls of balancing details, there are (according to Langer) some other elements too that go into the making of a dance. Two of these may be put thus: miming, of which *we* see a good deal in patterns portraying the pranks of Kṛṣṇa as a child, *and* stagy, theatrical motifs such as — to turn, again, to Kathak — keeping *Govardhan* aloft on the little finger and crushing (the serpent) *Kālīya's* hood to press out the venom. But, Langer would hasten to add, these elements serve only a *constructive* function; they are not the real creation of dance, but mere aids "to establish, maintain and articulate the play of 'Powers ' "[93]

Power as incarnate, radiated

What this particular remark means may be brought as follows:

That which the art of dance may be said to create essentially is, in Langer's view, 'the image of a world of vital forces, embodied *or* disembodied'. The meaning obviously is that a

93. Langer, *Feeling and Form*, p. 193.

dance seems to incarnate *and* radiate vital power or forces. Now, this is surely true. Generally, a well-timed posture in our dances appears as a moment of suspended animation: first, because it marks, even highlights, the end of a fluent pattern, or punctuates the flow as a kind of relief; and secondly, because (in Kathak) it is rarely quite severed from the cyclic rhythm (or the *ṭhekā*) which determines its duration. Even where the posture is soft and sensuous and employs *atibhaṅg*, as in Oḍissī dance, what meets the eye does not seem limp if the dancing is good, but only gentle and, so to say, as resting on its own self (*svātma viśrānti*). Mime, as representation adapted to a known text, suggests sentient agency. The histrionic motifs serve the *additional* purpose of making the agency appear out of the ordinary, so that in using them the dancer himself is, so to say, taken out of his everyday self and is transported to the region of dance. Yet, all this accounts (in the main) only for the aspect of *embodied* power in dance. The other aspect, the free play of powers, is worked up only by pure, rhythmic movement. Where the arms and the feet make patterns conjointly, though of course in a duly regulated way, one may speak, as (we have seen) Langer does, of a *play* or *interplay* of powers, a description which will not at all fit the sight of a massive machine lifting in one single movement heavy steel girders, though it may well be said to be a *display* of (mechanical) power. So, mime and histrionic motifs are not the only materials that go to make the total dance apparition.

Expression in dance and drama

Here, in passing, it may be noted that the aspect of pure movement also distinguishes dance from drama. Dramatic acting can, of course, be powerful, expressive, stirring; but in so far as it is done by regulated pauses, facial gestures and dialogues — which are all natural channels of expression — the expression here *appears* naturalistic, though inwardly the actor may not himself be feeling the suggested emotion at all. In a dance, on the other hand, we have the heightened contrast of *rhythmic beginning and attainment*; of steps, skips, or ample jumps, — all set, so far as *our* dances are concerned, in a chosen rhythmic frame; *and* of onward, sideway or circular movement — again in conformity with a rhythm-*cycle*, very clearly in the case of Kathak. So Langer *is* justified in saying that the projection of 'life-feeling' in dance is not naturalistic. But, though it may now be admitted that dance is essentially the creation of a realm of virtual (or artistically evoked) power, three important questions are yet to be discussed.

THREE QUESTIONS

First, how exactly does Langer distinguish the primary from the secondary illusions of dance? Second, how is the primary illusion of dance — or the realm of virtual powers — grounded in gesture? And, thirdly, is it possible to argue, justifiably, that (like every other art) dance projects the life of feeling?

Now, as to the first of these questions, Langer's answer is clear. A secondary illusion is that which *supports* 'the total creation or *enhances* its expressiveness'.[94] Here the key words are: 'supports' and 'enhances'. Thus, to cite one of Langer's own favoured instances, sculptural decoration can be called a secondary illusion of architecture where it serves for intensification of feeling in a structure. In the case of dance, the primary illusion of a play of virtual *powers or forces* is helped by uninhibited dance movement[95] which produces — for both the performer and the spectator — 'the (secondary) illusion of a conquest of gravity', so that the body, even where it is plump, appears weightless,[96] a fact which explains why 'lightness of movement is . . . the cardinal demand one has to make on a dancer'.[97] But, as Frank Theiss insightfully points out, this demand is

> nothing but the conquest of material resistance as such, and therefore is not a special phenomenon at all in the realm of [the] art [of dance]. Consider the triumph of sculpture over the stone, of painting over the flat surface, of poetry

94. Langer, *Feeling and Form*, p. 205.
95. *Ibid.*, p. 194.
96. *Ibid.*
97. *Ibid.*

> over language, etc. It is, then, precisely the material with which any particular art has to work that is to be overcome, and to a certain degree is to be rendered no longer apparent.[98]

The second question, relating to gesture as the basic abstraction of dance, has to be answered by focusing on the way Langer distinguishes between the actual and the virtual not only in respect of gesture, but also with regard to expression and feeling. The accepted meaning of *gesture* has been already brought out. But Langer would like us to mark that the gesture which a dancer makes has two clear aspects: the actual and the virtual. As a movement that is in fact willed by the dancer, the gesture is actual; as expressive (in dance) of the feeling of, say, embarrassment, it is virtual because real, felt uneasiness may be quite absent here. Within the dance, where it *is* effective, the 'actual' aspect is totally eclipsed. That is to say, if we know how to watch a (good) dance, we neither see in it the *dancer* as the agent of a particular movement of his own, nor register the movement (or gesture) as a mere means through which the dancer wishes to say *something of his own* personal life or present feeling. The former is superseded, so to say, by the personality of the *dance;* and the latter, by the created 'semblance of self-expression' to which the self-expressive quality of a properly made gesture directly conduces. In actual contemplation, of course, the two sides co-operate; and what we find, as *rasikas*, is *the dance as effortlessly itself* 'gathering here, spreading there — . . . resting, rising, and so forth'.[99] We do not here see the direct exercise of actual power. This power is, of course, used by the dancer; but *the power of the created dance apparition* can so possess, transfigure, and lift a dancer of even quite average physique that it may be said to be almost demoniac. I think it necessary to add that by the power in question Langer seems to mean not mere strength or energy, but a central agency that possesses power *and* is seen to exercise it. This agency, we may say, is the dancer's individual commitment to the art that he loves dearly,

98. Langer, *Feeling and Form;* a remark of Frank Theiss as cited by Langer.

99. *Ibid.*, p. 175.

in spite of its exacting demands; and it is this which really inspirits his performances. But what the onlooker direcly sees is obviously the interplay of movement with its variform dynamics; it is indeed this which distinguishes dance from the other arts. Yet, though the *rasika*s see only the display of *virtual* powers, the forces that make this display possible are *actual*; and are exercised by, and so are known to the dancer himself. *His* hearing and kinaesthesia support the rhythmic, moving image, to such an extent that though he does not *see* the dance illusion, he *knows* it is there; and it indeed exists as much *for the dancer* as for the spectators.[100]

But, be it noted, not only the dancer's gestures, but the very *feeling* which they may appear to express (in dance) are, in Langer's view, virtual. See, here, the following characteristic passage from her own writing:

> Real gesture springs from feeling (physical or psychophysical); the semblance of gesture, therefore, if it is made [as it obviously is] by means of actual movement, must be a movement that *seems* to spring from feeling. But *the feeling* that is implied in such an apparent spontaneous 'gesture' is itself a created dance element . . . and may even be attributed not to the dancer, but to some natural or supernatural power expressing itself through him. The conscious will that seems to motivate or animate him may be imagined to be *beyond his person which figures as a mere receptacle or even momentary concentration of it.*[101]

I may interpret the passage thus:

Real gesture, such as a mischievous wink, springs from actual feeling. But, virtual (or dance-) gesture only *seems* to spring from 'feeling'. Further, *this* feeling, from which the dance-gesture appears to issue, is itself created. It is not an event in the dancer's personal psychology. But what could this *created* feeling be? First, where the number to be danced *is* an essay in expression of some feeling, the feeling has to be visualised, and in that sense 'created' (instead of being actually

100. Langer, *Feeling and Form*, p.195.

101. *Ibid.*, p. 183.

experienced) by the dancer. Second, considering Kathak again, so far as the opening invocation and *thāṭa* are concerned, the feeling in question is the dancer's coming to feel attuned with the dance-situation: hence, the opt-repeated talk, here, of मिजाज़ बनाना. This feeling of attunement, induced by both conscious effort and the evocative impact of singing — say, of a *śloka* (providing the text of the *vandanā*) and to the *lahrā-ṭhekā* twosome — is quite different from the dancer's own relation to life. It is, on the one hand, a withdrawal from the context of everyday activity; and, on the other, a getting set to perform the opening intra-forms with such absorption — facilitated, of course, also by his entire past involvement with the art of dance — that for the moment he rises quite above his own personality of everyday concerns. The *dancer* in him is now brought to a focus; and *it is this superadded will* which animates the dance-gesture. The dance-figure may now be said to merely receive, and to serve as a channel for intimations from what may be called the *dance*-will; or to have grown, for the time being, one with this surpassing will to create.

Is it mere myth-making to speak thus? No, not in my view; and I can argue for my negative answer, say, as follows. The Kathak's world, though utterly different from the solid world of things and actual happenings, is yet quite objective. It comprises rhythm-cycles, *bol*s and patterns; *and everyone of these defies capricious handling*. The cycle has to be kept to, or at least all along remembered. The *bol*s have to be cut out — that is, not merely *marked* in respect of their relation to beats, but *shaped* in accordance with their euphonic character in *parhant*; which is why we speak of observing the *dharma* (or the essential character) of the syllables. And the patterns make their own demands in respect of accentuation, and accurate marking or intentional avoidance of the *sama*. All these contents and requirements make a realm which is quite objective. The dancer not only opens to, but dwells within this world; and whatever he does, so long as the dancing does not lose in quality, emanates from this felt suffusion and attunement. The 'will' which now animates him is the *dance*-will; the body merely obeys *or forthwith incarnates* it. The greater the Kathak's dedication to the largely pre-planned fabric of *bols*, rhythm-cycles, and *torhās*, the fuller is his feeling of being utterly available to dance. This is not to deny the role of improvisation, for which there is ample room in Kathak. But moments of creative abandon — or of what Milton called 'wanton heed and giddy cunning' — are themselves impossible unless the dancer has first saturated himself with the essential spirit of the art and with a clear awareness of its objective demands.

What, however, makes dance an art is, in Langer view, *not so much* its objective demands as its essential function of projecting the character of life as felt. But, one may wonder, how can the mere interplay of movements articulate felt life? Here, before we set out to frame a possible answer, we may remind ourselves that by 'feeling' Langer does not only mean emotions which bear separate names, but such general features of our affective life too as the rise and fall or accumulation of feeling, excitement and repose; and, what is more, *everything that can be felt'*.[102] As we have already noted in the opening chapter, 'feeling' in Langer's writing may, therefore, be taken as the whole of direct or non-relational experience, or as sentience simply.

Now, one clear form of sentience is the feeling of bodily vitality, experienced and manifest in such everyday movements as circling, gliding, jumping. In Kathak, as we know, these are all freely employed; and they may all be called *rhythms* in themselves not merely because they conform, on the whole, with the basic rhythm (or *tāla*) being danced, but because they have a clear beginning, a discernible course, and an end that strikes the eye as a kind of self-completion and not as abrupt termination. So 'pure' dance may be said to objectify vitality itself. But, here, the word 'objectify' is to be taken to mean not only 'to hold up before the eye', but also 'to present in an intelligible way', or as an object for contemplation. The latter end is achieved in some definite ways. Thus, the *movements* of jumping and gliding may be incorporated in a pattern that elicits and holds attention because of its very

102. Langer, *Problems of Art*, p. 15.

design. Or they may be made striking by being executed effortlessly, or as moments of aerial or merely intervallic relief in brisk patterns teeming with bead-like syllables that sound the floor in rapid succession, and yet decoratively. Far more easily, a movement may catch our attention by simply appearing to be co-extensive with a particular segment of the rhythm-cycle, a correspondence which the *rasikas* are quick to seize without conscious effort.

However, in every case — that is, whatever be the filling of a pattern of pure dance, and quite irrespective of the individual character of the movements it incorporates — the dance is able to hold our attention primarily because it is properly structured — besides, of course, being properly danced. What really counts is the formed expression of sentience or vitality. It is this character which makes what is projected (in dance) seizable by *rasikas* or, as Langer would put it, 'amenable to understanding'. The very sight of a rainbow may well appear to thrill *a child* through and through. But where a *rasika* reacts to good dancing the fullness of its impact on him is due not merely to what meets the eye or the ear, but to his ability to seize *with the intellect* the *formed* character of sentience which the dance (in Langer's view) projects. Here, as in contemplating the other arts, it is expressive *form* which is of paramount value.

In dance, as in the other arts, a semblance of living form is secured in some subtle ways too. According to Langer:

> (1) A small technical motif may create gesture, light, emotion, space and time. (2) And once an element is created, it influences the entire work. A transcendent moment effects a rarification of the whole piece and lifts it as a whole above the level of sensuous tensities. (3) Every abstraction, intensification . . . acts on it in this way; consequently even the most direct influence of one element on another seems to go via the implicit core of the art symbol.[103]

This is a tight passage, and the points it makes (as numbered by me) have to be brought out with care.

103. Langer, *Mind — An Essay on Human Feeling*, vol. I, p. 202.

1a. A single motif can indeed produce different elements in dance. As illustration, Langer here cites the following from Martha Graham's well-known dance, *Seraphic Dialogue*:

> . . . One and the same gestic motif — a shimmering shake of the fingers and hands — is first the sun in the window (without any actual play of light), then the tremor of the girl's fear, then the intensity of her compulsion . . . ; [and] at last it occurs in slower tempo as life awaking in the angelic form that has stepped out of the window. . . . [104]

This is a clear instance of 'the interplay of identity and diversity . . . [which Langer speaks of as] a major factor in the dialectical structure of the art symbol'.[105] She seems to regard it as a rarity; but almost all the *mudrā*s that our classical dances employ illustrate the truth which point (1) focuses on. Thus, the *patākā-mudrā* (flag-gesture) not only opens *alārippu,* which itself is generally the first number of a Bharata Natyam recital, but can also be easily used to convey such disparate ideas, in varying thematic situations, as welcoming a visitor, the undulating waves, or a resolute rejection of the advances of an unwelcome suitor. In no case, however, does the *mudrā* convey what it may, quite independently of the disposition of other parts of the dancing figure.

2a. And, of course, in every case the proper use of the *mudrā* influences the entire dance, may be, by way of appearing to invest the dance with a reality quite apart from the world, or by enriching the number with some moments of wordless eloquence. Some of these moments may be transcendent, or of exceptional value. In a good Kathak recital, two such possible moments are a well-designed access to the *sama* capped by a clear accent at it with split second accuracy (intensification) or a fleeting, but adroitly controlled withholding of the requisite footfall from its corresponding beat in the rhythm-cycle as marked by the drummer (abstraction). The one lends a look of *climactic attainment* to what would otherwise be a case of a colourless, if correct, completion of a rhythmic

---

104. Langer, *Mind — An Essay on Human Feeling,* vol. I, p. 202; fn.

105. *Ibid.*, p. 206.

passage; and the other leavens the dance with a touch of *wilful abandon*. But, it is noteworthy, first, that the two moments of artistic skill alike lend a measure of ideality to the dance; and, second, that in either case the moment gains its value essentially from its relation to the basic flow of *laya*. However, the rarefaction is marked and relished only by those who do not merely hear the beats (on the drum) and the footfalls (on the floor) but are able to follow discriminately the design of the flow of dance. This should make it clear how, as Langer says, the refinement effected by 'a transcendent moment . . . lifts . . . [the piece] as a whole *above the level of sensuous tensities'*.

3a. In other words, an artistic device — be it abstraction or intensification — not only creates a semblance, but does so essentially through the dialectical structure of the art symbol by which Langer means, essentially, the interplay of identity and diversity of forms.[106]

Above all, as Langer rightly says, dance can also create an image of the '*pulsating* organic life' which[107] we all commonly experience, may be as the regular throbbing of pulse or as occasional twitches of pain. However, what she says by way of emphasising this point is not all along clear. Consider the following, for instance:

> That creation will ever be the most pure and forceful in its effect, in which the most minute detail speaks of the vibrating, animated unity which called forth the *idea*.[108]

Langer here adds that dance which is art in this paradigmatic sense is a relatively recent emergence, *except possibly in some old Asiatic cultures*.[109] The qualification, in italics, should appear quite proper to lovers of Kathak dance, for what is called *nṛtta* in the region of this art is surely a well-knit fabric of

---

106. Langer, *Mind — An Essay on Human Feeling*, Vol. I., p. 206.

107. Langer, *Feeling and Form*, p. 207.

108. *Ibid*.

109. *Ibid*.

vibrant details. But, how exactly are we to interpret the *extract* just cited? I would say, as follows:

The 'idea' of which the extract speaks may be taken to mean a pattern *as conceived or contemplated*. When it is projected or 'called forth' — that is, danced, or played by the drummer — it has to appear not as a mere arrangement, but as a *vibrating and animated* unity. Now, this is indeed so in good Kathak dancing. The feet here not only cut out the *bol*s neatly, so that everyone of them appears quite distinct, but, what is more, they may even be expressly and adroitly varied in respect of emphasis or impact of the footfalls. Further, their set relation to the flow of rhythm can also be deftly changed, so that whereas one tuft of *bol*s may purposely overstep its allotted occupancy of beats in majestic leisureliness, the immediately following one may gently seem to quicken itself, so as to make due amends for the preceding deceleration. This *varying and consciously regulated adaptation* to an overall demand often makes Kathak appear quite 'living'. And the gentlest nod here, or an upturn of 'look' (or *nigāh*) may signal, as *sama*, the cessation of a flow that appears in the end to attain to what it has been moving towards — in the way, we may say, of directed endeavour.

Langer (we have seen) includes the following forms of sentience as well in 'the life of feeling' which dance may be said to objectify: 'the power to receive impressions, apprehend the environment and meet changes'.[110] Now, this again is clearly borne out by the practice of Kathak. Thus, one may find not only that in *āmad*, where the *aṅg* opens up, the confident visage and stepping seem a picture of vital power, but that sometimes — say, when he dances to a small and intimate gathering, and so can afford to be informal — his face reflects relish as the thought of a new pattern, to be danced next, dawns upon his mind. This little detail, I suggest, may be taken as a clear instance of 'the power to receive [and to

110. There is no reason to suppose that one can receive impressions only from the outside. Getting imbued with the power of noble thoughts which one may quietly cherish is an important means to moral growth.

respond to] impressions'.[111] Finally, the ability to apprehend the environment and to meet changes — nay, even challenges — is manifest where the danseuse first listens to, and then replicates with her feet, the playing of a subtle pattern by the drummer as a test of her ability to improvise.

Nor do I find it difficult to see the point of Langer's remark that a good dance can also clearly articulate 'the illusion of . . . wills in conflict'. In fact, I could add to this form of semblance the following as well: the sense of sudden enlivenment, the felt flightiness of movement, and a sense of constraint that may seem a little irritating. The warrant of what I here say is provided by language of the following kind which is seen to appear freely in our talk about Kathak:

> "वाह। क्या बोलों की लड़न्त है। इस बल ने तोड़े में जान डाल दी है; क्या उछलती हुई 'तिन' है। विलम्बित में फंस गया सा लगता है; धीमा त्रिताल अच्छे-२ नर्तकों के पैरों में बेड़ियां डाल देता है।"

Yet, in our anxiety to emphasise the semblance of life *as felt* (or as subjective) which dance can easily acquire, we sholuld not blink the slightly *representational* character of quite a few of our *rhythmic* patterns. The *paran*s, as our *rasika*s know, are classified as गौपुच्छा, पिपीलिका, according to the *shapes* they resemble. This aspect of the matter does not seem to be convered by Langer's treatment. And there is one detail of Kathak practice which is perhaps just unknown to her, but which lends added point to her emphsis of *expressive* form. In speaking of controlled, rhythmicised and formally conceived gestures, Langer makes ample provision for the following known elements of Kathak dance: the form and prefixed structure of our various *torhā*s, expression, and rhythmic movement. But our *bol*s (or mnemonic syllables) remain quite unnoticed. This defect *we* can hardly ignore; for the *bol*s of Kathak dance — nay, of our classical dances, generally — not merely lend a varied euphonic character to the dance itself,

111. In a way which has already been indicated in Note no. 110.

but enable *the audience* to identify the accents of rhythm. In brief, they make the entire *rhythmic form* of dance *more articulate or expressive*. The value of whole-form is paramount here. Indeed, good *parhant* (or recitation of syllables) is not only that in which the syllabic utterance is all along clear, but that in which the *śakla* — or what Croce would call, the individual physiognomy — of the pattern is duly brought out.

Some seeming oddities

We may now deal with some seeming oddities in Langer's writing on dance.

At places, her *language* is indeed a little odd. See, for instance, the following:

> In the dance . . . in . . . place [of] the actual personality [that we already possess] the created personality, a dance element which figures simply as a psychical, human or superhuman Being . . . is expressing itself.[112]

Language of this kind would appear questionable to many. Is it at all proper to speak of dance *as something over and above* the dancer himself, and as a *superhuman Being*? Now, questions such as these may be answered partly with the help of thinking which has already been done earlier, by way of explaining why the dancer is sometimes led to hypostatise the art which he cherishes. But it yet seems essential to add to it, in a way which may have a readier appeal. I may do it thus:

It is common knowledge that we freely speak of the dance, *without* making any mention of the dancer. Thus, when we say 'how सुबुक (that is, dainty, unhurried and neat) her dancing is' we do not admire the danseuse *as a person*; and, in spite of the lucid and reposeful quality of her dance, she may well be a complex and excitable person in actual life. Nor is the judgement that a particular male Kathak's *dancing* is robust (तगड़ा) the same thing as saying that *he* has a powerful physique.

Indeed, the energy one may find in a dance is not neces-

112. Langer, *Feeling and Form*, pp. 180-181.

sarily a direct clue to the dancer's own state of health. What *is* true on the other hand is that, in the process of dancing, the dancer ganerally becomes a different person; that there is often no straight road from his *refined* manner of dancing to his own way of life which may be pretty *coarse*; and that, as a devotee of dance, he may look on himself as a mere vehicle of the art's own vitality.

The dance may even be said to be a Being or personality, though of course not literally. A living being is something that *does* this or that; possesses an individual, identifiable physiognomy; and is internally more or less organised. Now, all these requirements are generally met (, if as mere semblance, I repeat) by a rhythmic pattern as properly danced. It may well seem to meander, sparkle, move on, expand and (in the end) to gather or complete itself. Again, a complete Kathak recital has its own 'life' with a clear beginning (say, as *thāṭa*), a climax in the closing, extra-fluent stages of *tatkār*: and its own moments of throbbing or subdued pulse. Further, just as the body has its own vital organs, the dance too may be said to be possessed of some subsidiary centres of 'life' in the *upāṅgs*, such as the wrists and the eyebrows; and, of course, in the feet which bring it so vividly to life. What is more, the thought that the dance is *a being with its own life* may also be taken to suggest that what the dancer creates on the stage is quite different from the mere *concept* of dance. Here, we have an actual spectacle with its own inner dynamics; and it is the 'interplay' of movements[113] which makes the dance appear as something in itself, *over and above the dancer*, exactly as the fluent thrust and parry of questions and answers (or counter-questions) in a seminar may make us admire the animated *discussion* without making any mention of the debators. Finally, by way of indicating the relevance of our present discussion to Langer's philosophy of art as a whole, I may add that just as when we speak of a powerful personality our meaning is that, though it may seem to be exuberant, the power is really *embodied in* the person, similarly Langer's talk of *the potent*

113. Cf. *Feeling and Form*, p. 187.

Being of dance is related to her favourite concepts of import (or *embedded* meaning), presentational (as opposed to discursive) symbol, and express*ive* form as distinguished from an arrangement which express*es* or transmits a kind of detachable meaning or singificance.

But, how can the dance-personality be even called *super-human*? Not, I suggest, in the sense of having powers above and beyond those of all mankind, but as exceeding an individuals *normal* ability or experience. Langer's meaning, here, may simply be that *during the course of dance*, the dancer (in a way) surpasses his actual limitations. If only for the duration of the dance, he forgets his own physical weakness or corpulence (assuming that he is in fact subject to such handicaps) and focuses instead on making his movements appear definite, streamlined and rhythmic; and the knowledgeable onlooker too utterly ignores, in case the dancing is effective, the physical trammels of the dancer.

I may illustrate this point by referring, once again, to the India International Centre Seminar of 1994 (November 11-13). On the final evening, as Briju Maharaj took the stage to begin his dance performance, I knew he was in a poor state of health. Heavy choreographic work over the preceding few weeks had aggravated his spinal discomfort and arterial hypertension; and he was visibly indisposed before he ascended the stage. But from the moment he began dancing he seemed to be bubbling with energy, and went on weaving a magical spell of rhythmic footwork like someone possessed. Out of sheer concern for his health, I interrupted him for a moment, and reminded him that he was not quite well; but he put me off politely with the words that, because he 'was dancing to an audience of genuine *rasika*s', he just could not help going on and on.

I may add, in the end, that the seeming oddity of Langer's language would be mitigated if we took care to remember that the Beings of which she speaks are all 'virtual'. We do not have to deal with Dance and its virtual powers in the way we deal with actual persons; and they sure do not, by radiating (seeming) energy, change the course of actual events.

But the oddity we have just discussed is not so commonly objected to as the one which appears to be there in the following words of Langer:

> *a.* The dance is an appearance, if you like, an apparition. It springs from what the dancers do, yet it is something else. In watching a dance *you do not see what is physically before you*, people running around or twisting their bodies; *what you see is a display of interacting forces*. But . . . these forces that seem to operate in the dance, are not the physical forces of the dancer's muscles, which actually cause the movements taking place. The forces we seem to perceive most directly and convincingly are created for our perception; and exist only for it.[114]

> *b.* In watching . . . an artistically successful ballet . . . one does not see *people running around*; one sees the dance driving this way, drawn that way, gathering here, spreading there — fleeing; resting, rising . . .; and all the motion seems to spring from powers beyond the performers.[115]

Both these extracts have been freely questioned. One pointed objection may be put thus:

> Langer wrongly ignores the simple truth of the matter which is "that in at least one ordinary sense of 'see', we see both physical movements and 'interactions of forces' . . . [Her] view that a dance is only a perceptual thing . . . an interaction of non-physical forces, is interestingly similar to the idealist conception of a work of art as something wholly ideal or imaginary . . . a view that has been much — and . . . convincingly criticised".[116]

Another protest runs as follows:

> What appears to perception, the dance 'apparition' as Langer puts it, may well be conceptually distinguished from the material; but it is wrong to suppose that conceptual distinc-

---

114. Langer, *Problems of Art*, p. 5.

115. Langer, *Feeling and Form*, p. 175.

116. H. Khatchadourian: 'Movement and Action in the Performing Arts', *The Journal of Aesthetics and Art Criticism*, Fall, 1978, p. 26.

> tions must stand for separate ontological entities, that the virtual image of the dance ("a display of interacting forces" etc.) is something *cut off* from the dancers ("People running around and twisting their bodies").[117]

In effect, such objections make the following points:

A. Langer wrongly maintains (or suggests) that, regarded as 'a display of interacting forces' or as an apparition, the dance is separate — rather than merely different — from the dancer's physical movements or forces;

B that, while watching a dance, we see only the merely perceptual (non-physical) forces, and not physical movements at all; and

C. that a work of art is something wholly ideal or imaginary.

A'. Now turning to A., we may begin by recalling our explanation of how the dance may be regarded as having its own objective being; and then set out to see, as follows, if Langer really *separates* the dance from the physical realities, that is, the dancer and his physical forces.

That she *distinguishes* the two is of course definite. I say so on the basis of Langer's own following words:

> . . . The physical materials of a dance *do not have* any direct similarity to the structure of emotive life; it is the created image (or the dance) that *has* elements and patterns like the life of feeling.[118]

> The physical realities are *given*; place, gravity, body, muscular strength . . . control. . . . All these are *actual*. . . . But . . . the moving forces of the dance, the *apparent* centers of power and their emanation, their . . . lift and decline, their rhythmic life . . . are elements, of the *created apparition*, and are themselves *not physically given, but artistically created.*[119]

---

117. L.A Reid, *Meaning in the Arts*, p. 84; italics added.
118. Langer, *Problems of Art*, p. 9. Italics added.
119. *Ibid.*, p. 6. italics added.

> [The dancers] do not create the materials of the dance — neither their own bodies, nor . . . the floor, ambient space, light, musical tone . . . nor any other physical provisions; all *these things they use, to create something over and above what is physically there*: *the dance.*[120]

Even a casual look at the italicised words in the above should make it clear that, in Langer's view, the given is quite different from the artistically created. But does she *disjoin* the two? I must answer in the negative; and I do so the basic of some of her own utterances. She says that the given realities disappear '*in* the dance',[121] and that 'the actual physical forces *that underlie it* (or the dance) disappear'.[122] Now if, as indeed is obvious and is also Langer's view, the dancers *use the given materials to create a dance*; and if, as is just as apparent, quite unlike a poem or a painting, a dance lasts only so long as it is *being created*, at no point of its course can its building materials, the given realities, really disappear. So where she says that they disappear '*in* the dance' Langer can only be taken to mean that they get thoroughly assimilated in dance, not that they vanish into thin air. The 'actual physical forces' that disappear all 'underlie' the dance; so their 'disappearance' can only mean the loss of their distinct identity in the dance as it appears to contemplation. And far from disjoining the two, Langer in fact insists that the actual and artistically created are and remain related in dance. Everything, she declares, that

> a dancer actually does *serves to create*, (and so is the cause of, or is related to) what we really see . . . (that is) a virtual entity . . . the moving forces of the dance.[123]

> The dance . . . apparition . . . *springs from what the dancers do, yet it is something else.*[124]

---

120. Langer, *Problems of Art*, p. 4. italics added.
121. *Ibid.*, p. 6. italics added.
122. *Ibid.*, p. 10. italics added.
123. *Ibid.*, pp. 5-6; italics added.
124. *Ibid.*, p. 5. italics added.

But, the critic may rejoin, even if a cause-effect relation be admitted between the actual and the 'forces' of dance, phenomenologically they remain separate *on Langer's account*; for she insists that in watching a dance we see *only* 'the virtual realities, the moving forces of the dance'.[125] This takes us to the second protest.

B'. How can we accept Langer's seemingly odd remark that 'in watching a dance you do not see what is *physically* before you'?

Here, I suggest, some points for a fair answer emerge if, along with close attention to the words just cited, we also take into account the following ones which provide a close to the para in which the words in question occur:

> The forces we seem to perceive most directly and convincingly are created for our perception; and they exist only for it.[126]

Now, as I widen my way of looking at the matter in the requisite way, I feel enabled to rejoin thus:

Langer here envisages a contrast between watching a dance (as art) and merely seeing something that is physically before us. She does not put it so clearly, but her meaning seems to be that whereas for the everyday seeing of things we do not need any special culture of our powers of apprehension, watching a dance as art (see, here, the words: *artistically successful ballet* in *Feeling and Form*, p. 175) is impossible without an adequate prior knowledge of the grammar of the art. Now, this should seem acceptable to all those who have experienced dance aesthetically. But the negative emphasis that in watching a dance one does *not* see what is physically before him, — that is, the given realities as such — can be accepted only after it has been shown to be individually true of the more important of these realities.

Now this, I believe, is quite possible. Consider, for instance,

---

125. Langer, *Problems of Art*, p. 6.

126. *Ibid.*, p. 5.

the stage space which every dance needs. There is, of course, no doubt about its being there. But from the very beginning of the dance it is the dancing figure that becomes the cynosure of all eyes; and what had so far been a mere stretch of vacancy, if well lit and commodious, is forthwith transfigured into the locus of a palpitant centre[127] which, on the one hand, determines the movement of our vision; and, on the other hand, turns the visible stage space itself into a mere environment of where the danseuse positions herself, *using* some stage space to be sure, but *revealing* nothing but the open or involute, leisurely or spirited quality of the dance itself. Of Kathak it is doubtless true that where it is well-formed and articulate — that is, a blend of clear accents and a manifest overall design — it captures attention and keeps us absorbed even if it is quite without representation of situations and expression of feelings, so that when it ends, the impression we are left with is one of the *dance's* disappearance, and not of the vacating of a solid floor.

Consider, again, the body of the dancer. When we watch the dance (properly) it is not that the dancing figure is not seen at all, but only that the body is not seen as it is in itself, or as apart from the dance. The figure is now seen as *aṅg*, that is, as adapted to the ends of dance. And if, as he sets out to dance, the Kathak's actual corpulence[128] does not disturb the (knowledgeable) onlooker's delight, how shall we put the matter except by saying that, as something unseemly in itself, it has disappeared *in* the dance? My own experience of watching Kathak suggests that, if the defect is not foreknown — *and if the dance does not grow feeble at places*, so as to let the viewer grow casual and turn to merely scanning the dancer's costume or figure — even a squint in the performer's eye does

127. In Kathak dance, because of the ceaseless suggestion of *laya*-flow, even the most quiescent posture does not appear quite so — except perhaps when it just reaches the *sama*; and, therefore, the dancing figure as a focus may well be called *palpitant*.

128. Many will here be reminded of the late Sri Acchan Maharaj. I wonder if his figure was ever admired as being streamlined, but did any one knowing Kathak ever fail to give in readily to the manifest grace of his dancing?

not disturb one's enjoyment except where the focus of the dance is on the act of looking (or *nigāh*) itself.

I would not categorically say that *no* actual detail *ever* disturbs the contemplator's delight. Sometimes, I distinctly remember, the loud colour of undergarments revealed during fluent *chukkurs* at once offends the eye. I would further like to press a point which Langer seems to undervalue. A recital of dance is not everywhere a matter of *movement*. It often begins with a *posture*; and, in respect of this detail, I would like to make two remarks:

> Where the dance is a fluent and rhythmically subtle or brilliant interplay of movement, or effective facial *abhinaya*, the dancer's *whole* (actual) figure — as against the eyes, face, and hands which may here seem to be eloquent, and so grip the watchful eye — may not be attended to.
>
> But where what meets the eye is just a quiet posture, and the lower limbs seem a little too filled out to make for the requisite symmetry or streamlined quality of the stance, one cannot but notice *the body's own* actual state, though *the dancer's disposition of limbs* may be perfect. The constraint is in fact heightened if the same *rasika* has been following with interest the past performances of a danseuse, and now suddenly finds her figure occupying more actual space.

Here I think it necessary to add that Langer too does not appear to hold that, in watching a dance, no actual detail is ever noticed. Her view only is that what is most directly convincing — or most naturally striking — about a dance is the fabric of its virtual elements; and this obviously implies that, if less directly and convincingly, the 'actualities' of dance are also sometimes perceived.

Be that as it may, *as the formulation of an ideal* we can certainly say that '*the more perfect* the dance, the less we see its actualities'.[129] But, I hasten to repeat, this will hold only where the contemplator is knowledgeable.

---

129. This, indeed, is Langer's net view on the matter. *Problems of Art*, p. 6; italics added.

To turn, once again, to Langer's words under discussion ('you do not see what is physically before you'), I may also point out that they are (in the passage) immediately followed by: 'people running around or twisting their bodies'. *These* everyday movements, all merely practical and not as such aesthetic, are indeed not *so* perceived when we watch a dance knowledgeably. As a work of art, a dance is a fabric of interacting forces; and the right attitude to the movements it displays — and to the beginning and cessation of its intra-forms — demands that we see how these two ends open, direct and consummate the individual numbers.

If the onlooker has no idea of what Kathak dance is, he will see the movements, to be sure; and postural abidance too. But whereas to him, in spite of all the attention he may lavish on it, the end of a movement (or of a pattern) will appear as a mere cessation — and postural abidance, just doing nothing or at best standing agreeably — by the discriminating *rasika* such incidental details of dance will be taken, respectively, as the expected advent of the *sama*-beat, and as a needful occasion which enables both the dancer and the *rasika*s — by means of the empty *āvṛtti* of the *lahrā-ṭhekā* twosome for the duration of which the posture is held — to patiently adjust themselves anew to the basic pace of the rhythm. Of the two details just referred to, one is, so to say, a climax; and the other, in its temporal aspect, the ground of all rhythmic work. The layman misses both, and so cannot be said to be watching a dance as the making of a work of art. I hasten to add that it is precisely under such undiscriminating notice that one only sees 'people running around' — purposelessly, or for some practical end. An instance would here help. If, while seeing a cricket match, a man who does not know the game at all suddenly hears a vigorous cry for a 'leg-before' decision from all over the field, he may well be struck by the very different postures of those who shout in chorus from places even far removed from one another, but he will not be able to see the unifying purpose; and so this would be merely a case of seeing the different, awkward postures and hearing the shouts, not of watching the game of cricket as it should be seen.

And with special reference to *movement*, I may defend Langer thus. Where do we see, directly, the exercise of physical power? In the delivery of a very fast service, we may say, by a tennis player; or in the sporting contest known as tug-of-war. A dance, it is clear, is not striking in this everyday manner. It is not that the dance is no real strain on the body. It sure is, palpably to the dancer; but the fact of this physical effort has to be kept cleverly hidden. Those who have watched a Kathak recital from the wings should be able to recall that it is only when, during spinning or some other movement, she is *not facing the audience* that the danseuse feels free to show signs of strain in her visage. So, in principle, what is displayed to and perceived by the audience in a dance is not the use of physical forces as such. Where *such* use is seen, it is (I repeat) invariably a moment of weakening. It is, as we know, very true of Kathak dance — in cases where the dancer is not very competent and seems to struggle in managing the course of an intricate pattern at a very fluent pace — that 'as soon as the beholder sees gymnastics and *arrangements*, the work of art breaks, the creation fails'.[130] An arrangement is a putting-together of pieces or parts — in some order, it may well be; but the dominant look here (in dance) is one of piecemeal and, more or less, laboured doing, not that of a process the essential character of which is so determined by that of the parts that the onward course may seem effortless and, so to say, natural rather than somehow contrived. Where a dance wears the former kind of look, we see actual effort; and the notice here *is* similar to seeing *'people running around* or twisting their bodies', and is not the watching of a *dance* as having its own life, its (virtual) 'moving forces' and 'centres of power'.[131] I therefore hazard to include in the list of 'actualities' — which (according to Langer) are *not* to be seen in watching a dance — the actual, conscious effort too of making the dance. This, I may add, is uniquely relevant to the occurrent arts where we see the work in the process of being made.

---

130. Langer, *Problems of Art*, p.10. Italics added.

131. *Ibid.*, p. 6.

What, on the other hand, we positively see in watching a dance (knowledgeably) is what Langer calls the 'purely apparent forces'. The presence of these forces in Kathak is easy to trace. The balancing of the two halves of a pattern, say as: तिटकता गदिगिन,गदिगिन तिटकता; the *sama* appearing to determine the flow of a well-designed pattern from the end-side, so to say; the build-up of a 'tension' as the pattern approaches its target, and its satisfying release as the *sama* is in fact attained, — all this, to be sure, is merely 'apparent'. None of the 'forces' that we here see — balancing, teleological determination, aesthetic tension and its subsidence — is at all the same as, or confluent with, the dancer's own exercise of actual energy, or with his own subjective experience at the moment. In fact, where in its shapely, rising access to the *sama* the pattern really shows a growing *tension*, the dancer's own experience may just be one of subdued satisfaction. Nor is dancing that appears fluent and sparkling necessarily a greater strain on a Kathak than leisurely movements. The truth rather is that, unless he is very well steeped in the *vilambit* idiom, presenting a *thāṭa in dhīmā* (*or slow*) *tritāla* is likely to make heavier demands on his concentration, and may even make him appear impatient, between the leisurely beats, to switch over to quicker dancing.

Yet, in watching a dance, which naturally demands attentive seeing, nothing that is in fact given can be said to go entirely unnoticed, if not in its independent non-aesthetic character.

C′. Nor do I find anything in Langer's writing to warrant the criticism that she thinks of a work of art as something 'wholly ideal or imaginary'. This (third) protest too can be met by paying careful attention to some of her own words. Consider, for instance, her following explicit utterance:

> The artist's most elementary problem is the symbolic transformation of subjectively known realities into *objective semblances* that are immediately recognised as their expression in *sensory appearances*.[132]

---

132. Langer, *Mind — An Essay on Human Feeling*, vol. I., p. 157; italics added.

Here, the suggestion is very clear that, far from being merely ideal or bodiless, a work of art is a transformation — that is, a complete alteration — of 'subjectively known realities' *into the objective and the sensory*. Langer, it is true, declares that art 'exists only for perception', not for use; and that, therefore, it is (in that sense) 'a virtual entity'. But she also at once adds that such an entity 'is not unreal. . . . We don't just dream that we see it';[133] and, in respect of 'the virtual realities' that make a dance she openly says that we 'see, hear and feel' them. How can such realities be called merely imaginary? Langer, in fact, insists that (far from being imaginary), a work of art expresses the nature of human feeling — . . . 'the stream of direct experience, *life as it feels to the living*'.[134] 'It is more than a perceivable entity . . . (it) strikes us as something charged with feeling'.[135]

Art is, of course, not the same as real life. But, just as clearly, it is not quite unreal either. It is (according to Langer) an *objective* presentation of how life feels, in more or less *material* terms. So, it is real and significant in a distinct sense. It projects the forms of feeling; and these are the 'life' of the work. One is here likely to wonder if such projection is possible even in that kind of dance which does not use any language, that is, in *nṛtta*. But a little close attention to the aesthetic character of the rhythmic patterns that abound in Kathak is enough to remove the uncertainty. If a 'pure' (or merely rhythmic) Kathak pattern is danced in such a way that the *bol*s which make it do *not* look like mere numerals in an act of counting, which is often quite impassive, but as how the inner elements of passages and processes in real life — say, moments in an hour of vacancy, billows on the surface of a lake, touches of humour and interjections or repartees in debate, or footsteps in a race — actually look, may be leisurely, meandering, surging, or wedged and incisive; and if, by virtue of their individual character and manner of movement, they seem to be inter-

133. Langer, *Problems of Art*, p. 5.

134. *Ibid.*, p. 7.

135. *Ibid.*, p. 6.

linked, so that the whole-form is all along clear to the knowledgeable, the entire intraform may easily appear as the rhythmic analogue of such life-expperiences as: अटखेलियां करना, इतराना, चुटकियां लेना, चमककर या बनकर आना.

These are indeed the words that a *rasika* often uses in admiring good Kathak; and, instead of complimenting the dancer straight, he may acclaim the aesthetic pace for its deftly varying manner: वाह! क्या लय की समेट है! ज़रा काट-तराश तो देखिए लय की!

All such language, we may note, relates to the very 'look' of the pattern being danced. Does it actually *remind* us of analogous features in our felt life? No; to say 'yes' here would be untrue phenomenologically, that is, to our actual experience at the moment. The focus of attention in such cases is all along on what is in fact there on the stage, facing us; the mind is not *led away* to thoughts of actual life; and so long as we remain confined or close to the experience, the use of language is not so much the deliberate ascription of predicates *by us* as a direct apprehension of the pattern's *own* character. Actual experience of life is, of course, of indispensable help in *recognizing* the 'look' or the aesthetic character of the pattern, but just as in the instantaneous recognition of a friend the aid of past experience is no distraction of attention from the immediately given, so when we identify in language how exactly a dance-*pattern* looks, its undivided hold on our attention does not suffer. Nor can the *dancer* be said to *represent* anything here. His aim is simply to present the pattern in what is (in his view) the best way. So, if we at all choose to speak of *expression* in such cases, we should take care to add that it is presentational rather than the pressing out of some inner content. A good dance, Langer says, seems *imbued with features of life as felt*. Where this is not so, and the dance only meets the requirements of the pace and ambit of rhythm, we too bemoan, as Kathak *rasikas*, that it is 'lifeless'.[136]

But the presentational aspect of dance is quite as important

136. Our words here are: ठंडा, बेजान, मुर्दा।

as its expressiveness. The postures that the danseuse assumes, or the movements she makes, are not the commonplace ones of everyday bearing, yawning, and stretching, but are in themselves good to look at; and are, what is more, accordant with the whole conception of the dance, so that we have not only to see, but to understand what we see. Correctness of *aṅg* is indeed not to be taken as mere beauty of postures and carriage, but their intelligible accordance with the other dance-elements. Yet, the visual element is not to be underrated. When Langer speaks of dance as an 'apparition', or as a dynamic, yet 'virtual image', she means not only that it is without the ordinary properties of a physical thing, nor merely that it is quite different from movements of the everyday kind, but also, and just as insistently, that it is 'given to the eye, or to the ear and eye'.[137]

In the face of this emphasis on actual *visibility*, how can Langer be accused of saying anything similar to the view "that 'virtual entities' can exist *independently of a perceiver*"?[138] She says explicitly that the dance forces 'we seem to perceive most directly and convincingly are created *for our perception*; and [that] they exist only for it'.[139] What *this* means is, however, to be brought out with care:

First, 'our perception', here, is not quite divided from the dancer's own. (This will be clarified a little later.) And secondly, though everything which can convince us that the dancing is good is *created* for perception, not everything that we *find* in an actual recital is *meant* for our (or the onlookers') perception, though it may *in fact be perceived* by us. Details of the latter kind, — that is, those that really concern the danseuse alone (and are not *meant* to be seen by us) — are easy to find in the region of Kathak dance. Her looking at the drummer, now and then, by way of just hinting as to whether the *laya* is to be slowed, accelerated or merely steadied; her letting a

137. Langer, *Problems of Art*, p. 6.

138. H. Khatchadourian: 'Movement and Action in the Performing Arts', *op. cit.*, p. 26; italics added.

139 Langer, *Problems of Art*, p. 5.

round of the cycle pass *sans* dance before beginning a new pattern, as a breather and as occasion to get a feel of the basic rhythm anew; the needful upgathering sometimes, during brisk footwork, of the *sārī*'s nether fringe; and, of course, the first few trial tinkles of the ankle-bells that enable the danseuse to check only if they are properly tied, — all this may well be *visible to* us, but it is merely done to facilitate proper dancing, not *created for our perception*. On the other hand, the entire expressional-representational exterior of the dance is meant for us; the danseuse does not *see* it,[140] and is, therefore, here dependant on the *rasika*'s reactions for determining if it at all bears out her artistic intention.

As for the rhythmic elements of Kathak, they are of course less hidden from the danseuse. The syllables are not only danced, but heard by her, as by us. She can also check the correctness of her rhythmic work by just looking at the drumming going on. But where she wishes to work up the *effect* of a climax, she can only try, but cannot really *watch* it; for, all her attention is here taken up by dancing the steps and syllables in a tasselled way of mounting accents. Or again, where a subtle turn of *laya* is to be shown, or such a *bol* is cut out by the feet as the tempo chosen would generally inhibit, the creative effort made is only *for the rasika* in so far as he alone can truly judge as to whether it really comes off or is merely attempted.

On the whole, it is certainly true that, though the audible elements of the dance, or its music and the rhythm with its sounding syllables on the floor and on the drums, are both alike checked also by the danseuse herself, so that the slightest slip from *laya* or unclarity in the making of a *bol* in her own footwork may make her visibly unhappy,[141] the *totality* of what she does, or the movements and postures and rhythm *as mutually accordant*, and the variform effects she seeks to work up — say, of a quiet mischief in both look and *layakārī*, or of

140. Though she of course *knows* what she does.

141. She may even *show* the dissatisfaction, provided she is dancing to a small and friendly audience in an informal way.

grandeur in *aṅg* and climactic attainment of *sama in parans*, — all this is surely meant for the *rasika*, in the main.

Where the dance is successful, and the onlooker knowledgeable, the 'watching' is done with 'our whole responsive sensibility';[142] and what elicits such fullness of notice at once appears to be 'charged with feeling'.[143] This 'feeling' may be a designable emotion, as it clearly is where the dancer projects a valorous theme — a *vīra rasa intra*-form — or one that shows amorous grief (*viyoga-śṛṅgāra*); but it may just as well be the 'feeling' of how matters come to a head through a labyrinth of details that make for it, though waywardly, or the felt relaxation of a tension. In either case, I repeat, the 'feeling' which appears *in the dance* is not necessarily (not even generally) the dancer's own feeling. He may be only feeling involved in whatever he does, and not himself suffer any distinct emotion. And where the leisurely, but shapely and confident attainment of the *sama* lends to the dance, thereafter, a look of *relaxation*, his own mind may straightaway be *keyed on to* the thought of the pattern that is to follow. Dancing (indeed) 'is not a symptom of how the dancer (himself) happens to feel'.[144]

Here, however, we must notice a difficulty which does not figure in the three protests listed. Is expression in dance *nowhere* symptomatic? In judging a (Kathak-) dance recital do we go only by what is intended and creatively organised for our perception, *or also* by what the dance automatically shows? Such questions, I suggest, may be answered as follows:

The most accurate following of rhythm is certainly not all that we do in watching a dance. We have to notice the *aṅg* too; and, of course, specially the face which is here not only *made to express* the various emotions, but often easily *evinces or betrays* the dancer's own *actual* attunement and swaying along with the rhythm of the intra-form being danced. Such

---

142. Langer, *Problems of Art*, p. 6.

143. *Ibid.*

144. *Ibid.*, p. 7.

expression is in itself symptomatic; *and* it makes for the overall appeal of dance. Are we not then forced to deviate from Langer's basic thesis that artistic expression is symbolic and organised, and not (at all) symptomatic and direct? And do we not here heed something that is actual? Notice, at this point, may also be taken of the fact that, according to our traditional theory of *rasa*, the *sāttvika bhāva*s — such as heightened pallor of the face and horripilation — which are direct signs of genuine emotion (not symbolic expressions of the artist's mere knowledge of the forms of feeling) are all held to be vital for the evocation of aesthetic experience.

However, the difficulty *can* be met; and the way I am going to do it should be acceptable to those who have also seen *bad* Kathak. Where the face of the danseuse duly registers, and even seems to beam at the subtle rhythm of the pattern being danced, the 'expression' is accepted by the knowledgeable not because a lit up face is a good sight, but because it duly *accords with* the way of the rhythm. So, what we here admire still remains the organised character of all that goes to make the total dance. Conversely, where there is nothing really likeable about the design of the pattern, nor anything of note in the way it is being danced, and yet the danseuse wears a smile — maybe, because she has been *instructed to appear enjoying* what she does — the *rasika* may even feel unhappy at the thought that only a lack (say, of skill in footwork) is being sought to be covered up — ineffectively.

It is indeed the dance's whole-form that ultimately counts. I am not suggesting that the onlooker can afford to ignore what have been called the 'regional qualities' of a work of art, but only that the details, here, are all seen as being *of* the total dance, mainly because of the form of the rhythm-cycle which all along continues, and which must ever be borne in mind, if but dimly and effortlessly. It is indeed the *sama*, the single pivotal beat, which generally encases an intra-form in a kind of flowing frame with a clear emanation and a definite close.

Summing up

In the end, because the run of the chapter so far has been rather loose and perhaps a little wayward too, I think it necessary, first, to consider if Langer's overall view of dance squares with her basic thesis that all art is the symbolic projection (or expression) of some forms of feeling; and, second, to give an integrated account of the more important concepts that distinguish her theory of dance. To facilitate understanding, I propose to proceed from the familiar viewpoint of a trained contemplator as actively engaged in watching a Kathak (solo) dance recital.

Now, what does the *rasika* actually see? A person, we may say, as traversing the stage with occasional pauses where he chooses to assume some quiet, but winsome or meaningful postures. Such an answer would, of course, not be irrelevant; but it would surely be superficial. For the movements that make a dance are all quite different from, say, a man's sauntering vacantly, or running to catch a bus. First, the dancer's moving figure appears to be intent all along. The intentness is generally visible in his eyes, and is specially manifest in his unremitting attempt to accord with a basic rule to which Indian classical dance is generally subject, namely, the requirement that the eyes have to follow the direction taken by the *hands*. But even generally — that is, including the *foot*falls in *tatkār* which is obviously not so subject to the rule just mentioned — every dance movement appears to be willed, if without seeming effort; and this justifies Langer's emphasis that *gesture* is the basic building material of dance. But, secondly, the intentness in question relates only to the making of the *dance,* and *not* to the pursuit of any personal end by the dancer; which is precisely why Langer holds that gestures in dance are all alike *virtual*. What is more, they are (as a rule) meant to be followed and understood by us; and we quietly acquiesce in this implicit demand of the dance; for if we at all go to see it, it is with the set purpose of letting it interest us in a way which is quite different from the way we care for everyday objects.

Yet, though what is presented to us in (or as) a dance is dissimilar to what we see and hear in our commerce with the real world, we do not find it odd or unfamiliar to the point of disagreeableness. On the other hand, where it is truly art, a dance may well fascinate and thrill us — thrill, I may add, in a fuller way than a beauteous spectacle of nature which, in general, only ravishes the eye and makes hardly any demand on our understanding; and it thrills us, where it does, because (in Langer's view) it is a projection of how vitality and the sense of agency feel in actual life.

Such an *explanation* of the appeal of good dance is, of course, not the same thing as the way we *experience* it. A distinction is indeed to be made btween the following: watching and enjoying a dance quietly; reacting to its charm, at times, in terms of approbatory, if very brief, *comments*; and coolly reflecting, well after the experience of watching, as to what a dance really is and why it appeals where it does. Yet the comments I have referred to appear only to support Langer's philosophical theory of dance, at least in respect of the rhythmic aspect of this art. It is indeed common to acclaim the excellence of 'pure' dance — and of the 'accompaniment' provided by the drummer — in terms of words that we freely use with reference to acts, passages, and processes as they are felt or directly experienced in everyday life; words like the following:

"इनकी लय डगमगाती नहीं; किस खूबसूरती से बनकर आए हैं, सम पर; कैसे लिपटकर संगत करते हैं! वाह! क्या काट–तराश है लय की!"

But, one may readily ask, what about those numbers in dance which are explicit essays in representation and expression? How can *they* we said to project forms of felt life, instead of *representing* facts and situations? Here, following Langer, our answer may run as follows:

As has been already pointed out, in the context of the specific art theory we are presently concerned with, *feeling* is not to be taken as emotion alone, but as signifying whatever is felt or directly experienced. If it is thus understood, the verb, *feel,* would appear to be clearly more comprehensive than *look* which relates to sight (in the main) and is inapplicable to what Langer calls 'subjectively felt realities', such as somnolence or embarrassment. Whatever be the outer situation we find ourselves in, along with a notice of its details or salient features, it is also (as a whole) always felt as having a specific character. Thus, it may be exciting or thrilling, or simply agreeable; manageable, intractable, or ominous; or explosive or congenial. So where the dancer has to project an emotion, which is always related to a situation, his emphasis has to be on capturing (in dance) the overall feel of the situation rather than on literal fidelity to details, without of course ignoring the features which make for its specific character, and which may even have to be heightened. If it be contended — as it may well be, in the light of a considerable amount of art and art theory today — that art need not bear any relation to life, Langer's answer would be that even where a work builds upon, say, straight lines alone, and is abstract in the sense of not representing any thing or situation, its distinctive look — of tenseness, maybe, or of convergence and diffusion — could not have been possible without the artist's own prior experience of these formal qualities in life; and that if the work in question is significant it is only because its form is able to capture the feel of these qualities.

The basic feel of life itself — comprising, we may say, sentience, physical and mental vitality or alertness, and the sense of agency — is the distinctive projection of the art of dance; and this is, according to Langer, precisely the reason why this art can not only give us the kind of disinterested delight which contemplation of art in general provides, but may even *thrill us*, or bring about a tremulous and joyous quickening of our inner being, just as the very sight of a child's ebullient spirit at play can almost coerce us to shake off our own torpor. A more obvious reason of such an impact is the fact that dance, in general, abounds in movement. Langer, I believe, has both these reasons in mind when she speaks of dance as a *dynamic* image: dynamic not only becasue, as already pointed out, it projects felt life, but also because it is an interplay of *powers* regarded (I repeat) as centres or sources of influence, and not as mere strength or energy; and *image* in the sense of a semblance or likeness rather than as a copy, and as possessed of a fairly determinate form, seizable by the cultivated eye or imagination without too much effort. A rainbow resembles a bow, and may, therefore, be said to be an image; a child too, if it resembles its father remarkably in appearance, may strike us as the very image of its father. But in neither case can the word *image* be duly replaced with *copy*.

But how is this dynamic image (or dance) *illusory*? We cannot say, it is clear, that it deceives us. The truth rather is that, where it is artistically successful, we take delight in the interplay of powers on the stage, and may even cherish it for long after the the watching is over. The dance is *illusory* only in the sense that it appears to be what it is not, that is, a *direct* expression of the dancer's own energy, thought, and feeling. Langer does not make the impossible suggestion that the dancing is quite unrelated to the dancer. What she insists on only is that it is not an act of his everyday personality, but of his being as (momentarily) transformed and enlivened by his attunement with the conception and execution of dance. But then, why does she not simply say that, where the dancing is good, the dancer gives an inspired performance? Why should she find it necessary to bring in ambiguous concepts of 'virtual power or entity' and illusoriness? Here, on behalf of Langer, our answer could be that whereas in the case of *such* inspired performance in regions other than those of the arts — be it in the form of a moving speech or in that of a dazzling display of strokeplay in tennis or cricket — the overt activity is truly (regarded as) a direct expression of the agent's own emotional states, energy, and power, the 'life' that we see *in dance* is not symptomatic or directly expressive (even) of the supercharged personality of the dancer. And the difference can be brought out easily. Whatever be the way in which a speaker gets and feels inspired, the thoughts that he puts forth in his talk are presently his own; and, similarly, the disgust that a player may show on playing a wrong stroke betrays *his own immediate* state of mind. In dance, on the other hand, the virile nimbleness that distinguishes an essay in *Śiva-tāṇḍava* — set in *sūla tāla*, let us say — expresses only the dancer's imagination of the quality in question, and is no index of his own present mental state which has, in fact, to remain peaceable, yet alert because of the exacting demands made by the number's intrinsic character.

Indeed, a dance is neither the sign or symptom of the dancer's own present state of mind nor a signal to be decoded for the sake of adapting ourselves to some practical situation. Yet it *is* meaningful. It is, of course, a visual spectacle; but what this spectacle signifies has to be understood. Even the appreciation of rhythm is not simply a matter of listening. This indeed is why the proper contemplation of a dance recital is impossible without a good deal of prior training on the part of those who watch it. So, to provide for its meaningfulness — *without*, at the same time, mistaking it as it as a sign, signal, or symptom — we have to say that a dance is a kind of *symbol;* and, because the understanding required, here, is inseparable from perceiving, we have to add that a dance is a *presentational* symbol, that is, an object the meaning of which imbues, and is not separable from its look or appearance.

Bibliography

Antony Flew, *A Dictionary of Philosophy*, Pan Books, 1979.

Beardsley and Schueller (eds.), *Aesthetic Inquiry*, Dickinson Publishing Co., Inc., Belmont, California, 1967.

Benjamin Lowe, *The Beauty of Sport*, Prentice-Hall, Inc., New Jersey, 1977.

C.J. Ducasse, *The Philosophy of Art*, Dover Publications, 1966.

E.Gilson, *Forms and Substances in the Arts*, Charles Scribner's Sons, New York, 1966.

George Santayana, *The Life of Reason*, Constable's, London, 1954.

———, *The Sense of Beauty*, Dover Publications, 1955.

G.V.D. Heuvel, *S.K. Langer, Abridged edition,* The John Hopkins University Press, PB. 1988.

H. Osborne, *The Art of Appreciation*, O.U.P., London, 1970.

Kathleen Raina, *William Blake* (The World of Art Library: Artists) Thames and Hudson, London, 1974 Reprint.

L.A. Jacobus (ed.), *Aesthetics and the Arts*, McGraw Hill Book Co., 1968.

L.A. Reid, *A Study in Aesthetics*, 1931.

———, *Meaning in the Arts, George* Allen & Unwin, London, 1969.

L.E. Hahn (ed.), *The Philosophy of Charles Hartshorne* (Library of Living Philosophers), vol. XX, La Salle. Open Court. 1991.

Matanga Muni, *Bṛhaddeśī*, Sangeet Karyalaya, Hathras, 1976.

Mohan Khokhar, *Traditions of Classical Indian Dance*, Clarion Books, 1979.

Monier-Williams, *A Sanskrit-English Dictionary*, Oriental Publishers, Delhi, 1899.

Monroe C. Beardsley, *Aesthetics — Problems in the Philosophy of Criticism*, Harcourt, Brace & World, Inc., New York, 1958.

N. Frye, *Anatomy of Criticism*, Princeton University Press, 1957, PB.

P. Daix, *Picasso*, Thames and Hudson, London, 1965.

Pandit Kedarnath (ed.) Bharata's *Nāṭya Śāstra*, 2nd edition, Bombay, Nirnayasagar, 1943.

Rudolf Carnap, *The Logical Syntax of Language*, 1937.

S.K. Langer, *The Practice of Philosophy*, Holt & Co., New York, 1930.

———, *Philosophy in a New Key*, Harvard University Press, Cambridge. Masachusettes, 3rd edn., 1976.

———, *Feeling and Form*, Routledge & Kegan Paul, 3rd Impression, 1963.

———, *Problems of Art*, Routledge and Kegan Paul, 1957.

———, (ed.), *Reflections on Art*, The John Hopkins Press, Baltimore, 1958.

———, *Philosophical Sketches*, A Mentor Book Softcover edn., 1964.

———, *Mind — An Essay on Human Feeling*, vol. I, The John Hopkins University Press, Baltimore & London, 2nd printing, PB. 1975.

Vol. II 2nd printing, PB. 1978.

Vol. III PB. 1984.

S.K. Saxena, *Aesthetical Essays*, Chanakya Publications, Delhi, 1981.

———, *Art and Philosophy: Seven Aestheticians*, Indian Council of Philosophical Research, New Delhi, 1994.

———, *Swinging Syllables: Aesthetics of Kathak Dance*, Sangeet Natak Akademi, 1991.

———, *The Winged Form: Aesthetical Essays on Hindustani Rhythm*, Sangeet Natak Adademi, New Delhi, 1979.

Stephen Spender, *World within World*, Hamilton, London.

Swami Prajnananda; *A Historical Study of Indian Music*, Anandadhara Prakashan, Calcutta, 1965.

Index